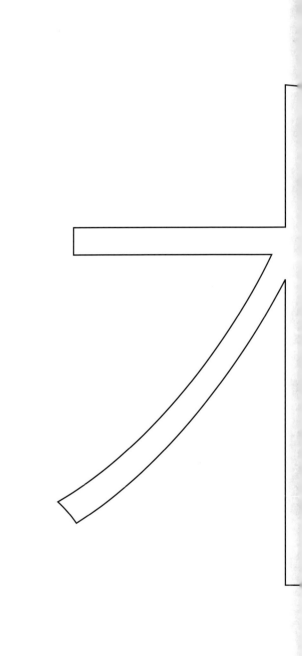

BENOÎT **JACQUET** | TERUAKI **MATSUZAKI** | MANUEL **TARDITS**

THE CARPENTER
& **THE ARCHITECT**
A HISTORY OF WOOD CONSTRUCTION IN JAPAN

Translated by Christian Hubert

EPFL PRESS

Graphic designer: Véronique Hours, www.a-p-arts.com

EPFL PRESS is an imprint owned by the Presses polytechniques et universitaires romandes, a Swiss academic publishing company whose main purpose is to publish the teaching and research works of the Ecole polytechnique fédérale de Lausanne (EPFL).

PPUR, EPFL – Rolex Learning Center, CP 119, CH-1015 Lausanne,
info@epflpress.org, tél.: +41 21 693 21 30, fax: +41 21 693 40 27.

www.epflpress.org

© 2021, First edition in english, EPFL Press
ISBN 978-2-88915-445-6

Printed in Czech republic
All rights reserved, including those of translation into other languages. No part of this book may be reproduced in any form – by photoprint, microfilm, or any other means – nor transmitted or translated into a machine language without written permission from the publisher.

8 FOREWORD: HISTORY, STORIES

— A STORY OF PRINCIPLES

28 — COMPLEXITY IN ARCHITECTURE… À LA JAPANESE
32 — THE DIFFERENT ARCHITECTURAL TYPES
78 — EVOLUTIONS OF THE PLAN
96 — CONSTRUCTIONAL COMBINATORICS
104 — TOWARDS ASYMMETRY
108 — INNOVATIONS WITHIN INTERIOR SPACE: FROM THE POST TO THE TATAMI
134 — IRREGULAR SPACES: THE ASSOCIATION OF HIROMA AND KOMA ROOMS
142 — NATURE AND ARCHITECTURE
162 — A FEW MORE RINGS IN CLOSING

二 A MODERN STORY

168 二 THE IMPORTATION OF WESTERN STYLES DURING THE MEIJI ERA
172 二 THE CREATION OF AN ORIENTAL JAPANESE STYLE
176 二 THE BEGININGS OF MODERN JAPANESE ARCHITECTURE: THE INFLUENCE OF EXPRESSIONISM
186 二 MODERN ARCHITECTURE IN WOOD: THE CORBUSIAN SCHOOL
202 二 POSTWAR: THE TANGE SAGA
214 二 TOWARDS AN ABSTRACT JAPANESE SPACE: THE SHINOHARA SCHOOL
230 二 THE COORDINATES OF IRRATIONALITY IN JAPANESE SPACE
236 二 TOWARDS AN ARCHITECTURE… IN WOOD
242 二 VARIATIONS ON THE STYLE
246 二 CONTEMPORARY SUKIYA ARCHITECTURE: AN EXCEPTION TO THE RULE?

三 A PARTICULAR STORY

266 三 AN EXAMPLE FROM TODAY
270 三 HISTORY AND CULTURE
294 三 IDENTIFICATION OF A CENTER
318 三 PRINCIPLES OF AN ONTOLOGY OF CONSTRUCTION
356 三 PAST-PRESENT

369 POSTSCRIPT: TRADITION, WHO ARE YOU?

403 JAPANESE TERMS

415 INDEX OF PROPER NAMES

418 PLACE NAMES

422 BIBLIOGRAPHY

429 ILLUSTRATIONS

436 CHRONOLOGY

437 ACKNOWLEDGEMENTS

fig 1. View of the Shinnyodo monastery 真如堂, from the Yoshida hill, Kyoto.

FOREWORD: HISTORY, STORIES

When Japanese architecture is mentioned today, images of temples or pagodas generally come to mind. Some may think of more contemporary works as well: massive modular walls of rough concrete poured in place and bearing imprints of their formwork in the manner of Andō Tadao, the lighter structures of Itō Toyō and Sejima Kazuyo, or the finely wrought facades of Kuma Kengo[1], to mention only a few. A generational chasm and, rather surprisingly, even a historical one seems to have opened up between the emblematic images of traditional architecture, in which wood is the material of choice, and more current and innovative work, in which its use has been reduced. Even though the carpenter has long been the lead builder, contemporary architectural culture appears to have forgotten this reservoir of construction experience accumulated over centuries. A similar forgetfulness seems to apply to music as well as to a number of other domains of art. Japanese children more often learn to play the piano or violin than the *shamisen* or the *koto*. Painting and sculpture have been taught according to Western canons since the Meiji restoration at the end of the nineteenth century. The decline of craftsmanship and the industrialization and modernization of practical knowledge and techniques are phenomena occurring on a global scale. But in Japan, the contrast between the ancient legacy and what is being built today in most Japanese cities is particularly striking, even worrisome.

Real estate development and the building industry are left free to destroy the majority of urban patrimony—in other words, all architecture built of wood—with the exception of registered monuments or a few protected historical areas. What can one still hope for? First of all, the situation must evolve towards greater protection of residential patrimony, which, because it belongs to private owners, is completely subject to the laws of the market. But to be realistic, one must first play devil's advocate: what could possibly convince the owner of a building on an urban site to conserve it, when making use of perfectly legal increases in building rights (linked to real estate speculation) make it possible to replace the older building with a new construction offering more space for sale or rent? High inheritance taxes do not encourage preservation or extending the lives of buildings either. The new owner is often obliged to subdivide a plot or sell it off to pay taxes, which leads *de facto* to the destruction of existing building stock. Economic considerations generally take precedence over aesthetic ones or the social dimension as well.

For example, in a city like Kyoto, wooden houses of a certain age—more than seventy years old (from the postwar), which does not seem old in Europe—are only conserved when an aesthete takes an interest in them, or as is more often the case, when they are restored

---

[1] Our references to Japanese names follow the local custom of placing the family name before the first name. We will use Japanese characters in their first occurrences in the text or footnotes and English spellings thereafter. Japanese terms are listed in the toponymic and onomastic indices located at the end of the volume.

for commercial purposes: for guesthouses, restaurants, or shared housing. There will be little change to this situation without active intervention by the Japanese government and local authorities to protect the urban patrimony. And on a smaller scale, efforts to revitalize the wood construction sector should be undertaken, using more varieties indigenous to the archipelago, in order to promote policies in which the entire cycle of production is part of a more balanced practice of sustainable development. Wood used in Japan today is scarcely Japanese at all; only 15% of wood used in construction originates in local forests. And much like what one observes in Europe, especially in Mediterranean countries where masonry remains the starting point of all construction, there has been a renewed interest in wooden architecture in recent years. This could help set in place a more efficient production system for wood.

WHAT IS TRADITION?

Addressing the issue of wood architecture in Japan requires starting out by invoking tradition. But what does that mean? The term has no separate existence or inherent meaning—nothing that has always existed or that perpetuates itself naturally like a genetic legacy. On the contrary, it is the product of a work process, of customs and rituals which themselves change over time.[2] The essence of tradition stems from the transmission of know-how and techniques. Some disappear because they are no longer passed on, while others appear, are practiced, recognized, respected, and followed. Historians tend to look for the origins of a tradition in monuments built of wood or described on paper, in the material legacy, and in archival documents. An anthropologist focuses more on human production, the ways in which customs are transmitted through human behavior and modes of life, and goes out in the field to interrogate those who know, define, and perpetuate the tradition in question. The geographer, the philosopher, and the sociologist all have still other theoretical and practical approaches, sometimes relying on written histories or oral traditions. The architect is situated somewhere between several disciplinary fields and finds inspiration in those aspects of a tradition found among prior productions of drawings and built objects.

The thesis of the first architect in Japan to obtain a doctoral degree, in 1898, addressed this subject in an almost prophetic manner. Itō Chūta was a pioneer in his field. He studied the architecture of Hōryūji,[3] a Buddhist monastery located near Nara, and based his work on the principle that careful study of its specific proportions and construction details could shed light on its history and its originality. Some of these edifices, which date from the seventh century, are considered today to be the oldest wooden buildings in the world. Through his study of the monastery's principal buildings, Itō sought to define the formation of a "Japanese" architectural style. This is a complex issue, as one of the principal characteristics of the architecture of Japan is that its origins are partly continental. There are differences between the typologies and techniques of Chinese, Korean, and Japanese carpenters, but in the course of developing their own tools and original solutions, the Japanese also copied much from their neighbors. Such "copying" was hardly considered a novice's shortcoming. Instead, it was seen as a necessary path for the transmission of traditional Japanese arts. In the eighth century, during the Nara period,

---

[2] Our reference on this point is to Gérard Lenclud, "Qu'est-ce que la tradition?" in *Transcrire les mythologies*, ed. Marcel Detienne (Paris: Albin Michel, 1994), 25–44.
[3] The study by Itō Chūta 伊東忠太 (1867–1954) was first published in the form of an article, "Hōryūji kenchikuron" 法隆寺建築論 [A study of the architecture of Hōryūji], *Kenchiku zasshi* 建築雑誌, vol. 7, no. 83 (November 1893), 317–50.

Buddhist architecture on the island was still very "Chinese," having come from the mainland with this religion, along with many other cultural features borrowed from the Tang dynasty, then at its height. Even the plan of the grand shrine of Ise, despite being devoted to the local Shintō religion, exhibits the influence of Chinese monuments, such as their typical axiality. In other words, Itō's undertaking was foundational on several levels: to show the historical importance of the Japanese contribution to world architecture, and in its attempt to define the Japanese itself, two issues that remain topical today.

Techniques, textures, and varieties of wood, followed by specific arrangements and then spaces began to flesh out Japanese architecture. Over the course of time, construction methods, not to say styles, came to shape an architectural culture and tradition, which in turn relied on local resources. Wood played the leading (if not the only) role although many local creators are unaware of this today, as it does not conform to the vocabulary of contemporary architecture derived from a modernism expressed primarily in metal, glass, and concrete. Although the current situation seems to be evolving, wood remains a material from the past, like stone in Europe, which most architects turn to for economic reasons or for local color: Japanese in this case. This is true for residential construction, for the renovation of older wood buildings, or for the construction of "Japanese"-type buildings, such as traditional hostels (*ryokan* 旅館). In the field of wood construction, the different tradespeople—framers, carpenters, and cabinetmakers—remain the true guardians of a temple, made of wood as it were, supported by the other agents of this chain: nursery owners, woodcutters, and dealers, who also continue to transmit a traditional culture linked to this material.

A LOCAL PASSION FOR WOOD

Japan remains a very wooded country, with two-thirds of its territory covered by forests—boreal forests in Hokkaidō to the northeast, temperate ones on the islands of Honshū and Shikoku, and subtropical forests on Kyūshū, to the southwest. Many villages earn their living from the cultivation of forests. Their village cooperatives stock posts, beams, and different wood planks destined for the construction market. And yet, more than seventy percent of the wood consumed in Japan today (for construction, the production of paper, or for heating) is imported from Asia and the Pacific, as well as from America, Russia, and Scandinavia. Areas dedicated to forest cultivation have become obsolete, too small to be profitable, and difficult to access in the mountain valleys. The village populations are aging, and occupations tied to forestry hold little appeal for the young and neo-rural populations.

The mountains north of Kyoto are a typical example of many of these various *terroirs* linked to the wood economy, where we were able to observe different actors in that sector (fig. 2). This area includes two major types of landscape devoted to silviculture: the mountains and valleys where trees destined for construction have been cultivated for more than 400 years, and a bit further to the north, the plateaus where the agricultural cooperative hangars are found, large warehouses for wood and factories for pre-cutting the various pieces of wood (from the English-Japanese "precut": *prekatto*), primarily destined for the fabrication of individual houses. These contemporary factories, entirely automated in operation, produce posts and beams precisely cut according to their intended position, and numbered according to the structural algorithms of the house. In this way, the wood structure of a house is defined as a set of parts, cut up and numbered before being delivered to the site and erected in a few days (fig. 3). According to the

fig 2. Landscape of the Keihoku 京北 plateau, northwest of Kyoto, 2016.

FOREWORD: HISTORY, STORIES   13

Keihoku factory manager, the factory operates twenty-two hours a day, approximately 360 days per year, and yet more than 90% of the wood it treats is imported. Next to it one sees a sawmill that looks abandoned, which serves to cut up domestic wood: primarily cedar (*sugi* 杉), cypress (*hinoki* 檜), and pine (*matsu* 松). A sad and recurring contrast between the success of foreign woods and the fate of those local species that once defined the beauty of buildings from the past, and still do.

WHAT IS CRYPTOMERIA?

This simple question brings up the issue of the relation between a specific architecture and its ecosystem. Which local woods are cut up by these sawmills, in such small quantity? What importance do they hold for our discussion? These are essentially the Japanese cypress (*hinoki*) and the Japanese cedar (*sugi*), whose scientific name is *cryptomeria japonica*. These two species constitute the bulk of the patrimony of wood in Japan, and along with some other less emblematic species found on the island, they define the tradition by virtue of their mechanical and aesthetic properties.

The very use of these trees was governed by rules based on their properties, their use, and aesthetics. Cypress was primarily reserved for visible and primary structures. When beams were hidden behind a false ceiling, other less expensive species would do. Cedar was used primarily in interiors. A prime example was the "cryptomeria of the Northern mountains" (Kitayama *sugi*) cultivated north of Kyoto (figs. 4, 5). Renowned for its pale color, it was prized by the nobility and bourgeoisie for the non-structural corner posts of ornamental alcoves (*tokonoma* 床の間) found in the tatami reception rooms of residences in the Shoin (書院) and Sukiya (数寄屋) styles of the sixteenth century. As this style continues to this day, these trees are still prized, even if decreased demand has jeopardized their production.

Commonly found in the subdivided mountain landscapes of central Japan, cypresses and cedars cover the slopes of relatively low but often quite steep ridges. There the cedar grows quick and straight, even in the valley shadows. After the Second World War, as part of poorly planned public policy, cedar was widely planted around major cities to serve as wood for construction, to the point of altering the ecosystem. Furthermore, its pollination periods that begin in mid-March are the cause of the hay fever that afflicts almost 20% of the Japanese population. As for the "Kitayama cryptomeria," it was "born" some five hundred years ago, at the beginning of the Sukiya style mentioned above, in the village of Nakagawa, today a neighborhood in the northern district (Kita-ku) of the city of Kyoto. The hamlet is also famous for having been featured in Kawabata Yasunari's novel about Kyoto, *Koto* (*The Old Capital*), which was published in 1962 and adapted three times for film and television (in 1963, 1980, and 2005). The chapter on "Kitayama cryptomeria" describes the location of this village constructed along a river: "The steep mountains on either side of the Kiyotaki River dropped into the narrow valley. One reason the famous cedar logs were raised here was that the area received ample rain and little sunshine."[4] But like the sawmills previously mentioned, the fame of the place and its cedars scarcely offsets the decrepitude of its houses, a further example of an ambiguous relation to the past.

[4] See Kawabata Yasunari 川端康成, *Koto* 古都 (Tokyo: Shinchōsha, 1962); English edition: *The Old Capital*, trans. J. Martin Holman (Berkeley: Counterpoint Press, reprint edition 2006), 68.

FOREWORD: HISTORY, STORIES   15

fig 3. Precut and numbered pieces (floor by floor), delivered to the construction site of the EFEO Center in Kyoto, 2014.

fig 4. At the start of the traditional felling (*honjikomi* 本仕込み) of the Kitayama cedars (Kitayama *sugi*), a woodcutter cuts the tree at its base, while another pulls it in order to make it tip onto the postern where it can dry. Kyoto, August 2016.

fig 5. Stripping the bark off a Kitayama *sugi*, Kyoto.

THE CULTURE OF THE CARPENTER

Posts made of "Kitayama cryptomeria" are primarily employed by carpenters in workshops specializing in the Sukiya style[5] that originated in the sixteenth century. Of the many workshops in Kyoto that existed previously, only three remain. They are entrusted with the restoration of the patrimony—tea houses, Buddhist temples, Shintō shrines, and old palaces—along with the occasional new construction (primarily luxury houses). These workshops are linked to a particular work ethic, in which the training of a master carpenter takes approximately ten years, and all the woods employed, with some few exceptions, are solid domestic ones, which also makes the work very expensive. The Sukiya master carpenter has an intermediary role, between artist and artisan, in the construction milieu. Although the aesthetic of his discipline is regulated by a specific system of proportions, he himself will adapt the organization of the rooms, their dimensions and construction details, as well as the choice of varieties, during the construction of buildings. In this sense, he plays the same role as the Sukiya carpenters, when they were the sole builders of large residences for the nobility in the past. The master carpenters work with an entire series of other participants or sub-contractors—installers for tiles, tatamis, paper sliding partitions, finish coatings etc.—not unlike artisans in France who specialize in the different arts of building, and who occupy a similarly precarious niche function like them.

One of the most famous of these master carpenters, Nakamura Sotoji (1906–1997) took part in the construction of buildings, tea houses, and Japanese gardens for wealthy clients around the world, notably for John Lennon and Yoko Ono, as well as for the Rockefeller family in the United States, in collaboration with the architect Yoshimura Junzō 吉村順三 (1908–1997). These projects provide living proof, as if that were required, that these artisans populate the imagination of clients belonging to a rich and often international elite, who hold a certain attachment to the image, even the stereotype, of Japanese traditional excellence. The American chieftains of Microsoft or Oracle recently called on the Sukiya carpenters and not the architects to build their private residences in Karuizawa and Kyoto. These artisans, whose work encompasses cabinetmaking as well, are also seeking new prospects. For example, the Nakamura Sotoji workshop, one of the principal Japanese fabricators of wooden furniture, has begun to collaborate with Danish designers under the umbrella of the Kohseki company, offering a selection of contemporary furniture compatible with the aesthetic of traditional architecture.

CODES AND CANONS

We will continue to examine the profession of the Sukiya carpenter, because today it exemplifies the mastery of wood construction for the most part, as well as the relation to tradition (or rather to one tradition). Yet one of the difficulties the profession faces, like most highly codified Japanese traditional arts, is how to remain alive and develop in a society whose architectural expression is constantly in flux, and whose range of available materials is so much greater than it was in the sixteenth century.

---

[5] The main carpentry workshops that still specialize in the Sukiya are Yamamoto kōgyō 山本工業 in Kinugasa 衣笠, at the northeast of the city, Nakamura Sotoji kōmuten 中村外二工務店, near the monastery of Daitokuji 大徳寺, Araki kōmuten 荒木工務店, in the Western part of the city, in the Ukyō-ku ward, and Yasui Moku kōmuten 安井杢工務店, in the city of Mukō 向日, Kyoto Prefecture.

The means by which technical knowledge is transmitted provides one of the main vectors for the perpetuation of tradition within a profession. This know-how is foundational and reflects an aesthetic. Manuals on framing carpentry essentially contain measurements and occasionally structural plans. Carpenters indicate the measurements and proportions of pieces of wood within the framing. This system is called the *kiwari* 木割, and makes it possible to determine the size of each element as a function of the ensemble of principal parts. The "stereotomy" of wood has been in use since antiquity, during the Nara period. Each master carpenter establishes his own system of proportions as a function of the intended building type, and these instructions are transmitted orally during construction. The oldest manual is said to have been written by the master carpenter of Hōryūji, but the first reference to it that has been found dates from a manual of the Muromachi epoch, in 1489. These manuals (*hinagata-bon* 雛形本) flourished in the seventeenth century, following the appearance of a collection of *kiwari* in 1608, which served as a reference during the Edo shōgunate (1603–1868). That collection was the *Shōmei,* edited by a master carpenter from the Wakayama prefecture.[6] The manual consists of five rolls: five books of notes for the construction of five types of building: gates (*mon* 門), Shintō sanctuaries (*sha* 社), Buddhist pavilions (*dō* 堂), pagodas (*tō* 塔), and palaces (*denya* 殿屋). The document helps one understand the general appearance of the main buildings of Japanese architecture, in that archaic form known as *kata* 形, which represents an ideal form, an archetype, or even a canon (fig. 6).

These cultural and "traditional" features—the techniques, dimensions, and proportions that are at the origin of the craft of carpentry—were transmitted from generation to generation over the centuries. Then at the end of the nineteenth century, knowledge and techniques imported from the West came to be taught in the universities and schools of art. These new approaches developed bit by bit to form a new architectural culture, bringing architects and carpenters into a kind of modern twinship.

THREE AUTHORS IN ONE

This volume was drawn up by three authors, each of whom has a specific relationship to Japanese architecture. As historians or practitioners, they decided to create this book together after several productive meetings in Kyoto between 2014 and 2017. 2014 was the inaugural year of the new Center for the French School of Asian Studies—École Française d'Extrême-Orient (EFEO)—in Kyoto. The commission for the design and construction of this wooden building was awarded to the Mikan architecture agency, one of whose four founders, Manuel Tardits oversaw the project. At the time, Benoît Jacquet was in charge of this research center, and by observing the construction process of a wood structure, he was able to discover firsthand the culture, the techniques, and the manner of execution that needed to be understood *in situ*, on the very site in which they were carried out. As proof of the successful understanding between the client, the project manager, and the contracting company, the project received

---

[6] See the preface by the historian Ōta Hirotarō 太田博太郎, to his modern edition of the *Shōmei* 匠明, "*Shōmei* no gendaiteki igi"『匠明』の現代的意義 [The contemporary significance of the *Shōmei*], in *Shōmei,* edited by Ōta Hirotarō, annotated and translated into modern Japanese Itō Yōtarō 伊藤要太郎 (Tokyo: Kajima shuppankai, 1971), 2 volumes, vol. 1, p. ii. The author of the five books of the *Shōmei* (1608) was Heinouchi Masanobu 平内政信 (1583–1645). An original copy of the *Shōmei* is located in the archives of the Graduate School of Architecture library at the University of Tokyo.

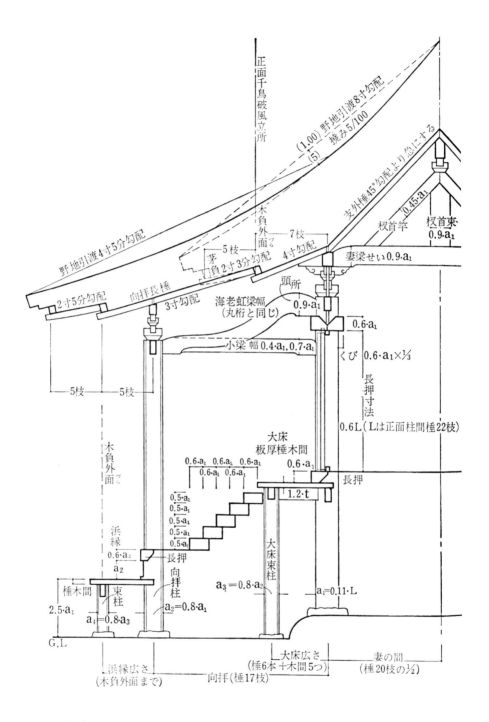

fig 6. Example of measurements and proportions for the construction of a Shintō sanctuary (*jinja*). Plate from the carpentry treatise *Shōmei* 匠明 (1608), republished in 1971 in the *Shōmei gokankō* 匠明五巻考 [An analysis of the five rolls of the *Shōmei*], plate 3.

FOREWORD: HISTORY, STORIES 21

a 2014 prize for sustainable construction from the LafargeHolcim Foundation.[7] In the end, the building also served as a starting point for our study on wood architecture in Japan. Historian of architecture Matsuzaki Teruaki was part of the research with the goal of bringing a deeper historical perspective, while Benoît Jacquet and Manuel Tardits addressed the modern period, starting with the transition from the old world to the contemporary one, and ending with a description of the construction process for the EFEO Center in Kyoto.

The authors met up on a regular basis in Kyoto to develop the concept for this book of stories and history. As each was in a position to share his own knowledge of the specialized domains of his colleagues, the intent of these meetings was to establish a common work plan and to create a coherent ensemble. While wood ("organic" matter *par excellence* and the essential constituent of traditional Japanese architecture) is of course the invariant factor for each of the "stories" detailed here, it also clearly conditions the traditions (cultures), the techniques, and by extension, specific spaces. Here we draw the reader's attention to a question that sheds light transversely on our study and the history of Japanese architecture in a latent and recurrent manner: the question of measure, of measurements, and of the dimensioning of spaces conceived in this manner. Indeed, a piece of solid lumber—from one of the species we have just mentioned—consisting of a tree trunk in a single segment, possesses limited physical properties. Along with the techniques used to overcome their limitations, these properties are characteristic of construction typologies essentially made up of posts and beams.

The first chapter of this study addresses in depth the work on spatial and structural dimensions linked to ancient palaces and religious architectures (from the sixth to the twelfth centuries), then to the residential spatial complexes linked to the ceremonies and art of tea during the medieval and modern periods (from the thirteenth to the nineteenth centuries). We should note that the development of these typologies, which stretches out over a millennium, is essentially conditioned and indebted to a post-and-beam system of solid wood pieces whose physical properties are limited. In this architecture, one finds an ever-present obsession for measure, measurement, and proportion in rooms that are described not only by their function, but also by their surfaces and the rhythms of their weight-bearing structure. This architecture consists of a "forest" planted by man. "Great rooms" were formed inside these lines of posts. By the end of the medieval period, the largest of these covered as much as 18 tatamis (approximately 29 square meters or 95 sf), while square-shaped "small rooms," measuring 4.5 tatamis in area, or even 2 tatamis (slightly over 7 square meters or 23 sf, or 3 square meters or 10 sf, respectively) were formed for the smallest spaces. If we take the tea pavilion (*chashitsu* 茶室) as an example, it developed first in the gardens of Zen monasteries, after monks returning from China in the twelfth century had discovered the virtues of green tea, especially for meditation.[8] It originated in the monastic habitat, as indistinguishable from the archetypal abbot's residence,

---

[7] See "High-Tech Low-Tech Sustainable research center featuring traditional woodworking methods." https://www. lafargeholcim-foundation.org/projects/high-tech-low-tech

[8] For an introduction to the history of the tea house, see Fujimori Terunobu, "The development of the tea room and its meaning in architecture" in *The Contemporary Tea House: Japan's top Architects Redefine a Tradition*, Isozaki Arata, Andō Tadao and Fujimori Terunobu, eds. (Tokyo: Kōdansha International, 2007), 7–25; See also Benoît Jacquet, "Dans les secrets du pavillon de thé, d'hier et d'aujourd'hui," *Sigila*, no. 28 (November 2011), 91–104.

the *hōjō* 方丈.[9] This room with an ideal square plan (of 4.5 tatamis, or approximately three meters or ten foot, one *jō* 丈, on a side) symbolizes a world in miniature. This architectural space, as we shall see, arises out of multiple spatial variations through the arrangement of its parts.

In the second chapter, we trace the passage to modernity, the assimilation of Western techniques, first turning away from and then back again towards an architecture considered "Japanese" by its designers, beginning in the 1920s and 1930s and once more after the Second World War, during the 1950s and 1960s. Traditional Japanese architecture is manifestly tied to the materiality of wood. Architects created hybrid modern expressions integrating the vocabulary of the masters of modernity, such as Le Corbusier or the Bauhaus, with the techniques of wood carpentry. This was particularly true of the architects close to Le Corbusier, such as Antonin Raymond, Maekawa Kunio, and Tange Kenzō.[10] During the 1960s wood was primarily used in the design of single-family houses. A certain regionalism resulted, for example in the renewal of the Sukiya style during the war and the nationalist period, exemplified by the work of Horiguchi Sutemi, Murano Tōgo, Taniguchi Yoshirō, and Yoshida Isoya. In a different register and one generation later,[11] Shinohara Kazuo employed the theme of the house as a vehicle for his reflections on architecture, and developed spaces according to his own interpretations of the Japanese vernacular dwelling (*minka* 民家). With the notable exception of the supporters of the Sukiya style, a sort of ambiguity remained because (like his contemporaries) Shinohara seems to have often used wood by default. Shinohara's interest is founded less on the expression of the nature of the material than on the spatial play which is nonetheless linked to it. Like cinderblocks in France or brick in England, wood in Japan remains the most economical and most frequently used material for residential or relatively low buildings (less than three stories high). It is easy to obtain. Its light structures can be erected quickly, and the carpentry contractors who have perfectly mastered its constraints remain the principal actors in this domain of the construction sector.

The third chapter addresses wood architecture in the contemporary world, at a moment when the relation to this material seems to be undergoing a certain revision. How can one pragmatically understand the relation between contemporary architects and the traditional methods of construction, especially in terms of the structural systems, the dimensions, the varieties, and their manner of implementation? What is the specific relation between the two traditions, the more recent one represented by architects, and the older carpentry tradition outlined in the previous two chapters? Here the construction of the EFEO Center is presented in detail, as a particular moment in the history of the dialectical relationship between theory and practice, between the old and the new as transposed to Japan. This particular story is the starting point of this essay as well as its conclusion.

---

[9] It is worth noting that is the same archetypal space built, dwelled in, and described by Kamo no Chōmei 鴨長明 (1155–1216) in his famous book *Hōjō-ki* 方丈記, in which the term *hōjō* is translated alternatively as "hut," hermitage, monk's hut, hermit's hut, or the ten foot square hut: see Kamo no Chōmei, *Hōjō-ki*, ed. Ichiko Teiji 市古貞次 (Tokyo: Iwanami shoten, 1989); English edition: *An Account of a Ten-Foot-Square Hut*, trans. Anthony H. Chambers, in Haruo Shirane, ed., *Traditional Japanese Literature: An Anthology* (New York: Columbia University Press, 2007); See also *Hōjōki: A Hermit's Hut as Metaphor*, translated and annotated by Matthew Stavros (Kyoto: Vicus Lusurum, 2020); See also Nicolas Fiévé, "De la villa de plaisance à l'ermitage de montagne. La chaumine carrée de dix pieds, allégorie architecturale et paysagère de la cabane de reclus," in Nicolas Fiévé, Yola Gloaguen, Benoît Jacquet (eds.), *Mutations paysagères de l'espace habité au Japon. De la maison au territoire*. Paris: Collège de France (2020), 9–55.

[10] Maekawa Kunio 前川國男 (1905–1986) worked for Le Corbusier from 1928 to 1930, then for Antonin Raymond (1888–1976). When he returned to Tokyo, Tange Kenzō 丹下健三 (1913–2005) worked for Maekawa from 1938 to1941. See Sasaki Hiroshi 佐々木宏, *Kyoshō e no shōkei: Ru korubyuje ni miserareta Nihon no kenchikukatachi* 巨匠への憧憬：ル・コルビュジエに魅せられた日本の建築家たち [Drawn to the master: the Japanese architects fascinated by Le Corbusier] (Tokyo: Sagami shobō, 2000), 167, 335, 373.

[11] Murano Tōgo 村野藤吾 (1891–1984), Yoshida Isoya 吉田五十八 (1894–1974), Horiguchi Sutemi 堀口捨己 (1895–1984), Taniguchi Yoshirō 谷口吉郎 (1904–1979), Shinohara Kazuo 篠原一男 (1925–2006).

DWARVES AND GIANTS

This book makes no claim to be exhaustive. Nonetheless, its three chapters follow a chronological course, whose goal is to provide an overview of the history of wood architecture in Japan. What are its essential features? The book sets out to show that despite the breaks and ruptures that resulted from the modernization of the country that began in the late nineteenth century, the construction principles and spatial typologies that were tied to traditions and techniques and set in place several centuries earlier still exert an influence on contemporary architectural creation today. The authors' main intent is to better define tradition, or rather traditions, and to understand what constitutes the "Japanese" in return.

The second preoccupation that underlies this research concerns the distinctive particularities of Japan itself, a topic that nearly monopolizes discourse on architecture in that country. At a time when travel and international exchange are the norm, when culture is globalized and information is made immediately available on the same social networks, where everyone in the world can consume the same products, use the same objects, the same furniture, and produce the same spaces in an increasingly unified way of life, other values are increasingly sought after: authenticity, handcraft, the local or regional, the artisanal. Japanese architects receive an education very similar to that of their Western colleagues. They also sometimes build projects in these same countries where architecture is born of tradition, but where they are expected to distinguish themselves as "Japanese" architects. A nagging question arises: how is a local architecture ("Japanese" in this case) any different, and how does it adapt to the universality of modern architecture?

We have sought to bring concrete elements of an answer to this question. Many creative individuals will recognize their own experiences in the apparently contradictory aspirations of being of one's time and also a reflection of one's past, of knowing the classics but being capable of innovation. The problem is an old, almost archaic one. It is one of the first paradoxes of modernity, for as early as the Middle Ages, the moderns (the evangelists) were already considered "dwarves standing on the shoulders of giants"—belonging to the classics— the prophets in this case.[12] Is the Japanese architect carried by the work of the carpenter? Is contemporary Japanese architecture just the legacy of a great architectural tradition? Architects do not seem to pose questions in those terms, nor do they attempt to answer them. Yet in the recent history of architectural debate, they cultivate a certain ambiguity between the proper use of local traditions and a desire for modernity.

In March of 1953, during one of those debates that the professional press of the archipelago likes to organize, the *Kokusai kenchiku* review brought together some of the principal protagonists of the period. Architects Maekawa Kunio, Sakakura Junzō, Tange Kenzō and Yoshida Isoya were invited to address the question of Japanese national identity, the specific effects of climate, and the importation of international values in architecture.[13] Each participant took advantage of the occasion to express his view of his relation to the Japanese context in his own

---

[12] The expression "*Nanus positus super humeros gigantis*," comes from Bernard de Chartres (twelfth century); see Antoine Compagnon, *The 5 Paradoxes of Modernity*, trans. Franklin Philip (New York: Columbia University Press, 1994); French edition (1990), 19.

[13] See Maekawa Kunio, Sakakura Junzō 坂倉順三, Tange Kenzō, Yoshida Isoya, "Kokusaisei, fūdosei, kokuminsei. Gendai kenchiku no zōkei o megutte" 国際性、風土性、国民性：現代建築の造形をめぐって [Internationalism, mediance, nationality. Around the formation of contemporary architecture] *Kokusai kenchiku* [International architecture] (March 1953): 2–15. See also the presentation of this discussion in Jonathan Reynolds, *Maekawa Kunio and the Emergence of Japanese Modernist Architecture* (Berkeley: University of California Press, 2001), 214–8.

fig 7. A combination of contemporary and traditional materials, techniques, and tools on the construction site of the EFEO Center in Kyoto, 2014.

creative work. Tange, who became one of the first "international" Japanese architects by virtue of being commissioned to build outside of Japan, considered the Japanese climate and tradition to be the "antithesis" of internationalism, and claimed that in his own practice, he tried to come naturally to an "international" form by using the "technical standards" of his country, even if these were not part of the general tendencies of contemporary architecture. Architect Yoshida Isoya, a proponent of a modern Sukiya architecture, was a bit lighter in tone but also more tendentious; he did not hesitate to invoke the influence of "Japanese blood" on the architects of the nation, the misfit between rugby and the Japanese body, or the absurdity of copying the supposedly international architecture of Brazilian Oscar Niemeyer, which was popular at the time among Japanese students, despite designing for a tropical climate, quite different from the Japanese milieu. As for the concept of a "Japanese" architecture, Yoshida considered that "the level of Japan-ness of a creation seems acceptable when it is not perceived as a Japanese thing by a Japanese person, although it can be seen as truly Japanese by a foreigner... Whereas if even a Japanese person sees it as something Japanese, that means that it has gone past the limit!" Here again, we see the pertinence or the impertinence of both endogenous and exogenous gazes.

The three authors of this book committed themselves to explore the process of creation of a local architecture in a given material, on the basis of historical documents and studies in the field, through interpretations of texts and writings by carpenters and architects, through the analysis of plans and conceptual drawings illustrating their concepts, and through the enlightened engagement in practice. The text was written by three sets of hands between Tokyo and Kyoto, primarily for Western readers. This "manual" is meant to be read by a variety of eyes, those seduced by images intended to be synthetic and to "speak," those seeking a specific reference, without fear of specialized knowledge or jargon, or those who seek to transversally reconstitute a longer history in a relatively compact format. Each of these readings corresponds to a goal of this volume, dedicated to the student as well as the scholar, to the practitioner as well as the user, to anyone interested in Japanese culture or simply interested in wood, that natural element that was once the essential material, in the etymological sense of the word, of Japanese architecture, and which is tending to become so once again (fig. 7).

A STORY OF
PRINCIPLES

fig a1. Ise shrine, Ise

COMPLEXITY IN ARCHITECTURE… À LA JAPANESE

"I don't know which god is to be found here… but I am grateful for all this grace, and I am in tears" (Saigyō)[14]

In 2013, the eighty-three structures of the Ise Shrine were reconstructed for the sixty-second time: first, the principal sanctuary (*seiden* 正殿 or *shōden* 昇殿)[15], where the mirror that symbolizes the divinity is housed, was rebuilt; then the major auxiliary building (*betsugū* 別宮); the minor ones (*sessha* 摂社 and *massha* 末社); and finally, the bridges and gates (*torii* 鳥居).[16] This periodic rite of reconstruction that entails the transfer of divinity has taken place approximately every twenty years since the year 690.[17] The shrine was originally built on a wooded site at some distance from the ancient capitals of Asuka (mid-sixth century–710) and Nara (710–794), the political centers of Japan in their respective eponymous periods. The main sanctuary is located within an enclosure erected in the middle of the forest. This enclosure is further subdivided into two plots of the same size and shape, one of them empty and the other built up. Every twenty years, a pavilion strictly identical to the existing one is constructed in the adjacent empty plot, alternating between the two. Once the transfer of the divinity is complete, the older building is completely dismantled. Despite its repeated demolitions, the current primary sanctuary (*seiden*) remains extremely close in form to the one mentioned in the historical documents of the Nara period.[18] The oldest-known detailed description of the form of a Shintō shrine is found in these documents, and it seems in fact to prove that the shrine has retained its original form throughout its cycles of reconstruction.

---

[14] Saigyō, *"Nanigoto no, Owashimasu o ba, Shiranu domo, Katajikenasa ni, Namida goboruru"* 何事の/おわしますをば/知らねども/かたじけなさに/涙こぼるる, in *Sankashū* 山家集; *Poems of a Mountain Home*, translated by Burton Watson (New York: Columbia University Press, 1991). This poem, in the waka 和歌 style, was to have been addressed to the Great Ise shrine (Ise daijingū 伊勢大神宮) by the monk Saigyō (Saigyō Hōshi 西行法師 [1118–1190]) who stayed there between 1180 and 1186. In 1186, the monk Keishun 慶俊 of the Tōdaiji Monastery (Nara), visited the sanctuary in the company of the monk Chōgen 重源 and also wrote that "In the buildings created for the gods (sanctuaries), everything is different, the ensemble is superb, one enters another world." (*Shinden seisaku, fuji yosha, chikei shôzetsu, iiki ni iru ga gotoshi* 神殿製作/不似余社/地形勝絶/如入異域). There is little doubt that the monks of the time shared this perception.

[15] We include Chinese characters for Japanese words when they are used for the first time. These words are also listed in the lexicon of Japanese terms in an annex to the work.

[16] For a detailed description in French of this reconstruction, see Jean-Sébastien Cluzel and Nishida Masatsugu (ed.), *Le sanctuaire d'Ise. Récit de la 62e reconstruction* (Brussels: Mardaga, 2015).

[17] It seems that the Ise shrine was the first to be reconstructed, but until the Edo period, the periodic rite of reconstruction (*shikinen sengū* 式年遷宮) took place in other sanctuaries as well, such as the shrines at Kasuga taisha 春日大社 in Nara, of Kamo jinja 賀茂神社 in Kyoto, or of Sumiyoshi taisha 住吉大社 in Osaka.

[18] In the document entitled "Order form for decorative metals" (*Kazari-kanamono chūmonjō* 鋜金物注文状), in the collection of writing *Shōsōin monjo* 正倉院文書 ("Archives of the Shōsōin"; 762), one finds a description of the metalwork for the main sanctuary (*seiden*), and dimensions are indicated in the "Register of ceremonies of the Inner Sanctuary of Ise" (*Kōtai jingū gishikichō* 皇大神宮儀式帳), *Toyu-kegū gishikichō* 止由気宮儀式帳 (dated from 804), that are almost identical with those of the sanctuary today.

The architecture of the oldest shrine in Japan has maintained its original form in this manner, despite being permanently renewed and rebuilt.

During the Kamakura period (1185–1333), six centuries after the first construction of the sanctuary, approaching it was forbidden. Pilgrims such as the monk Saigyō, quoted at the beginning of this chapter, offered their prayers from a distance, and could only see the shrine through the forest, from afar. Additionally, despite its ancient form, the shrine had already been reconstructed periodically. It may seem surprising that Saigyō was so moved by this single edifice whose existence was relatively ephemeral and was barely visible through the forest. Could this tearful monk even make out the sanctuary in the midst of the vegetation, and how could he experience such gratitude under those conditions?

This example clearly illustrates some characteristics of traditional Japanese architecture: a particular affinity for nature and a certain form of ambiguity, two features linked to the temperate climate and the geo-political position of this archipelago located at the edge of Asia. More precisely, its ambiguity resides in the coexistence of multiple meanings, and a tendency to value the relations with or between objects, rather than the objects themselves. Claude Lévi-Strauss characterized Japanese culture as an "alternation between borrowings and syntheses, syncretism and originality."[19] This coexistence of elements imported from the continent of Asia, from China and Korea, along with previously accumulated elements from ancient local cultures can give the impression that "it (Japan) retained what suited it and set aside the rest,"[20] by creating new compositions adapted to local conditions. Instead of formalizing an ensemble of parts within a framework predetermined by tradition, the original archetype will instead adapt to contingencies. This relativity, or establishment of relations, consists in its most developed form in "not building," or rather in conveying a spatial or spiritual sense not limited to construction alone.

The concept of the Ise shrine gives the impression that nothing is planned, but this appearance is deceiving. The access path (sandō 参道) through the forest to the main sanctuary (seiden) crosses a bridge before leading the pilgrims to the furthest part, in the depths (oku 奥) of the sanctuary. It describes a series of broad curves that maintain a sense of distance and preclude direct views of the home of the divinity. Over the course of the journey, one passes through a first portico (torii) at the purification point of the Isuzu river, then through a second one, each establishing a different zone. At the approach to the main sanctuary (seiden) the roof decorations appear between the trees and glint in the daylight. One ultimately circles the palisade before arriving in front of the sanctuary pavilions that rise up at the top of a stone staircase. The entire path is laid out to maintain a distance that makes one feel the sacred dimension of a hidden place in depths of nature. A nature that is itself "constructed," because cedars (sugi) and cypresses (hinoki) dating from the Heian period (794-1185) were planted along the access path (sandō) to orchestrate the approach to the sanctuary through the sacred laurel forest, which consists of broad-leaved evergreen trees, such as camphorwoods (kusunoki 楠).[21]

---

[19] Claude Lévi-Strauss, "The Place of Japanese Culture in the World," in *The Other Face of the Moon*, translated by Jane Marie Todd (Cambridge: Harvard University Press, 2013), 18.

[20] *Ibidem*, 39.

[21] For the species of trees in the Ise sanctuary forest, see Kawazoe Noboru 川添登, *Ki to mizu no kenchiku. Ise jingū* 木と水の建築・伊勢神宮 [The architecture of wood and water: Ise Jingū] (Tokyo: Chikuma shobō, 2010).

This aesthetics of ambiguity has evolved and been transmitted from one generation to another. To give a well-known example, the monk Urabe Kenkō wrote in his collection of thoughts *Essays in Idleness* that "Even when building the imperial palace, they always leave one place unfinished."[22] How has this aesthetic been developed in practice? Let us follow this path through the history of Japanese wood architecture from its origins up to 1868, at the beginning of the Meiji era.

[22] Yoshida or Urabe Kenkō 吉田兼好 (*circa* 1283–1352), *Tsurezuregusa* 徒然草 *Essays in Idleness*, translated by Donald Keene (New York: Columbia University Press, second paperback edition, 1998), 71.

fig a2. Wayō-style temple, Hōryūji monastery, Nara prefecture
fig a2-a. *kondō*

THE DIFFERENT ARCHITECTURAL TYPES

In order to better understand traditional Japanese architecture, let us begin by describing its different types and their stylistic characteristics. Although specialists on Japan speak of style, much in the way one can describe the orders in ancient Greece (Ionic, Doric, Corinthian, etc.), the term used is *zukuri* 造, corresponding more to a notion of fabrication, of constructive method/principle, or of form. So for example, the term *shoin-zukuri* 書院造り, translated as Shoin style, is literally the "construction principle" or the form of a *shoin* (construction), or a construction in the "library" style.[23] We will distinguish three categories of buildings: Buddhist temples, Shintō shrines, and residential constructions.

BUDDHIST TEMPLES: FOUR STYLES

The history of temple architecture consists of four main periods and styles. The first extends from the sixth century to the end of the Heian period in the twelfth century. It includes the ancient types of the Wayō style 和様 (literally, the "Japanese style") that began with the construction of the monastic complexes called *garan* 伽藍 in the capitals of Asuka and Nara. The first of them is the Hōkōji 法興寺 (also known as Asuka-dera, or the temple of Asuka 飛鳥寺), founded in 552, following the introduction of Buddhism from the Korean peninsula. Although none of the original buildings of this monastery remain, the five-story pagoda (*gojūnotō* 五重塔) and the treasure pavilion (*kondō* 金堂) of the Hōryūji, which are often considered the oldest wood buildings in the world, date from the same epoch (fig. a2). These were followed by the mountain temples of the Tendai 天台 and Shingon 真言 schools of Buddhism, which accompanied the transfer of the capital from Nara to Heiankyō, known as Kyoto today.

The second period includes the major temples in the Daibutsuyō style (literally, the "Great Buddha style"), which were built at the initiative of the warrior aristocracy during the Kamakura period, between the twelfth and fourteenth centuries, along with the *amidadō* 阿弥陀堂 buildings celebrating the Amida Buddha, whose cult was very popular at the time (fig. a3). This style is sometimes also known as Tenjikuyō (literally, "Indian style").[24] It began during the period of political unrest at the end of the Heian period, following the fire of the Tōdaiji 東大寺 temple of Nara, which housed a large statue of Buddha. Under the leadership of the monk Chōgen 重源 (1121-1206), its carpenters adopted new techniques that most likely came from

---

[23] See the nomenclature established in Nicolas Fiévé, *L'architecture et la ville du Japon ancien. Espace architectural de la ville de Kyôto et des résidences shôgunales aux 14ᵉ et 15ᵉ siècles* (Paris: Maisonneuve & Larose, 1996), 295-7.

[24] Up until the Second World War, this style was called Tenjikuyō 天竺様, but this term, literally meaning "Indian style" was inappropriate to designate a style that most likely came from China. Although it had been adopted for the reconstruction of the Tōdaiji temple, it was finally renamed Daibutsuyō 大仏様, see Ōta Hirotarō, *Shaji kenchiku no kenkyū* 社寺建築の研究 [A Study of the architecture of shrines and temples] *Nihon kenchikushi ronshū* 日本建築史論集 [Collected studies on the history of Japanese architecture], vol. 3 (Tokyo: Iwanami shoten, 1986), 2–5.

fig a2-b. from left to right, *kondō* and *gojūnotō*

THE DIFFERENT ARCHITECTURAL TYPES — 35

fig a3. Daibutsuyō-style temple, Tōdaiji monastery
fig a3-a. capitals and penetrating tie beams, Nandaimon gate

fig a3-b. *kondō*, Nara
fig a-3c. Nandaimon gate

China, in order to rapidly reconstruct the enormous buildings, both robustly and at the least cost. On the one hand, the strength of the building superstructures was no longer obtained by assembling and nailing beams/lintels (*nageshi* 長押) to the posts, that tied them together into a structural chain, as in the Wayō style, but instead the embedding was simplified and strengthened by standardized penetrating tie beams (*nuki* 貫) that intersect with the columns in which openings have been made. In addition, new kinds of corbelled capitols (*kumimono* 組物) were experimented with in order to better support the large roof canopies.[25]

The third period covers the various architectures of Zen Buddhism, Zenshūyō 禅宗様 (literally, the Zen school style), which was much appreciated by the military governments of the Kamakura and Muromachi periods (1336–1573), as well as the temples constructed by the new schools of Buddhism—Jōdoshū 浄土宗, Jōdoshinshū 浄土真宗, Nichiren or Nichirenshū 日蓮宗, to mention only the best-known ones—that appeared in succession during the Kamakura period (fig. a4). This style was contemporaneous to the Daibutsuyō, and was introduced in almost fully developed form by Zen monks in the thirteenth century, upon their return from pilgrimages to China. This latter style also employs penetrating tie beams (*nuki*), but it activates the supporting structure of the canopies in a more expressive manner,

---

[25] The *kondō* (Golden Hall) more commonly known as the Daibutsuden 大仏殿 (Pavilion of the Great Buddha) was reconstructed in the eighteenth century. The Nandaimon gate 南大門 (Great South Gate) is the only remaining original structure built under the leadership of Chōgen.

fig a4. Zen-style temple
fig a4-a. Kōzanji monastery, *butsuden*, Yamaguchi prefecture

fig a4-b. Murōji monastery, *hondō*, Nara prefecture

fig a4-c. Murōji monastery, *hondō*, Nara prefecture

THE DIFFERENT ARCHITECTURAL TYPES — 41

by replacing the exposed rafters (*taruki* 垂木) in parallel, with fanning rafters (*ōgitaruki* 扇垂木) in a manner similar to the continental archetypes[26] (figs. a33-a, a33-b).

The last period covers the Setchūyō 折衷様 style (literally, the composite style) (fig. a5). We should also note that beyond these issues of chronology, the construction principles, always based on assemblages of posts and beams, as well as the functions, all came from China, even if their forms were modified by the Japanese, who only retained some of the original elements. The stylistic variations touched primarily on the construction aspect (*zukuri*).

After the Kamakura period, the architecture of Buddhist temples concentrated on formal variations, while still combining elements of the three styles already described. But insofar as these developments had little effect on the construction methods, the builders and the users did not always consider them to be distinct styles. Such was the case with the new Wayō style (Shinwayō 新和様), which combined the Daibutsuyō and Wayō styles, whose spread was due to the initiative of the Nara monks. They were familiar with the great temple of Tōdaiji, which had been reconstructed in their own city, and developed the new style primarily in the area of the Inland Sea to propagate their faith.

[26] Sekiguchi Kinya 関口欣也, *Chūsei zenshūyō kenchiku no kenkyū* 中世禅宗様建築の研究 [Studies in medieval Zen architecture], *Sekiguchi Kinya chosakushū* 関口欣也著作集 [Works of Sekiguchi Kinya], vol. 1 (Tokyo: Chūōkōron bijutsu shuppan, 2011), 336–7.

fig a5. Setchūyo-style temple, Kanshinji monastery, *kondō*, Osaka prefecture

SHINTŌ SHRINES: LOCAL AND IMPERIAL MODELS

The architecture of shrines dedicated to the Shintō divinities, the *kami* 神, and that like Ise, also serve as a place to venerate the ancestors of the imperial family, is an ancient one. It is often considered older even than the architecture of Buddhist temples. Two pillars that supported the roof ridge (*munamochi-bashira* 棟持柱) of a construction at Ise have been discovered that are some two thousand years old.[27] Even if these vestiges, dating from the previous Yayoi period (BCE 350–250) resemble certain elements of the later main sanctuary (*seiden*), it still seems difficult to imagine that such elaborate buildings could have preceded the introduction of models coming from China in the sixth century. From the Nara period on, the shrine of Ise would thus have come under the influence of the architecture of Buddhist temples.[28] The symmetrical arrangement of the buildings attests to this as well, with axial access permitted because of the unequal arrangement of the bays of the central facade, its orientation to the south, and the presence of certain metal decorative elements (fig. a6).

Unlike the Ise shrine, the large regional sanctuaries of the local clans share typological characteristics such as double structural spans (two *ken*) in the cardinal directions and offset entries like those at Izumo taisha 出雲大社. Located on the west coast, the other major shrine in Japan that includes a central pavilion (*honden* 本殿), formerly called *seiden* or *shōden* 昇殿, was already mentioned in the oldest writings in Japan—the *Kojiki* 古事記 (*Records of Ancient Matters*), and the *Nihonshoki* 日本書紀 (*The Chronicles of Japan*) (fig. a7). This pavilion, *honden*, with its square plan and height of approximately twenty-four meters and its imposing central column, whose function is more symbolic than truly structural, remains one of the largest sanctuaries in Japan today. Archaeological explorations in the year 2000 revealed a central pillar assembled from three tree trunks, each one of which is one meter in diameter, and it is likely that the building reached a height of forty-eight meters until the middle of the thirteenth century (heights of 8 or 16 jō 丈, a traditional unit of about 3 meters). If the structural principle of a screen of posts is the same as at Ise, the entrance is offset laterally because the central axis is blocked by a post, an arrangement resulting from the even number of bays. The sanctuary of Izumo constructed at the same time as the Ise shrine, representing the imperial House, constitutes a sort of architectural counterpart, or another model devoted, like the regional sanctuaries, to the clans and the local divinities.[29]

From the eighth century on, various original architectural styles were adopted for sanctuaries, where the powerful families of the Kinai—the region that includes the five provinces in the immediate vicinity of Kyoto—held religious services. Three examples of these include: in Osaka, the *sumiyoshi-zukuri* 住吉造 or style of the Sumiyoshi taisha shrine, whose rituals were tied to offerings of rice made to the new emperor (the *daijōsai* 大嘗祭 imperial ritual); in Nara the *kasuga-zukuri* 春日造, the style of the Kasuga taisha shrine, and in Kyoto, the *nagare-zukuri* 流造, which is characteristic of the Kamo jinja sanctuary 賀茂神社. The two latter types, which

---

[27] Miyamoto Nagajirō 宮本長二郎, *Shutsudo kenchiku buzai ga hodoku kodai kenchiku* 出土建築部材が解く古代建築 [Architecture revealed through archaeological discoveries], *Nihon no bijutsu* 日本の美術 490 [Japanese art, vol. 490] (Tokyo, Shibundō, 2007). From the same author, see also: *Nihon genshi kodai no jūkyo kenchiku* 日本原始古代の住居建築 [Primitive residential architecture in Japan] (Tokyo: Chūōkōron bijutsu shuppan, 1996), 182-91.

[28] Maruyama Shigeru 丸山茂, *Jinja kenchikushi ron: Kodai ōken to saishi* 神社建築史論:古代王権と祭祀 [History of sanctuary architecture: Imperial authority and the rituals of antiquity] (Tokyo: Chūōkōron bijutsu shuppan, 2001), 30–106.

[29] Fukuyama Toshio 福山敏男, *Fukuyama Toshio chosakushū. Jinja kenchiku no kenkyū* 福山敏男著作集・神社建築の研究 [Collected works of Fukuyama Toshio. Studies on the architecture of sanctuaries], vol. 4 (Tokyo: Chūōkōron bijutsu shuppan, 1984), 34–41.

fig a6. central room (Asuka/Nara period)

moya: room, central core
kirizuma-zukuri: gable roof

ken: bay, span
men: side, face

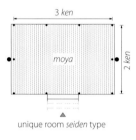

unique room *seiden* type

shinmei-zukuri shinmei style)
kirizuma-zukuri roof type
(e.g., Ise sanctuary)

sō-bashira local type

taisha-zukuri – Taisha style
kirizuma-zukuri roof type
(e.g., Izumo sanctuary)

THE DIFFERENT ARCHITECTURAL TYPES — 45

fig a7. Izumo taisha sanctuary, Shimane prefecture
fig a7-a. *honden*
fig a7-b. *honden* and *sessha*

fig a8. central room (Heian period)

gohai: space under canopy

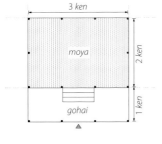

nagare-zukuri – Nagare style
kirizuma-zukuri roof type
(e.g., Kamo sanctuary)

kasuga-zukuri – Kasuga style
kirizuma-zukuri roof type
(e.g., Kasuga sanctuary)

were easier to build and also to move, subsequently spread throughout the whole country (figs. a8, a9). Near Hiroshima, the Itsukushima jinja shrine 厳島神社, which sits above the water, is a remarkable example of those provincial complexes in which the various structures are linked by pontoon/passageways (fig. a10). Thus, by the Heian period, the main styles or types of sanctuaries were fixed: the principal sanctuary (*seiden/shōden*), dedicated to the primary divinity, and the adjoining devotional pavilions (*heiden* 幣殿) and oratories (*haiden* 拝殿). Numerous divinities (*kami*) were honored in the same sanctuary, with auxiliary outbuildings (*sessha* or *massha*) completing the complex.

Subsequently, starting in the Kamakura period, and under the influence of Buddhism, the shrines of the Heian period, whose wood had been left exposed, were painted, and curves were introduced into the two-tiered roofs (*nagare-zukuri*), which had been rectilinear up to then (*kirizuma-zukuri* 切妻造) (figs. a11, a12). New architectural elements appeared as well, such as various sorts of sitting dogs (*chidorihafu* 千鳥破風), curved porches (*noki karahafu* 軒唐破風), and decorative details progressively added to the roofs. As in residential architecture, sliding panels (*shōji* 障子) appeared at the beginning of the Muromachi period (fourteenth century), with sculpted and perforated transoms (*ranma* 欄間) above, along with partitions (*wakishōji* 脇障子) covered with bas-reliefs, which were set on either side of the exterior gallery running around the buildings (fig. a13).

fig a9. canopies in front of the *moya*
fig a9-a. *nagare-zukuri* style, with *gohai* space, Mikami jinja sanctuary, *sessha*, Shiga prefecture
fig a10. Itsukushima jinja Sanctuary, Hiroshima prefecture

fig a9-b. Kasuga style with *gohai* space, Kanshinji monastery, Kariteimotendō, Osaka prefecture

fig a11. roof construction principles

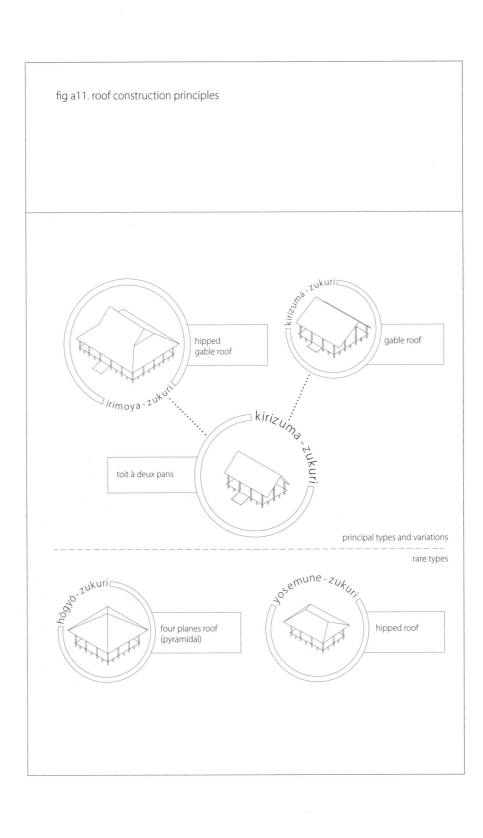

fig a12-a. *kirizuma* roof type, Hōryūji monastery, *denpōdō*, Nara
fig a12-b. *irimoya* roof type, Tōshōdaiji monastery, *kōdō*, Nara

fig a12-c. *yosemune* roof type, Tōshōdaiji monastery, *kondō*, Nara
fig a12-d. *kirizuma* roof type, *nagare-zukuri* style, Fushimi Inari taisha sanctuary, *honden*, Kyoto

THE DIFFERENT ARCHITECTURAL TYPES — 51

fig a13. architectural details
fig a13-a. "seated dog" *chidorihafu*, Yoshino Mikumi jinja sanctuary, *honden*, Nara prefecture
fig a13-b. curved canopy (*noki karahafu*), Hiunkaku pavilion, Nishi Honganji monastery, Kyoto
fig a13-c. *wakishōji* screen, Kunōzan Tōshōgū sanctuary, Tochigi prefecture
fig a13-d. *wakishōji* screen, Kanshinji monastery, Kariteimotendō, Osaka prefecture

fig a-14. residential architecture

Shinden-style palace, Heian period, Kyoto

moya
hisashi

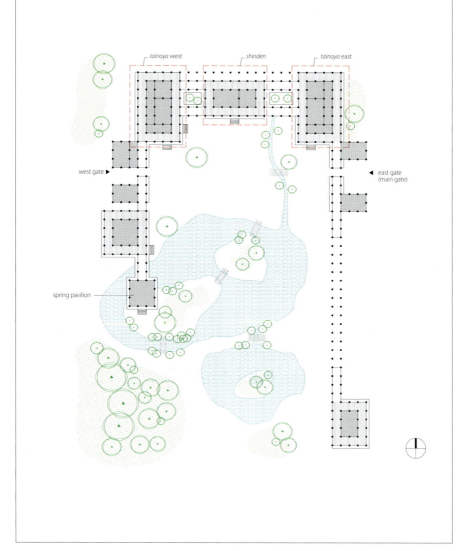

RESIDENTIAL CONSTRUCTION: THE SHINDEN, SHOIN, AND SUKIYA STYLES

Three successive styles constituted the residential architecture of the upper classes: the Shinden style 寝殿, or *shinden-zukuri* 寝殿造 of the aristocracy during the Heian period (794–1185), the Shoin style, or *shoin-zukuri*, which appeared during the Muromachi period (1336–1573), and the Sukiya style 数寄屋, or *sukiya-zukuri* 数寄屋造, which dates from the subsequent Azuchi-Momoyama period (1573–1603) and the beginning of the Edo period (1603–1868).

While there are no original palaces in the Shinden style remaining, their layouts are well known (figs. a14, a15, a16).[30] In ensembles of this type, the main building, *shinden*, is oriented to the south opposite a garden bordered by annexed pavilions (*tainoya* 対屋). These are located on the east, west, and occasionally north sides and are connected to each other by large corridors. Each building consists of a main boarded room (*moya* 母屋; literally, the "mother beam" and by extension the space it covers) surrounded by an open gallery, with a projecting roof (*hisashi* 庇 or canopy, that also designates the covered space by extension). The rhythms of the spaces are established by the alignments of circular bearing posts (*maru-bashira* 円柱). There were few separations inside these palaces, which served both as residences and reception halls, and only some moveable elements–that included screens and silk curtains (*kichō* 几帳)—as well as a few swinging doors and some suspended shutters that partially and temporarily closed off the rooms and served to modulate this large boarded space (*itajiki* 板敷き).[31]

[30] Nicolas Fiévé, ed., *Atlas historique de Kyôto. Analyse spatiale des systèmes de mémoire d'une ville, de son architecture et de ses paysages urbains* (Paris: Centre du Patrimoine Mondial, Editions de l'UNESCO–Editions de l'Amateur, 2008), 85–94.
[31] Ōta Seiroku 太田清六, *Shinden-zukuri no kenkyū* 寝殿造の研究 [Study of the Shinden style] (Tokyo: Yoshikawa kōbunkan, 1987), 23–37.

fig a15. Shinden-style palace
fig a15-a. Gosho imperial palace, Shishinden, Kyoto

fig a15-b. Byōdō-in temple, "Phoenix Hall," Kyoto prefecture

THE DIFFERENT ARCHITECTURAL TYPES — 55

fig a15-c. Gosho imperial palace, Shishinden, *irimoya-zukuri* roof type, Kyoto
fig a15-d. Gosho imperial palace, Seiryōden, Kyoto

fig a15-e. framing and spatial structure

kirizuma-zukuri basic type
gable roof

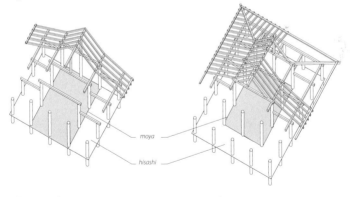

moya
hisashi

kirizuma-zukuri type
roof with two extended gables

irimoya-zukuri type
hipped gable roof

fig a-16. Shinden palace, interior view
fig a-16-a. Gosho imperial palace, Seiryōden, view from the *moya*, Kyoto

fig a-16-b. *shinden* of the Higashi sanjō dono residence

example of typical layout (*shitsurai*)
according to the roll of illustrations of the "ruijū zatuyōshū sashizukan" 類聚雑要指沙巻

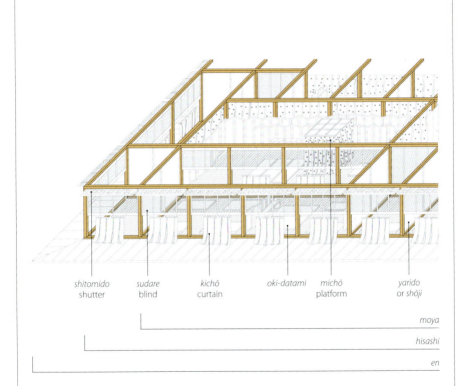

| shitomido shutter | sudare blind | kichō curtain | oki-datami | michō platform | yarido or *shōji* |

moya

hisashi

en

fig a17. aristocratic residential architecture: evolutionary principles (1)

1. Shinden-style palace – Heian period
2. palace (intermediary type between *shinden* and *shoin*) – Muromachi period

hisashi
en
shutter

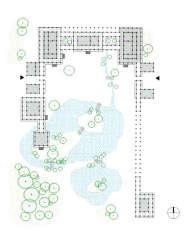

1. Shinden-style palace

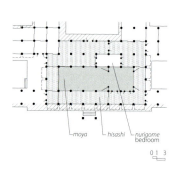

Higashi Sanjō dono residence

— moya — hisashi — nurigome bedroom

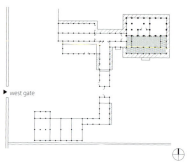

2. Ashikaga Yoshinori palace

▶ west gate

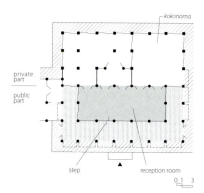

— kokonoma

private part
public part

step   reception room

fig a18. aristocratic residential architecture: evolutionary principles (2)

3. Zen abbot residence *tachu hōjō* - Muromachi period

1. main reception and ceremonial room
2. reception room main hosts
3. reception room hosts
4. bedroom
5. study cabinet, *shoin*

ochien
hiroen
en
shutter

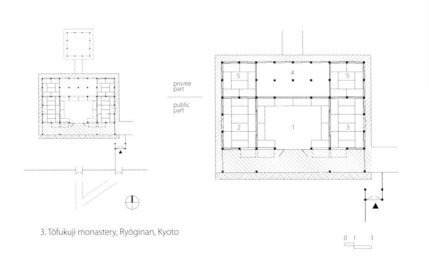

3. Tōfukuji monastery, Ryōginan, Kyoto

fig a19. Shoin architectural details
fig a19-a. from left to right: *kuroshoin* and *ōhiroma* pavilions, Nijō Castle, Ninomaru, *kyakuden*, Kyoto

THE DIFFERENT ARCHITECTURAL TYPES — 63

The *shinden* evolved over the course of the following periods, the Kamakura and Muromachi, and many modifications were made as part of the renewal of the interiors and their organization. The single central space (*moya*) disappeared and was replaced by a new ensemble divided into several rooms by sliding panels—all of them designated by the generic term of *shōji*—made of wood or paper, translucent or opaque, which continued to afford a certain flexibility of use. These new rooms were then finished off with ceilings of different height, depending on their size. At the same time, most of their floors were covered with tatamis, that were originally simple mats made rigid and modular. Certain elements of built-in furniture appeared as well: staggered shelving (*chigai-dana* 違棚) used to display books and precious objects often imported from China or Korea (*karamono* 唐物), low, long, and thick tablets (*oshiita* 押板), which became deeper and developed into alcoves (*tokonoma*) and served as spaces of representation where the ("lettered") master of the house displayed a painted scroll, a calligraphy, or a floral arrangement (*ikebana* 生け花), depending on the season and his mood; small studies (*tsukeshoin* 付書院), a term often shortened to *shoin*, were often placed next to the *tokonoma*, in the form of additional alcoves equipped with shelving as well as tables for writing or reading. A post served to mark the separation between these two alcoves, along with a small dividing wall. This post represented a tree trunk that could shelter a hermit, out in the midst of nature, far away from the affairs of society. This ideal also inspired the first designs of tea rooms, that emerged at this time. This room, the *shoin*, lent its name by extension to the pavilions devoted to tea, and later to a style (figs. a17, a18, a19).

The last major development appeared during the Azuchi-Momoyama period, in which Toyotomi Hideyoshi 豊臣秀吉 (1537–1589) had become the leader of Japan, despite his modest origins. He was inspired by the residences of the military leaders (*shōgun*) of the previous Muromachi period and employed buildings in the new Shoin style to receive his vassals. The Tokugawa shōguns who succeeded him, did the same during the Edo period that followed, by developing this style in their residences. These building projects were linked to a moment of violent change and claims to political power. They reflected the social status and the power of

fig a19-b. from left to right: the new palace, the music room, the main Shoin and the old Shoin, Katsura Villa, Kyoto

their occupants. They now consisted of a combination of large and small rooms: the *hiroma* 広間 on the one hand (literally, "large room"), large and luxurious Shoin style formal rooms equipped with tatamis—*taimenjo* 対面所, *shiroshoin* 白書院, and *kuroshoin* 黒書院—and on the other hand, the *koma* 小間 (literally, "small rooms") devoted to the tea ceremony, among other things, which were also known as *kakoi* 囲い, *kozashiki* 小座式, or Sukiya style rooms[32] (figs. a20, a21).

The ornamentation and size of the major rooms, the *hiroma* or *ōhiroma* 大広間 (literally, the "great *hiroma*" for the most impressive among them) varied according to their use: those reserved for official events or dealings with guests and vassals, contained painted frescoes on the walls, and sliding partitions finished in gold leaf, with sculpted openwork transoms above (*ranma*).[33] Less important rooms in the Shoin style, the *shiroshoin* and *kuroshoin* (literally, "white reading cabinet" and "black reading cabinet"), which served for auditions or more private meetings respectively, remained formal and ostentatious in the former case, but were more sober and decorated with paintings in China ink (*suibokuga* 水墨画) in the latter, hence their appellation as "black." As for the *koma* rooms, they are small rooms measuring less than four

[32] Horiguchi Sutemi 堀口捨己, *Rikyū no chashitsu* 利休の茶室 [The tea pavilions of Rikyū] in *Horiguchi Sutemi hakase chosakushū* 堀口捨己博士著作集 [Collected works of professor Horiguchi Sutemi] (Tokyo: Kajima shuppansha, 1987).
[33] Hirai Kiyoshi, *Feudal Architecture of Japan* (New York-Tokyo: Weatherhill-Heibonsha, 1973); Inoue Mitsuo, *Space in Japanese Architecture*, trans. Hiroshi Watanabe (New York: Weatherhill, 1985), 133–6.

fig a19-c. Tōfukuji monastery, Ryōginan, Kyoto
fig a19-e. *jōdannoma* high room in the *ōhiroma* pavilion, Nijō castle, Ninomaru kyakuden, Kyoto

fig a19-d. *tokonoma* alcove with a flower vase and a *kakejiku* hanging roll and *tsukeshoin* study cabinet, Tōji monastery, Kanshinin, Kyoto
fig a19-f. *chigai-dana* shelving, Gokokuji monastery, *gekkōden*, Tokyo

fig a20. aristocratic residential architecture: evolutionary principles (3)

4. Shoin-style palace – Momoyama period

0. *jōdannoma*
1. *ichinoma*
2. *ninoma*
3. *sannoma*

hisashi
hiroen
ochien

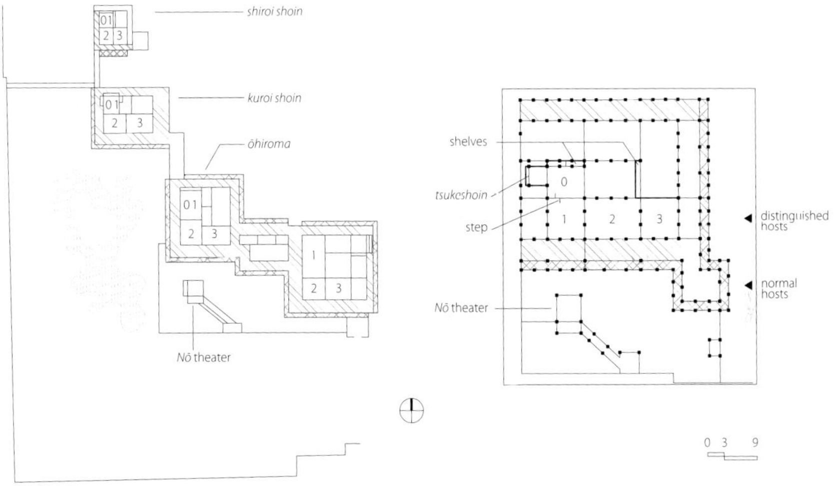

shiroi shoin

kuroi shoin

ōhiroma

Nō theater

shelves

tsukeshoin

step

Nō theater

distinguished hosts

normal hosts

0 3 9

4. Nijō palace
Ninomaru
taimenjo (reception rooms)

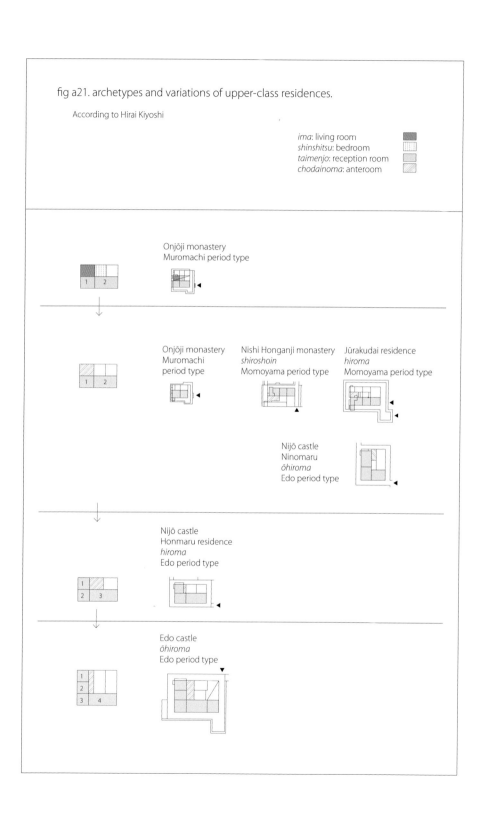

and a half tatamis (approx. 7.3 square meters or 24 sf), often used for the tea ceremony, which was originally introduced and practiced by Zen monks, before being adopted by the military elites of the fifteenth century. Sen no Rikyū 千利休 (1522–1591) was inspired by them, following Murata Jukō 村田珠光 (1423–1502) and Takeno Jōō 武野紹鴎 (1502–1555), and codified a new style of tea pavilion of rustic appearance, called Sōan 草庵[34] (figs. a49, a50).

According to Yamanoue Sōji 山上宗二 (1544-1590), Takeno Jōō, a disciple of Rikyū and also Sōji's master, had begun to simplify the richly decorated Shoin style by creating tea pavilions that retained only the decorative alcove, the *tokonoma*, and eliminated the other types of shelving, as well as the *tsukeshoin* and *shoin* alcoves that served as reading cabinets[35]. He also employed bamboo, a simple and natural material, for a certain number of elements, such as the ceilings. Following in his wake, Rikyū continued this process of simplification. Among other "inventions," he eliminated the paper that covered over its walls to reveal the cob behind. He also chose to reduce the number of windows: the light required by the tea ceremony enters through a single window (*shitaji mado* 下地窓; literally, the "window—with what exists—underground"), which exposes the bamboo lath that comprises the internal structure (*shitaji*) of the walls. He created various tea pavilions, including miniscule rooms, which were rustic, dark, and two tatamis in size (approximately 3.3 square meters or 10.8 sf).[36]

Subsequently, his disciples the feudal lords (*daimyō*) Furuta Oribe 古田織部 (1544–1615) and Oda Uraku 織田有楽 (1548–1622), who considered these pavilions to be too bare, conceive larger and more modular spaces, ones more suitable for use by the nobility. They modified Rikyū's archetype through various procedures (offsets, angled elements, intersections) to create elegant and well-lit tea pavilions. Kobori Enshū 小堀遠州 (1579–1647), a disciple of Oribe and the last great creator of tea pavilions further refined this tendency with his pavilions in the Kireisabi 奇麗さび (beautiful *sabi*) style, whose ornamentation and less rustic materials ran counter to Rikyū's famous Wabisabi 侘び寂び style. He incorporated them into Shoin style pavilions and thus developed a new residential style called Sukiya today. The Katsura Villa 桂離宮 in Kyoto is one of its masterpieces[37] (figs. a22, a44).

---

[34] The philosophy of Murata Jukō and Takeno Jōō, the masters of Rikyū, is described in *Chadō shiso densho* 茶道四祖伝書 [The first four books of the Way of Tea]. Rikyū no doubt developed a new aesthetic that built upon his two predecessors. See Matsuyama Ginshoan 松山吟松庵 (ed.) and Kumakura Isao 熊倉功補 (revised), *Chatō koten sōsho* 茶湯古典叢書 [Classics of the tea ceremony], vol. 1 (Kyoto: Shibunkaku shuppan, 1974).

[35] See the "Yamanoue no Sōji-ki" 山上宗二記 (The Notes of Yamanoue Sōji), 1588, in Kuwata Chikatada 桑田親忠, *Sadō koten zenshū dai 6 kan* 茶道古典全集第6巻 [The Classics of the Tea Ceremony. Complete works, volume 6], revised and annotated edition (Kyoto: Tankōsha, 1977).

[36] A detailed description of the successive architectural contributions of Jukō, Jōō et Rikyū is to be found in French in Nicolas Fiévé, "Les pavillons du thé: philosophie et fonctionnalisme d'une architecture," in Christine Shimizu (ed.), *Les arts de la cérémonie du thé* (Dijon: éditions Faton, 1996), 48–85, and in English, by the same author, "Origins of the Tea Pavilion," in *Acta Universitatis Ouluensis, Humaniora*, special issue: "Japani: Culturi, Nainen, Murros" (Oulu: Oulu University Press, 1998), 25-38 ; Hayashiya Tatsusaburō, Nakamura Masao, et al., *Japanese Arts and the Tea Ceremony* (New York-Tokyo: Weatherhill-Heibonsha, 1974); Paul Varley and Kumakura Isao (eds.), *Tea in Japan: Essays on the History of Chanoyu* (Honolulu: University of Hawai'i Press, 1995).

[37] Horiguchi Sutemi, *Shoin-zukuri to sukiya-zukuri no kenkyū* 書院造と数寄屋造の研究 [Studies on the Shoin and Sukiya styles] in *Horiguchi Sutemi hakase chosakushū* [Collected works of professor Horiguchi Sutemi] (Tokyo: Kajima shuppankai, 1978).

fig a22. Katsura Villa (exterior view), Kyoto

fig a23. *tateana* construction type (on the right)
fig a24. *takayuka* construction type

THE WORKING-CLASS HABITAT

The main archetypes of wood architecture in Japan are embodied in the temples, the sanctuaries with all their secondary buildings, and the aristocratic residences in all their stylistic variations. Nonetheless the dwellings of the working populace (*minka*; literally "popular dwelling"—peasants, artisans, merchants) remain a significant part of traditional construction, which is not to be ignored. These are usually divided into two different categories: farms (*nōka* 農家) and city dwellings (*machiya* 町家).

There were two sorts of dwellings among the first known of them. The oldest kind date from the Jōmon period (BCE 14,000 – 300). Archaeological evidence reveals groups of half-buried houses (*tateana jūkyo* 縦穴住居) cut directly into the surface of the earth. They were often laid out in circular plans, with wood posts around the perimeter supporting the roof, while a central pillar served no doubt as an altar, with clay figurines placed on it. A second and more recent type of dwelling has also been discovered, depicted on a bronze mirror of the Yayoi period and pottery from the imperial tumuli, the *kofun* 古墳 (250-700), which depict constructions with a raised floor (*takayuka jūkyo* 高床住居). On one of those mirrors four constructions are represented with elevated floors which probably served as warehouses, places of power, popular dwelling, or places of worship (*saiden* 祭殿) preceded by an open entry terrace (*rōdai* 露大), that already prefigured the intermediary spaces between interior and exterior (figs. a23, a24).

The plans and forms of farms (*nōka*) varied as a function of the social status of their owners and the regions in which they were located. Nonetheless, many common features characterize this type of construction: a parallelepipedic volume, a spatial organization separated into two main parts: a beaten earth floor (*doma* 土間) entry at the ground level and rooms with slightly elevated wooden plank floors equipped with mats; a tripartite or quadripartite layout of the plank parts, whose checkerboard organization recalls the patterns of rice fields (*ta* 田). Despite the existence of numerous typologies whose names derive from their roof shapes, such as the *honmune-zukuri* 本棟造, the *kabuto-zukuri* 兜造, and the *chūmon-zukuri* 中門造, along with yet other regional variants, the basic spatial organization of the different rural habitats remains stable and is found in the cities as well.

If the separation of the lower spaces in beaten earth and the plank floors in the raised areas corresponds to the distinction between the functions proper to the countryside—agricultural work on one hand, and daily domestic activities, linked to food preparation on the other—a similar spatial differentiation appears in city dwellings (*machiya*) of merchants and artisans as well. These dwellings are laid out along the streets and generally consist of a store at the front, which corresponds to the rural space in beaten earth (*doma*), while the different dwelling spaces along with the warehouses (*kura* 倉) are located in the back and are elevated[38] (figs. a25, a26, a27).

However, in most cases, where the plot is narrow and deep, this differentiation is not serial, but rather parallel. The living spaces are thus juxtaposed one to another in the deep direction and are separated by small interior gardens (*tsubo niwa* 坪庭, literally, "two-tatami garden") that admit natural light. A long passageway in beaten earth (*tōri niwa* 通庭)—a development of the

---

[38] On the architectural form and uses of the urban house, see in French: Katō Kunio, "Structure de l'habitat, tentative de compréhension théorique de l'habiter," in Augustin Berque (ed.), *La maîtrise de la ville: urbanité française, urbanité nippone* (Paris: EHESS, 1994), 189-220; Nicolas Fiévé, "Les transformations morphologiques des quartiers populaires," in Fiévé (ed.), *Atlas historique de Kyôto*, op. cit. (2008), 121–6.

fig a25. residential architecture

variation of *minka* in central Japan, Kinki region

minka: popular habitat
⊠ : hearth
● : *daikoku-bashira* post
doma: entry space with earthen floor

salon: also bedroom, *zashiki*
living: occasional bedroom, *ima*
st: storage, *nando*

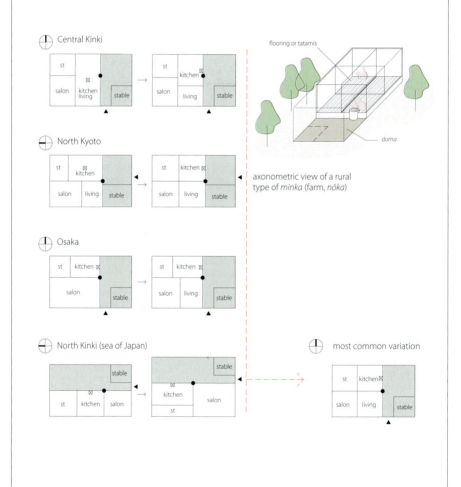

THE DIFFERENT ARCHITECTURAL TYPES — 73

fig a26. *nōka* farm (Kakehashi house, Kōchi prefecture)
fig a26-a. exterior view
fig a26-b. *doma* room
fig a26-d. salon (*zashiki*)

fig a26-c. living room (*ima*)
fig a26-e. roof detail. In rural architecture, the purlins and rafters are often bound together, without joints.

fig a27-a. urban house, *machiya*

Murata house, Kyoto, early twentieth century

S: shop
O: back room, *okunoma*
Z: *zashiki*
N: interior garden, *nakaniwa*

To: *tōriniwa*
BR: servant's room, storage
E: extension, tea pavilion
T: *tokonoma*

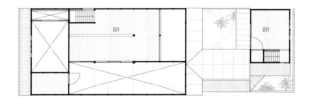

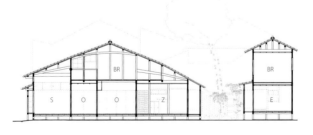

fig a27-b. urban house, *machiya*, Gion neighborhood, Kyoto

doma—runs alongside, which serves as a kitchen and workspace, as well as connecting them with each other.[39]

This duality extends beyond the regions and the types of activities that take place in these habitats. Another point in common is that the *minka* are often configured in a dual fashion, similar to the couplet of *moya-hisashi*—spaces located below the main roof and the canopies respectively—a characteristic feature of the architecture of palaces in the Shinden style. A higher central portion (*jōya* 上屋) indeed often stands in contrast to peripheral additions with lower roofs (*geya* 下屋).

SHINTŌ AND BUDDHIST SYNCRETISM: MOUNTAIN MONASTERIES AND MAUSOLEUMS

The intermixing of places of worship is an ancient and frequent occurrence in Japan. As early as the eighth century, Buddhist temples (*jingūji* 神宮寺) were erected in the principal sanctuaries, and conversely Shintō shrines (*chinjusha* 鎮守社) were often to be found in temples. Although they did not establish an actual style, two other particular types of religious buildings devoted to the divinities of both pantheons can be mentioned here.

The first representative examples of this syncretism are the places of worship linked to the mountain, known as *kake-zukuri* 懸造,[40] or overhang style (fig. a28). They were built during the Heian period and are supported by posts against steep cliffs in rocky terrain. Another form of architecture appeared at the same time in the new capital Kyoto that was linked to the belief that sees the dead and worships them as divinities in the form of *kami*. During the Muromachi period, the new syncretic Shintō-Buddhist doctrine (*shinbutsu konkō* 神仏混淆) took up this belief and borrowed one of the principal rituals of the Shingon school, the sacred fires (*goma* 護摩), to honor Toyotomi Hideyoshi and Tokugawa Ieyasu 徳川家康 (1543–1616) the two principal politico-military unifiers of the country at the end of the sixteenth century. The two dead are honored under the names of Hōkoku daimyōjin 豊国大明神 and Tōshō daigongen 東照大権現 in the grandiose and profusely ornamented mausoleums (*reibyō* 霊廟) of Hōkuko shrine 豊国神社, Kyoto (subsequently destroyed) and Nikkō (fig. a29).

[39] On the rural house, see the work of the geographer Pezeu-Masabuau, *La maison japonaise* (Paris: POF, 1981); *La maison japonaise et la neige. Études géographiques sur l'habitation du Hokuriku (Côte occidentale du Japon central)*, "Bulletin de la Maison franco-japonaise," New Series Volume 8, No 1 (Paris: PUF, 1966).

[40] Matsuzaki Teruaki 松崎輝明, "Kake-zukuri to iu meishō ni tsuite" 懸造と言う名称について [On the the appellation *kake-zukuri*], *Nihon kenchiku gakkai ronbun hōkokushū* 日本建築学会論文報告集 [Annual symposium of the Architectural Institute of Japan], 1989; by the same author "Kodai chūsei no kakezukuri" 古代中世の懸造 (The *kake-zukuri* in Ancient and Medieval times), *Nihon kenchiku gakkai ronbun hōkokushū*, 1991.

fig a28. construction of the *kake-zukuri* type, Kiyomizu-dera monastery, Kyoto
fig a29. mausoleum of the Shintō sanctuary of Tōshōgū, *haiden*, Nikkō, Tochigi prefecture

fig a30. surface area units

1 ken / 1 ma / 1 ken

1 ken / 2 tatamis / 1 ken

hitoma room (1 *ma*, 2 tatamis)

futama room (2 *ma*, 4 tatamis)

yoma room (4 *ma*, 8 tatamis)

muma room (6 *ma*, 12 tatamis)

kokonoma room (9 *ma*, 18 tatamis)

EVOLUTIONS OF THE PLAN

MA: CONCEPT AND ORGANIZING PRINCIPLE

The sino-Japanese character 間 allows for multiple readings and meanings: *aida, ai, kan, ken,* and *ma*. But *ken* and *ma* remain the most commonly used in the domain of architecture. *Ken* has a double meaning: a bay or the distance between two posts, and a specific unit of length to measure a span. In its second acceptation, its dimension decreased over the course of the centuries: a *ken* is equal to ten *shaku* 尺 (approximately three meters) during the Heian period, then seven during the Kamakura period, six and one-half in the Azuchi-Momoyama period, and then finally only six during the Edo period. Their respective sizes, which had also fluctuated over time, were officially normalized in 1886: the *shaku* at 30.303 cm, and the *ken* at six *shaku*. The other reading *ma* is more complicated, because it refers in a conceptual manner to a space or interval—in an architectural context, between two posts—a distance between two elements, but also a room–as in dining room or bathroom. *Ma* is also an ancient unit of surface area for measuring the size of a room one *ken* on the side. Rooms measuring one, two, or three *ma* are called *hitoma* 一間, *futama* 二間, and *mima* 三間 respectively. One can see that this terminology is multiple and equivocal. But despite these difficulties, given that Japanese construction was more often defined by its plans than by its volumetric arrangements, we should consider the architectural *ma*, with all its semantic variations, as the essential organizing element in the layout of buildings (fig. a30).

The Bay and the Post, Basic Units of Japanese Architecture

In a country where most buildings, from the prehistoric Jōmon to the Meiji restoration in the latter half of the nineteenth century, are built with a post and beam structure of wood, construction starts with the erection of posts (*hashiratate* 柱立て). From that point on, this step takes on symbolic meaning, consecrated through propitiatory ceremonies similar to those described in chapter three. The posts are then erected at regular intervals, at the intersection points of an orthogonal construction grid. In this system, called *sō-bashira* 総柱, the regular bays are called *ken* and are counted in *ken*. In other words, a *ken* is both the interval/bay between two posts, and the distance/span of a unit of the same name, as we have just described. The remains of rectangular construction of two *ken* by one have been found which back to this ancient prehistory and confirm this spatial organization, with two bays in the long dimension and one across, and an elevated floor (*takayuka*). In some cases however, the presence of central pillars could be a drawback for functional reasons, in which case these were eliminated and the basic interval of one *ken* became a virtual one, as opposed to the *sō-bashira* system. Buildings from the subsequent Yayoi period have been found in the villages that measure three *ken* by two, in which both of the central pillars were omitted (fig. a31).

fig a31. *moya* archetype

ma: center-to-center surface
ken: bay, span

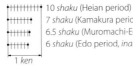

10 *shaku* (Heian period)
7 *shaku* (Kamakura period)
6.5 *shaku* (Muromachi-Edo period, *kyōma* type /Kyoto)
6 *shaku* (Edo period, *inaka ma* type /Edo)

takayuka and *saiden* type
Jōmon period~
religious buildings

sō-bashira type
Yayoi period~
dwellings, temples (auxiliary buildings), sanctuaries (rare type)

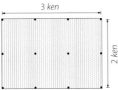

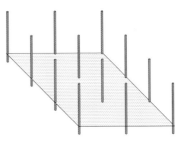

moya type
Yayoi period~
dwellings, temples, sanctuaries (main buildings)

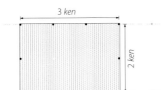

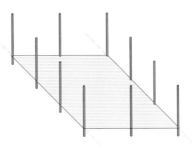

Now let us compare the more recent Shintō shrines of Ise and Izumo. As in the previous constructions, the first presents a so-called *mima* (three *ma*) structure in length and *futama* (two *ma*) in width, that is to say, three *ken* by two, with the two central posts omitted.[41] The second, on the other hand, is an architecture of the *sō-bashira* type, in which all the posts are present. Aside from the examples from the Yayoi period referred to above, of which only traces remain, these two sanctuaries can be considered archetypes of wood construction (fig. a6). Aligning beforehand the posts on a raised wood floor, with their location based on an orthonormal grid, cutting out some, retaining or adding others in order to create a physical or symbolic space—this is how the original principles of Japanese architecture were expressed from the seventh century on.

Rules of Composition according to the "Bays and Sides" Method

In the majority of writings relative to the later periods of Nara and Heian, one finds references to the number of bays (*ken*) and faces/sides (*men*), or face-galleries (*men hisashi*).[42] This method for describing constructions is called *kenmen kihō* (間面記法, "rule of bays and sides"). As we have already seen, the Shinden style palaces, as well as temples, consist of a central room (*moya*) and perimeter galleries (*hisashi*). A building called out as "three *ken*, four *men*" thus consists of a central room three bays across (in other words along the east-west axis for a pavilion whose main facade is generally oriented to the south) surrounded by galleries on all four sides. Strictly speaking, however, the building thus described measures five *ken* by four in all, but it is striking to note that the basic description according to this method does not take into account or mention the two-ken depth of the *moya*, or the one-*ken* width of the various galleries. This is due to the implicit fact that some dimensions (the depth of the *moya* and the width of the galleries) are considered to be invariant. The third term, *men hisashi* (face-gallery) is used to describe the number and location of peripheral galleries arranged around the central room. Thus *ichimen hisashi* 一面庇 (single face-gallery) refers in principle to a single anterior gallery on the south; *nimen hisashi* 二面庇 (two face-galleries) refers to two galleries, one at the front on the south, the other at the back on the north; *sanmen hisashi* 三面庇 (three face-galleries) refers to three galleries, one on the front and two on the sides, and so on[43] (fig. a32).

This method also informs us about the size and configuration of the buildings it describes. In most religious constructions, the maximum span of the central bay, without intermediate posts, is three *ken* in the long direction of the *moya*, and two *ken* in the short direction—in other words a rectangular archetype of three bays by two, without any posts in the room. Even in the pavilion of the Great Buddha (*daibutsuden* 大仏殿) of the Tōdaiji temple of Nara, the largest wood structure in Japan, in the only room in which certain central posts are omitted in

---

[41] Miyamoto, *Nihon genshi kodai no jūkyo kenchiku* [Primitive residential architecture in Japan], op. cit. (1996), 180–91.

[42] See the evaluation reports on the holdings of their monasteries prepared for the Hōryūji during the Nara period (*Hōryūji garan engi narabi rukishizaichō* 法隆寺伽藍縁起並流記資財帳) and for the Yakushiji during the Heian epoch (*Yakushiji engi* 薬師寺縁起).

[43] Ōta Hirotarō, *Nihon kenchiku no tokushitsu. Nihon kenchikushi ronshū* 日本建築の特質・日本建築史論集 [The characteristics of Japanese architecture. History of Japanese architecture], vol. 1 (Tokyo: Iwanami shoten, 1983), 408–12; and the detailed illustrations in Ōta Hirotarō (ed.) and Nishi Kazuo 西和夫, *Zukai kokenchiku nyūmon. Nihon kenchiku wa dō tsukurarete iru ka* 図解古建築入門：日本建築はどう造られているか [Illustrated introduction to ancient architecture. How are Japanese buildings constructed?] (Tokyo: Shōkokusha, 1990).

fig a32. principal layouts of central room/galleries (*kenmen kihō* method)

moya: central room, core
hisashi: canopy, canopied space
sanctuaries (rare), temples, residences

ken: span, bay
men: side, face

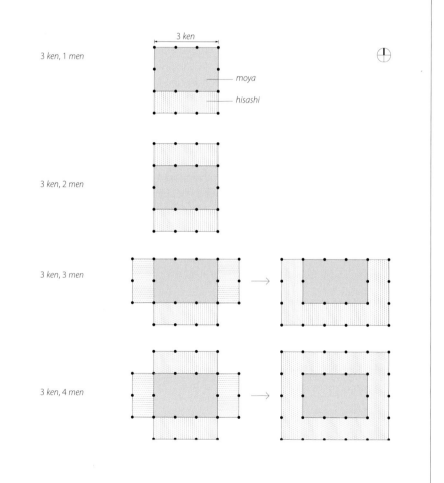

order to house the statue, the spans do not exceed three *ken* by three.[44] Later, during the Edo period, the Tokugawa government regulated the construction of large-scale buildings, such as temples, residences of the aristocracy or merchants, and it forbade spans between posts of more than three *ken*—or less than six meters at the time, with a *ken* of six *shaku*.[45] And in this same method, one observes that the transversal interior span of two *ken* is implicit and constant. With few exceptions, for example in the Tōdaiji temple, this invariant feature is most likely the result of an empirical compromise between structural concerns and use. In a country prone to earthquakes, a clear span of two *ken* leaves a useful central open space, without jeopardizing the stability of construction.

These principles of composition by the addition of exterior galleries (*hisashi*) to a central core (*moya*) are also to be found in the transition from the older gabled roofs (*kirizuma*) to more complex hipped-and-gable roofs (*irimoya* 入母屋). The *irimoya* form is a response to an aesthetic impulse, a need for ventilation, and is also a response to the structural and geometric problem of adding an exterior gallery of one *ken* along the four faces (*men*). This can be accomplished along the sloped sides of the roof, most often oriented north-south, by simply extending the roof with canopies (*hisashi*) that are used as names for these spaces, as in the *nagare-zukuri* type. But if one wants to maintain the height and width of the two other galleries north and south without cutting into the high ends on the east and west gables, then the *irimoya* form is particularly well suited (fig. a15-e). While the galleries are necessary for moving about, they are lower than the central space, usually housing statues of Buddha in temples, or used for habitation and reception in residences in the Shinden style. These additive and concentric compositions, with their separations between low and high spaces, between central and peripheral, dynamic and static constitute one of the primary characteristics or the basic spatial organization of wood constructions in Japan.

As a last remark, this method of understanding space, which was in vogue during the Heian period, clearly underscores the entire ambiguity of the *ken* as a spatio-structural unit. As long as the length of the interval between two posts varies relatively little, remaining around ten *shaku* (approximately 3 meters), there is little difference between the *ken*-bay and the *ken*-dimension or span. But as soon as posts are omitted in the *moya* and the layout is still defined by counting *ken*, the confusion resulting from the double meanings of *ken*-bay and *ken*-span comes into play. To give a concrete example of this ambiguity, let us return to the previously cited example of the three by two *ken* room with its two central posts eliminated. In the strict sense, one would need to describe it in a redundant and convoluted way as a pavilion three *ken*-bays wide, with each bay measuring one *ken*-span, by one *ken*-bay wide, whose span is two *ken*! And to further complicate the calculus, the size of the *ken*-span varies over time, decreasing over the course of eight centuries from ten *shaku* to six (from approximately 3 meters to slightly less than 1.82 meters). If the principle of organization by bays is retained, the physical dimensions will change, and buildings with the same number of *ken*-bays will have very different *ken*-spans.

---

[44] We should nonetheless keep in mind the ambiguity of the term *ken*. Although the number of bays remains constant, the spans are unusual in this case: with eight meters, or approximately twenty-six *shaku* between posts.

[45] Mitsui Wataru 光井渉, *Kinsei jisha keidai to sono kenchiku* 近世寺社境内とその建築 [Temples and shrines of the modern period and their architecture] (Tokyo: Chūōkōron bijutsu shuppan, 2001), 121–66.

Rules of Proportion (kiwari): From the Part to the Whole

During the Heian period, all posts were round in section, with only their diameters varying between those of the central rooms and those at the periphery. But towards the middle of the medieval period, square sectioned posts came into use in the galleries. In the Azuchi-Momoyama period, when the Shoin style was blossoming, all posts in important buildings became square, with their sections varying only in relation to the loads they had to bear in the different parts. There were a number of reasons for these changes, other than purely stylistic ones: a general intention in relation to economy of construction due to the scarcity of material—among others, the increasing scarcity of cypresses (*hinoki*) due to their overexploitation—technical improvements such as more rigid assemblages of posts and beams with penetrating tie beams (*nuki*), which required less material due to their thinner sections, as well as the appearance and generalized use of sliding panels and tatamis, that joined more easily to flat surfaces at the posts than to rounded ones.

In the Shoin style, the posts in the peripheral galleries maintain a five to seven ratio with the posts of the principal rooms. The visitor who takes one of these passageways will encounter thinner and thicker posts that follow a rhythm inspired by the classic Japanese *waka* poems that consist of lines of five, seven, five, seven, and seven feet. More specifically, an entire system of proportionality, a sort of stereotomy of wood called *kiwari*, regulates the dimensions of the main elements of wood construction. The *Shōmei* one of the best-known carpentry manuals, which became widely available at the beginning of the seventeenth century, describes in detail the dimensions relating to the large rooms, *hiroma*: the relation between the size of pieces and their floor to ceiling height, the *tokotenjō* 床天井 (the ceiling of the *tokonoma* alcove), the height of the shelves, the thickness of their planks etc.[46] Chapter Three provides a precise example of these relations (fig. c9).

The emergence of an important difference between the local system of the *kiwari* and the system that originally regulated these architectures imported from China is also worthy of note. In religious buildings of the Asuka period, the proportions of the ensemble were based on the spans between the posts of the central axis (*nakanoma* 中の間), and on the standard spacing of posts in residential construction. The thickness of these same posts is in proportion to their spans. But starting in the Kamakura period there is a reversal of perspective, and the proportional relations are established on the basis of the spacing (*isshi* 一枝) between the rafters of the roof.[47]

A similar phenomenon appears in Zen architecture, also imported from China around the same time. The relative proportions of the ensemble, initially based on the size of the central bay of the temple, evolved during the subsequent Muromachi period. The center-to-center distance (*aita*) of the corbelled capitals (*kumimono*) formed from an assemblage of parts supporting purlins and rafters served as a starting point for establishing a proportional system. No longer did it operate from the "whole"—the main constructional system—to the "part," in this case, a roof detail, but instead from the "part" to the "whole."

---

[46] This is a reference to the book on *kiwari* as set out by Heinouchi Yoshimasa and Masanobu father and son, master carpenters of the Edo government, and translated into modern Japanese under the title *Shōmei* by Ōta Hirotarō (ed.) and Itō Yōtarō, op. cit. (1971).

[47] Itō Nobuo 伊藤延男, *Bunkazai kōza. Nihon no kenchiku 3. Chūsei* 文化財講座:日本の建築3中世 [Lectures on cultural property, Japanese architecture, volume 3, The Middle Ages] (Tokyo: Daiichi hōki, 1977), 212–18.

Although the reasons for these changes remain unclear, one can set forth a hypothesis that demonstrates once again the ties between modular construction and the emergence of styles: it is a matter not only of establishing the least common denominator, but also of starting out from the most expressive and most complicated parts for the carpenters to build. If the spans are not all completely identical—the central span (*nakonoma*) often being larger in order to emphasize the symmetry—the spacing between rafters, on the other hand is identical. This it was doubtlessly simpler and more coherent to start with their module and spacing. But in the case of Zen temples, their fanning rafters (*ōgitaruki*) did not afford a basis for regularity, since their spacing increases as one approaches the corners of the canopies, so it turned out to be more practical to start with the assembled capitals (*kumimono*) that remain constant instead (figs. a33, a34, a35, a36).

The Relation between Use and the Continuity of Interior Space

In Shinden style residences, the space structured by posts affords a fluid suite of rooms, echoed by a powerful continuity between interior and exterior. As the monk Urabe wrote, "In conceiving a house, one should primarily consider the summer."[48] More concretely, in domestic space priority is given to summer comfort, because in the capital Kyoto, the hot and humid summer is the most grueling season. The promotion of good air circulation in that part of the year is one reason why walls are so few in number and partitions rare and mobile (in the *shinden*) or sliding (in the *shoin*). But even more importantly, the grand nobility organizes ceremonies in its *shinden* residences and seeks to combine the rooms with flexibility in order to optimize the ensemble they can form with the garden. In the subsequent pavilions in the Shoin style, a number of posts were omitted in the suite of rooms which replaced the older central foyer (*moya*) in the Shinden style, although they remained recurrently aligned in the large peripheral hallways (*hiroen* 広縁).

One can also see that the terminology evolved along with changes in the composition and nature of the spaces: there is less talk of canopies and canopied galleries (*mago-bisashi* 孫庇), and more references to different types of verandas, wide or low (*en* 縁, *hiroen*, *ochien* 落縁).[49] The reason is the clear separation between places devoted to everyday life or to formal functions on the one hand, and on the other the verandas and galleries that served as passageways. The size of the latter have diminished since the Heian period as well, when their size accommodated uses other than simple movement; not only did the *ken* diminish in size from ten *shaku* to six and a half (from approximately 3 meters to less than 2) in the Kyoto region, but at that point in time, the corridors rarely exceeded a half *ken* (approximately 90 cm), with the exception of the grand verandas (*hiroen*) of the imperial and aristocratic residences (figs. a15-d, a37, a38).

---

[48] Urabe Kenkō, *Essays in Idleness*, op. cit. (1998), 50.
[49] In French, see Nicolas Fiévé, "Les ermitages impériaux et la villa de Shugakuin au XVIIe siècle," *Annuaire. Résumé des conférences et travaux*, 145e année, 2012-2013 (Paris: EPHE SHP, 2014), 346–60. For the construction stages of a *shoin*, see "Les techniques de construction d'un corps de logis au XVIIe siècle. Le *shoin* 書院 de la villa secondaire de Katsura," *Annuaire. Résumé des conférences et travaux* (Paris: EPHE SHP, 2013), 276–88.

fig a33. architectural details
fig a33-a. fanning rafters (*ōgitaruki*) Tōdaiji monastery, Nandaimon, Nara

fig a33-b. rafter (*taruki*), Tōdaiji monastery, *daibutsuden*, Nara

fig a33-c. console beam (*hanegi*) Kazuragawa monastery, *gomadō*, Shiga prefecture
fig a33-d. lintel (*nageshi*) Tōji monastery, *gojūnotō*, Kyoto

fig a33-e. capital (*kumimono*) Daigoji monastery, *kondō*, Kyoto
fig a33-f. penetrating tie beam (*nuki*), Kanshinji monastery, *kondō*, Osaka prefecture

fig a33-g. collar beam frame, Kusabe house, Takayama, Gifu prefecture

fig a34. structural principles in the Heian period: roof truss and foundations

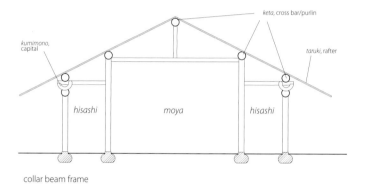

collar beam frame

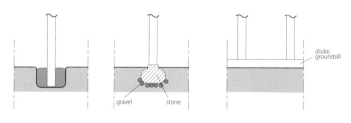

foundations

EVOLUTIONS OF THE PLAN — 91

fig a35. capitals, *kumimono*. Principles (1)

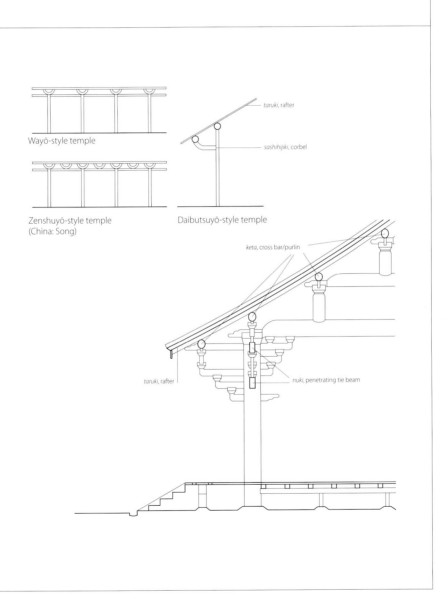

fig a36. capitals, *kumimono*. Principles (2)

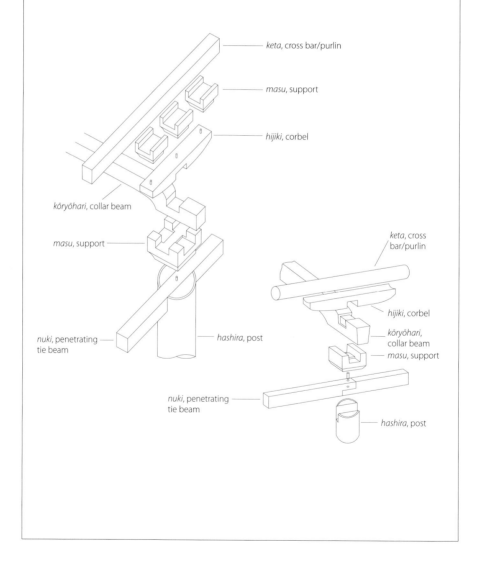

fig a37. structural principles in the Momoyama period: sections through a *tachu hōjō*

collar beam frame

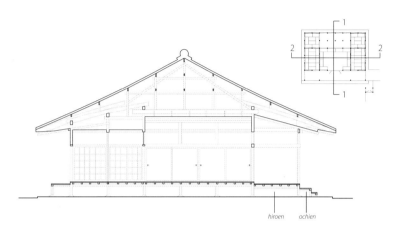

1. Tōfukuji monastery, Ryōginan, Kyoto

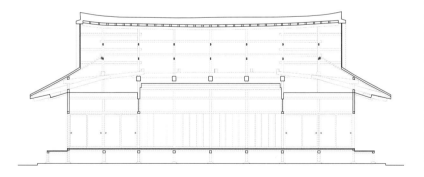

2. Tōfukuji monastery, Ryōginan, Kyoto

Another important point: although the space appears visually continuous, it was precisely structured at the time according to very strict rules of precedence and use. Unlike the visions of modern architects, and despite their open aspects, these residences were far from providing fluid spaces to freely pass through and use. This is evident from the fact that a number of documents pertaining to ancient architecture are drawings by monks or noblemen on the occasion of specific ceremonies and events, in which the position of the different hosts required being set down on paper beforehand.[50]

---

[50] The functioning of aristocratic residences during the Heian period is described in detail in the study by Kawamoto Shigeo 川本重雄, *Shinden-zukuri no kūkan to gishiki* 寝殿造の空間と儀式 [Space and Ceremony in the *Shinden*] (Tokyo: Chūōkōron bijutsu shuppan, 2012). On the usage and the architecture of the Imperial Palace in pre-modern times, see also Nicolas Fiévé, "Les reconstructions du palais impérial de la période pré-moderne" [The reconstructions of the Imperial Palace over the course of the pre-modern period] in *Annuaire. Résumé des conférences et travaux* (Paris: EPHE SHP, 2016), 346–60 (first part); ibid. (2017), 388–95 (second part); ibid. (2018), 388–403 (third part).

fig a38. architectural details
fig a38-a. from left to right: central room (*moya*); canopy (*hisashi*); veranda or large terrace (*hiroen*); low terrace (*ochien*), Gosho imperial palace, Seiryōden, Kyoto
fig a38-c. Tōji monastery, Kanshinin, Kyoto

fig a38-b. Tōfukuji monastery, Ryōginan, Kyoto
fig a38-d. Kikugetsutei residence, Takamatsu, Kagawa prefecture

EVOLUTIONS OF THE PLAN — 95

fig a39. methods of enlargement
fig a39-a. pavilion with multiple wings, Enjōji temple, Kasuga and Hakusan sanctuaries, Nara
fig a39-b. aligned pavilions *narabidō*, Hōryūji monastery, *jikidō* and *hosodono*, Nara prefecture

fig a40. attempts to establish symmetry in Shingon Buddhism
fig a40-a. the only pagoda built out of two originally proposed by Kūkai: Konpon *daitō* of the Danjō garan monastery, Kōya, Wakayama prefecture

CONSTRUCTIONAL COMBINATORICS

SYMMETRY AND ASYMMETRY

Aligning and Pairing

The enlargement of already existing pavilions, thinking of them like onions with successive layers, is a recurring issue for Japanese builders. The simplest solution is to add a new thickness, in the concrete form of an additional gallery (*mago-bisashi*), usually one *ken* wide, to the existing galleries (*hisashi*) that already run around the four faces of the central space (*moya*). But this method of extension has its physical limitations, and rather than rebuilding a larger edifice, creating a new one while retaining the proportional relations is often preferred. In the Nara and Heian periods, rows of new pavilions appeared (literally, aligned pavilions *narabidō* 並堂), with the addition of another building of the same length at the front of the main building, whose purpose was to increase the capacity of the latter for ceremonies and visits. Aligned or doubled warehouses were also built (*narabikuradō* 並倉堂) according to a similar principal. Vestiges of these two types, *narabidō* and *narabikuradō*, are to be seen in the precinct of the Hōryūji monastery at Nara. Here, the refectory (*shokudō* 食堂) and the narrow pavilion (*hosodono* 細殿) are *narabidō*, and the two warehouses *narabikuradō*, which clearly illustrates the additive principles.

This same structure with two parallel wings, which seem to have been clearly inspired by the *narabidō*, is also to be found in other ensembles. In Oita, for example, the principal pavilion (*seiden*) of the Usa jingū 佐神宮 sanctuary consists of two strictly identical buildings placed one behind the other. Here the front pavilion is considered the place where the divinities (*kami*) manifest themselves during the day, and the back building the one they use at night, even if both are used for rather similar religious purposes.[51] Additionally, since antiquity every Japanese shrine was dedicated to a single divinity, and when one began to venerate a second one, it was logical to place an identical construction next to the first. The same process of addition can also be repeated several times over: representative examples include principal pavilions (*honden* 本殿) consisting of multiple elements, as in the Kasuga taisha sanctuary at Nara, with its four similarly sized constructions aligned with one another, or those at the Sumiyoshi sanctuary of Shimonoseki, whose buildings are aligned with each other and one *ken* apart, to present an extended facade nine *ken* in length (fig. a39).

---

[51] Inagaki Eizō 稲垣榮三, *Jinja kenchikushi kenkyū. Inagaki Eizō chosakushū* 神社建築史研究・稲垣榮三著作集 [Historical studies on the architecture of sanctuaries. Works of Inagaki Eizō], vol. 2 (Tokyo: Chūōkōron bijutsu shuppan, 2008), 45–8.

These symmetrical groupings, *a priori* very influenced by Chinese models, are to be found both in Buddhist temples and Shintō shrines. They were nonetheless regularly called into question. In Shingon Buddhism, that appeared in the Heian period, prayer and ceremonial pavilions, the *mandaradō* 曼荼羅堂 or *kanjōdō* 灌頂堂, which served to display the pantheons or mandalas of the two worlds—the Taizōkai 胎蔵界 and the Kongōkai 金剛界, the world of the Matrix (feminine principle) and the world of the diamond (masculine principle) respectively—were constructed under the direction of the monk Kūkai 空海 (774-835), the founder of this school.[52] He had brought his doctrine back from China, where it seems that ceremonies and prayers linked to the two mandalas, which symbolize different worlds, took place in separate but symmetrical buildings. Nonetheless, in the first *kanjōdō* pavilion, at the monastery of Jingoji 神護寺, the

[52] Fujii Keisuke 藤井恵介, *Mikkyō kenchiku kūkanron* 密教建築空間論 [A spatial analysis of the architecture of Esoteric Buddhism] (Tokyo: Chūōkōron bijutsu shuppan, 1998), 16–22.

fig a40-b. two mandalas symmetrically arranged in the main room, Kanshinji monastery, *kondō*, Osaka prefecture

original seat of this school, that measured six *ken* by four, the even number of bays precluded the presence of an axial entry, and this asymmetry was further reinforced by the prominent projection of part of the main facade. Kūkai sought to modify the liturgy at the time, by placing paintings of the two mandalas on facing and symmetrical walls in the central room (*moya*), and he organized ceremonies and prayers in between[53] (fig. a40-b). Upon the relocation of the Shingon school to Mount Kōya 高野山 to the south of Nara before his death, he planned to create two immense pagodas, *tahōtō* 多宝塔 or *daitō* 大塔 (literally, "pagoda of many treasures" or "great pagoda"), with a pavilion for the monks' training and study (*kōdō* 講堂) tucked in between them. The divinities of the Taizōkai were worshipped in the former, and the divinities of the Kongōkai in the latter. Despite their different uses, these two constructions were to create a symmetry about the entry to the monastery. The notable asymmetries of the Jingoji, that were only offset in the internal layout of the mandalas within the central room (*moya*), had thus disappeared in the initial project for the Mount Kōya. But when the ensemble was constructed posthumously, with the formal differences between the two pagodas, due in part to the features of the terrain, this symmetrical composition was abandoned once and for all (fig. a40-a).

In the palaces of the aristocracy during the Heian era, unlike in the spatial compositions of Shingon Buddhism, one finds smaller pavilions to each side and sometimes behind the main building (*shinden*). These are called *tainoya* and are connected by wide corridors. The *shinden* and its annexes present a strict symmetry as a whole, probably an adaptation of the Chinese models of houses laid out in a U-shaped plan around a courtyard, of the Siheyuan 四合院 type.[54] But in the Higashi Sanjō dono residence 東三条殿 of Fujiwara no Michinaga 藤原道長 (966-1028), the most powerful regent of the imperial court during the Heian period, the west *tainoya* has been eliminated. As a source sprang up during the reconstruction initiated by Michinaga, the latter replaced it with a spring pavilion (*izumidono* 泉殿), which broke the symmetry.

Let us cite a last example of this questioning of an initial symmetry. According to Chinese tradition, prune trees were placed to each side of the central axis at the entry to the Shishinden pavilion (紫宸殿, "palace of the North Star") at the Imperial Palace of Kyoto (Kyōto gosho 京都御所), which was used by the emperors for various ceremonies. But during the Heian period, these were replaced by a pair of wild cherry-mandarin trees (*tachibana* 橘) of different appearance. It is clear that unlike China, which upheld the principles of symmetry, Japan did not cease to alter them[55] (fig. a15-a).

Linking

In the other great school of Buddhism from that time, the Tendai founded by the monk Saichō 最澄 (767–822), four rituals called *shishu-zanmai* 四種三昧 were practiced. Over the course of them, monks could either remain sitting in the lotus position in the prayer hall or turn around

---

[53] Masaki Akira 正木晃, *Kūkai to mikkyō bijutsu* 空海と密教美術 [Kūkai and the art of Esoteric Buddhism] (Tokyo: Kadokawa gakugei shuppan, 2012).

[54] Ōta Hirotarō, *Nihon jūtakushi no kenkyū* 日本住宅史の研究 [Study on the history of the habitat in Japan], in *Nihon kenchikushi ronshū* [Collected studies on the history of Japanese architecture], vol. 2, op. cit. (1984), 21–31.

[55] Among others, in the *Shoku Nihon Kōki* 続日本後紀 [Suite of the Later Chronicles of Japan], under the date of February 1, 845, there is mention of "prune tree flowers... in front of the Shishinden" (紫宸殿...前之梅花). But on the date of August 24, 874, in the *Nihon sandai tennō jitsuroku* 日本三代天皇実録 [True Chronicles of the Three Reigns], the author describes a "cherry tree in front of the Shishinden" (紫宸殿前桜); One can thus estimate that the prune tree was replaced by a cherry tree between those two dates. On the origins of these trees, see also Nicolas Fiévé, "The reconstructions of the Imperial Palace during the Pre-modern Period," First part: The Imperial Palace at the end of the Medieval Period (15th-17th centuries), op. cit. (2016), 354.

the statue of Buddha. Some pavilions were exclusively dedicated to these practices in the monastery of Enryakuji 延暦寺, the home of this school, which was constructed during the Heian period on several sites spread out over Mount Hiei 比叡山, to the northeast of Kyoto. On Saitō, the western site, two identical oratories Hokkedō 法華堂 and Jōgyōdō 常行堂, that retain the square plan of three *ken* by three (five by five counting the galleries) typical of pavilions of the Tendai school at the time, are linked to each other by a corridor.

In the Hokkedō, ascetic exercises were practiced for ninety days at a time in front of a representation of a bodhisattva placed in the middle of the square room. These were based on a meditation (*zazen* 座禅) called *hangyō hanza* 反行反座: "half walking and half seated" and on prayer. In the neighboring Jōgyōdō oratorio, the monks circled around the statue of Amida Nyorai (the Amida Buddha) in a clockwise direction. While the nature of the practices differed between the two neighboring oratorios, they nonetheless formed a symmetrical pair, unlike the examples of Shingon Buddhism referred to above. Thus, Japanese creators did not eschew axial and symmetrical compositions. While these were sometimes consciously retained, following the Chinese tradition, they were nonetheless more often adapted (fig. a41).

EXTENDING AND ENLARGING

Influenced by the Buddhist text Ōjōyōshū 往生要集 ("The essentials of rebirth in the Pure Land"), drawn up by the monk Genshin 源信 (942–1017) in 985, the period known as Mappō 末法 (The Latter Day of the Law), which began in 1052 at the end of the Heian period, saw members of the nobility competing to construct pavilions dedicated to the savior Buddha Amida (*amidadō*). The Jōgyōdō oratorio on Mount Hiei, referred to above, provides an example. Despite abandoning the square plan usual to Tendai Buddhism, Fujiwara no Michinaga, who was the first to create an *amidadō* in the capital, at the Muryōjuin temple 無量寿院, commissioned at that time a long and narrow pavilion known as *kutaidō* (九体堂, "pavilion of the nine bodies"), where nine statues of Amida Nyorai (the Amida Buddha) were venerated. The building with its central *moya*, giving pride of place to the statues, along with its peripheral galleries, measures eleven *ken* in length (nine plus two with the galleries). The only building of this type to remain today is the *amidadō* of the Jōruriji monastery 浄瑠璃寺 near Nara, although there were up to twenty-nine of them in Kyoto during Heian period.[56] One of the advantages of this type of construction lies in the fact that it is structurally relatively simple to increase the size of a wood-framed building with a gable roof, by simply extending the roof purlins. Drawing on the example of Michinaga, the elites launched into a contest for length. The sacred hall of Rengeōin 蓮華王院 near Kyoto, better known by the name of Sanjūsangendō (三十三間堂, "pavilion of thirty-three *ken*-bays"), dedicated to the thousand-armed goddess Kannon, was built by Taira no Kiyomori 平清盛 (1118–1181) the military chief towards the end of the Heian period, for the emperor Go Shirakawa 後白河天皇 (1127–1192). This pavilion, which was rebuilt after a fire during the Kamakura period, measures 35 *ken* in length (33 plus two for the galleries) by seven *ken* (five plus two) in width, that is to say 120 meters by 22.

---

[56] Shimizu Hiroshi 清水擴, *Heian jidai bukkyō kenchikushi no kenkyū. Jōdokyō kenchiku o chūshin ni* 平安時代仏教建築史の研究: 浄土教建築を中心に [Historical studies on Buddhist architecture during the Heian period. The architecture of Pure Land Buddhism] (Tokyo: Chūōkōron bijutsu shuppan, 1992), 252–6.

CONSTRUCTIONAL COMBINATORICS — 101

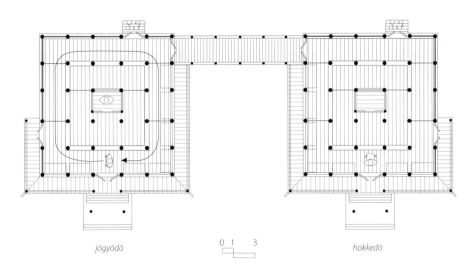

jōgyōdō   0 1 3   *hokkedō*

fig a41. attempts to establish symmetry in Tendai Buddhism
fig a41-a. exterior view
fig a41-b. hokkedō and jōgyōdō oratories, Enryakuji monastery, plan, Kyoto

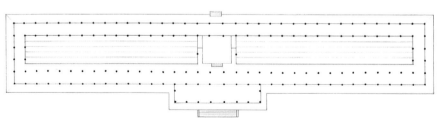

fig a42. Sanjūsangendō temple, Kyoto
fig a42-a. exterior view
fig a42-b. plan

With one thousand and one statues of the goddess on display—the principal statue placed at the center along the entry axis, with five hundred others to either side—this construction is a clear expression of that individual's taste for excess. Nonetheless, despite its inordinate proportions, the building adheres to the binary principle of a central space surrounded by galleries (*moya-hisashi*). His son Taira no Shigemori 平重盛 (1138–1179) was to have built an even longer *amidadō* within the precinct of his residence, measuring fifty *ken* (forty-eight plus two with the galleries) containing forty-eight statues of the Amida Buddha, one in each bay. Very long buildings were also built subsequently for beliefs tied to the sacred mountains (*sangaku shinkō* 山岳信仰) where ceremonies were held for pilgrims coming from different provinces. This type of architecture is called *nagatoko* (長床 literally, "long-floored"). The oratory (*haiden*) of the Heisenji monastery 平泉寺 in Katsuyama, northeast of the city of Kyoto is to have reached 35 *ken* in length[57] (fig. a42).

[57] See the document "Chūgū Hakusan Heisenji keidai ezu" 中宮白山平泉寺境内絵図 [Illustrated view of the Hakusan Heisenji precinct], collection of the Heisenji Hakusan shrine 平泉寺白山神社.

fig a43. Zuiganji monastery

Matsushima, Miyagi prefecture

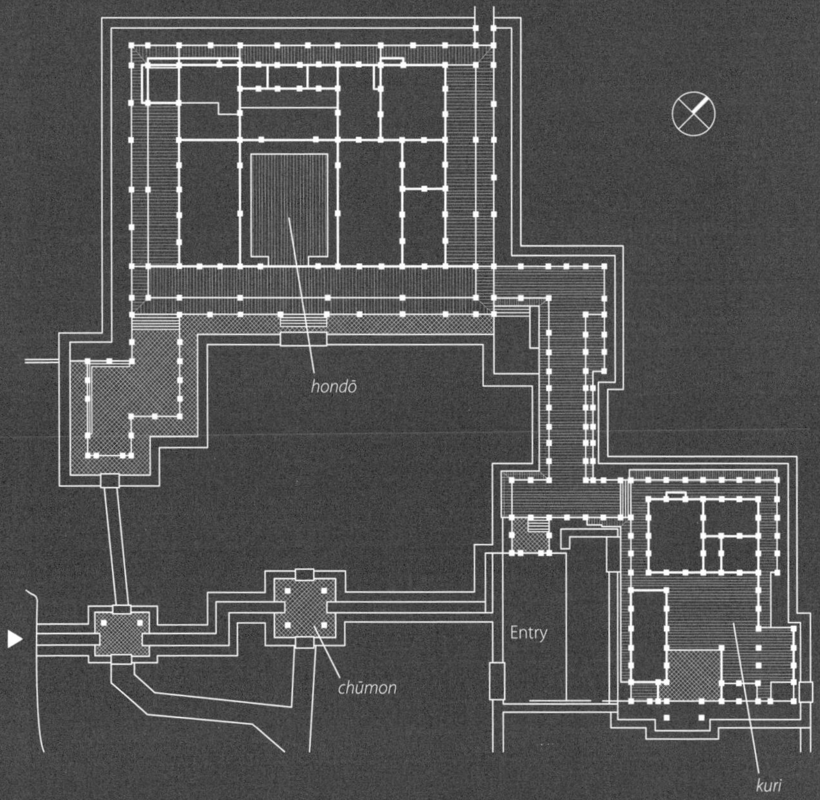

hondō

chūmon

Entry

kuri

TOWARDS ASYMMETRY

OFFSET ENTRIES

In palaces from the Heian period built on large urban plots one *chō* 町 (approximately 120 meters) on a side, two lateral pavilions (*tainoya*) were placed symmetrically opposite to the east and west of the main building (*shinden*). Long covered corridors, (*chūmonrō* 中門廊) connected them to pavilions located near the garden pond towards the south end of the property. But in the Kamakura period, the need for building such imposing palaces disappeared, and smaller residences, called *shuden* 主殿 progressively replaced them. There are no remaining examples of these residences, but the principle of the corridor (*chūmonrō*) now reduced to a single element, was to remain and create an asymmetry in plan[58].

An asymmetry appeared as well in new types of pavilions called *tachū hōjō* 塔頭方丈, constructed within the precincts of Zen monasteries during the Middle Ages. The *tachū* 塔頭 originally served to house the tombs of the Zen abbots who had founded the temples, and the monks who guarded them. But over time, the powerful protectors who supported or patronized the monasteries started to build their own tombs there, along with the *hōjō* 方丈 pavilions where the Zen monks resided. Together, these two constructions ended up playing an increasingly public role for receiving visitors and various other functions. Those new complexes for residence and prayer, the *tachū hōjō* more commonly known as *hōjō*, proliferated near the main temple. At the outset, their main entrance was through a gate set into the south wall of the property, on its axis of symmetry, but this arrangement evolved in the fifteenth century and finally disappeared, to be replaced by gates on the east or west, as in the residences of the *shuden* type.

In the oldest surviving example of a *hōjō*, the Ryōginan 龍吟庵 (1387), in the Tōfukuji monastery 東福寺 in Kyoto, one still enters from the south in an axial manner (figs. a18, a37). But in another example, the Shūonan pavilion 酬恩庵 in the Ikkyūji monastery 一休寺, built later to the south of Kyoto in the sixteenth century and rebuilt in 1650, one enters from west and then turns north to proceed towards the *hōjō*. In the Zuiganji 瑞巌寺 monastery (early seventeenth century) in Matsushima close to Sendai, the entrance is even laid out in a chicane, preventing the visitor from going straight ahead (fig. a43).

---

[58] Hirai Kiyoshi 平井聖, *Nihon jūtaku no rekishi* 日本住宅の歴史 [History of the habitat in Japan] (Tokyo: NHK shuppan, 1986), 107-12; see also Fiévé, *L'architecture et la ville du Japon ancien*, op. cit. (1996), 191–228.

fig a44. aristocratic residential architecture: evolutionary principles (4)

  4. Sukiya-style residence – Edo period

    0. *jōdannoma*
    1. *ichinoma*
    2. *ninoma*
    3. *sannoma*

    hiroen
    en

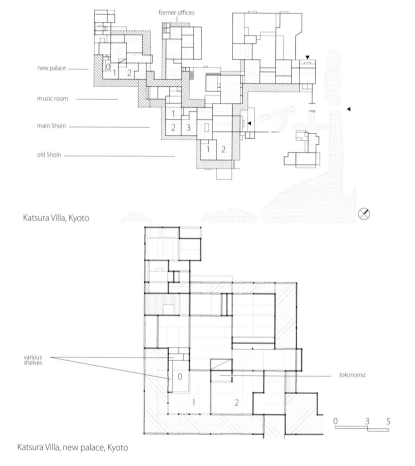

Katsura Villa, Kyoto

Katsura Villa, new palace, Kyoto

STAIR-STEPPED LAYOUTS

Residences for the Zen abbots (*hōjō*) developed to such a point that at one time there were more than two hundred of them in the Tōfukuji[59] monastery in Kyoto alone. Their newfound importance thus influenced the styles of many later constructions. In principle, they consist of a building element with a symmetrical plan, containing two parallel enfilades of three rooms each. In the first series located on the south and facing the garden, the central room where ceremonies are held (*shichū* 室中) is preceded on its right by the space for ordinary visitors (*gekan* 下間), near the entryway placed on the east; on the left and to the west is the reception room for guests of higher standing (*jōkan* 上間)[60]. Along the enfilade at the back, facing north, the center is taken up by the head abbot of the temple, and is flanked at either end by the study cabinets, *shoin*.

These residences mark an important step in the history of typologies. Their plans still reflect their Chinese origins by their symmetry in the east-west direction and the affirmation of a central axis, but the entrance offset to one side introduces an equally explicit asymmetry. Furthermore, the relation between front and back reveals a relation between public and private that was otherwise absent from the palaces in the Shinden style. If the long gallery that extends along the south remains indebted to the canopied spaces (*hisashi*) of the Heian period, the exterior corridors along the three other sides are much narrower than before, and can only be used for circulation, which highlights the new formation of veranda spaces (*en*). Another important trait is the tripartite arrangement of the ceremonial spaces, prefiguring the alignment of the three rooms *jō* 上, *chū* 中 and *ge* 下 (high, medium, and low), also known as *ichi* 一, *ni* 二, and *san* 三 (one, two, three) of pavilions in the Shoin style. And as a last important point, this type of organization prefigures the play of translation that will subsequently come to break the original symmetry by fragmenting the unified volume composed out of these rooms. Between the end of the sixteenth century and the beginning of the seventeenth, these stylistic developments flowered in tea pavilions and architecture in the Sukiya style with stair-stepped compositions, or to use a more poetic formulation, in the "flying geese formation" (*gankō haichi*), as in the Katsura Villa[61] (figs. a19-a, a19-b, a20, a22, a44).

---

[59] Ōta Hirotarō, *Chūsei no kenchiku* 中世の建築 [Architecture of the Middle Ages], vol. 2 (Tokyo: Shōkokusha, 1957).

[60] Sekiguchi Kinya, *Gozan to zenin* 五山と禅院 [The Five Mountains and the Zen monasteries], *Sekiguchi Kinya chosakushū* [Works of Sekiguchi Kinya], vol. 3 (Tokyo: Chūōkōron bijutsu shuppan, 2016), 263–4.

[61] On Katsura Villa, see Saitō Hidetoshi 斉藤英俊, *Katsura rikyū* 桂離宮 [The Katsura villa] (Tokyo: Shōgakkan, 1990). On the arrangement in «flying geese formation» (*gankō haichi* 雁行配置), see also Benoît Jacquet, "La villa Katsura et ses jardins: l'invention d'une modernité japonaise dans les années 1930," in Fiévé and Jacquet (eds.), *Vers une modernité architecturale et paysagère. Modèles et savoirs partagés entre le Japon et le monde occidental* (Paris: Collège de France, 2013), 114–5.

fig a45. *hiroma* and *koma*

hiroma: large formal room, *zashiki* (4.5 tatamis or more)
kokonoma: 9 *ma hiroma*
koma: small room/tea pavilion (less than 4.5 *tatamis*)

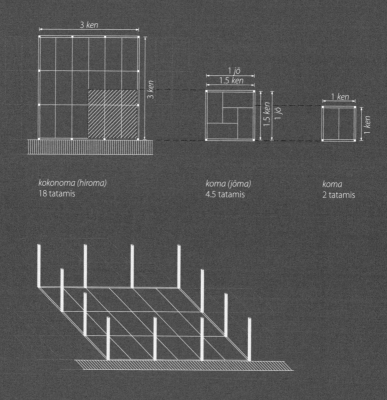

kokonoma (hiroma)
18 tatamis

koma (jōma)
4.5 tatamis

koma
2 tatamis

INNOVATIONS WITHIN INTERIOR SPACE:
FROM THE POST TO THE TATAMI

LARGE AND SMALL ROOMS (*HIROMA* AND *KOMA*)

It seems that the term *hiroma* or "great room" first came into use during the Azuchi-Momoyama period. At that time, it was opposed to the term *koma*, which designated small rooms, in particular tea pavilions or tea rooms, *chashitsu* 茶室. One of the most celebrated manuals of carpentry, the *Shōmei*, which appeared in 1608, precisely called out the defining sizes for these two types of rooms in the architecture in the shoin style: "*koma* refers to rooms one and one half *ken* on a side, whose area is four times smaller than that of *kokonoma* 九間, which are squares three *ken* on a side"[62] (figs. a45, a46).

THE SQUARE *KOKONOMA* ROOM

In the Kamakura period that followed, a new fashion emerged for festive gatherings in the residences of high-ranking warriors or in temples. These were called *yoriai* 寄合, in which the guests participated in various social activities, including *renga* 連歌 (collaborative poetry) or *tōcha* 闘茶 (tea drinking contest). They took place in meeting rooms (*kaisho* 会所) whose dimensions are called out in a text referring to Sasaki Dōyo 佐々木道誉 (1296-1373), a famous *daimyō* of the Muromachi period, as three *ken* by two, or a *muma* (六間 "a room of six *ma*" or twelve tatamis)—a very common size at the time[63]. Later, during the shogunate of Ashikaga Yoshimitsu 足利義満 (1358–1408), an organizer of these festivities (*yoriai*), the term *kaisho* seems to have been extended to apply to the pavilion that contained a room used for this purpose. There was a multiplication of *kokonoma* ("rooms of nine *ma*" in area, or eighteen tatamis, that is to say more than thirty square meters or 323 sf), the largest rooms it was possible to build free of posts, with spans of three *ken* by three (approximately 6 m x 6 m), as attested by the fact that his son Yoshinori had three of them built in his own residence[64] (fig. a31). The meeting rooms for entertaining one's friends were decorated with antiquities imported from China or Korea (*karamono*), that were very sought after at the time. The game winners sometimes even received them as prizes. It was common for scrolls of poems to be hung on the walls. These rooms were also equipped with alcoves (*tokonoma*) for displaying precious objects, with shelves (*tana* 棚) for presenting tea bowls and other utensils, or with study cabinets/alcoves (*tsukeshoin*) in which

---

[62] "The first tea room *kakoi* (*koma*) comes from the division of a space of eighteen tatamis into four as was done by (the master) Jukō in the Higashiyama dono palace." 囲の始りは珠光東山殿正寝十八畳の間を四ツ一と分がこひたるが濫觴なり, in *Sadō sentei* 茶道筌蹄 [Introduction to the Tea Ceremony] (Tokyo: Ōsaka kashiwabara gihei shuppan), 184.

[63] According to the principle stating that "In meeting rooms (*kaisho*) of six *ma* (*muma*), the tatamis are to be aligned" 六間の会 所には大文の畳を敷きならべ, in *Taiheiki* 太平記, chapter 37 (late fourteenth century).

[64] Kōjiro Yūichirō 神代雄一郎, "*Kokonoma ron*" 九間論 [A Study on the *kokonoma*], in *Ma: Nihon kenchiku no ishō* 間(ま):日本建築の意匠 [*Ma*, the conception of Japanese architecture] (Tokyo: Kajima shuppankai, 1999), 128–47.

fig a46. *hiroma* room in the *shoin*, Tenryūji monastery, Kyoto

INNOVATIONS WITHIN INTERIOR SPACE: FROM THE POST TO THE TATAMI — 111

fig a47. *shoin*: reception room

jōdannoma space

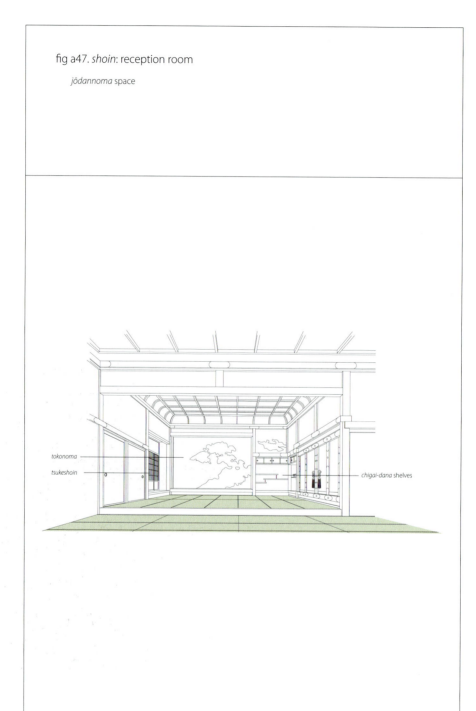

to keep calligraphy materials. This new spatial ensemble, with the subsequent addition of an antechamber (previously the room for the master of the house), and most often composed of *kokonoma* rooms, is characteristic of this new architecture in the Shoin style[65] (figs. a19, a47).

In the first residences in this style, which date from the end of the sixteenth century, a series of three reception rooms with tatamis, similar to the *hōjō* already described, makes its appearance. These rooms are separated from one another by sliding partitions and are laid out in an *enfilade* facing the garden, which always lies to the south. In order of precedence, the first room is called *ichinoma*, the second *ninoma*, and the third *sannoma*. At the back of the *ichinoma* room, one sometimes encounters an appended space, called *goza no ma* 御座の間 or *jōdan no ma* 上段の間, one step up and reserved for the host. Later, at the beginning of the seventeenth century, with the Tokugawa shōgun coming to power, a tatami room adjacent to the *sannoma* room was added for purposes of social display. In the Edo period, this addition also influences the geometry of the *shoin*, which passes from and I-shaped plan to an L-shaped or U-shaped configuration[66] (figs a20, a21).

---

[65] Horiguchi Sutemi, *Shoin-zukuri to sukiya-zukuri no kenkyū* [A Study of the Shoin and Sukiya styles], in *Horiguchi Sutemi hakase chosakushū* [Collected works of Professor Horiguchi], op. cit., 1978; Koizumi Kazuko 小泉和子, *Kagu to shitsunai ishō no bunkashi* 家具と室内意匠の文化史 [A cultural history of furniture and interior design] (Tokyo: Hōsei daigaku shuppansha, 1979).

[66] Hirai Kiyoshi, *Shiro to shoin* 城と書院 [Castles and *shoin*] (Tokyo: Heibonsha, 1965), 45–59; and Yamato Satoshi 大和智, *Shiro to goten* [Castles and palaces] (Tokyo: Shibundō, 2000), 43–59.

fig a48. architectural details
fig a48-a. translucent paper sliding panel (*shōji*) and blind (*sudare*), Yoshijima house, Takayama, Gifu prefecture

fig a48-b. hanging shutter (*shitomido*) and lattice (*kōshi*), Tenryūji monastery, Kyoto

Settings for Nō theater, which were developing at the same time, occupied independent constructions, placed in the garden opposite the existing *shoin*, instead of the preexisting ponds. They were most often *kokonoma* types, which underscores once again the importance of these rooms.

SPACE IN TATAMI OF THE TEA PAVILIONS IN THE SŌAN STYLE

Aside from the large rooms of the *kokonoma* type, which were proliferating at the beginning of the fifteenth century, small square rooms four and a half tatamis in size (less than 8 square meters or 86 sf) appeared during the epoch of the shōgun Ashikaga Yoshimasa 足利義政 (1435–1490), the patron of the Silver Pavilion (Ginkakuji 銀閣寺) in Kyoto. They form small reception rooms (*kozashiki* or small *zashiki*) that measure one and a half *ken* on a side, or approximately one *jō* 丈—a unit of length which has since fallen out of use—or ten *shaku* (close to three meters) at the time—whence their other designation of *jōma* 丈間, in other words a "room (or *ma*) of one *jō* (squared) in area."[67]

In Japanese Buddhism, the term *hōjō* which refers to a space one *jō* on a side—also refers back symbolically to the myth of the shelter and dwelling place of Vimalakīrti (in Japanese Yuima Koji 維摩居士), a famous hermit and contemporary of Shakyamuni, the historical Buddha.

[67] During the course of repairs to the Tōgudō a painting in China ink the size of one *jōma* was discovered on one of the ceiling planks. See the *Kokuhō jishōji Tōgudō shūri kōji hōkoku-sho* 国宝慈照寺東求堂修理工事報告書 [Report on the restoration of the National Treasure of the Tōgudō at the Jishōji (Silver Pavilion)], 1965.

fig a48-c. sliding exterior shutter (*amado*), Rinshukaku villa, Sankeien park, Yokohama

Rooms called *jōma* are thus *hōjō* in the etymological sense of the term—a small space transcended by meditation and vigil to become a world—as opposed to the *tachū hōjō* or much larger *hōjō* in which the Zen abbots dwelled much more comfortably. In the northeast part of the Tōgudō pavilion 東求堂, constructed within the temple of the Silver Pavilion, the private salon (*zashiki*) of the shōgun, that bears the name of Dōjinsai (同仁斎, "cabinet of the same virtue") is the oldest square room of four and one-half tatamis known today. Such a geometry shows the adaptation of a space based on a former structural grid of *jō* units into the closest possible room measured in modules of tatamis, which helps recalling the size, shape and meaning of the original shelter of the hermit. The room contains dedications to the ancestors of Yoshimasa and an image of the Buddha, and traces of a hearth were discovered under the floor, leading one to think that gatherings for the tea ceremony (*chayoriai* 茶寄合) also were held there. It is likely that this was a miniature version of the ceremony that had been practiced until then in the great rooms of the *kokonoma* type, revised in the light of the simplicity of the Buddhist *hōjō* and Vimalakīrti's original and mythic archetype. The only spatial additions to the simple square of the Dōjinsai were the shelving (*tana*) and the study cabinet (*tsukeshoin*), but there was no alcove (*tokonoma*) yet. Although one cannot say with certainty that this room was devoted to the tea ceremony, it represents the only vestige of the spaces that served as models for the tea pavilions of the Sōan style that followed, that were also based on the archetypal *jōma* square spaces measuring four tatami and a half.

With the advent of these small rooms, a radically new way of dividing space came into being. For the first time since the ancient establishment of buildings regulated by successions of full bays, this cardinal principle was set aside in the creation of a half-bay. Since the *jōma* had a surface area of one-fourth of that of a *kokoma*, with sides measuring one *ken* and a half, it was necessary to place intermediate posts, called *manaka no hashira* (間中の柱, literally, "the middle post," the post in the middle of the bay), by omitting the post that previously was located on the edge of the bay (fig. a45). Another revolution was that this division was no longer directly linked to the spatio-structural grid, but rather to the size of the tatamis that had recently come to cover the floors of all formal rooms. This method of conceiving, called *tatamiwari* 畳割 (division by tatami modules), is based on the number of tatamis, as opposed to the method known as *hashiwari* 柱割 (division by the distance between columns or post spans), which was dependent on the distances between posts, measured in *ken*. The dimension of the tatami is close to that of a human figure lying down and is particularly well suited to the small intimate spaces of the tea pavilions in the Sōan style (literally, "a thatched pavilion," in other words, a rustic style).

FROM REGULAR ORTHOGONAL FORM TO IRREGULAR FORMS: THE *KOMA* TEA PAVILIONS

At the end of the sixteenth century, Sen no Rikyū, known as Rikyū, formalized the tea ceremony (*chanoyu* 茶の湯), and created the first tea pavilions (*chashitsu* 茶室) in the Sōan style to house them. These spaces of reduced dimension and rustic appearance play a contrapuntal role to the splendid *hiroma* rooms that express social standing. One of Rikyū's disciples, Yamanoue Sōji, wrote that the success of the pavilion derived from the "creative idea," that is to say, from its originality.[68] And changes, even improvements continued to be added. These small tea rooms, regulated by the half-*ken* module and following the *tatamiwari* principle (planar division by

---

[68] Kuwata, *Sadōkotenzenshūdai6kan* [The classics of the tea ceremony. Complete works, vol. 6], op. cit. (1977).

tatamis), in the end called into question the parallelepipedal forms linked to the *hashirawari* (planar division by posts ie structural bays) which had been employed up to that point, and enabled the creation of irregularly formed and complex pavilions. Procedures that would have been difficult to imagine up to that time were employed. Posts were sometimes eliminated for aesthetic reasons, sometimes added without structural necessity, thus leading to new spatial configurations. The architecture for the tea brought with it a sort of revolution, whose influence extends to contemporary architecture today.

From Tea Pavilions for Rich City Dwellers to Sen no Rikyū

We have little information on pavilions from before the Azuchi-Momoyama period, as no examples remain. Yamanoue Sōji reports nonetheless that Murata Jukō had already created a tea room of four and a half tatamis in the fifteenth century. A hundred years earlier, this example paved the way for the Wabicha style (詫茶, literally, "tea in the Wabi style")—in other words the tea ceremony practiced in the spare and rustic setting of a pavilion known as Wabisabi, as codified by Rikyū and still practiced today. Even if there is no really tangible proof to corroborate this assertion by Yamanoue Sōji, this small square room, without a center or direction, nonetheless affords a form well adapted to a new ceremony in which all participants have an equal place.

After Murata, Takenoo Jōō, the master of Rikyū, was to have built a room of four and one-half tatamis that was much more closed off. Unlike the subsequent pavilions from the Azuchi-Momoyama period, in which two of the four sides opened up on to adjacent spaces, this new pavilion was closed off on three sides. It was also simplified, as the elimination of any decoration (suspended rolls, *kakejiku* 掛軸) on the walls emphasized their presence and the form of the space. If the celebrated tea masters (*chajin* 茶人, "man of tea") of the time all reproduced this room of four and one-half tatamis, Rikyū's originality lays nonetheless in the explicit rupture with the richness of the other rooms and the introduction of elements of rusticity. Using "poor" materials—wattle and daub walls (*tsuchi kabe* 土壁), unsquared tree trunks for the beams, windows leaving the construction lattice exposed (*shitaji mado*), thatched roofs (*kayabuki yane* 茅葺屋根)—he created the Wabi style of the Sōan tea pavilions. Upon his arrival in Japan at that time, the Jesuit missionary Luis Fróis (1532–1597) wrote about the tea pavilions in the Rikyū style, in one of the first comparative studies about this country by a Westerner, that "their *chanoyu* (tea ceremony) rooms are made from raw wood as it comes from the forest, in order to imitate nature," and that "the *zaxiqis* (*zashiki,* salon) of the *chanoyu* are dark and windowless."[69] (figs. a49, a50).

The Rikyū Square, or the Association of a Confined and Closed-off Space

Rikyū's tea pavilions are thus characterized by their bare and rustic appearance, but his primary intention was probably something else. In reality, he seems to have sought just as much if not more to reduce the size of the room, in addition to reorienting it to the south instead of to the north as it had until then. This was to avoid any distraction for the guests, whose attention

---

[69] See Luís Fróis, *Européens et Japonais. Traité sur les contradictions et différences de mœurs, écrit par le R.P. Luís Fróis au Japon, l'an 1585* (Paris: Chandeigne, 1998), 69–70. English edition: Daniel T. Reff, Richard K. Danford, Robin D. Gill (eds.), *The First European Description of Japan, 1585: A Critical English-Language Edition of Striking Contrasts in the Customs of Europe and Japan by Luis Frois, S.J.*, Japan Anthology Workshop Series (New York: Routledge, 2014).

fig a49. Sōan tea pavilion: principles

   three tatamis and one *daime-datami* room

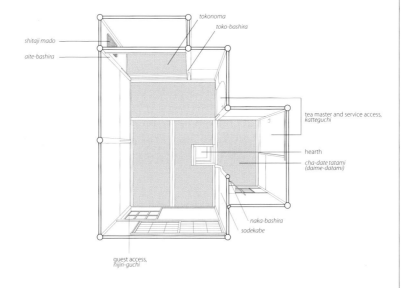

could then be focused exclusively on the ceremony. Over its course, as the accent was on the utensils—hanging scrolls (*kakejiku*), tea bowls (*chawan* 茶碗) etc.—it was customary to admit a uniform light from the north in order to light them properly.[70] Instead, Rikyū inverted this organization in the only original pavilion existing that may have been constructed under his care: the Taian (待庵, "waiting pavilion") at the Myōkian temple 妙喜庵 in Yamazaki, between Kyoto and Osaka (figs. a51, a52).

This tea pavilion, structurally independent and oriented towards the south, is attached to the main building (*shoin*) of a Zen monastery. It consists of three rooms: one square, two tatamis in size and an alcove (*tokonoma*) for the ceremony, the second, called the "next room" (*tsuginoma* 次の間) of one tatami in size, through which the tea master entered, and the last one, which served for the preparation, the "water room" (*mizuya* 水屋). The two first spaces are separated by a double sliding door (*fusuma* 襖, in opaque white paper, and a wing wall (*sodekabe* 袖壁). A small and low entry is located on the south facade, a crouching entry (*nijiri-guchi* 躙口) the height of a wood half door, through which one (literally) "enters on one's knees." The corners of the room are rounded off and coated in such a way as to conceal the posts at the corners of the room, which are all uniformly made of wattle and daub. The space is deliberately closed off and dark, punctured only by two small windows covered with translucent paper (*shōji*) that diffuse

[70] Yamanoue Sōji has noted that "The Jōō style is always with the hearth to the left (*sa-katte* 左勝手) and oriented towards the north" (紹鴎の流は悉く左勝手、北向也), and that "Sōeki (Rikyū) likes the orientation to the south, with the hearth on the left" (宗易は南向、左勝手を好く), in *Yamanoue no Sōji-ki* [Notes of Yamanoue Sōji], cited in Kuwata, *Sadō koten zenshū dai 6 kan* [Classics of the tea ceremony. Complete works, vol. 6], op. cit. (1977).

fig a50. tea pavilion, Sōan style, Meimeian, Matsue, Shimane prefecture

fig a51. tea pavilion (1)

cha-date tatami: tea master's tatami
nijiriguchi: lowered entry for guests
T: alcove, *tokonoma*
S: study cabinet, *tsukeshoin*
E: shelves, *chigai-dana*

☐ : hearth
•— : *naka-bashira* and *sodekabe*
∘ : *toko-bashira*
▸ : tea master access
▹ : guest access

before Sen no Rikyū:
Dōjinsai
4.5 tatamis
Jishōji temple (silver pavilion)
Tōgudō, Kyoto
Shōgun Ashikaga Yoshimasa

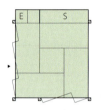
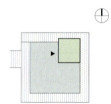

1 before Sen no Rikyū:
4.5 tatamis
Takeno Jōō

2 rotation, *tokonoma* on the north
Yūin
4.5 tatamis
Urasenke house, Kyoto
Sen no Rikyū

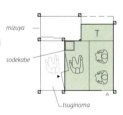
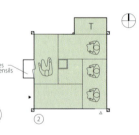

Taian
2 tatamis
Myōkian temple, Oyamazaki
Sen no Rikyū

INNOVATIONS WITHIN INTERIOR SPACE: FROM THE POST TO THE TATAMI — 121

fig a52. Taian pavilion, Kyoto prefecture
fig a52-a. exterior view (reconstruction for the "Japan in Architecture" exhibition, Mori Art Museum, 2018)
fig a52-b. interior view
fig a53. Joan pavilion, Aichi prefecture
fig a53-a. exterior view

fig a53-b. interior view showing the angled *sujikai kabe* wall with the *tokonoma* alcove

INNOVATIONS WITHIN INTERIOR SPACE: FROM THE POST TO THE TATAMI — 123

the light. One of them illuminates the utensils that are placed on the "tatami where the tea is set" (*cha-date tatami* 茶立畳), where the host prepares the beverage, seated in front of the white surface of the two closed *fusuma*. The other one, placed above the small entry door on the south facade, directs the light on to the guests, who drink the tea and admire the bowls, in order to help them concentrate on the ceremony.[71] The ceiling is divided into two parts: an L-shaped lower and flat area (*hiratenjō* 平天井) sits above the *cha-date tatami* and the place for the main guest to sit, who is thus set on an equal footing. The other part of the ceiling, which is higher and inclined, dominates over the zone where another guest could be seated, one of lower rank. The exiguous dimensions of the room do not allow more than two people, aside from the master of ceremonies, to comfortably occupy the space. This arrangement is not as paradoxical as it may seem. In residences of the Shoin style, only the rooms occupied by the hosts have ceilings, while the peripheral corridors (*en*) that one merely passes through and which are occupied by servants, follow the inclined forms of the canopies. The parts of the pavilion, on one hand low and finished off with ceilings, and the others, higher and inclined, and following the form of the roof, indicate this difference in status. Thus, Rikyū created an original tea pavilion, recentered on the tea ceremony, which also subtly modifies the perception of rank at that time. The tea master is set at the same level, even though the social status of his host may be superior.

The architects and professors Horiguchi Sutemi—whose work takes inspiration from this architecture and will be addressed in the next chapter—and Nakamura Masao indicate the strong possibility that the Taian pavilion was dismantled, transported, and reconstructed in its current location. There is no proof that the garden was by Rikyū either, but in Horiguchi's estimation, his style can be clearly discerned. If one analyzes the path that leads from the Taian to the temple, the reorientation to the south assumes its full meaning. The visitor heads along a path made of disjointed stone steps (*tobi ishi* 飛石; literally, "jumping stones") and heads south with the sun in his eyes, before turning left and mounting a large stone sill and penetrating the small door (*nijiri-guchi*) while lowering his head, in a space that has suddenly become dark. The blinded visitors, who enter this dark place with its uniform walls and deliberately rounded corners, find it difficult to apprehend its dimensions; the space of the room appears larger and deeper to them than it is in reality. All the subtlety of Rikyū's composition lies here, starting from a small square room (*koma*) of four tatamis and a half, which he decomposes by homothetic transformation into a double square: the smaller one constitutes the space of the ceremony per se, and the larger one the initial *koma*. With this organization, that conserves the regularity of the archetypal of a *jōma* despite its transformation, he created the first Japanese example in which the modular wooden structure takes a back seat to a spatial conception based on the walls.

Rikyū killed himself in 1591 as commanded to by his master, Toyotomi Hideyoshi. According to a piece of writing by his disciple Hosokawa Sansai, he was thinking at the time about a four-and-a-half-tatami tea pavilion with a non-structural central post (*naka-bashira* 中柱).[72]

---

[71] In regards to this aesthetic intent, see Aikawa Hiroshi 相川浩氏, *Hikaku kenchikuron: Rikyū to Aruberuti no sakui* 比較建築論:利休とアルベルティの作意 [A comparative architectural study: the conceptions of Rikyū and Alberti] (Tokyo: Chūōkōron bijutsu shuppan, 2003); Horiguchi, *Rikyū no chashitsu* [The tea pavilions of Rikyū], *Horiguchi Sutemi hakase chosakushū* [Works of Professor Horiguchi Sutemi], op. cit. (1987); and Nakamura Masao 中村昌生, *Chashitsu kenkyū* 茶室研究 [Studies on the tea pavilion] (Tokyo: Bokusui shoten, 1971).

[72] Hosokawa Sansai 細川三斎 (1564–1646) wrote that "Rikyū already wanted to build a four and a half tatami pavilion with a *naka-bashira*, before Oribe failled in turn." (利休ハ四畳半ニ中柱立てべきとたく候中に相果候、其後、織部 殿四畳半に中柱を間半目に立て候得共、しまぬよし被仰候), in *Hosokawa Sansai odenjusho* 細川三斎御伝受書 [The initiation book of Hosokawa Sansai]. See Nakamura Masao (ed.), *Sukiya koten shūsei* 数奇屋古典集成 [Collection of Sukiya classics], vol. 2 (Tokyo: Shōgakkan, 1989).

This idea, which was pursued by his successors Oribe, Uraku, and Enshū, no doubt came to him from a desire to make the spatial relationship between the *cha-date tatami*, the seat of the tea master, and the rest of the room more dynamic. In the Taian and in another pavilion built inside Toyotomi Hideyoshi's Jūrakudai palace 聚楽第 in Kyoto, one finds a very short wall plane (*sodekabe*) between these two zones. This light separation masks the utensils from the eyes of the guests and reduces their relation to the dramaturgy of the beverage's preparation. The future association between this wall and the post (*naka-bashira*) which terminates it and introduces an "incident" in the room, gave rise to a multitude of formal variations.

TOWARDS AN IRREGULAR FORM, THE TEA PAVILIONS OF THE GREAT LORDS

Although Rikyū was the tea master of Toyotomi Hidetoshi, he was only a merchant from the port of Sakai near Osaka. His disciples, on the other hand, were practically all local aristocrats (*daimyō*). The ideal in his pavilions was to practice the tea ceremony in a simple and serene manner in a two-tatami space. This presented a certain number of inconveniences in their eyes, and they wished to develop their own styles as well. Progressively abandoning the austerity of their master, they played with the archetype of the square plan they had inherited, created irregularities, multiplied the openings in the walls and ceiling, and reintroduced ornamentation borrowed from the great formal rooms (*zashiki*) of the time, which Rikyū had deliberately eliminated.

Furuta Oribe (1544–1655), known as Oribe, who succeeded Rikyū as the tea master of the shōgun Tokugawa Hidetada 徳川秀忠 (1579–1633), the ruler of Japan and the second Tokugawa shōgun, created tea rooms of a minimum of three tatamis with the addition of the *cha-date tatami* reserved for the tea master. Some of his works contained as much as ten windows, a number that was less a function of the need for lighting than for some spatial construction or for a "landscape" (*kei* 景) of which the Enan pavilion 燕庵 at the Yabunouchi house 薮内家 is a perfect example (fig. a54). To sum up their differences, if Rikyū placed stone steps (*tobi ishi*) in the garden "sixty percent for facilitating their use and forty percent for aesthetic reasons" (*watari roku bu ni kei yon bu* 渡り六分に景四分). It was later said that in applying this formula to the ensemble of the pavilion, Oribe inverted it.

Oda Uraku's Transformations and Rikyū's Post

Oda Uraku, known as Uraku, was a younger brother of Oda Nobunaga 織田信長 (1534–1582), the predecessor of Toyotomi Hideyoshi He created a new style of tea pavilion by modifying Rikyū's square plan through geometric transformations such as magnification, extension, curvature, and displacement. The high point of these developments was the Joan pavilion 如庵, conceived at the end of his life (figs. a53, a54). Built inside the Shōdenin pavilion 正伝院 of the Kenninji monastery 建仁寺 of Kyoto, it served originally as Uraku's retreat. It has subsequently been relocated and reconstructed by integrating it into a *shoin*, in the Urakuen 有楽園 Inuyama garden near Nagoya. The edifice consists of a large square main room of eight tatamis, and a "following" or secondary room (*tsuginoma*) of six. The small room (*koma*) constitutes the tea pavilion proper. It is unusual in form, with a space of two and one-half tatamis and one *daime-datami* 台目畳—a small tatami three-quarters of the normal length, which serves as a *cha-date tatami*—and includes a number of original devices:

— A central post (*naka-bashira*) appears, although it is tied to the wall by a partition (*sodekabe*) pierced by a rounded opening (*katō-guchi* 花頭口).

— An angled wall (*sujikai kabe* 筋交い壁) separates the *cha-date tatami*—on which the tea master officiates—from the alcove (*tokonoma*), curiously integrated into the room instead of being attached to it from the outside in order to maintain the regularity of the plan of the room, as is usually the case.

— Windows placed to the side of the *cha-date tatami* are provided with thin lengths of bamboo held tight against each other—called "in the Uraku manner" (*urakumado* 有楽窓). Although the exterior is not directly visible through them, they let natural light filter through their bars.

Even though the pavilion is small in size, when one enters by the low door (*nijiri-guchi*), these detailed differences in concept, along with the movement of the guests, gives them a sense of dynamism and containment. Once the guests are seated in the room, if they look back, they can see the round window in the lateral wall of the projecting exterior canopy, through the window that sits above the low door. The gaze is thus drawn to the distance and dilates the space. The old recycled calendars, that cover the lower part of the walls, contribute as well in a humorous manner, to the sense of depth, of temporal depth this time, all the while underscoring the continuity of the wall surfaces, which tends to blur the outlines of the form and to visually enlarge this narrow space (fig. a53-b).

The Joan tea pavilion is an irregularly shaped room, and yet if it is considered in its totality, including the alcove (*tokonoma*), it remains practically square, like Rikyū's Taian. Furthermore, by the addition of the (*naka-bashira*) post, Uraku proposed a spatial solution to the spiritual legacy of his predecessor. If one looks specifically at where to place a post in the middle of the four and a half tatamis of the pavilion, only two places seem possible, in the corner of the *cha-date tatami* or at its center (fig. a54).

In the first case, the post is offset in relation to the ensemble of the room and the space for putting the utensils on the *cha-date tatami*. In the second case, when the post is placed in the angle of the *cha-date tatami*, there is no spatial tension to be felt. Uraku thus thought to reduce the size of the room by including the alcove (*tokonoma*) into the original space of four and a half tatamis. Since a depth of one-half *ken* (approximately 90 cm) was a bit too big for this space, Uraku shortened it slightly by five *sun* 寸 and five *bu* 分 (that is, one half *shaku* or 16.7 cm), and reduced the *cha-date tatami* in the process, which became a *daime-datami* (a tatami with a smaller module). To fill in the gap which appeared next to the alcove (*tokonoma*), he introduced an angled wall joining the post of the *tokonoma* (*toko-bashira* 床柱) to the entry door for the tea master (*katte-guchi* 勝手口). But then judging the space in front of the master to be too open with only the central post (*naka-bashira*), he added a plank partition (*sodekabe*), with no more structural function than the post. The latter is nonetheless interrupted in its lower portion so as not to completely close off the space.

This painstaking description is a clear illustration of all the infinite subtleties of the spatial culture of the tea pavilion. Down through the centuries, all the way down to contemporary architects, it provided a continuous repertoire of references, of variations, and of copies. We will see this clearly, among other examples, in Chapter Two in the case of modern Sukiya architecture. And even if the structural role of wood is often obscured by the emphasis on partitions of wattle and daub, its structuring and decorative role remains highlighted through the grace of various decorative posts, the variety of profiles, and the different species of wood.

fig a53-c. interior view from entry, with the *sodekabe* partition terminated by a *naka-bashira* ornamental post and *"Uraku"* windows
fig a53-d. *"Uraku"* windows

fig a54. tea pavilion (2)

daime-datami: cha-date tatami reduced in size (3/4)

☐ : hearth
: *naka-bashira* and *sodekabe*
• : *toko-bashira*
▶ : tea master access
▷ : guest access

① first attempt
Oda Uraku
② Joan
2.5 tatamis and 1 *daime-datami*
originally in Kyoto,
relocated near Nagoya
Oda Uraku

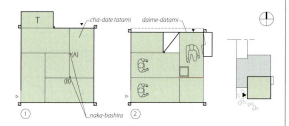

Enan
3 tatamis and 1 *daime-datami*
Yabunouchi house, Kyoto
Furuta Oribe

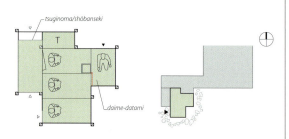

Hassōseki
3 tatamis and 1 *daime-datami*
Nanzenji monastery, Konchiin,
Kyoto
Kobori Enshū

INNOVATIONS WITHIN INTERIOR SPACE: FROM THE POST TO THE TATAMI — 129

fig a55. architectural details
fig a55-a. full-sized model of a tea pavilion. Detail of internal structure of the walls before being covered in cob, Takenaka Carpentry Tools Museum (*Takenaka daiku dōgukan*), Kobe

fig a55-b. crouching entry (*nijiri-guchi*), Shōkintei pavilion, Katsura Villa, Kyoto

fig a55-c. *tokonoma* alcove with its *toko-bashira* angle post, Shunsōro pavilion, Sankeien park, Yokohama
fig a55-d. ornamental post *naka-bashira* in front of a *daime-datami* and the *sodekabe* partition, Shunsōro pavilion, Sankeien park, Yokohama
fig a55-e. *shitaji mado* window, Takenaka Carpentry Tools Museum, Kobe

fig a55-f. earthen floor entry space (*do-bisashi*), Shōiken pavilion, Katsura Villa, Kyoto

fig a-56. the tea pavilion (3)

□ : hearth
: *naka-bashira* and *sodekabe*
∘ : *toko-bashira*
▸ : tea master access
▹ : guest access

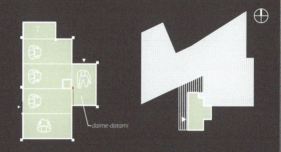

Kanunken
4 tatamis and 1 *daime-datami*
Iwashimizu Hachiman sanctuary, Kyoto
Kobori Enshū

daime-datami

daime-datami

Mittan
4.5 tatamis and 1 *daime-datami*
Daitokuji monastery, Ryūkōin, Kyoto
Kobori Enshū

IRREGULAR SPACES:
THE ASSOCIATION OF *HIROMA* AND *KOMA* ROOMS

ASSOCIATION OF STYLES

With his tea pavilions in the Sōan style, Sen no Rikyū defined the forms and rules of the tea ceremony in the *wabicha* style at the end of the sixteenth century and put the final touches on a sober and rustic aesthetic, devoid of any ostentation and centered on the ceremony itself. Conversely, his disciples Furuta Oribe and Oda Uraku sought to develop new types. The *kireisabi*, a style invented by Kobori Enshū, known as Enshū and himself a disciple of Oribe, pushed this inversion even further in the opposite direction from Rikyū's *wabisabi* by giving, as it was said, "sixty percent" to aesthetics.

The Kireisabi of the Little Tea Pavilion Koma of Kobori Enshū

In general the notion of the beautiful, *kirei* 奇麗, in other words the aesthetic of Enshū, is essentially based on the following devices: the inclusion and arrangement of multiple windows that produce a very brightly lit room; the visibility of a series of decorative elements, such as wall paintings and openwork transoms (*ranma*), or finely worked metal trim (nail heads on the beams, door handles etc.). But Enshū's true revolution lays in his adaptation of Rikyū's *wabicha* aesthetic of the tea pavilion for use by the nobility (fig. a56).

In the case of the small rooms (*koma*), Enshū's master Oribe added one supplementary tatami, called *shōbanseki* 相伴席, to a space initially consisting of three tatamis and one shorter tatami (*daime-datami*) (fig. a54). This contiguous space, the size of the new tatami and separated by a sliding partition, made it possible to place guests of lower rank and to increase the number of participants without affecting the main room. But Enshū also proposed a larger room of four tatamis and one *daime-datami*, as in the Kanunken pavilion 閑雲軒 in the Iwashimizu hachiman 石清水八幡宮 sanctuary near Kyoto. The added tatami at the end comes to serve the role of *shōbanseki*, which is now integrated into the room. In the course of enlarging the original space, Enshū created a subtle threshold by repositioning the crouching entry (*nijiri-guchi*), normally placed in the corner, to stand between the three original tatamis and the new additional one. The design of the ceiling over the latter is different from the rest of the room and helps "distance" the less important guests, both symbolically and equally efficiently. The central post (*naka-bashira*), linked to the tatami reserved for the tea service (*cha-date tatami*) and added by Enshū, constitutes another important feature of this pavilion.

Two celebrated works located in Kyoto also illustrate these manipulations by enlargement, addition, or displacement of the elements that are attached or integrated into the basic square: The Mittan 密庵 tea pavilion of the Ryōkōin temple 龍光院 at the Daitokuji monastery 大徳寺, and the Hassōseki (or Hassō no seki) 八窓席 of the Konchiin temple 金地院 at the Nanzenji 南禅寺

monastery (figs. a54, a56). In the first example, a smaller-sized tatami (*daime-tatami*) is added to a four-and-a-half-tatami room, which exceeds the previous limits of this little room (*koma*). Enshū established a balance by the further addition of an alcove (*tokonoma*), a shelf (*tana*), and a study cabinet (*tsukeshoin*), all of them joined to the basic room. In the second case, on the other hand, a shallow *tokonoma* and a *cha-date tatami* complemented by a shelf are repositioned side to side within the four-and-a-half-tatami room, opposite the low door (*nijiri-guchi*).

The Hassōseki pavilion also illustrates another important development, in that the adjoining secondary room (*tsuginoma*), which originally served as a place to prepare the tea, becomes a ceremonial space in turn. This intermediate type will lead to the integration of a room called *kusarinoma* 鎖の間, which started out as a link between the larger and smaller rooms, *hiroma* and *koma*, into the pavilion complex itself. These spaces will all add to the range of locations for the tea ceremony, in a more varied and informal manner. These new forms of organization will also lead to further questioning the original sobriety of the designs of the *koma*, which would now be influenced by the wealth of decoration of the large halls for reception and formal events (*hiroma*) of the Shoin style (fig. a58).

fig a-57. example of the multiplication of windows leading to Oribe and the *kireisabi* of Enshū. Oda Uraku, Shunsōro pavilion, Sankeien park, Yokohama

Enshū's Combinations: The Kusarinoma Space

The *kusarinoma* was originally an intermediate space between the large and small rooms, *koma* and *hiroma*, in which the tea was prepared. Rikyū is often credited with introducing the aesthetic of the tea pavilion into the great room (*hiroma*), but he seems to have nonetheless considered the more modest one (*koma*) as the appropriate place for the tea ceremony. For Rikyū, the main and auxiliary rooms *hiroma* and *tsuginoma* were to be used for meetings and exchanges before and after the ceremony itself. On the other hand, Oribe started to organize tea ceremonies by setting up a hearth in the *kusarinoma*, whose dimensions varied from four and a half to eight tatamis and exceeded the size of a *koma*. In addition, he disrupted the usual layout of Shoin style rooms, in which the alcove (*tokonoma*) and shelf (*tana*) were generally placed side by side on the main wall, with the study cabinet (*tsukeshoin*) on the side wall along the exterior corridor (*engawa*), in an L-shaped layout (fig. a47). With the legacy of this aesthetic, in which these three elements could be combined more freely by displacing them or increasing their number, Enshū sought in turn other even more complex layouts, which enabled him to create new spaces.

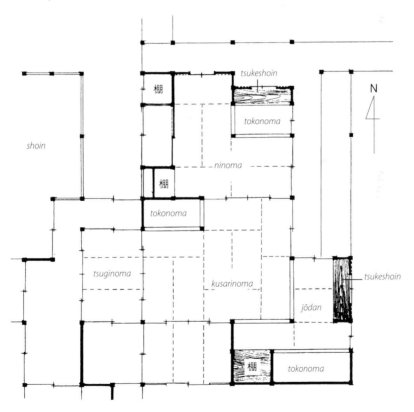

fig a-58. *kusarinoma* space
fig a-58-a. example of a *kusarinoma* room in plan

fig a-58-b. example of *kireisabi*. Kobori Enshū, reconstruction of Kobori Enshū's residence in Fushimi. Fuji no kuni cha no miyako Museum, Shizuoka
fig a-58-c. example of *kireisabi*. Kobori Enshū

In the Manner of

In the literature on the tea pavilions of Rikyū and his successors, the Shoin and Sukiya styles tend to become fixed. Many expressions illustrate this, referring to new pavilions being designed "in the manner of" Rikyū (*Rikyū-gonomi* 利休好み), of Oribe (*Oribe-gonomi* 織部好み) or of Enshū (*Enshū-gonomi* 遠州好み), or referring to "copies" (*utsushi* 写し) of some pavilion by such and such master. Thus, for the first time in the history of Japanese architecture, styles are attributed to some original type and to a particular person, a recognized master builder for example—in a manner not unlike the terminology that was beginning to be applied to the Renaissance architects in Europe—and was subsequently reproduced or modified as such.

The tea pavilions of these masters, in which the new aesthetic of the Sukiya style was being developed, also adopt a ternary spatial structure, characteristic of many buildings. Starting in the Edo period, in the seventeenth century, the aesthetic principles of the *shingyōsō* 真行草, that was originally applied to calligraphy, came to be applied to architecture by analogy. The term is made up of three characters: *shin, gyō*, and *sō*, and it initially defined the three classic styles of writing imported from Tang China during the Nara period: angular, half-cursive and cursive, either formal (*shin* 真), more relaxed (*gyō* 行), or rapid and untied (*sō* 草). Thus, by analogy, the *shin* principle applies to large formal spaces whose floors are covered in tatamis, *zashiki* or *shinzashiki* 真座敷 (or *hiroma*); *gyō* describes intermediate and less formal spaces like the *kusarinoma*, and *sō* is applied to small rooms, *sōzashiki* 草座敷 (or *koma*), and rustic pavilions in the manner of Rikyū.[73]

Interior and Landscape

The tea pavilion did not only influence architectural design with the advent of the Sukiya style. It also entailed a redefinition of the relationship between interior and exterior space. The two last examples we will mention, the Kohōan 孤篷庵 and the Jikōin 慈光院 are thus celebrated archetypes of new spatial organization (figs. a59, a60).

During the first half of the seventeenth century, Enshū built the Kohōan in the monastery of Daitokuji in Kyoto for his own sepulcher. As such, it is of the *tachū* type, built to commemorate the passing of a monk. Here Enshū created a new space, the *chazashiki* or *zashiki* for tea, which does not resemble a tea pavilion at first glance. If its basic form is simple and does not diverge from the square plan, the author not only enlarged the small room in bringing it to eight tatamis, but he also made several additions: on the east side, he added a supplementary *tatami* for the tea service (*cha-date tatami*) to which he added an alcove (*tokonoma*) of the same length; on the adjacent side to the north, he added a group of three tatamis for additional guests (*shōbanseki*); opposite the tea master's space, including the *chadate tatami* and the *tokonoma*, the west side opens on to a veranda, consisting of one *hiroen* and one *ochien* in a row. The veranda itself is open on its lower part and partly closed in its upper part by short partitions of translucent

---

[73] For these terms, see *Yamanoue no Sōji-ki* [Notes of Yamanoue Sōji] who describes the tea pavilions of Takeno Jōō; *Matsuya kaiki* 松屋会記 (The record of Matsuya tea gatherings) (1634) which mentions the Sekishū pavilion, in the *Nanpōroku* 南方録 (The Southern Record), known as Rikyū's "Book of Secret Teachings." There is much uncertainty around the origins of this work, which was no doubt drawn up approximately one hundred years after the death of the master, with written additions that are not from his hand. Nonetheless, it is generally believed that the term *shinzashiki* came into common usage for tea pavilions at this time. See Kuwata Chikatada and Kumakura Isao 熊倉功夫, *Nanpōroku seiritsu to sonohaikei* 『南方録』成立とその背景 [The *Nanpōroku*: its genesis and context], *Chanoyu* 茶湯, no. 11 (1977).

fig a-59. Jikōin temple, Nara prefecture
fig a-59-a. view of the garden from the *shoin*

paper (*shōji*). These no longer serve to close off the space but to cut down on the glare from the setting sun, and they allow first and foremost the framing of a landscape consisting of a basin and a stone lantern, with a garden behind. In this way, Enshū tied the interior to an exterior, the view of which is limited and centered on a single scene that lacks any perceptible scale, and paradoxically gives the impression of a space without depth, in other words infinite. In the Kohōan, the absence of successive planes to be seen from the pavilion establishes the relation between interior and exterior.

In the Jikōin family temple near Nara, the tea master Katagiri Sekishū 片桐石州 (1605–1673), who time and again had participated in ceremonies organized by Enshū, created a new relational arrangement at the beginning of the Edo period, as opposed to that of the Kohōan. By playing with the arrangement of posts on the gallery outside of the temple's reading room (*shoin*), the placement of the guests, and the direction of their views, he put the relation between interior and exterior into play. Thus, the garden when seen from the main room (*hiroma*) and the veranda (*hiroen*), seems to extend the landscape to the Nara cliffs seen at a distance to the east, beyond the azalea bushes that conceal the immediate background and create a spatial continuum. Critics called this arrangement *shakkei* 借景 or "borrowed landscape." Little more than a half-century after Rikyū, the concept of tea pavilions founded on a large room, *hiroma*, had reached its fruition.

fig a-59-b. view of the *shoin* from the garden
fig a-59-d. *shakkei* principle

fig a-59-c. *hiroma* room with a *tokonoma* alcove, a *tsuke shoin* alcove on the right, and the entry of a tea pavilion from the *engawa* veranda
fig a60. Kohōan pavilion, Daitokuji monastery, Kyoto

fig a61. jetty, Golden Pavilion (Kinkakuji), Kyoto

NATURE AND ARCHITECTURE

THE EXTERIOR ASPECT: CONCAVE AND CONVEX CURVES IN THE ROOFS

The original forms of wood architecture, which came from China during the Asuka period in the sixth and seventh centuries, display their strong symmetry, but other architectonic principles have also played a role, such as the proportions of buildings, their coloration, and their roof forms.[74] With the introduction of Buddhist monasteries from the continent, buildings of greater height—pagodas, halls and main pavilions (kondō)—were built with painted structures for the first time, with emphasis on their verticality and topped by roofs that adopted the concave curves called sori 反り. The "indigenous" buildings with elevated floors (takayuka shiki), such as the Ise shrine or the majestic central pavilion (shōden) of the Kasuga taisha sanctuary, had slender silhouettes of course, but these were religious constructions. It was more difficult, on the other hand to imagine that the first ordinary dwellings, half-buried or not, had been marked by a strong verticality.

The monasteries in the Daibutsuyō or Zenshūyō styles, that were imported as well, but later, between the twelfth and fourteenth centuries, were also characterized by an emphatic slenderness in contrast to the types of architecture found on the islands. Nonetheless, local influences are visible in the case of the former style, which was adopted to allow for the rapid reconstruction of the Tōdaiji temple in Nara. For example, radiating chevrons were used only at the angles of the canopies, not the entire length, as they were in the Chinese archetypes, and the palisades were constructed with horizontal weatherboards and not vertical ones. The curves of the roofs were also limited, in order to reduce their complexity as well as the duration and cost of construction. In the latter case, a style imported by the Zen monks arriving from the Asian continent and no doubt influenced by Chinese architecture of the Southern Song, the first buildings had a slender allure, resulting from the relation between the height of the posts and the length of the beams, and the very strongly marked curvature of the roofs.[75]

Other details appeared such as the new types of arched windows (katōmado 花頭窓). But as this style spread in Japan, its slenderness was reduced over time, and the curvature of the roofs softened. In addition, buildings initially intended to have an earth floor (doma) were provided with elevated wood floors and were surrounded by exterior galleries, measures that accentuated their horizontality. But how does one explain this evolution of continental types over the course of their propagation? While it is difficult to give a definitive answer, on can suppose that in Japan, more than in China, there is greater concern for the spatial whole that the construction forms with its environment, on its relation to nature, than on the edifice alone.

---

[74] Ōta Hirotarō, *Nihon kenchiku no tokushitsu* [Characteristics of Japanese architecture], in *Nihon kenchikushi ronshū* [Collected studies on the history of Japanese architecture], op. cit., vol.1 (1983), 18–20.

[75] Kōjiro Yūichirō, *Nihon kenchiku no kūkan. Nihon no bijutsu 9 No. 244* 日本建築の空間・日本の美術 9 No. 244 [Space in Japanese architecture. Art in Japan, vol. 9, no. 244] (Tokyo: Shibundō, 1986), 22–3.

fig a62. architectural details
fig a62-a. convex roof (*mukuri*), Sakamoto Hanjirō house, Fukuoka prefecture

If elevated floors and the addition of exterior galleries are comprehensible adaptations in the end, since these measures had already affected practically all types of construction for a long time, the reasons for evolution of the roofs are less obvious. When their curvature is powerfully expressed and their edges raised, as in the Zen style (Zenshūyō), their "presence"—and that of the temple they cover—is visually reinforced. The converse is also true: more gently curved roofs are less expressive, with a more restrained identity that allows them to be more easily integrated into the surrounding context. From a geometric and construction point of view, aside from their formal variations, these roofs almost always follow segments of catenary curves, such as those that obtain from letting a light chain hang, that are consequently "natural" forms.

Later, with the introduction of the Sōan tea pavilions, new roof shapes began to be adopted with convex inflections (*mukuri* 起り), which according to some authors echo the forms of mountains.[76] Yet other curves, like those of the gables (*hafu*) and the edges of the awnings (*nokisaki* 軒先) are inflected towards the center and slightly raised at the extremities; in that case, they follow the shapes of long pieces of wood called *tawamijaku* 撓尺, which are themselves planed and curved in order to serve as templates during construction. We should also keep in mind that the curves obtained in the roof shapes of various buildings are made from solid wood beams that have been precisely cut according to detailed descriptive drawings before being assembled with each other. This task gives some idea of the complexity of the forms and of the joints to calculate and draw in two dimensions before realizing them in three (fig. a62).

Another remarkable and recurring characteristic is the marked projection of the canopies in relation to the exterior walls. While wood has its advantages in terms of its strength, lightness, and workability, it must be protected from the rain in order to prevent any rot or loss of resistance. As opposed to the Chinese continent, where there is less precipitation in general, and where brick is more often used, the overhang of the roof is much more important in Japan. In order to support or even strengthen the roof, carpenters created corbelled capitals (*kumimono*) consisting of an assemblage of superimposed pieces that tended to proliferate and become a stylistic element beyond being a purely structural one. The main pieces are the sorts of supports (*masu* 斗) that alternate with the corbels (*hijiki* 肘木) (figs. a35, a36). This double play between construction and aesthetics occurs with the rafters as well, that were so present in the architectures from antiquity and medieval times: the lowest row is the most visible, sometimes even doubled, but it is more decorative than load bearing, while the true structural rafters are hidden at the underside of the roof. Other reinforcing elements for the frame, such as the console beams called *hanegi* 桔木, are sometimes also required to help support the depth of the overhang[77] (fig. a33c). The full length of the canopy, extended through these various procedures, covers a broad space around the exterior walls, which are held back within the shadows, and helps bring a visual lightness to the roofs, which then seem to float. These canopies that most clearly illustrate the technical progress in the stereotomy of wood architecture in Japan, also reinforce the relation to the immediate exterior context by virtue of the peripheral transition spaces they create.

---

[76] Sekiguchi Kinya, *Chūsei zenshūyō kenchiku no kenkyū* [Studies on Zen architecture in the Middle Ages], in *Sekiguchi Kinya chosakushū* [Selected works of Sekiguchi Kinya], op. cit., vol. 1 (2011), 337–8.

[77] Itō Nobuo, *Bunkazai kōza. Nihon no kenchiku 1. Kodai* 文化財講座:日本の建築1古代 [Lectures on cultural property, Japanese architecture, vol. 1, Antiquity] (Tokyo: Daiichi hōki, 1977), 216–8.

fig a62-b. extremity of the canopy (*nokisaki*), Kōzanji monastery, Yamaguchi prefecture
fig a62-c. concave roof (*sori*), Tōdaiji monastery, *hokkedō*, Nara
fig a62-d. convex roof (*mukuri*), Manshuin monastery, great *shoin*, Kyoto
fig a62-e. gable (*hafu*), Kanshinji monastery, *kondō*, Osaka prefecture
fig a62-f. *katōmado* window, Tōfukuji monastery, *zendō*, Kyoto

fig a62-g. wood shingle roofing (*kokera-buki*), Silver Pavilion (Ginkakuji), Kyoto
fig a62-h. template (*tawamijaku*), Silver Pavilion, Nara

fig a62-i. three-dimensional assembly of beams with the angle rafter (*sumigi*), Yakushiji monastery, Nara
fig a62-j. assembly of a roof canopy with the angle rafter (*sumigi*), Takenaka Carpentry Tools Museum, Kobe
fig a62-k. (*tsugite* type) joint between two collar beams
fig a62-l. assembly at top of angle capital (*kumimono*), Yakushiji monastery, Nara

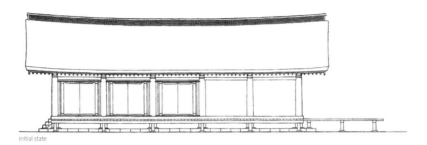
initial state

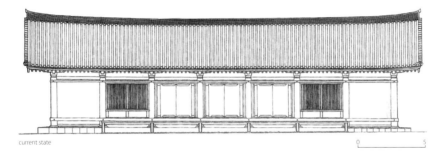
current state

fig a63. study pavilion, Hōryūji monastery, *denpōdō*, Nara prefecture
fig a63-a. elevation, initial and current state
fig a63-b. exterior view

THE INTERIOR - EXTERIOR RELATION

Continuous Space (fukihanachi) and Transition Spaces (en)

In many examples of Japanese architecture, and particularly in the residences of the nobility (*shinden*) during the Heian period, the interior is often continuous and uninterrupted by fixed partitions, a solution that is particularly well adapted to the humid heat of summer and for ceremonies. These interior spaces are extended by the peripheral gallery (*hisashi*) and frequently by an uncovered veranda (*nureen* 濡れ縁) as well. These forms of spatial organization seem quite ancient. A bronze mirror from the fourth century was found in an imperial funerary tumulus (*kofun*), at Samita Takarazuka 佐味田宝塚 near Nara, one of whose faces shows four constructions. These represent habitations in which one can distinguish a sort of uncovered terrace of the *nureen* type.

Two celebrated examples of residences from the middle of the eighth century, during the Nara period, the "Lady Tachibana" house and Fujiwara no Toyonari's 藤原豊成 are concrete examples of these arrangements. While the latter has been transmitted down to us only through descriptions from the period, which mention different parts of the building and their dimension, the former still exists. It was relocated and subsequently rebuilt to become the study pavilion (*denpōdō* 伝 法堂) of the Hōryūji temple. It initially consisted of a hypostyle hall called *fukihanachi* (吹き放ち), without any partitions and prolonged towards the exterior by a terrace (fig. a63). Another building from the Nara period, located in the center of the Tōin 東院庭園 garden of the Heijō palace 平城宮, was discovered during an archaeological excavation, and was preceded by an open terrace (*rodai*)[78].

The sequence of relations to nature as symbolized by the garden in this construction consisting of three spaces—a closed hall, an open hall, and a terrace open to the sky—was intended to create a unity with the outside. This building clearly prefigures the spring pavilion and the fishing pavilion (*izumidono* and *tsuridono*) built above the pond, at the end of the corridors of the *shinden* palace.[79] More recently, during the Muromachi period, the Golden Pavilion (Kinkakuji) and the Silver Pavilion (Ginkakuji), the two celebrated medieval pavilions located in the monastic ground of Rokuonji 鹿苑寺 and Jishōji 慈照寺 respectively, were erected partly over ponds. As structures inspired by the now-lost Ruriden pavilion 瑠璃殿 in the garden of the zen temple Saihōji 西芳寺 (also known by the name Koke-dera 苔寺, "the moss temple") or as possible successors to the source and fishing pavilions, they illustrate once again these new spatial organizations, where once the moveable partitions of the ground floor have been opened or withdrawn, a guest sitting in the space has the impression that the building floor is extended in the surface of the water in a continuous manner (figs. a61, a64).

---

[78] See the report on the excavations by the Nara National Research Institute for Cultural Properties: Nara bunkazai kenkyūjo 奈良文化財研究所, *Heijōkyō hakkutsu chōsa hōkokusho 15: Heijōkyō Sakyō sanjō-nibō teien* 平城京発掘調査報告書15 平城京左京三条二房宮跡庭園 [Report on the archaelogical excavations of the Heijōkyō, no. 15. Garden of the remains of the Heijōkyō Sakyō sanjō-nibō Palace] (Nara: Nara bunkazai kenkyūjo, 2003).

[79] Inagaki Eizō, *Jinja kenchikushi kenkyū* [Historical studies on the architecture of sanctuaries], in *Inagaki Eizō chosakushū* [Works of Inagaki Eizō], op. cit., vol. 2 (2008), 45–8.

Another well-known example is the reception hall *kyakuden* 客殿, of the Kōjōji pavilion 光浄院, at the Onjōji 園城寺 monastery, built in Ōtsu, on Lake Biwa. Here, the central space is extended by a series of verandas *hiroen* and *ochien*. When the sliding partitions are open, and with the pond that comes under the lowest terrace (*ochien*), the garden and interior spaces become one. Later still, one finds more of these transition spaces constituted by these same *hiroen* and *ochien* verandas in the first Shoin style residences, before being replaced by Nō theater stages.

The custom of adding a veranda (*en* or *engawa*) as a transition space under the projection of the roof is thus an ancient one, of which there are many examples in Japanese residences—starting with aristocratic habitations, before they influenced other ones. This zone constructs the relation between interior and exterior; depending on whether the panels—tilting shutters (*shitomido* 蔀戸), sliding partitions in translucent paper (*akari shōji*), or other types of partitioning—are closed or raised, open or closed, these peripheral veranda/galleries either appear as belonging to the inside or as part of the outside.

"The Earthen Floor Space under the Canopy" Do-bisashi

Another space of transition appeared in turn in the tea pavilions. For Rikyū and others inspired by him, the focus of attention was essentially on the single building, which consisted of an enclosed space, closed off and separated from the garden. For his disciples, on the other hand, in the Joan and Enan 燕庵 pavilions, drawn up by Uraku and Oribe respectively, an open space called *do-bisashi* (土庇, literally, "earthen floor—space—under the canopy") precedes the low door (*nijiri-guchi*). In the tea pavilions in the Sukiya style, the constructions were henceforth provided with a large *do-bisahi*, as in the Gepparō 月波楼, Shōiken 笑意軒 and Shōkintei 松琴亭 pavilions, which were laid out in the gardens of the Katsura Villa, to the west of Kyoto. Here too, water plays a connecting role between the garden and the building through an earthen floor space (*doma*), as in the Seikōken pavilion 清香軒 of the villa Seisonkaku 成巽閣 in Kanazawa, with a stream running across it. This relation is so powerful that it sometimes makes these entry spaces disappear, rendering the limit between interior and exterior even more tenuous: in the Hiunkaku pavilion 飛雲閣 at the Nishi Honganji monastery 西本願寺 near Kyoto, visitors cross a pond on a skiff before passing under the piles of the building; in the Ryūten pavilion 流店 of the Kōrakuen garden 後楽園, which was part of the Okayama domain, the river flows through the building, and when the moveable partitions are removed, all that remains are the posts. The variety of these transition spaces in Japanese architecture attests to a constant concern for spatial unification (figs. a55-f, a65, a66, a67).

AFFINITY WITH NATURE: "HANGING ON"

Mountains and Architecture: Places of Prayer of the Kake-zukuri Type

Religious architecture maintains a particular relation with nature as well. As we have already noted, the mixture of Buddhist and Shintō is an ancient one. During the Nara period (eighth century), the different schools of Buddhism were based in the monasteries (*garan*) located in this capital, but the monks also pursued their ascetic practices in the mountains. At first, they probably selected flat sites for their rudimentary dwellings, which also lent themselves to syncretic prayers. But over time, the mountain temples (*sangakujin* 山岳神) became increasingly

fig a64. overall view, Golden Pavilion (Kinkakuji), Kyoto

fig a65. Seikōken tea pavilion, Seisonkaku villa, Kanazawa
fig a65-a. plan
fig a65-b. exterior view

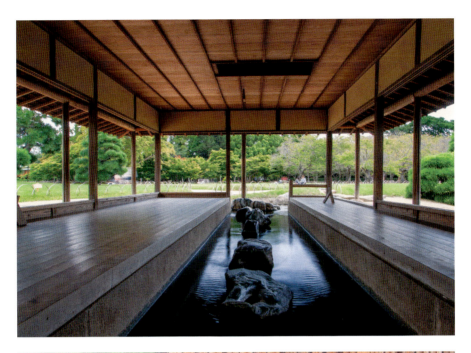

fig a66. Ryūten pavilion, Kōrakuen garden, Okayama
fig a66-a. view from the interior
fig a66-b. view from the exterior

important places of worship *shōdō* or *hondō*. Exterior galleries were added to the initial pavilions, in keeping with the *moya-hisashi* principle that was the rule at the time. Beginning in the ninth century, during the Heian period, and with the introduction of Vajrayāna Buddhism at a large scale, through the Shingon and Tendai schools, there was a significant increase in the number of rites for the nobility, as well as the number of ascetics and persons who isolated themselves to pray in places of worship. Oratories, *raiden* 礼殿, were added in front of the existing *hondō*. In Kyoto, in the complexes built on constrained sites at the limits of the town and the mountain, the additional pieces were not added on flat planar surfaces obtained by reshaping nature, but by adapting to the topography instead. Thus, towards the tenth century was born the characteristic style known as *kake-zukuri*.[80] This term, which comes from the verb *kake-zukuru*, signifies "building by attaching," and the construction in fact attaches to the natural element which is the object of veneration. The Kiyomizu-dera monastery 清水寺 in Kyoto, Ishiyama-dera 石山寺 in Ōtsu on the Biwa lake and Hase-dera 長谷寺 in Sakurai near Nara are the most representative examples of this hybrid style (figs. a68, a69, a70).

[80] Matsuzaki Teruaki, "Kake-zukuri to iu meishō ni tsuite" [On the appellation *kake-zukuri*] and "Kodai chūsei no kakezukuri" [The *kake-zukuri* in Antiquity and the Medieval Era], in *Nihon kenchiku gakkai ronbun hōkokushū* [Acts of the annual symposium of the Architectural Institute of Japan], op. cit., 1989 and 1991.

fig a67. Hiunkaku pavilion, Nishi Honganji monastery, Kyoto

fig a68. Ishiyama-dera monastery, Shiga prefecture
fig a69. Hase-dera monastery, Nara prefecture

fig a70. Kiyomizu-dera monastery, Kyoto

NATURE AND ARCHITECTURE — 159

fig a71. Nageiredō pavilion, Sanbutsuji monastery, Tottori prefecture

Becoming One with Nature

The Buddhist monks were not the only ones to practice asceticism in the mountains during the Heian period; shintō priests and lay persons did as well. By means of ascetic exercises practiced in these remote places, these anchorites, known as *yamabushi* 山伏, or *shugenja* 修験者, communicated with the Buddhist shintō deities.[81] This belief and the architecture that went along with it, was not limited solely to the capital Kyoto but extended to the province as well. Buildings that were built directly on places of worship devoted to these new practices, increasingly became one with nature (rocks, caves, etc.) The oldest example is the Nageiredō pavilion 投入堂 at the Sanbutsuji monastery 三仏寺, near Tottori on the Japan sea. Built during the first half of the eleventh century, it is a clear expression of this osmosis between architecture and its environment. The construction seems literally attached to the sacred cliff. It includes a part that is supported on columns and another that sits on the flank of the rock. Where the building touches this part, its form adapts to the steep terrain by means of sixteen posts of different length. The building also belongs to that register of antiquity architecture that still places an emphasis on symmetry. The central part (*moya*), which faces north, is thus embellished with three galleries (*hisashi*) on the east, west, and north sides (the cliff takes up the south), although the east side, (whose floor steps down) and a small additional element called *aizendō* 愛染堂, which is attached to the same side, introduce an element of asymmetry. Once again, one can see that the relation between inside and outside generates deformations of the archetype (fig. a71).

---

[81] Wasokamori Tarō 和歌森太郎, *Shugendōshi kenkyū. Tōyō bunko 211* 修験道史研究・東洋文庫 [Historical studies on the *shugendō*, Tōyō bunko], no. 211 (Tokyo: Heibonsha, 1972); see also Bernard Faure, D. Max Moerman and Gaynor Sekimori (eds.), *Shugendō. The History and Culture of a Japanese Religion, Cahiers d'Extrême-Asie*, no. 18 (2009), 2011.

fig a72 Shōkintei tea pavilion, Katsura Villa, Kyoto

A FEW MORE RINGS IN CLOSING

The aesthetic principles of Japanese wood architecture recurrently rely on ambiguity, repetitive modularity, and establishing a relation to nature (fig. a72). Another particularity of traditional architecture is the propensity to go from the part to the whole, unlike Western architecture, in which one often arrives at the desired object by starting with an original form conceived or preconceived in its entirety. In Japan, on the other hand, each constituent part is thought through independently, albeit in a coordinated way, as in the buildings of the Heian period, starting towards the end of the eighth century. Independent unitary elements such as the pavilions, united by a similar modular principle (*ken*) are then added to a main body, consisting of a central space (*moya*) and its peripheral galleries (*hisashi*). Another example of these additive principles lies in the disposition of different spaces or rooms (*ma*) in a single construction. One obtains the whole by cutting back or adding posts to the starting point for practical reasons, all the while respecting modular and proportional rules linked to the stereotomy—the cutting up or assembling of wood elements—the *kiwari* (fig. a73).

Flexibility is also one of the consequences of construction grids. Although the organization of religious, public, or political ceremonies and their sequences are fixed, the places themselves are temporary or evolving, as one can see in the periodical reconstruction of shrines (*shikinen sengū*) or in the seasonal interior decorations in Shinden style (*shitsurai* 室礼) residences.

Wood, cypress (*hinoki*) in particular, is the material of choice for the structures of religious buildings and residences for the nobility (fig. a74). Builders have tried to highlight its material qualities in their use of wood: posts left unplaned or put it to use in its unaltered state in tea pavilions (*chashitsu*), and most often left it unpainted in various other kinds of buildings, as continental influences diminished. The materials are shown in their "natural" state. This manner of responding to nature is equally visible in architectonics and spatiality; rather than attempting to transcend the physical context, Japanese builders favor an aesthetic of symbiosis. The different verandas (*en, hiroen*, or *ochien*) of residential architecture, or the galleries (*hisashi*) of sanctuaries, temples, and palaces enable the linking of gardens and interior spaces; in tea pavilions, water flows directly into the very interior of the buildings; the gentleness of the roof curves is a softer affirmation of the building's identity than is the case in their Chinese archetypes. Religious buildings attached to steep mountainsides (*kakezukuri*) also illustrate this will to create a relation to the environment.

Starting out from continental models, Japanese builders transformed, eliminated, or added elements and created architectures whose forms and construction place less emphasis on their identity in favor of greater integration of space and landscape, with its symbolic benefits. In general, these wood-structure traditional architectures, with their parallelepipedal shapes are characterized by a will to simplify. But this apparent reticence is considered to be enriching: for example in the tea pavilion, when the "*tokonoma-tana-shoin*" ensemble of space and furniture (alcove, shelf, and cabinet) in the Shoin style comes to be reduced to the simple *tokonoma* alcove, a spatial structure

fig a73. proportion system, Gosho imperial palace, Kyoto
fig a74. plank barrier and cypress (*hinoki*) post, Ise shrine

influenced by the three types of classical calligraphy, *shingyōsō*, will appear by analogy. If the formal spirit (*shin*) of the canonic form that was imported from Tang China during the same period as the Nara, suffuses the main calligraphy and remains the model for the large and luxurious formal rooms (*hiroma*), the subtle and precious stripping of the rooms (*koma*) of the Sukiya style, linked to the cursive and free (*sō*) calligraphy, in which the richness has only apparently disappeared, suggests it just as much.

Japanese construction is marked by alternating periods of fertile contact with the culture and models of Chinese architecture—during the Asuka and Nara periods (sixth to eighth centuries) as well as the beginning of the Kamakura period (twelfth and thirteenth centuries)—followed by periods of retrenchment. The evolution of types, styles, and techniques has been subject to this duality. Nonetheless, despite the differences between these moments of exchange and influence and the periods during which Japan appropriated these legacies by closing in on itself, the developments have always been slow and have never called into question the central role of wood nor of carpenters. But on the other hand, the second encounter with the West, which started at the end of the Edo shogunate, radically changed the history of architecture in Japan.

A MODERN
STORY

fig b1. Honganji dentōin honkan 本願寺伝道院本館 building (formerly Shinshū shinto seimei hoken 真宗信徒生命保険 "Life insurance for adherents of the Shinshū Buddhist school"), built by Itō Chūta, Kyoto, 1912

THE IMPORTATION OF WESTERN STYLES
DURING THE MEIJI ERA

New architectural forms developed in Japan at the end of the Edo shogunate (Bakumatsu, 1853–1868) and during the Meiji era (1868–1912), when the country opened to the West once and for all. In Japan at the end of the nineteenth century, the social order that had come down from the Edo period and divided the world between the warrior aristocracy, the peasants, the artisans and merchants (*shi, nō, kō, shō* 士農工商), as well as the outcasts, the "hamlet people" (*burakamin* 部落民) was officially abolished, but still seemed palpably present. New social classes emerged as well, with the modernization of society. Former warriors occupied important political positions in both public and private administrations,[85] while a new rural and industrial proletariat developed in tandem with the formation of new bourgeois classes, linked to the industrial and commercial economy and to urban growth. Architecture and the cities were transformed fairly rapidly to accommodate these new activities. Almost all the new buildings—banks, administrative buildings, railway stations, post and telecommunications offices, prisons, etc.—were based on European architectural styles, or sometimes on an eclectic interpretation of so-called "oriental" styles.

The first examples of modern architecture in Japan appeared with the construction of residences for the missionaries and "merchant adventurers" who lived in foreign concessions where international commerce was permitted—near the ports of Nagasaki, Kobe, or Yokohama. These houses were built by Japanese carpenters and were not technically very different from the urban dwellings (*machiya*) being built at the time. Yet they reflected a new way of life and modes of dwelling that had not existed before. The lifestyle associated with this new architecture resembled that of colonial houses that had developed in Asia from the time of the first Portuguese and Spanish colonization at the end of the sixteenth century, as well as the more recent British colonies in India and French ones in Indochina.

In the history of Japanese modern architecture, these houses are referred to as colonial with a veranda, "veranda colonial"[86] in style. In the first type to be constructed, pretty much one-third of the floor area is taken up by a two-floor veranda, on both the ground floor and on the second floor just above. Tall and narrow windows extend from floor to ceiling and let light into the house. This type of architecture is typical of the houses built in the old concessions for foreigners, and with some few exceptions, they were generally built in those neighborhoods. In Kyoto, for example, where there was no zone specifically designated for foreign merchants, Joseph Hardy Neeshima (Niijima Jō 新島襄, 1843–1890)—the Japanese aristocrat who converted to Protestantism in the United States before founding the Dōshisha university upon his return to Japan—built his residence near the Imperial Palace (Gosho 御所, fig. b3) in this style.

[85] For example, the *daimyō* lords become "prefects" or "provincial governors." See Pierre-François Souyri, *Nouvelle histoire du Japon* (Paris: Perrin, 2010), 447.
[86] Fujimori Terunobu 藤森照信, *Nihon no kindai kenchiku* 日本の近代建築 [The modern architecture of Japan], vol. 1 (Tokyo: Iwanami shoten, Iwanami shinsho, 1993), 9.

fig b2. Christian Orthodox church of Kyoto (Kyōto Harisutosu seikyōkai 京都ハリストス正教会), built by Matsumuro Shigemitsu 松室重光, Kyoto, 1903

This veranda space that extends out from the south, and sometimes from the east and west sides as well, distinguishes these houses from their Japanese homologues, whose street facades remain rather closed (figs. a27, b4). In the traditional working-class house (*minka*)—whether built in the city (*machiya*) or in the countryside (*nōka*)—it provides protection from the sun, the weather, and the neighbors. In the veranda house, on the other hand, the master of the household is exposed to the view of others and shows that he has the means to live in comfort. He has space around his house and can appreciate the landscape. Sitting comfortably in a reclining chair he expresses a new way of living, in which he can take full advantage of his free time at his leisure.[87]

Many other "Occidental" building types (yōkan 洋館), built in the European styles—and called English, French, or German—have a wood structure but are clad in stone. This was especially true of public buildings, banks, prisons, insurance agencies, and department stores, as stone was a symbol of a certain form of affluence and security (fig. b1). More utilitarian and industrial constructions (workshops, warehouses) were built with wood structures and brick infill. Some buildings for new institutions were built in a style that more closely resembled American and Northern European examples, with a wood facade covered in weatherboarding, attached in place and often painted in pastel colors.[88] The new primary schools, occasionally town halls, but especially churches belong to this type (fig. b2). This style stands in contrast to the great religious buildings of the past, as well as the traditional habitat, in which wood is usually left exposed, even if one can find burnt wood facades (in the mountains) or ones treated with tannin (along the coast).

---

[87] Jordan Sand, "Tropical Furniture and Bodily Comportment in Colonial Asia," *Positions: East Asia Cultures Critique*, 21:01 (2013); "Mobilier tropical et comportement corporel dans l'Asie coloniale," in Nicolas Fiévé and Benoît Jacquet (eds.), *Vers une modernité architecturale et paysagère. Modèles et savoirs partagés entre le Japon et le monde occidental* (Paris: Collège de France, 2013), 261-93.

[88] Fujimori, *Nihon no kindai kenchiku*, op. cit., vol. 1 (1993), 32.

fig b3. Former Niijima house, Teramachi street, east of the Imperial Palace, Kyoto, 1870

fig b4. Example of a *machiya* facade, Kyoto. Hata House (Hatake 秦家), Aburanokōji street, Bukkōji, Kyoto, 1869. Registered as a tangible cultural property of the City of Kyoto (Kyōto-shi tōroku yūkei bunkazai 京都市登録有形文化財)

fig b5. Kiko Kiyoyoshi and Ito Chuta, Heian Shrine, Kyoto (Okazaki), 1895

THE CREATION OF AN ORIENTAL JAPANESE STYLE

Architecture in Japan in the Meji era suffered the same fate as all the traditional arts, letters, and skills that were exposed to and then adapted themselves to Western criteria. "Foreign advisors" were recruited by the Japanese state to train the Japanese elites in modern sciences and techniques. After 1877, architecture was taught as a scientific and artistic discipline, at the Graduate School of Engineering of the Imperial University by a young British architect, Josiah Conder (1852–1920). The latter was tasked with introducing students to architecture as it was practiced in Europe. The first architecture graduates of the Imperial University of Tokyo were called upon to create buildings in the Western style, without any relation to Japanese tradition. Local architecture only came to be taught towards the end of the 1880s.

Itō Chūta (1867–1954) was one of the first to be initiated into Japanese architecture. After joining the architecture department of the Imperial University in 1889, he followed the course on Japanese architecture taught by master carpenter (*tōryō* 棟梁) Kiko Kiyoyoshi 木子清敬 (1845–1907). This latter was in charge of the restoration of the properties of the Imperial House (Kunaishō 宮内省), and served as consultant for the restoration of the Tōshōgū shrine at Nikkō, as well as the Tōdaiji monastery at Nara. Itō acquired a practical knowledge of Japanese architecture by working with him, and also studied ancient buildings *in situ* in the Kansai, in Kyoto and Nara. Itō also collaborated with Kiko on the Heian shrine, which was a reconstruction of part of the former Imperial Palace of Heian-kyō, the early name for Kyoto, for the National Industry Exhibition in Kyoto (Okazaki) in 1895 (fig. b5).

Itō Chūta can be considered an orientalist, insofar as he studied the architecture of the different countries of the Asian continent and drew in part on them for his inspiration. In 1898, he was also the first architect to obtain a doctorate in architecture from the Imperial University of Tokyo, on Japanese architecture, moreover. We should emphasize the pioneering aspect of his work, as no one before him had studied traditional architecture. The first part of this work was "A Study of the Architecture of the Hōryūji," which appeared in 1893 in the journal *Kenchiku zasshi*, published by the Architectural Institute of Japan (Nihon kenchiku gakkai 日本建築学会)[89] (figs. b6, a2). This analysis of one of the first Buddhist monasteries built in Japan—the pagoda (*gojūnōto*) and the treasure pavilion (*kondō*), which are parts of the oldest wooden buildings to be found in the world (seventh century)—is a study of the proportions, the system, and the construction details of three of the main buildings. The author also compared the plans and dimensions of this seven-pavilion complex (*shichidō garan* 七堂伽藍) with those of other Buddhist monasteries from the same epoch.[90]

---

[89] Itō Chūta, "Hōryūji kenchikuron," *Kenchiku zasshi*, op. cit. (1893): 317–50.
[90] Benoît Jacquet, "Itō Chūta et son étude architecturale du Hōryūji : comment et pourquoi intégrer l'architecture japonaise dans une histoire mondiale," *Ebisu*, no. 52 (2015): 89–115.

fig b6. Buddhist monastery of Hōryūji,
Ikaruga, Nara prefecture, seventh century

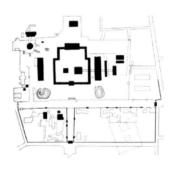

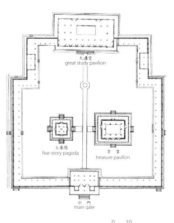

At the same time that Itō became interested in cultural heritage, the Ministry of the Imperial Household undertook an inventory of national treasures (1888–1897). Itō's own project was clearly intended to be part of these steps towards the conservation of ancient architecture, but went even further: he sought to demonstrate that the architecture of Hōryūji was the first Japanese style, even though its origins were complex. He wrote at the time that "this architecture is all the more interesting in that its forms clearly retain aspects of the Chinese style, some traces of the Indian style, in addition to a legacy from the Greek style."[91] Itō referred to the gently curved shapes of the posts at the main gate (*chūmon* 中門) of the Hōryūji as being related to *entasis*—a technique for swelling the shaft of a column—as in Greek temples and later the Graeco-Indian temples built in western Asia, particularly in Gandhara (Afghanistan and Pakistan today). In this respect, Itō took up contemporary speculation regarding the distant Hellenic origins of the Hōryūji temple.[92] With one thing leading to another, the latter was the inheritor of a long tradition leading back to the edges of the continent of Asia and even to those regions that had been in contact with Greece in antiquity—even as it included new dimensions and details of construction. For Itō it thus represented both the origin and the quintessence of Japanese architecture. And as a result, the Hōryūji deserved a special place in the history of art, on equal footing with the greatest monuments of world history.

[91] Itō, "Hōryūji kenchikuron," op. cit. (1893): 327; Jacquet, ibid. (2015): 105.
[92] This Hellenic origin is evident in the entasis of the Hōryūji posts, and it is pointed out today in school texts as well as in the most widely consulted encyclopedias such as the *Kōjien*.

fig b7-a. Shiensō Clubhouse

HORIGUCHI Sutemi, Saitama, 1926

LR: living room
BR: bedroom

THE BEGININGS OF MODERN JAPANESE ARCHITECTURE: THE INFLUENCE OF EXPRESSIONISM

While Itō Chūta was one of the first professors of Japanese and oriental architecture, he was also a builder and even a champion of a modern Japanese style. However, his output was all the more ambiguous, insofar as it was conflated with the political agenda of the Japanese Empire. But the subsequent generation of architects tended to disassociate itself from his "historicist" style, as the influence of modern movements in European architecture made themselves felt after 1910. During the entire Taishō period (1912–1926), Western modernity and science generally held pride of place, with architecture following the major European currents as well. Itō's successor at the Imperial University of Tokyo, Kishida Hideto, who spoke German and was the author of a thesis on Otto Wagner,[93] invited Bruno Taut to teach at the university in July 1934.[94] Like many architects of his generation, Taut's first architectural works were very influenced by Expressionism. Around the same time, one of the first Japanese movements in modern architecture, "The Association for the Architecture of the Secession" (Bunriha kenchikukai) or Bunriha 分離派, created by six students at the Imperial University of Tokyo in February 1920, drew on the Viennese Secession movement, as well as various movements influenced by German expressionism, the Jugendstil and the Amsterdam School, and subsequently the Bauhaus. These young architects sought to differentiate themselves from the "historicist," neo-classical, or eclectic architecture that was in favor in Europe as well as in Japan at that time, and to provide a new way of looking at tradition.

Thus, after Horiguchi Sutemi, one of the best-known members of Bunriha, returned from travelling to Europe, he published a book on contemporary Dutch architecture.[95] This work met with a certain success and enabled him to obtain a commission for a building whose style owed as much to the architecture he had been able to observe in 1924 in Holland, as it did to the architecture of Japanese pavilions.[96] This building, which dates from 1926, is a clubhouse for a horse owner, Makita Seinosuke 牧田清之助, who, like Horiguchi, was also an aficionado of the tea ceremony (*chanoyu*). The Shiensō 紫烟荘 (literally the "hermitage of purple smoke," (fig. b7) was built in the countryside of Saitama, near Tokyo, in the middle of a field of ferns. It was inspired

---

[93] Kishida Hideto, *Ottō Wagunā: kenchikuka toshite no shōgai oyobi shisō* オットー・ワグナー：建築家としての生涯と思想 [Otto Wagner: The life and thought of an architect] (Tokyo: Iwanami shoten, 1927).

[94] Bruno Taut (1880–1938), lived in Japan between May 3, 1933 and July 15, 1936 and had several occasions to meet Kishida Hideto 岸田日出刀 (1899–1966), in particular between the ninth and seventeenth of July, 1934, when he gave a series of six lectures on the theme of "Western Architecture and its importance for Japan." The original text of these lectures is available for consultation in Berlin, at the *Archiv des Akademie der Künste*, BTA-01-300). See Benoît Jacquet, "La villa Katsura et ses jardins : l'invention d'une modernité japonaise dans les années 1930," in Fiévé and Jacquet (eds.), *Vers une modernité architecturale et paysagère*, op. cit. (2013), 119.

[95] Horiguchi Sutemi, *Gendai Oranda kenchiku* 現代オランダ建築 [Contemporary Dutch architecture] (Tokyo: Iwanami shoten, 1924).

[96] On Horiguchi Sutemi (1895–1984), see Taji Takahiro, "Le regard et la sensibilité de Horiguchi Sutemi." in Fiévé and Jacquet (eds.), *Vers une modernité architecturale et paysagère*, op.cit. (2013), 141–81.

fig b7-b. exterior view (1926)
fig b7-c. exterior view (1926)

by Dutch thatched-roof houses that also shared this feature with the "rustic" architecture of certain areas in the Japanese countryside—in particular those houses known as "thatch-roofed" (*kaya-buki* 茅葺). Even though it was already the period of concrete and steel, Horiguchi favored more traditional materials for an architecture he qualified as "non-urban" (*hitoshiteki* 非都市的). In this clubhouse, "the roof is made of grass, the posts of wood, and the walls of earth."[97] More precisely, the walls are built from cob: subsoil and straw (*juraku tsuchi* 聚楽土) left exposed on the interior like in the Sōan tea pavilions, and covered in a white glaze on the exterior. This reference holds true of the convex roof (*mukuri*) as well, and the latter thus brings out the expression of materials such as the cypress (*hinoki*) joinery, the cob interior, the "overcooked" bricks (*yakisugi renga* 焼き過ぎ煉瓦) at the foundations, and the thatched roof.

The Chōchikukyo 聴竹居 House (literally, the "house of the sound of bamboo"; fig. b8), was built in 1928 by Fujii Kōji 藤井厚二 (1888–1938) in the commune of Yamazaki, on the border between the Kyoto and Osaka prefectures. It is in a different style, yet draws on both Western and Japanese inspiration, and is also an example of modern architecture in wood. This commune, not only known for its whiskey production, also includes one of the most celebrated tea pavilions in all of Japan: the Taian (*circa* 1582), built by Sen no Rikyu, and described in the previous chapter (fig. a52). It seems that the very name Chōchikukyo comes from the calligraphy that was on display in the alcove (*tokonoma*) of the Taian the day that Fujii visited it for the first time.[98]

A graduate of the Imperial University of Tokyo like Horiguchi Sutemi, he was initially employed by the Takenaka Corporation (Takenaka kōmuten), a carpentry enterprise based in Osaka and Kobe. He subsequently joined the Department of Architecture at the Imperial University of Kyoto, recently created by Takeda Goichi 武田五一 (1872–1938), where he studied environmental architecture. His research led to the construction of a few experimental houses, including his own—the Chōchikukyo house, which was the first bioclimatic dwelling to be built in Japan. It is ventilated naturally (to the "sound of bamboo") and incorporates a ventilation system that allows warm air to evacuate, and to bring in geothermal cooler air through the floor—thanks to an earth tube, a ground heat exchanger known as a "cool tube" in Japan. Each room has its own roof as well, providing air circulation at both the level of the ceiling and the floor.[99]

As for its architecture, it reflected a number of different influences: the traditional carpentry of the Sukiya style—evident in the choice of materials, the design of the ceilings—as well as the tea pavilions, and the contemporary style of the time, in an "Art Nouveau" register. Fujii was particularly interested in the Arts and Crafts movement of the Scotsman Charles Rennie Mackintosh (1868–1928) as well as the architecture of Frank Lloyd Wright (1867–1959). His house in Yamazaki was built on a single level and, like Wright's Prairie Houses, highlighted the horizontal lines of the roofs, obtained from their gentle slopes and strong projecting eaves. The reference to Mackintosh is more visible on the interior, in the design of the furniture and some of the woodwork.

---

[97] Horiguchi Sutemi, *Shiensō zushū* 紫烟荘図集 [Catalogue of the plans of Shiensō] (Tokyo, Kōyōsha, 1927), 3.
[98] Fujimori Terunobu and Shimomura Junichi 下村純一, *Fujimori Terunobu no gen, gendai jūtaku no saiken* 藤森照信の原・現代住宅再見 [Fujimori Terunobu's re-reading of the origins of contemporary housing] (Tokyo: TOTO shuppan, 2002), 28.
[99] For these ventilation principles, see Matsukuma Akira 松隈章, *Chōchikukyo. Fujii Kōji no mokuzō modanizumu kenchiku* 聴竹居：藤井厚二んの木造モダニズム建築 [Chōchikukyo: the modernist wood architecture of Fujii Kōji] (Tokyo: Heibonsha, 2015 [2017]), 24.

fig b8-a. Chōchikukyo House

FUJII Kōji, Kyoto, 1928

LR: living room
SA: salon
DR: dining room
EN: *en*

ST: study
KI: kitchen
BR: bedroom

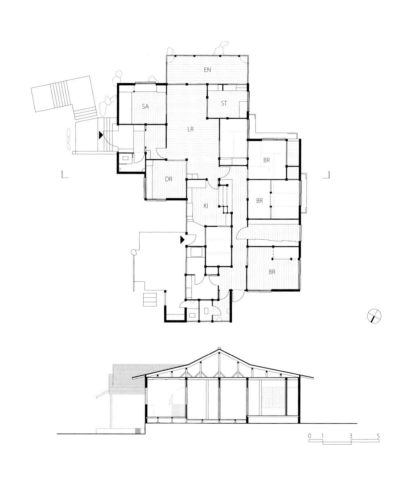

Fujii also explored innovations on the design of traditional motifs, notably in the rounded curves of the dining room, which is located at one of the northern corners of the house, and consequently cooler in the summer. A brief anecdote on the particular ties between the carpenter and the architect in this project: Sakatoku Kinnosuke 酒徳金之助 (1896–1946) was descended from a family of *miyadaiku* from Ise. When he was a young carpenter, he lived near the University of Kyoto and had already constructed four houses for Fujii before that one. He was particularly close to his client and had, at the latter's request, adopted a builder's square (*kanejaku* 曲尺) graduated in centimeters and millimeters (rather than *shaku* and *sun*) and lived on the construction site at Yamazaki.[100] He apparently had to redo the famous curve at the entrance to the dining room six times before meeting the architect's expectations.

These two houses, Shiensō and Chōchikukyo, have a particular status in the history of modern Japanese architecture, because they were the first examples of the so-called "expressionist" school (*hyōgenha* 表現派). The historian and architect Fujimori Terunobu considers that at Shiensō, Horiguchi succeeded in incorporating a Japanese style into a piece of architecture in the modern style, while at Chōchikukyo, Fujii did the reverse: by incorporating a modern ambiance into a piece of traditional Japanese architecture.[101] In the former example, the inspiration comes from modernism, from the white houses of the "International Style" and from the Amsterdam School, and the author endows the house with a "Japanese" essence. In the latter example, the overall appearance is that of a "Japanese" house, with its plan composed of an agglomeration of rooms with different roof profiles and walls out of wattle and daub covered with an ochre coating.

The Chōchikukyo House employs various details and woodwork designs in the interior that lend it a certain form of modernity. The use of corner windows without posts at the large enclosed veranda, for example, is one of the innovations of modern architecture not found in vernacular construction. One senses a modern interpretation of traditional dwelling in various details, as well as in the layout of rooms in relation to each other, and in references to the Sukiya style that are sometimes deliberately quirky. This is evident, for example, in the emphasis on different flooring elevations—sometimes slightly raised and terminated by a corner piece of very thick solid wood (*kamachi* 框), as between living and dining rooms, by the free-standing posts in the living room or sloped ceilings, by the offset posts and shelves in the annex, or in the choice and combinations of local materials (cedar planks, bamboo). Furthermore, the central living space plays a surprising role in the distribution of the different rooms, each clearly defined and laid out to fulfil specific functions (dining room, bureau, living room, veranda, tatami rooms). Even if it is relatively spacious, this living room remains a circulation element like the earthen floor space (*doma*) in popular dwellings *minka* (fig. a26-b). It is difficult to furnish and it is the negative outline of the forms of the rooms it opens on to, as well as setting the stage, similar to the connecting space, *kusarinoma* (fig. a58), for the tea rooms (*chashitsu*).

---

[100] Yagasaki Zentarō 矢ケ崎善太郎, *Sakatoku to iu daiku* 酒徳という大工 [The carpenter Sakatoku], ibidem, 136.
[101] Fujimori, *Nihon no kindai kenchiku*, op. cit., vol. 1 (1993), 178.

fig b8-b. exterior view
fig b8-c. living room, dining room, and tatami room

fig b8-d. dining room

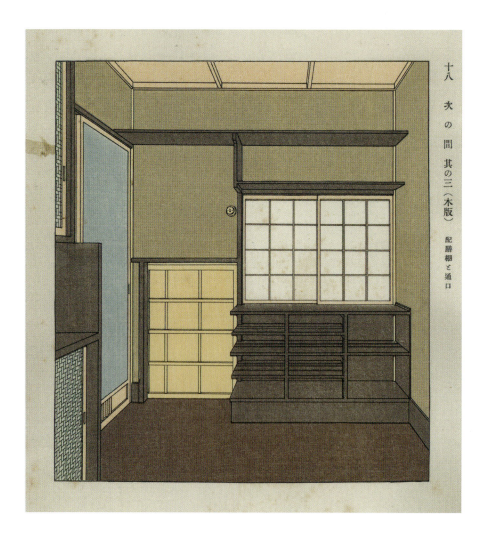

fig b8-e. annex, *tsuginoma* room 次の間, cabinet (*haizen-dana* 配膳棚), passage (*kayoi-guchi* 通口), author's print; Fujii (1932), plate 18

fig b8-f. annex, low room (*gedannoma* 下段の間) or salon; storage shelving with door (*to-dana* 戸棚); desk (*tsukue* 机), sofa (*koshikake* 腰掛), author's print; Fujii (1932), plate 13.

fig b9-a. Karuizawa Summer House

Antonin RAYMOND, Karuizawa, 1933

LR: living room
DR: dining room
KI: kitchen
BR: bedroom

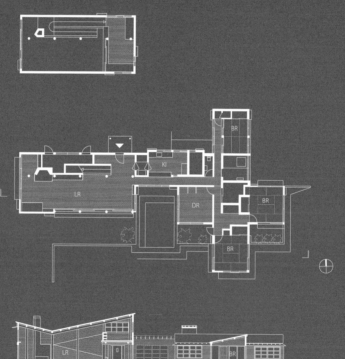

MODERN ARCHITECTURE IN WOOD: THE CORBUSIAN SCHOOL

Examples of wood construction are infrequent in modern Japanese architecture in the twentieth century, and they are constrained by fire codes. In addition, the language of modern architecture is rarely associated with wood as a material—over the new technologies of concrete, steel, and glass—and its use usually remains limited. As was the case with the buildings in the Western style built in the Meiji era, economic considerations are usually at the fore when structures are made of wood. Relatively small buildings still remain within the reach of most carpentry contracting companies. The Great Kantō earthquake (1923) and the fires that followed also contributed to strengthening fire regulations. For example, social housing built by the Dōjunkai, the new bureau for collective housing founded in 1924 after the earthquake, were initially built out of concrete.[102] But during the 1930s, the escalation of military conflicts resulted in a lack of steel (and thus of reinforced concrete), as metal was earmarked for the war effort and the armament industry. In the light of this constraint, architects developed a form of modernism out of wood.

Like the modern movements in European architecture, most of the Japanese "expressionists" turned towards the international architecture of the Bauhaus or of Le Corbusier. Horiguchi and the Secessionists (Bunriha) turned to the former, while others, who were closer to Kishida, developed a Corbusian style and built in wood in a similar manner to the way they would have built in concrete. A particularly eloquent example is Antonin Raymond's "Summer House" in Karuizawa.[103] The latter was an American architect of Czech origin who came to Japan in the employ of Frank Lloyd Wright, assigned to follow the construction of the Imperial Hotel built in Tokyo in 1923 on-site. The hotel was constructed of reinforced concrete (for the foundations) and brick. It was one of the few buildings to survive the earthquake and the fires that followed. Raymond, who remained in Japan after Wright departed, was one of the first, along with Motono Seigo 本野精吾 (1882–1944) to work in concrete in that country. His style become Corbusian in the creation of his own house in Tokyo in 1923, which was the first local building entirely constructed out of reinforced concrete.

---

[102] At least initially. It seems that later they would also be built with a wood structure. On the housing of the Dōjunkai 同潤会 (1924–1941), see Marc Bourdier, "Production du logement et usage de l'habitat : les premiers logements sociaux au Japon (1924–1941)," in Augustin Berque (ed.), *La qualité de la ville. Urbanité française, urbanité nippone* (Tokyo: Maison franco-japonaise, 1987), 272-93; Satō Shigeru 佐藤滋, Takamizawa Kunio 高見澤邦雄, Itō Hirohisa 伊藤裕久, Ōtsuki Toshio 大月敏雄, Mano Yōsuke 真野洋介, *Dōjunkai no apātomento to sono jidai* 同潤会のアパートメントとその時代 [The Dōjunkai apartments and their times] (Tokyo: Kajima shuppankai, 1998).

[103] On this "Karuizawa Summer House" (Natsu no ie 夏の家) and the work of Antonin Raymond (1888–1976), see Yola Gloaguen, "L'expression de la nature dans le parcours architectural d'Antonin Raymond. Vers la maison d'été à Karuizawa (1933)," in Fiévé & Jacquet (eds.), *Vers une modernité architecturale*, op. cit. (2013), 223–59. On the work of Raymond in Japan, see also the thesis by the same author, *Les villas réalisées par Antonin Arthaud dans le Japon des années 1920-1930. Une synthèse entre modernisme occidental et habitat vernaculaire japonais*, PhD dissertation, EPHE, January 13, 2016; see also Christine Vendredi-Auzanneau, *Antonin Raymond: un architecte occidental au Japon* (Paris: Picard, 2012).

fig b9-b. interior view of the living room
fig b9-c. exterior view

His Summer House (*Natsu no ie*) was built a few years later in 1933, in the alpine landscape of Karuizawa, a summer holiday destination for the wealthy foreign community (fig. b9). In this vacation residence, Raymond simply reproduced part of the unbuilt project of Le Corbusier for the villa Errázuris in Chile of 1930, which had been planned to be constructed "with elements to be found on site and simple construction: walls out of large stone blocks, tree trunks used for framing, and a roof made of local tiles."[104] At Karuizawa, with its double height living room, cylindrical columns and ramp, we encounter some of the features of the architecture of the villas designed by the Franco-Swiss architect. But more relevant for our purposes, this borrowing clearly illustrates that a modern architecture is conceptually possible without recourse to concrete, and that its use does not necessarily need to be justified by structural considerations when the spans between walls or posts remain fairly small. Le Corbusier's architectural vocabulary is expressed here in a wood structure, even though the ideal of the free plan, which could allow for the free partition of interior spaces, was initially conceived with the greater spans of concrete post and beam structures in mind.

While the spatial conception is distinctly Corbusian, the construction details and the materiality of wood transform this building from a simple copy of modern architecture in concrete and inscribe it into its context. Raymond employed local materials, solid wood posts and beams, circular in section, in a manner that hearkens back to the Sukiya style and the rustic quality of the log house. Wood is also employed as an interior finish on the walls, but not on the columns—so as to differentiate between structural bearing elements and infill. The posts are made from un-squared chestnut tree (*kuri no ki* 栗の木) trunks, the beams are made of cypress (*hinoki*), and the floors and walls are lined in cedar (*sugi*) planks[105]. On the facade, the wooden weatherboarding further accentuates the horizontality of the building. As in the project for the villa Errázuris, Raymond designed a roof with two inverted planes, known as a "butterfly" roof, far better suited to wood construction than a flat roof terrace. The waterproofing is ensured by a covering in metal, which is covered in larch (*karamatsu* 唐松) twigs, that lend it the appearance of Japanese farms (*minka*) with thatched roofs, whose construction systems Raymond had studied[106] (fig. b9-c). Even if setting a low inflection point is not the ideal solution for a roof with a wood structure—it was a feature of the Corbusian model that had been proposed for the much dryer climate of central Chile—the architect inserted a gutter to resolve the problem. The subtlety of this solution is to have partly concealed it with the "thatch," which aside from its symbolic function, also slows down the flow of rainwater and conceals this device. The Karuizawa Summer House is probably the first example of modern architecture, Corbusian on top of it all, built out of wood in Japan. But there are two lines of descent here, for the plan of this house, built by Japanese carpenters, is both modular and based on traditional spans of 2.7 by 3.6 m (1.5 and 2 *ken* respectively), and the bedrooms are defined by tatamis.

Raymond's work in wood, which continued through the end of the 1960s, consists of private houses, churches, and small utilitarian buildings. The originality of his contribution, which goes far beyond the impressive "borrowed" house in Karuizawa, lies in the relation between

---

[104] Le Corbusier and Pierre Jeanneret. *Œuvre complète de 1929-1934*, ed. Willy Boesiger (Zurich: Les Éditions d'Architecture [Artemis], 1964 [1935]), 52.

[105] Antonin Raymond, "Towards True Modernism," *Lectures and Articles*, manuscript, 1940, p. 13, citation in Gloaguen, "L'expression de la nature dans le parcours architectural d'Antonin Raymond," in Fiévé & Jacquet (eds.), *Vers une modernité architecturale*, op. cit. (2013), 13.

[106] Christine Vendredi-Auzanneau, "Tradition/Traditions de l'architecture japonaise," in Benoît Jacquet, Philippe Bonnin, and Nishida Masatsugu (eds.), *Dispositifs et notions de la spatialité japonaise* (Lausanne: Presses polytechniques et universitaires romandes, 2014), 222.

fig b10. Antonin Raymond, Adachi House, Karuizawa, 1966
fig b10-a. interior view of living room

his interests in modernity and the Japanese vernacular habitat along with the excellence of the culture of carpenters. He used their traditional module of the *ken* in all his houses, which is also a sort of reply to the Corbusian modulor.[107] He often included thatch roofs, which gave an almost anachronistic look to his houses—but which we can regard as prescient in the light of today's interest in sustainable development. In a similar manner, the architect still often played with the contrast between the very rustic and barely squared tree trunks sandwiched together in the framing—the double tie beam being an arrangement not specific to Japan—which he mastered with brio, against the paneled surfaces of the walls (of solid wood or plywood) and floors (fig. b10).

His work marks an important point of passage between Japan and the West. He was educated in old Europe, then worked with Wright in New York, and subsequently built the first reinforced concrete house in Japan in 1923, where he was one of the initiators of Corbusian ideas. In addition, he published a seminal as well as practical book, *Architectural Details*, in 1938, in a tradition that was as much German (Neufert catalogue) as it was Japanese (the carpentry manuals). Illustrated with many sketches, plans, and photographs of his own buildings, it mixed contemporary architecture (concrete and metal details) and exemplary features of the Japanese vernacular tradition (wood details).[108] The book was widely distributed in the United States, and

[107] Kurt Helfrich, "Antonin Raymond in America, 1938–49," in Kurt Helfrich and William Whitaker (eds.), *Crafting a Modern World: The Architecture and Design of Antonin and Noémi Raymond* (New York: Princeton Architectural Press, 2007), 58.
[108] Antonin Raymond, *Architectural Details* (Tokyo: Kokusai kenchiku kyōkai, 1938).

fig b10-b. interior view of living room and dining room

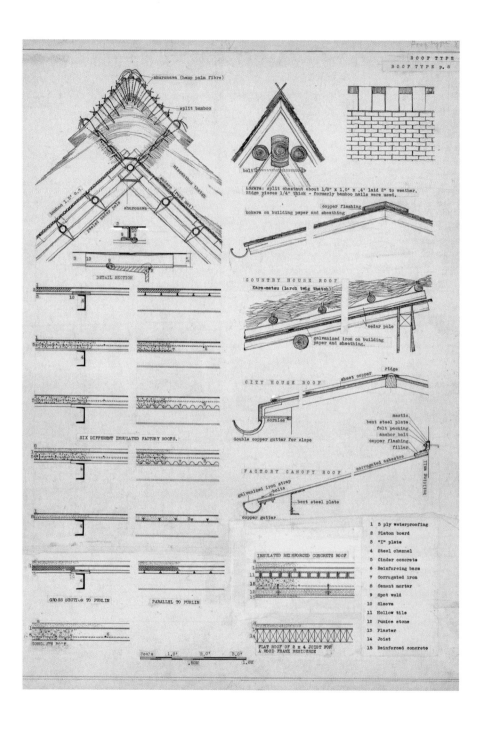

fig b11. Construction details for traditional roof types, Antonin Raymond, *Architectural Details*, 1938

even republished in 1947. With its wide range of references, it marked an entire generation of young American architects like Joseph Esherick in California (fig. b11).

Among his better-known collaborators, Raymond attracted young architects such as Yoshimura Junzō and Maekawa Kunio, who had worked under Le Corbusier between 1928 and 1930 and returned to Tokyo yearning to create architecture in the modern style of his mentor. Due to the worsening political climate, the Raymond atelier closed in 1935 and did not reopen until 1949. Maekawa then opened his own office and had several opportunities to build in wood, even if that material was not the obvious choice for the Corbusian architect he sought to become, and was necessary only by default. Towards the end of the 1930s the use of steel had become pretty much impossible. Its price was too high, as it was reserved for armament and military equipment. The only affordable construction material was wood.[109] The Maekawa studio turned to wood exclusively, as illustrated in its first three houses. In the first one, the M House (M-tei M邸) built in 1936 but subsequently destroyed, the main body of the house was in a Western style (yōfū 洋風) with a single-slope roof plane (katanagare yane 片流れ屋根) and stained wooden walls. The "Japanese" part (wafū 和風) consisting of a zashiki—a term that had appeared in the dwellings of the medieval period to designate the reception space—is clearly separated

[109] Especially after the government measures of 1938 regulating materials in wartime (senji shizai seigen 戦時資材統制). On Japanese modernism in wood, see Fujimori, Nihon no kindai kenchiku, op. cit., vol. 2 (1993), and Fujimori Terunobu & Tange Kenzō, Tange Kenzō (Tokyo: TOTO shuppan, 2002), 67–71; and on Maekawa Kunio 前川國男 (1905–1986) in particular, see Matsukuma Hiroshi 松隈洋 et al. (ed.), Kenchikuka Maekawa Kunio no shigoto 建築家前川國男の仕事—The Work of Kunio Maekawa: A Pioneer of Japanese Modern Architecture (Tokyo: Bijutsu shuppan dezain sentā, 2006).

fig b12. Maekawa Kunio, Kasama House, Tokyo, 1938

and is constructed independently of the rest of the house. In the tradition of the *hanare* 離, the *zashiki* became a pavilion "apart" from the house, a distant annex from the main foyer, where one withdraws to gain some distance from daily affairs.

For his second project, the Kasama House (Kasama tei 笠間邸, fig. b12), which dates from 1938, Maekawa adopted a different approach. Tange Kenzō, who had just joined his office, worked on its drawings and design. This house, inhabited until very recently, is located in the central neighborhood of Meguro in Tokyo. With its gabled roof (*kirizuma yane*) and a coated wall running its entire length that separates it from the street, it has the appearance of a Japanese villa. The ensemble of the roof is made up from several planes that cover different spaces and are slightly offset from each other. The house is divided into three parts linked together by a central longitudinal axis, parallel to the street. The service areas are located along one side: the entry, an interior garden, a kitchen, a staircase, and a parking spot. The living spaces on one hand, and the bedrooms on the other, are located along the other side, facing the garden. An office is located on the upper floor, which has its own roof plane, that is higher than the main roof. Along the exterior facade, this dwelling conveys a Japanese or traditional character, with its woodwork and its large and projecting tile roof; but on the other hand, its plan and interior furnishings are modern, that is to say Western in style.

The third project was his own residence (Maekawa jitei 前川自邸), built in 1942 in the Shinagawa neighborhood of Tokyo, which has since been moved and rebuilt in the Edo-Tokyo Open Air Architectural Museum on the outskirts of the capital. At that time, the country was fully engaged in the Second World War and local architects, including Maekawa, were involved in research on a national architecture. The Architectural Institute of Japan organized several conferences and competitions with the goal of establishing a unified vision of what a "Japanese national architecture" might be,[110] and Maekawa was himself very fecund on the subject. In the early 1940s, when he had little work because of the war effort, he participated in competitions for memorials organized by that same institute, and for the first time in his career, devoted himself to the study of the architecture of his country. After his marriage, he aspired to create a work that represented the archetype of the Japanese house for his own home. Like Raymond several years before, he was particularly inspired by the vernacular dwelling of the *minka* type, a Japanese version of the chalet, which symbolized a return to his country, to the earth and its *terroir*, and by extension to the national homeland itself.

The historian Matsukuma Hiroshi, who had the opportunity to work with him, has found documents from the time that show the ideological orientation of this Corbusian architect. Several of his sketches for the Maekawa villa are to be found on blank pages of books that belonged to his personal library.[111] The works in question are by Marxist historian Aikawa Haruki (1909–1953) on contemporary technique,[112] by philosopher Tanabe Hajime (1885–1962) on the relation between philosophy and science,[113] and two volumes of the *Shōbōgenzō*, the

---

[110] See Benoît Jacquet, "Les mots et les discours sur la monumentalité de l'architecture japonaise," in Jacquet, Bonnin & Nishida (eds.), *Dispositifs et notions de la spatialité japonaise*, op. cit. (2014), 169–89.

[111] See the account of Matsukuma Hiroshi's research, *Maekawa Kunio no senzenki ni okeru kenchiku shisō no keisei ni tsuite* 前川國男の戦前期における建築思想の形成について [On the development of Maekawa Kunio's architectural thought in the prewar period], unpublished research summary, September 2008, 359–63, 519–33 (drawings).

[112] Maekawa owned the third edition of Aikawa Haruki 相川春喜, *Gendai gijutsuron* 現代技術論 [A theory on contemporary techniques] (Tokyo: Mikasa shobō, 1940).

[113] See Tanabe Hajime 田邊元, *Tetsugaku to kagaku to no aida* 哲学と科学との間 [Between philosophy and science] (Tokyo: Iwanami shoten, 1937). Maekawa's copy is from the seventh edition (1941).

masterpiece of Zen monk Dōgen (1200–1253).[114] The first two had recently been published at the time, and their content was potential food for thought for a contemporary architect. Maekawa had access to a recent translation of Dōgen into modern Japanese. The text consists primarily of *kōan* 公案, brief dialogues between master and disciple and sources for meditation, with the potential for awakening (*satori*). The texts of this Zen monk, often considered to be the origin of Japanese philosophical thinking, have been studied and translated by the Japanese schools of philosophy, notably the Kyoto School (Kyōto gakuha 京都学派). No doubt Maekawa was searching for spiritual inspiration from this source.

After deciding to set up a home, Maekawa undertook research on "national housing" (*kokumin jūtaku* 国民住宅). This theme was precisely the subject for a competition proposed by the Architectural Institute in August 1941, and he was a member of the jury. In his private journal (*nisshi* 日誌), he wrote that "the principal issue for national housing is innovation in material and techniques. For the purposes of mass production, it would be strange to have recourse to the old techniques for wood construction."[115] Despite his "modernist" intentions to modernize and industrialize building systems, his work from the time indicates nonetheless that he did not want to, or maybe could not, abandon these "old" techniques.

The composition of the Maekawa House is symmetrical, centered on a large living room that extends from one side to the other, with bedrooms and two bathrooms on each side. The entrance and the kitchen are also located to either side of the living room. The latter is a double-height space, as in Le Corbusier, and a stair leads to a mezzanine taken up by a study. The garden facade, in its proportion and gabled roof, refers just as much to the architecture of the alpine chalet, with its open gable, as it does to the vernacular Japanese dwelling (*minka*). Under the broad roof, Maekawa inserted three cubic volumes, whose white plaster ceilings contrast with the woodwork and floorboards of brown wood. The exterior facades are clad in stained wooden weatherboards, with a distinctive central pillar detached from the large double-height bay held back from the front face of the two lateral volumes. Maekawa employed classical elements of Japanese architecture, such as *shōji*, those sliding frames covered in paper (*washi* 和紙), even if they were doubled by glazed exterior frames for the sake of modern comfort. Despite the ambiguity of this facade and the roof with two planes and a central gable, the double-height elevation remains very Corbusian.

The architect's intention to produce "mass housing" with a wood structure did not see the light of day during the war, but he was able to launch a prefabricated wood house company at the war's end, in 1945. The PREMOS project's name was derived from the prefix "pre" for prefabrication and from the three initials of Maekawa, the structural engineer Ono Kaoru 小野薫, and the Sanin construction company (Sanin kōgyō 山陰工業). This was one of the first attempts to create prefabricated wood houses in Japan, and between 1946 and 1951, PREMOS built a thousand of them, especially for workers involved in coal mining. The seventh version of the prototypes tested by Ono was erected along with three versions of the model (71, 72, 73), using a "honeycomb structure" (*hanikamu kōzō* ハニカム構造). The bearing walls were hollow core wood panels and the framing consisted of trusses place 91 cm apart (three *shaku* or half a *ken*) (fig. b14).

---

[114] The edition Maekawa consulted is: Dōgen 道元, Hashida Kunihiko 橋田邦彦 (translated into modern Japanese), *Shōbōgenzō shakui* 正法眼藏釋意 [Translation and interpretation of the *Shōbōgenzō*], 4 vols. (Tokyo: Sankibō busshorin, 1939–1950).

[115] Written on August 7, 1941. Quoted in Matsukuma, op. cit. (2008), 309–10.

fig b13-a. Maekawa House

MAEKAWA Kunio, Tokyo, 1942

LR: living room
ST : study
KI: kitchen

BR1: bedroom
BR2: guest room
BR3: maid's room

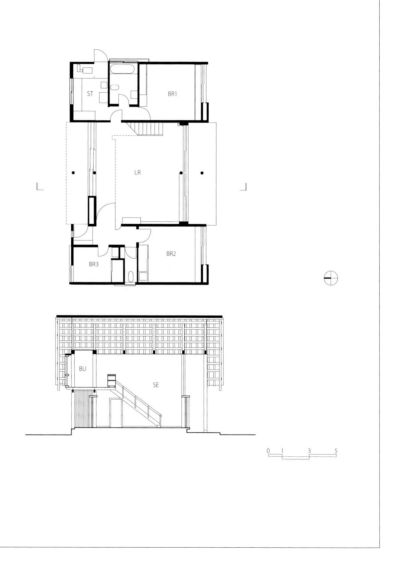

MODERN ARCHITECTURE IN WOOD: THE CORBUSIAN SCHOOL   197

fig b13-b. reconstruction of the Maekawa House in the garden of the Edo-Tokyo buildings (Edo Tōkyō tatemonoen), exterior view
fig b13-c. interior view

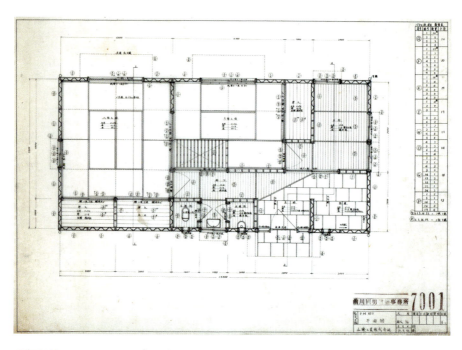

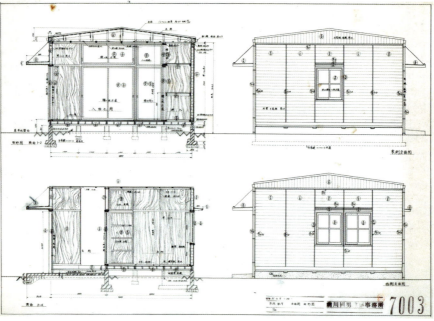

fig b14. PREMOS (Maekawa, Ono, Sanin) prefabricated housing, 1946-1951
fig b14-a. plan
fig b14-b. sections and elevations

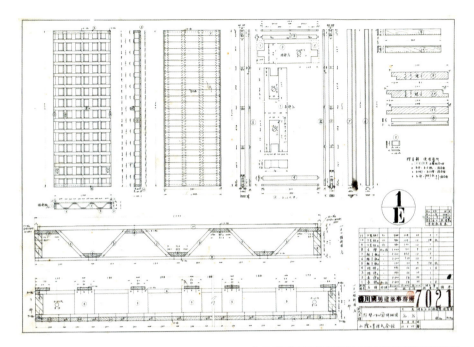

fig b14-c. details
fig b14-d. exterior view under construction

The end of the 1940s was a particularly difficult period for the Japanese economy, and Maekawa developed other projects in wood with a modern vocabulary at that time, as if he was building them in concrete. This was the case for the Kinokuniya bookstore in the Shinjuku neighborhood of Tokyo (fig. b15). In a Japan in ruins, in the midst of shantytowns and precarious housing, this store was intended as symbol of renewal and modernity, at a time when the printed book remained the principal vector of information and one of the most accessible means of entertainment. This 600-square-meter (6458 sf) building on two levels employs a post and beam structure, with trusses spaced approximately every 3.6 m (two *ken*). The main rectangular facade suggests a roof terrace at the top, for a more modern expression, but the fascia hides a gabled roof. During this same period, Maekawa also created the Keio hospital at Shinjuku (1948) and three regional offices for the public radio and television chain NHK in the towns of Okayama, Gifu, and Wakayama (1949–1950), all of them with wood structures.

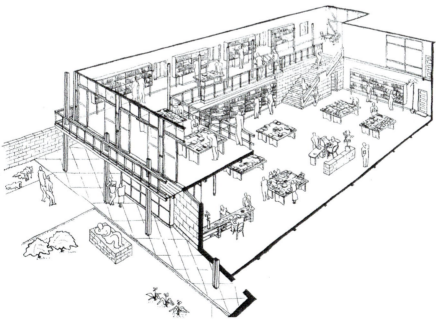

fig b15. Maekawa Kunio, Kinokuniya bookstore, Tokyo, 1947
fig b15-a. front elevation
fig b15-b. perspective

fig b16. photograph of the Katsura Villa by Ishimoto Yasuhiro in 1953

POSTWAR: THE TANGE SAGA

The residence that Maekawa built in 1942 was an expression of his desire at the time to create a house of Japanese (or national) inspiration, while the research he undertook subsequently, after the Second World War, favored a modern expression using an inexpensive wood structure in lieu of concrete or steel. Nonetheless, the postwar period was also a time for returning to tradition. All the architects who had started their careers in the 1930s were confronted with the emergence of nationalist ideologies and commissions that conformed to these particular aspirations. Most of those projects were not built, and we will not present them here, but it is important to note that this generation, in the grip of Japanese imperialist politics, came to address architecture in a different way. Although the major architectural tendencies up to the middle of the 1930s were propelled by the modern movements in Europe, Japanese architects subsequently came to reflect on their own tradition.

Tange Kenzō was undoubtedly the most emblematic architect of postwar Japan. He started out by winning the competition for the Hiroshima Peace Memorial in 1949, but he also exerted a powerful influence on his generation as well as the next one, through his teaching at the University of Tokyo. However, the competitions he won during the war and the fairly eloquent discourse he developed regarding a monumental national architecture are generally less known. And finally, one of the first projects he was able to build, during the construction of the Peace Memorial (1949–1955), was his own residence in Tokyo. The Tange House of 1953 (Tange jitei 丹下自邸) turned out to be contemporaneous with his interest in certain selected moments from the past, including the Katsura Villa in Kyoto. As Maekawa had done some ten years before, Tange looked to Japanese architecture and took a villa as a model whose modern filiation had been revealed (or "invented") by his peers—notably Kishida Hideto, then by Bruno Taut at the former's invitation. In the 1950s Katsura and the shrines of Ise—that were reconstructed in 1953—were the occasion for numerous lectures and controversies around the subject of tradition.[116] These monuments that symbolized national identity and the nation's distinctive characteristics in different ways then became theoretical models for a concept of contemporary creation.

In 1960, Tange published a work on Katsura with the American architect of German origin Walter Gropius (1883–1969) and the Japanese-American photographer Ishimoto Yasuhiro (1921–1969) to illustrate his thoughts on the relation between tradition and creation in

---

[116] On the views of modern architects on Katsura, see Benoît Jacquet, "À la croisée des chemins : l'ambivalence des discours sur les villas impériales de Kyōto," in Dejanirah Couto and François Lachaud (eds.), *Empires éloignés. L'Europe et le Japon (XVIe–XIXe siècles)*, (Paris: EFEO, 2010), 255–77; Benoît Jacquet, "La villa Katsura et ses jardins : l'invention d'une modernité japonaise dans les années 1930," in Fiévé and Jacquet (eds.), op. cit. (2013), 99–139.

Japanese architecture.[117] Two years later, with the critic Kawazoe Noboru (1926–2015) and the photographer Watanabe Yoshio (1907–2000), the Ise site was presented in turn as an archetype of Japanese architecture.[118] The two volumes thus present a modern vision of tradition. The photographs in the first are in black and white. They present an architecture that highlights its main structural elements: the verticality of the posts, the horizontality of the floors and beams, and the modularity of the facade elements (*amado, fusuma, shōji*). The qualities of the materials, the diversity of species of wood, everything that conveys the expression and nature of the material—its texture, color, and patina—do not appear in the photographs. In the book on Katsura, the photographs are often taken frontally. The images are lacking in depth and fragmented; the buildings are practically never seen in their entirety; the high roofs are often cropped, and the details convey a feeling of relatively modern abstraction.

The photographs of Ise, taken by Watanabe, are different from the ones taken by Ishimoto at Katsura, but here again the frontal views are very strong in contrast. In addition, we know that he photographed the buildings in fine weather without a single cloud,"[119] when the "white" light of the sun was most direct. In neither of these collections did the texts of Tange, Gropius, or Kawazoe address the question of wood construction itself. Gropius stressed the modernity of the construction principles of Japanese architecture and the rationality of a proportional system as resembling contemporary processes of industrialization.[120] The style of the residential part of the villa, of the *shoin* with their raised floors, their verandas (*engawa* or *hiroen*) that open to the garden, and the slender posts with their square sections, are the most intrinsically modern aspects, in our eyes (fig. b16).

In 1953, Gropius was invited by the International House of Japan to travel to Japan.[121] His principal host was Tange, whom he had met at the *Congrès International d'Architecture Moderne* (CIAM) in London (Hoddesdon) in 1951, and again in Cambridge (Massachusetts) that same year. They travelled together to the construction site of the Peace Memorial in Hiroshima, as this was the project that the Japanese architect had been asked to present to the community of architects from the modern architecture movement. The monumentality of this work is the result of an ingenious composition combining several Japanese architectural traditions. Local historians of architecture, from Kawazoe in the 1950s[122] to Inoue Shōichi more recently,[123] have clearly demonstrated that this urban project was indebted to the old architecture of granaries and attics in which monasteries stored their treasures, especially the architecture of solid logs

---

[117] Tange Kenzō 丹下健三, Walter Gropius, and Ishimoto Yasuhiro 石元泰博, *Katsura: Tradition and Creation in Japanese Architecture* (New Haven: Yale University Press, 1960).

[118] Tange Kenzō, Kawazoe Noboru, and Watanabe Yoshio 渡辺義雄, *Ise: Nihon kenchiku no genkei* 伊勢：日本建築の原形 (Tokyo: Asahi Shinbun, 1962); English translation: *Ise: Prototype of Japanese Architecture* (Cambridge: MIT Press, 1965).

[119] Cited in Jonathan M. Reynolds, "Ise Shrine: Modernism and Japanese Tradition," *The Art Bulletin*, Vol. 83, No. 2 (June 2001): 332.

[120] Walter Gropius, "Architecture in Japan," in *Katsura: Tradition and Creation in Japanese Architecture*, op.cit. (1960), 103.

[121] Walter Gropius was invited to spend three months in Japan, from the 20th of May to the 18th of August, benefitting from a grant from the Rockefeller Foundation. See "A Report on the Visit of Dr. and Mrs. Walter Gropius in Japan," Rockefeller Archive Center (Collection: RF, Record Group: 1.2, Series: 609R, Box: 36, Folder: 406), document consulted in March 2011 in Sleepy Hollow, New York.

[122] One of the foundational articles in the discussions on the relation to tradition in modern architecture was by Kawazoe Noboru, on the subject of Tange, written under the pseudonym of Iwata Tomō 岩知夫, "Tange Kenzō no nihonteki seikaku," 丹下健三の日本的性格 [The Japanese character of Tange Kenzō] *Shinkenchiku*, Vol. 30 (January 1955): 62–70.

[123] Inoue Shōichi was one of the first to study the history of Japanese architecture during the Second World War and its controversial relation to tradition. See especially Inoue Shōichi, *Senjika Nihon no kenchikuka: āto, kitchu, japanesuku* 戦時下日本の建築家：アート、キッチュ、ジャパネスク [Japanese architects during the war: art, kitsch, Japanesque] (Tokyo: Asahi shinbunsha, Asahi sensho, No. 530, 1995), 180–279; first published in 1987 by Seidosha.

of the Shōsōin 正倉院 at Nara, and the Shinden style palaces whose different buildings were arranged facing a garden with a water feature (fig. a14); on the central island of Nakashima at Hiroshima, a cenotaph was placed in a park surrounded by a river. Despite the modern appearance of its concrete construction, its horizontal lines and flat roof, this architecture symbolizes a modern Japanese regionalism.

Tange was probably the first Japanese architect to work closely with photographers. Like others before him, notably Kishida Hideto, he was experienced in architectural photography himself. We know for a fact that he often placed his lens on a very high tripod in order to capture the frontal elevations of the main facades of his buildings. Ishimoto Yasuhiro in particular photographed the Hiroshima Memorial and the Katsura Villa in this manner, and showed that Tange's modern architecture owed much to the elegance of classical Japanese architecture, and to his knowledge of the Shinden, Shoin, and Sukiya styles (fig. b17).

Like Raymond and Maekawa, Tange had been able to create modern expressions of architecture out of wood before the war, given the impossibility of doing them out of concrete. In his first projects in this more modern material, he later distinguished himself in the design of details and elements of construction that were conceived "in the manner" of elements of wood construction. If one compares certain details of traditional architecture with those developed at Hiroshima, one can see that there is undeniably a sort of Baroque inspiration to his work: especially in his taste for dynamic geometrical compositions (the double trapezoid of the massing plan), and the monumental constructions (fig. b18).

This relationship between historical and contemporary forms, which subtly appeared in the design of the Hiroshima Memorial, was far more explicit in the design of his own house. It was built after his marriage, on a lot belonging to his wife, in the posh Tokyo neighborhood of Seijō, and holds a special place in his work. First of all, it is the only project he built out of wood. It was also the only private house he designed: the rest of his career was primarily devoted to larger scale institutional or monumental buildings, for the most part constructed out of steel and concrete. Although it is a unique example, the Tange family house is a testimony to his capacity to draw up an essentially modern Japanese architecture, and at the same time an architecture that is essentially Japanese (fig. b19).

This project is remarkable for its exposed wood structure. It is built on two levels, with its upper floor elevated on *pilotis* that leave the ground floor garden completely open. Tange's arrangement embodies both the recognizable typology of Corbusian villas as well as the Japanese model of houses with raised floors (*takayuka*). The archetype for this kind of dwelling traces back to prehistory (the Yayoi period), based on structures for grain storage raised up on large *pilotis*. This arrangement was subsequently widely adopted for both functional reasons (ventilation of the floorboards) as well as aesthetic and social ones, as it symbolizes a form of opulence. Beyond this primitive type, the style of the shoin of the Katsura Villa, which is built on a flood plain, and Le Corbusier's Villa Savoye are the most obvious references. Tange's residence adopted some of the proportions of the latter: in addition to the tripartite elevation of *pilotis*, main living areas, and roof, they share the same breadth.[124]

---

[124] Sendai Shōichirō 千代章一郎, "La notion de 'mur' dans le dispositif de 'façade': le croisement entre Le Corbusier et les architectes modernes et contemporains," in Jacquet et al. (eds.), *Dispositifs et notions de la spatialité japonaise*, op. cit. (2014), 266–267.

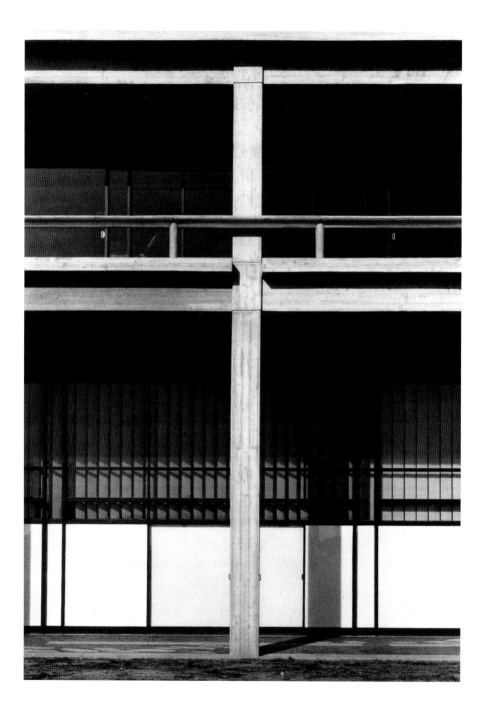
fig b17. photograph of the Hiroshima Peace Memorial, by Ishimoto Yasuhiro (circa 1953)

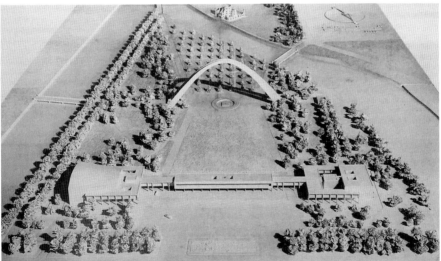

fig b18. Tange Kenzō, Hiroshima Peace Memorial, 1949–1955
fig b18-a. site plan
fig b18-b. model showing the state of the project during the competition phase,1949

fig b19-a. Tange House

TANGE Kenzō, Tokyo, 1953

LR: living room
ST: study
KI: kitchen
DR: dining room
T: *tokonoma*
BR: bedroom

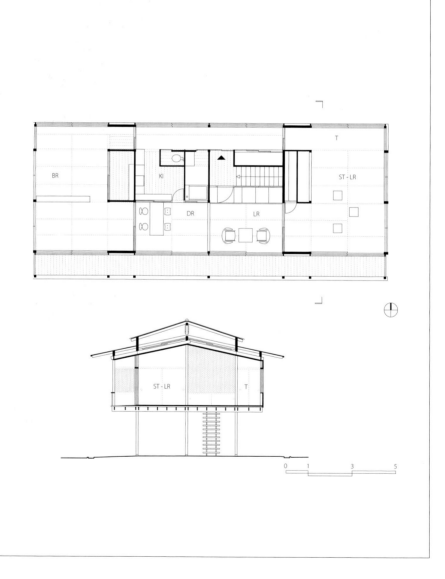

fig b19-b. main facade with artificial mound
fig b19-c. main facade

Taking inspiration from the Katsura Villa, Tange reinterpreted the Shoin style: thin columns square in section, a facade whose horizontality is emphasized by the width and depth of the veranda (called here *hiroen* or *nureen*) that is covered by a projecting canopy (*hisashi*). The gently sloped roof has two planes (*kirizuma* type) which seem to float above the glazed transoms, and it sets up a system that is different in appearance from the *shoin* of Katsura, that are in effect dominated by four-planed hip and gable roofs (*irimoya* type) with solid wall returns above white sliding panels. But resemblances still remain: the composition of the *shoin* at Katsura is tripartite as well, and if one puts aside their differences in matter and texture at the upper floor, Tange simply substituted the lower part taken up by sliding panels (glass against white paper) and the upper transoms (glass against whitewashed cob). Aside from a few variations, the rhythm of the posts in the main grid, which is approximately two *ken* (slightly over 3.6 m), is similar in both buildings. And similarly, the smaller sides of Tange's two-planed roof are held back like the cut-in gables at the four-planed roof of Katsura. The central portion of the roof, that has no structural or spatial reason for being raised since it is concealed on the inside by a false ceiling, and the lower overhangs at the edges (which, on the other hand, extend the sloped ceiling of the rooms) form a figure that recalls the couplet of *moya-hisashi* of the Shinden style residences, equally as well as referring to the exterior forms of modern wood houses, such as those built by Maekawa in the 1930s.

fig b19-d. a heightened focus on Japanese wood in a 1/3 scale model built out of cedar by a carpenter specialized in the construction of temples (*miyadaiku*); reconstruction for the "Japan in Architecture" exhibition, Mori Museum, 2018

The house is thus a certain form of hybrid. Its wooden elements, the carpentry details, the design of the guard rail, the exposed rafters (*taruki*) of the roof, all belong to a Japanese building tradition, and yet in other respects the house expresses a certain modernity. As part of Tange's search for fluidity and spatial dynamic, the ceilings of the rooms are inclined and extend out to the porch. In Sukiya houses, on the contrary, one experiences a sequence of different adjoining spaces: first, reception rooms with flat ceilings are interrupted by the dropped heads at the walls above the sliding partitions, and are followed by an exterior gallery (*engawa*) whose ceiling follows the slope of the overhang. But the rhythm of the facade, in which longer spans (approx. 3.6 m) alternate with shorter ones (approx. 1.3 m), and the presence of planed double beams, along with large gabled panes of glass or transoms—all of which are modern elements—do not conflict with the Sukiya aspect of the house.

In fact, it is the rafters—two of them at the extending eaves of the gables, two for the short structural spans, and six for the long ones—that most clearly establish a regular meter for the building, especially as Tange extended them visually by baguette moldings at the ceilings inside. This insistence recalls the proportions that once established the relations between the part and the whole—a principle referred to in the previous chapter regarding the spacing between rafters and the structural grid of the building—in the religious buildings of the Kamakura period, at a time when Chinese influences were on the wane. Without necessarily being an explicit intent to fall back on the ways of carpenters from the past, this nonetheless indicates a sensitivity on Tange's part to such architectonic expressions. The house also benefitted from an immediate context suited to these mixtures of genres, with a garden and local species of large pines that are reflected in the windows.

On the inside, the same feeling of hybrid space predominates. *A priori*, the plan seems indebted to a division based on the tatami module in the alternating rhythm of the facade, as some tatamis measure 1.8 m in length and others only 1.3 m. But this layout is in fact paradoxical. Despite the emphasis placed on this kind of floor divisions, which directly express the Japanese quality of a space, the architect proceeded to cut up the mats at his convenience to fit this small and unusual grid, which he could have avoided by keeping the dominant module, and he also replaced them intermittently with floorboards. In fact, as one can see from the photographs of the interiors, Tange placed wood boards with the same proportions as the tatamis in the study / living room so as to allow furniture including lounge chairs to be integrated, as usually one sat directly on the mats and avoided furniture with legs that could damage the surface. Only low tables with large base frames are arranged in them in a temporary manner. In reality, the Tange family often placed Western chairs and tables directly on the tatamis, but everyone sat on the floor when there were guests. These two forms of accommodation were far from insignificant, because the unusual module of 1.3 m and the replacement of tatamis by wooden planks was a form of contemporary inventiveness. They showed a modern architect freely playing with elements of the past and giving pride of place to structural rhythms (established by the posts and rafters) and functional spatial organization. As for the glazing, it was used for the bays, but also for the transoms between rooms, over the rails/lintels (*nageshi* and *kamoi*), in locations where one normally placed decorative transoms (*ranma*) in the *shoin*. In this way, all the structural elements, as well as the frames and sliding panels, are highlighted. The roof in particular is elevated above the rest of the house. The *fusuma* and *shōji* appear in the primary function as screen and frame within a space made even more transparent and modern, especially by the glazed transoms.

fig b20-a. The Tange family with painting on the *fusuma* by Shinoda Tōkō in the *tokonoma* of the main room

This notion of hybridity, between tradition and modernity, can be seen as well in the Tange family's way of life. In photographs published at the time, one often sees the mother of the family (Toshiko) wearing a kimono, while the daughter (Michiko) and husband (Kenzō) are wearing western attire, as if the mistress of the house needed to remain the principal guardian of traditions. Behind them in this same photograph, one sees calligraphy painted on a *fusuma* and not in the alcove of a *tokonoma*, as would be the case in a more traditional space in the Sukiya style (fig. b20). It is a calligraphy by Shinoda Tōkō 篠田桃紅 (1913-2021), an artist who is known for her compositions that combine calligraphy and abstract painting in China ink—the ultimate hybridity.

fig b20-b. reception room (ST-LR on the plan)

fig b21. Frontal view of the post, the door, and the wall. Shinohara Kazuo, House in White, Tokyo, 1966

TOWARDS AN ABSTRACT JAPANESE SPACE: THE SHINOHARA SCHOOL

The generation that entered the profession during the 1950s was also involved in the debate about tradition. But residential architecture remains built primarily out of wood, and in many cases this is more for reasons of cost than aesthetics or historicist orientation. In addition, as if it were still necessary to show, architectural expression is not always tied to some structural truth, nor to the use of a particular material, even if modern architecture defended the claim that these are the primary engines of creation. One of these newcomers, representing an architectural discourse that can be considered post-modern, or at least critical of the ideals of modernity, is Shinohara Kazuo (1925–2006). His approach to architecture is a shift from that of Tange Kenzō and his disciples.

While the latter, who taught at the University of Tokyo, was the principal actor of Japanese large-scale projects after the war, Shinohara, an "architect-professor" at the Tokyo Institute of Technology, dedicated himself almost exclusively to the design of the house. Until the end of the twentieth century, the teachers at the university architectural laboratories (design studios) could engage in professional activity, with students working on practical projects. Given the scale of his projects, Tange was one of the first "architect-professors" to establish a design practice outside of the university, but most of the other teachers developed their practices within the university structure, up until retirement age. Thus, over the course of some thirty years, until 1985, Shinohara designed each of his most radical house projects with his students. He also left behind a great many texts and aphorisms that serve as references for his disciples, and for a number of architects that comprise what one might call the "Shinohara school," whose current proponents include Tsukamoto Yoshiharu (Atelier Bow-Wow), himself a teacher at the Tokyo Institute of Technology, and less directly, SANAA (Sejima and Nishizawa Architects and Associates).

It might seem strange to consider Shinohara as an example in a study on wood architecture in Japan, but his case is actually fairly emblematic of the relation that contemporary Japanese architects maintain with this material. With few exceptions, most Japanese houses have a wood structure; this was the case of 90% of non-collective housing in 1960, and is still true of more than 60% today. So at the beginning of his career, Shinohara thus primarily built houses out of wood. And like most of his contemporaries, during the 1950s, he consequently developed a discourse and reinterpreted the architectural tradition of his own country.

As a researcher, he published articles and works primarily concerned with the concept of the habitat. Ideas on housing (*jūtakuron* 住宅論) and on living space (*seikatsu kūkan* 生活空間) are to be found within his many publications. He was also the author of a series of studies submitted to the Japanese Institute of Architecture on "the Methodology of Japanese Architecture."[125]

---

[125] Between 1957 and 1964, Shinohara Kazuo published, in the annals and lectures of the Architectural Institute of Japan a series of 12 papers devoted to different aspects of Japanese architecture. The first two of them have as subtitles "The Character of Japanese Architecture" (*Nihon kenchiku no seikaku* 日本建築の性格), before he adopted the title of the series, "The Methodology of Japanese Architecture" (*Nihon kenchiku no hōhō* 日本建築の方法).

fig b22-a. Kugayama House

SHINOHARA Kazuo, Tokyo, 1954

H: *hiroma*
DR: dining room
KI: kitchen
BR: bedroom

H: *hiroma*
SM: salle à manger
CU: cuisine
CH: chambre

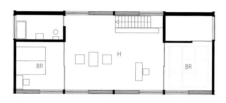

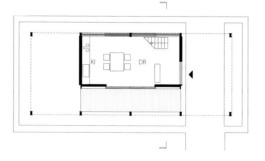

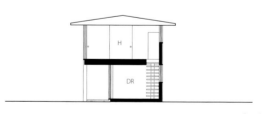

fig b22-b. main facade
fig b22-c. interior view

His theoretical work has been informed by his architectural practice, and the original ideas that he has propounded in the form of aphorisms reveal his personal outlook on the mission of the architect. He considers tradition as a "starting point for creation," and not a "regression." He insists that residential architecture in particular has the character of a work of art. One of his most famous sayings, "the house is an art" (*jūtaku wa geijutsu de aru*) was formulated in reaction to the strictly functional architecture and to the industrialization of housing that was being advanced in Japan at the end of the 1950s. His first works were motivated by both a return to tradition and a creative artistic will. While this position may not be all that different from those of other architects who addressed the Japanese architectural tradition with the intention of integrating it into modern expressions, Shinohara's particular contribution lay in his capacity to theorize his own design practice. He started out studying and even teaching mathematics before undertaking his architectural studies in 1949. Although he rarely referred to his first field of interest, his analysis of the principles of composition of Japanese architecture demonstrated his capacity for developing theoretical concepts that he sought to put into practice. Until the end of the 1960s, his work evolved in the direction of a "Japanese" sense of space, and an architecture in which reference to Japanese space became symbolic, or even abstract.

The first of his houses should probably not appear in a work on wood architecture, since contrary to what one might imagine—by the scale and very proportions of the object—it is in fact not a wood building. As opposed to Maekawa's Corbusian house built out of wood for lack of concrete in Japan during the 1930s, the House in Kugayama (Kugayama no ie 久我山の家, (fig. b22), built in 1954, has a steel and concrete structure. Its facade strikingly resembles Tange's residence, as illustrated in the architecture magazines of the time—through photographs by Hirayama Chūji in both cases. And in both houses, the references to the Villa Savoye are unmistakable.

The facade of the House in Kugayama is modular and divided in a binary manner, but unlike Tange's project, the veranda is located on the ground floor, not on the second. The plan is simple and symmetrical; the kitchen and dining room are located at ground level, with the bedrooms above. The plan reveals a common feature of Japanese space: the absence of corridors, the direct relations between different rooms that are separated from each other by sliding panels only. The organization of functions is nonetheless different from Tange's "hybrid" project; here the servant spaces—the kitchen and dining room on the ground floor—are separated from the served spaces—the living room and bedrooms on the upper floor, and this vertical superposition is underscored by the fact that these rooms are either equipped in the "occidental" way, with wood floors, tables, and chairs, or in a more "Japanese" manner, with tatamis.

Given its dimensions, this house could very well have been built out of wood, but Shinohara did not want to identify that material with his architectural discourse at the time. In the Umbrella House (Karakasa no ie から傘の家, fig. b23) though, built eight years later, wood had become a more essential part of his architectural expression. This house was one of the first true architectural prowess by the Tokyo architect. Its structure derives from a model of industrial architecture with an "umbrella" arrangement (*karakasa kôzô* 唐傘構造), in which the framing of beam-rafters radiates out from a central post. But by building this structure out of wood, Shinohara's "umbrella" becomes reminiscent of the Japanese objects out of oiled paper (*karakasa* 唐傘) in a Chinese style—a distant importation from the Tang civilization during the Nara period (eighth century).

The Umbrella House is laid out on a square plan with a small footprint of about 50 square meters (538 sf). The aphorism "the house is an art"[126] was the title of the article that Shinohara published upon the publication of photographs of this house in the periodical *Shinkenchiku* in May 1962. With this small dwelling, he was moving in the opposite direction from the monumental architecture being imagined by his Metabolist colleagues. The house was built in one of the new neighborhoods of detached private dwellings, in the Suginami ward, and it also ran counter to the "rationalist" industrial logic of prefabricated housing construction that was proliferating in the outskirts of Tokyo. The scale and composition of the umbrella house into a "total" space—a single space without separations, where "everything" can be apprehended in the same room—links it to the spatial qualities of the tea pavilion (*chashitsu*), a celebrated example of which, the Karakasatei 傘亭, is to be found at the Kōdaiji monastery 高台寺 in Kyoto. This pavilion is known for the design of its ceiling, in which rafters radiate out from the center of the roof and recall the ribs of an umbrella. From a more contemporary point of view, this was also a reference to metal structures very often used in the 1960s. Even though in this case, the structure does not actually belong to this type—since the central post is not truly bearing—this reference is also a gentle nod to the generation of his old professor, Seike Kiyoshi 清家清 (1918–2005) who sought to develop modular housing through the use of industrial processes.

Here Shinohara conceived of a roof supported by eight posts around the perimeter. The "central"—but de-centered—post is located at the intersection of two doubled beams (called "composite" beams, *gōsei-bari* 合成梁) that contribute to the division of the spaces by forming two axes for the framework of beams. The main column is a simple peeled cedar trunk (*sugi*) that does not extend to the ceiling and which in fact only serves to support the beams attached to either side that stabilize the entire frame. At the edges of the roof, the rafters are placed on eaves beams (*noki-geta* 軒桁) of Douglas fir (*beimatsu* 米松) and fan out from a square frame "keystone." The four corner rafters come together at the top of the ceiling. The square plan of the house is then divided as a function of the hierarchy of different rooms that make it up.

The Umbrella House is divided into two types of spaces: intimate ones, including bedrooms and sanitary facilities, and common ones, such as the living room and kitchen. It is worth noting that Shinohara used the archaic Sukiya term of *hiroma*, or "great room," to designate the living room. The reception rooms have no ceilings and are open to the underside of the roof structure. On the other hand, the main bedroom with its tatami floor, unlike the other wood planked spaces, has a ceiling formed by the underside of mezzanine that opens to the living room. In the pictures published by Shinohara, access to the mezzanine is by a ladder placed against one of the transverse beams that form the main axes dividing the space. The ladder element complements the bamboo screen (*sudare* 簾), that is suspended from the beam and separates off the kitchen, and it adds to the rustic quality of the house.

Despite its name, the house evokes the popular house *minka* more than the tea pavilions of the elite as its spatial referent. In a text on old and new forms of living, published a few months after completion of the work, Shinohara emphasized that "the plan of the Japanese popular house (*minka*) is considered to come from the Chinese character for the word 'field' (*ta* 田)," but that in his estimation there was a more essential reason for this archetypical form: "The spatial

---

[126] Shinohara Kazuo, "Jūtaku wa geijutsu de aru" 住宅は芸術である [The house is an art], *Shinkenchiku*, Vol. 37 (May 1962): 77–8; republished in *Jūtaku kenchiku* 住宅建築 [Residential architecture] (Tokyo: Kinokuniya shinsho, 1964): 76–82.

fig b23-a. Umbrella House

SHINOHARA Kazuo, Tokyo, 1961

H: *hiroma*
BR: bedroom

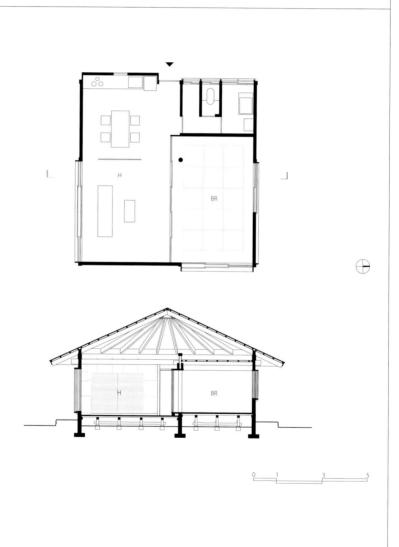

TOWARDS AN ABSTRACT JAPANESE SPACE: THE SHINOHARA SCHOOL 二 221

fig b23-b. interior view

unit is usually divided in two, and this form is divided into two again."[127] According to him, the organization of the *minka* rests on these principles (fig. a25). He thus tried to apply them to the plan of the Umbrella House. The single space is first divided along a line of separation on the axis running the length of the two structural beams, before a second subdivision is established.

We should also point out that like Tange, Shinohara had a particular interest in photographic representation. We can place the book on the *minka* by the photographer Futagawa Yukio (1932–2013)[128] alongside the works on Katsura and Ise published by Tange. Shinohara's interest in vernacular dwellings that Futagawa photographed after the war was the inverse of Tange's and explains his feeling that there was something lacking in the old architecture embodied in Katsura and the palaces of Kyoto.

In his own terms, Shinohara tried to rigorously "abstract" (reduce to the essentials) the basic principles of Japanese space by interpreting the plan of the *minka*. This theorization was facilitated by a certain recurrence of vernacular morphologies in the entire archipelago, unconstrained by variations in climate and geography. But aside from these principles, he also drew on symbolic elements of local residential architecture. In the Umbrella House, he drew up a "Japanese" room, in which he placed a "central" post at the intersection of the two dividing axes. The post is relatively slender and sleek, compared to the two beams it supports. It carries a primordial symbolic charge that Shinohara emphasizes by detaching it from the wall plane, unlike the posts at the edges of the house, that are integrated into the facade walls and only visible from the outside (*shinkabe* 真壁 style, in which the post remains exposed). It is important to note that the central post is not centrally located! The architect preferred to offset it along the diagonal to form two virtual squares (3.18 m x 3.18 m on the sanitary side, and 4.26 m x 4.26 m on the living side). This location clearly demonstrates the double geometrical logic at work: on one hand, the symmetrical form centered on the roof, and on the other hand, the division into independent rooms, with the de-centered post which ties the two systems together. This figure of a central post, which represents one of the principal structural elements of the house, is frequently to be found. The Daikoku-bashira (大黒柱, literally, Post of the Great Black), the seat of the divinity Daikoku, is charged with ensuring the prosperity of the home.

Shinohara again took up the theme of the vernacular house (*minka*) in the project for the House with an Earthen Floor (Doma no ie 土間の家, fig. b24) built in the Nagano prefecture, in 1963. He designed this small house for the photographer Ōtsuji Kiyoji 大辻清司 (1923–2001) in the Japanese Alps, with a square plan and a floor area of approximately 50 square meters (538 sf). This wood construction, which owes as much to the chalet as it does to the rural *minka* (*nōka*), borrows from the latter its earthen floor (*doma*) entry, which he considered to be an "organic" element. The house is built on a single level and is divided into two raised rooms on tatamis and the earthen floor area that includes the dining room and kitchen. The bathroom and the toilets are tiled for sanitary reasons. The division between spaces occurs under the main ridge beam, and sliding partitions separate the bedrooms from the rest of the house. The roof is gabled, and the exposed framing is built out of round sections, as is the main post of the house.

---

[127] Shinohara Kazuo, "Karakasa no ie" から傘の家 [The umbrella house] *Shinkenchiku*, (October 1962): 149–51; also cited in Shinohara, *Shinohara Kazuo* (Tokyo, TOTO shuppan, 1996).

[128] Futagawa Yoshio 二川幸夫, *Nihon no minka* 日本の民家 (Japanese popular houses) (Tokyo, Bijutsu shuppan-sha,1962); republished: *Nihon du minka 1955 nen* 日本の民家一九五五年 *Minka 1955 Japanese Traditional Houses* (Tokyo, A.D.A edition, 2012).

In comparison, the plan of this house is even simpler than the Umbrella House's. The models of the square and double division are also taken up in a more literal manner along a longitudinal axis of symmetry, and the house appears even more as a minimal dwelling. The finishes of the woodwork are left raw ("*bruts*" in French)—with the posts simply stripped of their bark, and the beams barely planed. Shinohara used plywood panels for the transoms (*ranma*) of the sliding panels—a very modern "wood" that contrasts with the solid wood and traditional aspects of the tatami rooms. The transoms are very tall, approximately two-thirds of the full height of the partitions, and serve only to demarcate the subdivision of the rooms all the way up to the ceiling. This partition deliberately reinforces the division of spaces down to the earthen floor (*doma*) and creates the impression of a two-dimensional screen inside the house. The architect already introduces an element of frontality that will be much more evident in the following project.

The House in White (Shiro no ie 白の家, fig. b25) was constructed in 1967 in the outskirts of Tokyo. It was the last in the first series of houses designed by Shinohara that refer to tradition and to "Japanese" spatiality. After studying its characteristics and extracted certain "principles," he believed he had developed a way of conceiving and creating a "Japanese space," based on what the architect considered its "irrational" coordinates (*higōriteki* 非合理的). In a text published in English and entitled "The Japanese Conception of Space,"[129] he explained that the "closing off" of Japan during the Edo period, between the beginning of the seventeenth century and the end of the nineteenth—when the government had decided to ban pretty much all foreign relations—had a considerable impact on the traditional notion of space in Japan. One concrete result, according to him, was that the development of Japanese spatial culture had not followed the same path as the evolution of sciences and the history of art in the West. This was the case of the three-dimensional perception of space, specifically linked to the creation of perspective. Although there is no proof that these forms of spatial representation were unknown during the Edo period, this opinion is based on the Japanese carpenters' manner of drawing, on the absence of perspective in their construction drawings—that are essentially structural and organizational plan drawings (*itazu* 板図) and detailed descriptive drawings (fig. c3)—as well as the representation of space in paintings exclusively by means of oblique projection (cavalier perspective, fig. a16-b). In his interpretations of various kinds of construction, from popular to aristocratic dwellings, Shinohara will define the "coordinates of irrationality" of an essentially Japanese architecture and spatiality.

---

[129] Shinohara Kazuo, "The Japanese Conception of Space," *The Japan Architect* (June1964): 57. This text is a translation of the passage "kūkan no ronri" 空間の論理 (The logic of space), in the first chapter, on Japanese space, ("Nihon no kūkan" 日本の空間), in his study of residential architecture. See Shinohara, *Jūtaku kenchiku*, op.cit. (1964), 29–41.

fig b24-a. House with an Earthen Floor

SHINOHARA Kazuo, Kita-Saku, 1963

Ta: *tatami no ma*
D: *doma*

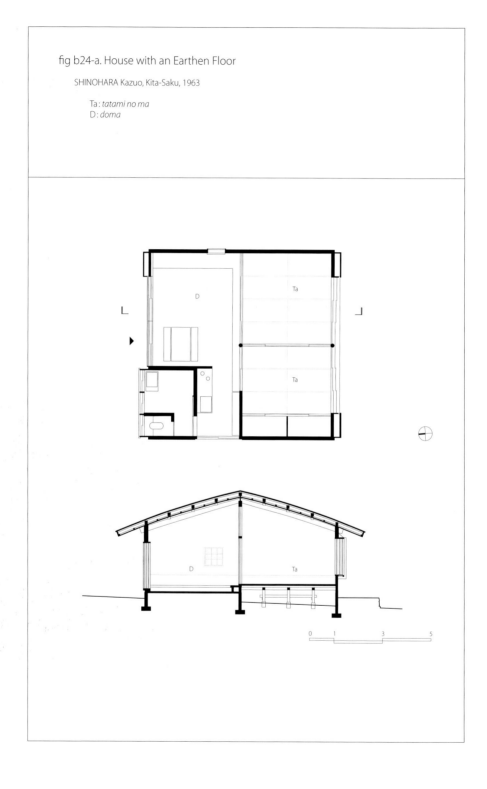

fig b24-b. interior view

fig b24-c. exterior view

fig b25-a. House in White

SHINOHARA Kazuo, Tokyo, 1966

H: *hiroma*
BR: bedroom

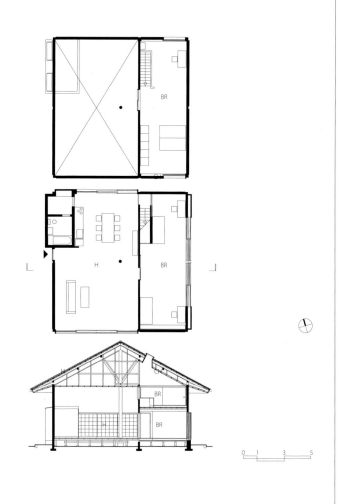

TOWARDS AN ABSTRACT JAPANESE SPACE: THE SHINOHARA SCHOOL 二 229

fig b25-b. exterior view
fig b25-c. interior view

日本には空間はなかった

「日本には空間はなかった」という意見を中心とした「開放的な空間という意味」を書いた。ヨーロッパ・モダニズムの〝ガラスの箱〟を空間と言うならば、桂離宮書院に代表される、繊細な木造柱梁でつくられる、広びろと庭に向かって吹き抜ける〝開放的な空間〟は同じ空間という語を使えない。基準の空間性をヨーロッパに置けば、必然的に日本のそれには〝空間はない〟。

しかし、50年代、日本の伝統とモダニズムとの見えがかりの親近性を拠りどころにして、日本の現代建築は急速な展開をした。私もその雰囲気のなかで最初の建物をつくった。しかし、日本的開放性とガラスの箱の透明性との相違の確認によって、日本の伝統の本質が現われると気づいた。モダニズムのガラス空間を〝実〟とすれば、日本近世の開放的な空間は〝虚〟と言うべき。これは価値の上下を意味しない、空間の定性である。日本的感情を代表する、吹き放たれた近世書院の空間は見事な〝空虚〟。

"In Japan there was no Space"

I have written about "the meaning of open space" as an expression of my opinion that "In Japan there was no space." If we consider the "glass box" of European modernism, then the "open space" represented by the *shoin* of the Katsura Villa—created by a delicate structure of wooden posts and beams which spreads out and extends towards the garden—cannot be designated using the same concept of space. If one takes European spatiality as a reference, then one necessarily comes to the conclusion that in Japan, "there is no space."

And yet during the 1950s it was precisely because of this apparent familiarity between the Japanese tradition and modernism that contemporary Japanese architecture was able to develop so rapidly. I too designed my first buildings in this context. But I realized that the essence of the Japanese tradition appears precisely where the difference between the very nature of Japanese open space and the transparency of the glass box comes to be emphasized. If one considers the space of modernism in glass as a "content," then the open space of medieval Japan is an "emptiness." This is not a value judgment. It is simply a question of spatial quality. The Japanese emotion represented by this space which emanates from the *shoin* of the medieval period is a splendid "emptiness."

民家はきのこである

書院造の背景には古代の寝殿造がある。貴族生活のなかの開放的な空間意識と結びついているとすれば、その対として、竪穴住居を原形にもつという民家がある。そしてその空間の特性は土間に現われる。雰囲気の印象を越え、その構成の特徴を論理的に定性することは可能か。

「民家はきのこである」という、冷たい断定から私はその定性を始めた。恵まれた自然のなかに美しい民家集落があり、厳しい自然のなかにひっそりと耐えぬいてきた民家の集落がある。人口の構築物であるよりは、自然の産物、たとえばきのこの群生のようであると。貴族的背景をもつ住宅の系列に住んだ少数の例外を除いて、人びとはこの懐かしい表情をもった空間で生活をしてきた。それを引き継ぐことの大切さを否定したのではない。たとえば民家調と呼ばれる、形や素材の断片的な使用を越えた、現代の方法を見いだすことができないか。

"The *minka* is a Mushroom"

In the background of the Shoin style of medieval residences, there is the Shinden style of ancient palaces. As opposed to the open spatiality of the aristocracy's way of living, the popular house, the *minka*, has as its archetype the partly buried prehistoric habitat (*tateana jūkyo*). The specific quality of this space is materialized in the earthen floor, the *doma*. Is it possible to get beyond the impression created that this simple materiality and to qualify the composition of this space in a logical manner?

I started by qualifying this particularity in the form of the cold judgment that the "*minka* is a mushroom." There are beautiful villages of *minka* to be found in a blessed nature. The *minka* villages sprang up silently in a hostile nature. They do not have the structure of a human population, because their growth is more like the products of nature, like mushrooms that sprout up in a gregarious fashion. Leaving aside the few residences that originate in aristocratic culture, the bulk of men have lived in this space with its nostalgic expression. One cannot deny the importance that this more recent habitat has taken for the former. And if one considers the model of the *minka*, beyond the simple and isolated use of forms and materials, would it be possible to extract a contemporary method of composition?

fig b26. "In Japan, there was no space" and "The *minka* is a mushroom," in Shinohara Kazuo, op. cit. (1996), 61–2

THE COORDINATES OF IRRATIONALITY
IN JAPANESE SPACE

If space as conceived in the West from the Renaissance to the first industrial revolution was meant to be a representation of a certain kind of rationality, for Shinohara, space as produced in Japan up until the Meiji period afforded *a contrario* a certain form of irrationality, or lack of rational logic. Like Le Corbusier, who defined his "Five Points of a New Architecture" in 1927 (*pilotis*, roof terrace, free plan, ribbon window, and free facade), Shinohara too proposed a certain number of concepts that could be used to create a Japanese space (frontality, division, useless space, and central post). Employing the vocabulary of mathematics, he called them spatial "coordinates."

The first of these, "frontality" (*shōmensei* 正面性) is directly linked to a two-dimensional perception of space. In concrete terms, one experiences this notion when a space—three-dimensional by definition—seems to be projected on to a single plane and comes to be perceived as two-dimensional. The visual effect thus produced tends to eliminate depth and the distance between the different elements present in the space. The division of space, through the use of sliding panels (*fusuma*) also tends to produce this effect. The succession of screens heightens this perception, but the facade of the building also produces a similar effect. While the canopies and the floorboards of the exterior galleries (*en*) project from the plane of the facade, all the other elements that comprise it (posts, beams, sliding frames, shutters— are pretty much aligned along the same plane, within the thickness of the rows of posts. This perception is also at work when one is seated on the tatamis in one of the rooms looking out, as in the famous Kohōan tea pavilion drawn up by Kobori Enshū in the Daitokuji temple in Kyoto (fig. a60). The very notion of "frontality" is not defined in dictionaries of architecture. It came to be conceptualized and employed by architects after the Second World War.

Shinohara was probably influenced by his colleague at the Tokyo Institute of Technology, the historian Inoue Mitsuo (1918-2002). In his major study of space in Japanese architecture,[130] Inoue showed that the monumental architecture of temples and palaces since Nara period (eighth century) had evolved towards increased "frontality." This tendency was characterized by a "flattening" (*henpeika* 扁平化) of the plan, and a diminution in the relation between the depth and width of buildings (fig. a15-e). In addition, the non-perspective representations of pre-modern Japanese pictorial art, as well as the flat areas in prints from the Edo period are so many elements that contributed to a two-dimensional perception of space.

Did the architectural photographers we have already mentioned, such as Ishimoto Yasuhiro and Watanabe Yoshio, willingly accentuate this tendency? It seems fairly evident that they too worked on "flat" representations of Japanese architecture, in their frontal views. In his text on "The Japanese Concept of Space," and like Inoue in his work, Shinohara refers to the example

---

[130] *See* Inoue Mitsuo 井上充夫, *Nihon kenchiku no kūkan* 日本建築の空間 (Tokyo: Kajima shuppankai, 1969); English Edition, *Space in Japanese Architecture*, op. cit. (1985).

of the Kōnoma 鴻の間 reception room in the Nishi Honganji monastery, in which an elevated frontal space, the *jōdan no ma* is set up. This slightly raised space, at the back of the hall, serves as a podium and frame that can highlight the presence of special guests in the *shoin* (figs. a20, a47). Shinohara uses this device in the projects already referred to: in the Umbrella House, the tatami room is raised by about 15 cm, enough to mark a threshold and to distinguish it from the living rooms. In the House with an Earthen Floor, this elevation is actually 30 cm (one *shaku*) and the difference in floor height is even more emphasized.

The second coordinate, which is directly tied to frontality, sets up the device of "division" (*bunkatsu* 分割) of space. It often occurs between the lines of posts that provide the structure of the construction, and where the tracks for the sliding partitions are placed. Shinohara opposes this Japanese concept of "division" of space in order to form rooms, from the western practice of creating a "connection" (*renketsu* 連結) between closed rooms (by walls). In the free plan "liberated" from its walls, as Le Corbusier described it, space is modulated thanks to sliding screens placed between the posts, whereas in a space constituted by walled-off rooms, the architect must create links between them. The hallway is one; the door is another. From this point of view, the logic of architecture as produced by masonry construction is the story of connection and openings pierced into closed spaces; in an open space between posts, spatial creation is a matter of division and juxtaposition.

One of the particularities of Japanese residential architecture was offering multifunctional rooms that accommodate the different moments of dwelling: eating, sleeping, playing, and working. But today modernization entails a certain kind of spatial specialization. As a result, the tatami, which was ubiquitous until the end of the Edo period, aside from rooms with earthen floors (*doma*) and open spaces (like the paneled living room/kitchens in farmhouses and verandas, *engawa*), has become reserved for the so-called "Japanese" reception rooms—the *zashiki* that evoke the salons of the grand residences of the Sukiya style, or the more recent *washitsu* 和室, a vague term that simply means a Japanese room, in other words, on tatamis—even bedrooms, although most Japanese sleep in beds today. In reaction to the "functionality" of the forms of industrialized dwelling being built in massive quantities in the Japanese megalopolis starting in the 1960s, be they prefabricated private houses or standardized collective housing in which there is no longer any space that is not reduced to a specific function, Shinohara proposed to create spaces which had no use, no function. He considered the capacity to create a "useless space" (*muda na kūkan* 無駄な空間) to be another one of those coordinates of Japanese space.

More than an empty space or a space that magnifies nothingness, the "useless space" is a spatial layout which can produce a particular spatial sensation, without being linked to a precise or utilitarian function. Through this rather provocative formulation, Shinohara proposed to reverse the rational logic of functional spaces, so dutifully measured in "modern" housing, by creating a spatiality which gives an impression of "total" space, that is almost over-scaled and encompasses the whole house, but for no particular function. The fact that the "divided" space can expand, by virtue of the flexible opening of the partitions, is an advantage in this respect. But other measures are also put in place, such as the ceiling height, the open spaces under the roof (at mezzanine height) and the contrasts established between the different spatial scales, with some rooms reduced in size to favor other larger volumes. In most of these cases, as in the Umbrella House, the bedrooms are minimized, while the living room takes up the full available ceiling height.

The last coordinate to be pointed out is the central post that contributes both to the structure—the main house beams rest on it—and to the symbolism of the home. It is usually located at the center of the *minka*, or sometimes slightly offset, near the kitchen, and is called the Daikoku-bashira, the "Post of the Great Black" (figs. a25, b21). It is traditionally the first to be erected in the house, and it is larger in size than the other posts. It is named in honor of Daikoku 大黒 or Daikokuten 大黒天, the "Great Black," one of the Seven Gods of Fortune, and symbol of prosperity. Chubby-cheeked and often represented seated on a sack of rice, known by the name Mahākāla in Indian Buddhism, Daikoku is the pacified form of Shiva in Japanese Buddhism. In his architecture, Shinohara incorporates this post as one of the most elementary and constitutive coordinates of the space. For example, in the Umbrella House, the central post maintains its status, even if it is slightly offset, along with the axes of the two main transverse beams. Positioned as it is in the tatami room, its thick round shaft (*maruta* 丸太) contributes to giving a Japanese character to this space. We find this same post in the House with an Earthen Floor, but with a more rustic expression. It is a "natural" piece of wood with exposed knots (*fushi* 節) that came from a tree that had not been grown by a nurseryman. However, here it is in a more classical position, central and not detached from the rows of sliding partitions. In the House in White, the central post is a round section, out of cedar (*sugi*), as in the Umbrella House. Here it plays a structural role and can also be considered the unifying element for the coordinates of "irrationality" in this house. This column is both central and eminently symbolic. It is also the only structural element made of wood from Japan, as economic logic otherwise dictated the use of imported wood (most often American Douglas fir).

With the House in White, one of his most fully developed projects, Shinohara reached the ultimate stage of his creative process of abstraction whose goal was to found a Japanese space. The house is divided in two. One enters directly from outside into a large double-height volume, a sort of white cube, which includes the living room and the kitchen, along with a small volume for the bathroom. The other half of the house is dedicated to the bedrooms, on two levels. A window opens on to the living room from the upper bedroom, again called *hiroma*. The "frontality" is established here thanks to the dividing wall that separates the house into two parts. As soon as one opens the entry door, the view is blocked by this double-height surface without any transition—a rather rare arrangement in Japan, as houses almost always include an entryway in which to remove one's shoes. The double-height partition (3.7 m or close to two *ken* in height) is held back from the axis of the house (by a distance of 1.38 m, or 4 *shaku* and 6 *sun*, as specified in the plans) (figs. b25, c5). The central post is highlighted by this spacing; a high window and a door (to the bedrooms) create an abstract landscape, composed of the essential elements of architecture. We should also note that the architect, who was very meticulous about the photographs of his work, placed two well-known Scandinavian chairs by Poul Kjaerholm in the picture. These were both foreign and very contemporary at the time.[131] The effort to define a new tradition did not preclude familiarity with the latest trends in international furniture. More importantly, it seems that Shinohara hesitated for some time about putting a ceiling in this room. Through this fundamental choice, he broke with the aesthetic of his preceding houses, in which the roof and its beams were always very present. Instead, he created a white cube, of the sort one comes across in most art galleries. In this

---

[131] This does not hold true of recent photographs that were obviously not supervised by the architect.

fig b27. Living room (*hiroma*) of the House in White

abstract landscape, the cedar (*sugi*) post comes to be seen as an "organic" element. The architect invokes the "construction of an artificial nature" (*jinkō shizen no kōchiku* 人工自然の構築). In his terminology, this "nature" (*shizen*) derives not just from the organic origins of the wood but is instead "an abstract concept produced by the interaction between a white-painted cubic box, abstract and simplified, with the cedar post."[132]

[132] Shinohara Kazuo, *Shinohara Kazuo 16 no jūtaku to kenchikuron* 篠原一男16の住宅と建築論 [16 houses and architectural reflections by Shinohara Kazuo] (Tokyo: Bijutsu shuppansha, 1971), 161.

fig b28. Shinohara Kazuo, House for Mister Tanikawa (Tanikawa san no jūtaku), Naganohara, 1974
fig b28-a. interior view

TOWARDS AN ARCHITECTURE... IN WOOD

After working extensively on the theme of the Japanese architectural tradition and revisiting its different moments of expression in pre-modern Japan (pre-Western modernity, that is), Shinohara then spent the next ten years building an architecture that had little to do with his earlier interest, but was instead more focused on the interpretation of the forms of modern architecture from the West. He started working with the notion of "the cube" in particular, as an element inherited from modernist thinking. He had crossed a threshold typical of traditional arts in Japan: once one has copied a model, a master, or a school, one can then experiment with a completely different model and ultimately create one's own personal style. Shinohara himself distinguished four styles (*yōshiki* 様式) in his work. Was he making some reference to these obligatory passages? While he has not addressed this question directly, it is still worth noting that beginning in the mid 1970s, he developed an architecture free of references to tradition, and after building in concrete, he came to free himself from the modern vocabulary altogether.

In 1974, Shinohara created a secondary residence for the poet Tanikawa Shuntarō, whose main home in Tokyo he had already designed in 1958. The House for Mister Tanikawa (Tanikawa-san no ie 谷川さんの家) from that time consists of two spaces with independent structures, a first "shelter" of 40 square meters (430 sf), with two rooms, north and south, separated by sliding panels (*fusuma*), and a second area for the wet spaces. The architect and client retained the idea from 1958 of building two structures underneath the same roof. The second House for Mister Tanikawa (Tanikawa-san no jūtaku 谷川さんの住宅, fig. b28) is built in the mountains near Karuizawa. The client's only "written" statement is a short poem:

> A winter home or a pioneer's shack (a house).
> A summer space or a pantheistic church (which could as well not be a house).[133]

The house is built on a sloped site surrounded by the trees of the forest. In a text entitled "When Naked Space is Traversed," published alongside the plans and photographs of this project in the architecture review *Shinkenchiku*, Shinohara explained that he did not seek to reproduce the surrounding natural features on the inside of the house, but rather to interpret the topography and materiality of the site. While the exterior, with its gabled roof and wood siding, gives the house the look of a simple chalet, the arrangement and furnishing of the interior convey a completely different impression. It seems to be divided into two spaces juxtaposed under a single roof, one dedicated to "winter" and the other to "summer," in keeping with the owner's request. The winter space is equipped and furnished for minimal comfort. It occupies two levels, with a tatami bedroom on the upper floor, in the archetypical form of a wood hut. The summer

---

[133] *Fuyu no ie mata wa kaitakusha no koya (jūtaku)* 冬の家又は開拓者の小屋（住宅）*Natsu no kūkan mata wa hanshinronsha no kyōkai (jūtaku de nakute ii)* 夏の空間又は汎神論者の教会（住宅でなくていい）. Poem by Tanikawa Shuntarō 谷川俊太郎 (b. 1931) cited in Shinohara Kazuo, "Ragyō no kūkan o ōdan suru toki" 裸形の空間を横断するとき *Shinkenchiku* (April 1975): 34; English ed.: "When Naked Space is Traversed," *The Japan Architect* (February 1976): 64–9.

fig b28-b. House for Mister Tanikawa

SHINOHARA Kazuo, Naganohara, 1974

H(s): summer *hiroma*
H(w): winter *hiroma*

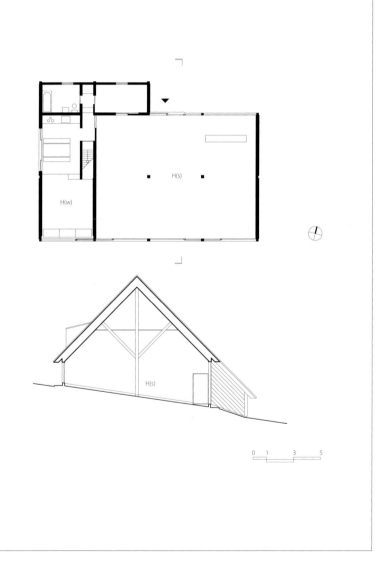

fig b28-c. exterior view
fig b28-d. exterior view of gable

fig b28-e. interior view

space is empty and along the lines of a "useless space"; it contains a single bench and two posts located along the central axis. The floor is left as is, "naked," like the earth outside, and following the same slope.

As he often does, Shinohara favors the term *hiroma* for the rooms (fig. b28-b). Given the importance he attaches to the meanings of terms, the floor is not a true *doma* as one might first think; the dirt is not compacted, but rather trampled by the inhabitants. Here he seeks to evoke the architectural emotion of an "anti-space," (*hankūkan* 反空間) to use his terms. This paradoxical feeling results from the contrast which results from the encounter of the raw materiality of the soil—a nature that is both abstract and organic at the same time—and the artificial and pared down geometry of the posts and struts. As opposed to the preceding houses, here the post is no longer a barely squared cylindrical trunk made from local cedar, but something fundamentally different: a square post, milled by man and machine out of imported Douglas fir (*beimatsu*).

The Tanikawa house was the last one to be built by Shinohara out of wood, who reprised several of the principles and measures that he defined as being essential to the spatiality of the Japanese house. Among them, the earthen floor (*doma*), with the qualification noted above, the useless space (*muda na kūkan*), and the symbolism of the central post, although it is split off and foreign, are all composed together in a manner that runs counter to the functional logic of architecture. Although the architect does not draw attention to this feature, we could also stress the hypertrophy of the roof–it practically comes down to the ground, leaving room for narrow bands of glazing only–a common feature in mountain farm buildings (*minka*). The summer space, which takes up three quarters of the floor area of the house, calls into question the very reason for a residential dwelling. The architecture has become uninhabitable, for Shinohara considers it a "spatial machine" that places the user in a situation best suited for experimentation involving his own body, within a strange and unusual space. From the outside, it appears to be a simple wood house with a large roof, whose two surfaces intersect to form a right angle, that sits on a wooded slope, while on the inside, it is split into a little cabin and a sort of barn: an ultra-modern reinterpretation of a farm for a single animal, in this case, a human being in search of creativity.

fig b29-a. Villa at Karuizawa

YOSHIMURA Junzō, Karuizawa, 1962

LR: living room
DR: dining room
BR: bedroom
HA: hall

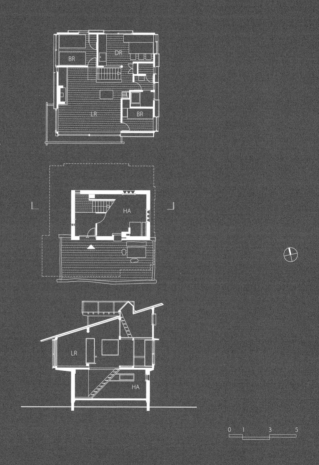

VARIATIONS ON THE STYLE

The houses of Shinohara Kazuo from the 1960s and 1970s represent an explicit effort to produce, by means of a theoretical method, a contemporary Japanese space, and the use of wood was an integral part of this Japanese character. What is true for Shinohara is also the case for other architects who employ a modern vocabulary. We have already pointed to Raymond, Maekawa, and Tange, each of whom reinterpreted a Corbusian tradition. We should also draw attention to the work of Yoshimura Junzō, a close collaborator of Raymond's during the 1930s. Along with the American in his churches, he is one of the few to have completed buildings out of wood, other than residences. One example is the Cunningham Harmony House in Karuizawa (1983), which despite its name is a small concert hall, and the Hall of Chamber Music in Yatsugatake (1988), which is a combination of concrete and wood. But his most striking work is without a doubt his little "Forest House" (Mori no ie 森の家). Also known as the villa at Karuizawa (Karuizawa no sansō 軽井沢の山荘, fig. b29), that he designed for himself and his family in 1963, in this vacation place much prized by the Tokyo elites, as Raymond had done a few years before.

The planning rules for this commune located at the foot of the Japanese Alps require that a certain density of trees per hectare be conserved. This lush quality is one of the main features of the local landscape, which serves to enhance the villa as literally a "mountain retreat" (sansō). Yoshimura drew up a raw concrete basement or pedestal (socle) supporting a wood structure, thus creating the figure of a belvedere (kaku 閣). This type is also an ancient form of "rustic" architecture—the celebrated gold (Kinkakuji) and silver (Ginkakuji) pavilions in Kyoto afford refined examples (fig. a64). With its 18-square-meter footprint (193 sf) and its 45 square meters (484 sf) of flooring at the upper floor, the architect created a minimal shelter. The ground floor includes a wood terrace, sheltered by the cantilever of the upper floor, and by the concrete base that provides entry to the house. This enormous hollow pillar, which takes the place of pilotis, serves as an entry and utility space, but most of all, it lifts the house off the ground, all the while anchoring it in the humid ground of the forest. Above it, the living space forms a square that extends beyond this pedestal on all sides, to differing extents. The overhang is greatest on the south and west sides. This small offset, which protects the ground floor terrace, also projects towards the access path below in that same direction and energizes the entire composition of what nonetheless remains a modest vacation home. Yoshimura further fortified this arrangement by installing a large angled window that is extended by a small balcony with two simple trunks for guardrails.

We should note that all dimensions on the original drawings, as was the case for all wood houses built until the mid-1960s, are indicated in traditional units of length, that is to say, in ken and shaku, not in metric units. The upper floor thus breaks down into two homothetic squares: one of them makes up the whole upper floor, measuring 24 x 24 shaku (7.2 m x 7.2 m), and the

fig b29-b. exterior view
fig b29-c. interior view

other smaller one, which measures 16 *shaku* x 16 *shaku* (4.8 m x 4.8 m), defines the living room. This geometrical relation between two square rooms recalls what we have seen previously in some of the houses drawn up by Shinohara, particularly in the Umbrella House. In this way, the two architects make fairly clear reference to the ideal tea pavilion, in which the square of 4.5 tatamis (9 x 9 *shaku* or 2.7 m x 2.7 m) derives from both a homothety based on the large reception rooms of Sukiya style residences, such as the *kokonoma* of 18 tatamis (18 x 18 *shaku* or 5.4 m x 5.4 m) (figs. a20, rooms 1 and 3, a30), and from the archetype of the minimal shelter such as the Buddhist *hōjō*, addressed in the first chapter—or even a retreat like that of Karuizawa. And if the living room of the "Forest House" is only 16 *shaku* on a side rather than 18, this is because the architect considered the original Sukiya room a bit too large and preferred to use multiples of two *shaku* rather than three; modern as he is, Yoshimura still knows his classics!

The roof cuts obliquely into the volumes that compose the facade—the rectangular parallelepiped of concrete and the cube made of wood—with a single roof plane sloping to the west. The eastern side of the house that is most exposed to the sun is double height, which makes it possible to add a supplementary mezzanine room. It overlooks the living room, and provides access, via a ladder, to a wooden terrace mounted on the roof; an element that once again accentuates the building's function as a belvedere. On the facades the glass bays slide in caissons integrated into the walls, like the wooden shutters (*amado* 雨戸) in older buildings, particularly the *shoin*, and they bring a "Japanese-style" detail to the ensemble. One should also take into account the presence of round cedar beams (*sugi*), barely squared, that add to the rustic quality of the two-story space of the living room, which is also clad in cedar on all its sides.

Yoshimura does not refer explicitly to vernacular architecture in his secondary residence; nor does he claim any particular relation to tradition. The presence of a base and a pronounced concrete cantilever, the chalet aspect, the horizontal glazed bay and the internal mezzanine underscore the modernity of the project with expressivity. And yet, a double reading subtly emerges as soon as one examines the materiality, the geometry, and the dimensions of the project in any detail.

fig b30. Yoshida Isoya, villa Inomata, Tokyo, 1967. Entry door to the *roji* 露地 pathway that leads to the tea pavilion.

CONTEMPORARY SUKIYA ARCHITECTURE: AN EXCEPTION TO THE RULE?

Any consideration of wood architecture in the twentieth century, as opposed to preceding centuries, requires one to concentrate on domestic space. However, the difficulties of dealing with the period between the 1920s and the 1980s lies in finding one's bearings within the discourse on tradition and modernity. While the recurrence of this questions of identity is remarkable in itself, the works are varied, and the discourses sometimes contradict each other. But beyond the differences, it is this protean dialectic between (local) tradition and (Western) modernity that is at the foundation (if one can put it that way) of Japan-ness. As soon as one touches upon the domain of wood, all works refer back one way or another to this ontological debate. Yet it is important to specify which tradition one is talking about. Creative artists do not all draw on the same aspects of the past, and even when they refer to it, these choices are not neutral. References that are not always explicit can refer as easily to spatiality and to its arrangements, to materials and their use, to styles from the past, to certain known typologies, or even to older buildings in whole or in part. What can one say about tendentious readings of tradition like those by Kishida, Taut, and their consorts on the subject of Katsura?

All the architects have one point in common, however. Despite their variety in expression, their houses are always built by carpenters, and beyond theory and style, they all conform to the same spatio-structural regime, based on pre-modern measurements (in *shaku* and *ken*). In other words, these residences share the same spans, most often 2.7 m or 3.6 m, made from solid wood components, and consequently of similar dimensions. There is a simple reason why this point is rarely brought up by architects: it is scarcely subject to debate, founded as it is on invariant criteria of economy of construction. A few selected examples bypass this constraint: Raymond's doubled collar beams that were typical of his houses and churches from the 1930s to 1960s; the sandwiched beams in Tange's house, certain structures of Shinohara, including the umbrella house. One could certainly find others, notably in the pre-war public or utilitarian buildings, which required longer spans in their framing. But not only are these examples limited in number, they also result primarily from economic considerations. As one can see, the exceptions are rare.

Among the architects already discussed, Maekawa and Tange are no doubt the most modern, and Shinohara the most radically inventive. But as we have already noted, strictly speaking, they are not interested in wood as a material. With the other protagonists, at least in that aspect of their work that makes use of this material, traditional construction techniques play the central role. Horiguchi, published detailed research on the tea pavilion (*chashitsu*) in parallel with his projects.[134] Through his writings and his book on construction details, Raymond revealed his interest in local carpentry on an equal footing with the contemporary technologies of his time.

---

[134] See especially Horiguchi Sutemi, *Shoin-zukuri to sukiya-zukuri no kenkyū* and *Rikyū no chashitsu*, in *Horiguchi Sutemi hakase chosakushū* [Collected works of professor Horiguchi Sutemi], op. cit. (1978–1987).

This is an indication of a subtle but important difference between the American architect and his Japanese colleagues, who were equally interested in this material: whereas he gives priority to the detailing as the most intrinsically constructive aspect, the others always combine spatial or typological references with this practical knowledge. One insists on the living quality of a particular form of craftsmanship—while the others, while admiring it, also see it as the historical prerogative of a culture. This pragmatic and ideological admiration for the quality of wood construction, directly linked to tradition, brought Yoshimura, Raymond's former partner, to work in the United States, at MoMA in New York (on the construction of a Japanese wood house)[135], or for the Rockefellers (residence and Tea Pavilion at Pocantico, in New York State, 1974), with the Sukiya carpenter Nakamura Sotoji as a guarantor of this building culture.

An illuminating example of this understanding and shared approach is given by the architect Arata Isozaki 磯崎新 (born in 1931), in connection with a tea pavilion that he drew up in Tokyo in the 1990s and called on the very same artisan to build.[136] Isozaki proceeded to explain that his pavilion was intended to have a contemporary quality, and that he was using a number of materials to renew the genre. But when he showed his drawings to the old Kyoto master, the latter reflected in silence before delivering a compliment… and suggesting that he reduce the height of the sliding panels (*shōji*) and add transoms above them. The architect took the advice. We can see signs of the same sort of empathy when looking at Yoshimura's construction drawings for the Rockefeller house, where it is noted on the interiors to refer to Nakamura's plans. The set also contains specifications on the species of wood—written in Japanese, on plans and notes drawn up in English, or spelled out phonetically, such as *akamatsu, akasugi*, for red pine and red cedar—to be used for built-in furniture, partitions and their woodwork or to indicate the flooring out of camphorwood (*kusunoki* 楠). In other words, the Japanese quality, for a modern designer such as Yoshimura, passes through a style: the Sukiya, itself born on a materiality. But although not all the architects were interested in the same elements from the past, neither did the carpenters make up a unified body with identical skill sets, and Sukiya was simply one among them. In the next chapter we will address the trade in greater detail, along with its precise definition and attributes.

This notion of a common and underlying grammar of construction, albeit varied in its expression, brings us to consider a significant approach to contemporary architecture that seeks to continue or even promote tradition. Here again, the terms are important, and they differ from author to author, even if today we tend to lump them all together under the dominant concept of Sukiya. Along with Horiguchi Sutemi, cited above, the best-known contributors to this renewal, or this continuation, are Murano Tōgo (1891–1984), Yoshida Isoya (1894–1974) and Taniguchi Yoshirō (1904–1979). While Yoshida uses the term contemporary Sukiya or new Sukiya (*gendai sukiya* 現代数寄屋) to describe his practice, the three others prefer to speak more broadly of traditional architecture (*dentō kenchiku* 伝統建築) or architecture in the Japanese spirit (*wafū kenchiku* 和風建築). These differences make it clear that this is not a fixed scene, and that the actors are far from sharing the same vision as to the role of history, and hence what meaning to give to the notion of reference. It might at first glance seem to be an exotic archaism to claim filiation with the Sukiya, a style that emerged at the end of the medieval period, in the sixteenth

---

[135] Japanese Exhibition House, MoMA, New York, June 1954–October 1955.
[136] "Shin nichiyōbi no bijutsukan" 新日曜日の美術館 (The new Sunday museum), television program for national public radio and television NHK, 05-07-1999, entitled, "Sukiya kenchikuka Nakamura Sotoji no sekai" 数寄屋建築家中村外二の世界 (The world of the Sukiya architect Nakamura Sotoji). This video is available online.

century. This might seem as fleeting and superficial as certain post-modern architectures from the late twentieth century. And yet, not only have these ideas informed Japanese architecture over time, but they have not precluded the production of houses and certain types of buildings (tea pavilions, inns and hotels in Japanese style) that go far beyond pale imitations of past examples—even if home builders and many architects cannot seem to avoid the platitude of stereotypes. How is one to explain this persistence, this pertinence, and the fact that some architects seem capable of working simultaneously, as if twinning themselves, in two apparently so dissimilar registers, contemporary for certain types of buildings, and traditional for others?

A first cause that we have already referred to, allows one to grasp what is more of a phenomenon than a truly concerted movement—rather than the promotion, even the reconstruction of a mythicized past, it is more a case of historical continuity. The construction culture centered around carpentry, which represented the entire local model, survived the shock of the brutal opening to the West at the beginning of the Meiji era during the 1860s. But this adaptation occurred in a double sense. On the one hand, the carpenters redefined themselves around certain domains of excellence; the new culture of construction, propelled by the architects, pushed them aside and limited them to patrimonial or domestic space, fundamentally more resistant to change. In turn, they influenced the architects, when the latter were called upon to work on these types of buildings. But as soon as different typologies of construction, and new materials such as concrete or steel are addressed, then these references start to fade away. On the other hand, and in the opposite direction one might say, a certain number of carpenters founded general contracting firms. Takenaka Corporation (Takenaka kōmuten), one of the five major construction firms in Japan, has for example opened the new Takenaka Carpentry Tools Museum (Takenaka daiku dōgukan 竹中大工道具館), near Kobe, drawn up and built by the company, and showcasing its past by displaying tools, materials, and full-size models of framing elements and a tea pavilion. One can consider this a form of self-promotion and a celebration of an enduring excellence, originating with the artisans that were the core of a prestigious enterprise that start in Nagoya at the beginning of the seventeenth century, but one can also think of it as a superb source of ethnographic information. The widely recognized quality of contemporary Japanese construction derives as much from the influence of these builders as it does from the architects they work with. Rather than seeing this as a duplication, it would be better to distinguish the variety of changes within the carpentry trade, and the emergence of the architect as a new agent, that often influence each other in reciprocity.

Another cause: as soon as a certain resistance to the Western ideas and models appeared, one that prized local culture and sought to showcase Japan-ness, the only possible references remained the traditional ones. The nationalist period of the 1930s and 1940s provides an example that reoriented individuals such as Horiguchi and Taniguchi and influenced others, even if only temporarily, like Maekawa and Tange. The resistance to the international movement of the 1960s, represented by Shinohara in his own way, the proliferation of shops, restaurants, and hotels with Japanese themed interiors of the 1980s, along with the economic expansion of the country that thought to export a Nippon model, provides other examples. In this sense, the contemporary Sukiya style is not so much a somewhat extreme and archaic version of this view of tradition but is instead more a facet of construction practice in Japan. But beyond this now commonly accepted nomenclature, we were discussing different versions of the role of history and what meaning to give to the notion of reference; Horiguchi, Yoshida, Murano, and Taniguchi offer us a compendium of answers.

fig b31. Yoshiya House, YOSHIDA Isoya, Kamakura, 1962
fig b31-a. exterior view
fig b31-b. interior view

The architect Yoshida Isoya is someone who has most explicitly called for exploration of a new Sukiya style, and who has chosen to favor a relation to national tradition over more contemporary architectural expression. In 1962, he created the house of Yoshiya Nobuko (Yoshiya tei 吉屋邸, fig. b31), a successful author of novels for teenage girls (*shōjo* 少女), in Kamakura, the former capital of medieval Japan, and today a favorite spot for surfers near Tokyo. The house has since been turned into a museum in his memory, dedicated to promoting the education and culture of women. It is managed by the city and clearly conveys the architect's preoccupations. The house is the third one he built for the same client. In this case, Yoshida proposed an arrangement meant to conform to her private life, as she shared it with a woman companion and sought to protect that intimacy. The residence, which the writer conceived as her very last one, is a large renovated single-story home. With its raised main roof and its lower side eaves, it refers to the medieval archetype of a building consisting of a central section (*moya*), with peripheral galleries (*hisashi*) attached. An exposed structure, in a style known as *shinkabe*, or literally "true wall,"—where walls reveal the truth of their structure—provides a rhythm of post and beams, with an infill of earth finished off in white plaster (*shikkui* 漆喰), a typical expression of the Shoin and Sukiya styles.

Past the exterior portico (*mon*) on the street, one follows a long access path made from disjointed stepping stones (*tobiishi*) and laid out in a chicane, an arrangement often found in the access paths (*roji*) of tea pavilions. After some thirty meters, one finally reaches a covered exterior entryway. This layout, completed by a low wall that projects out from the main body of the building, conceals the house and its garden from the visitor over the course of the approach. The building plan is simple. It is divided transversally into three juxtaposed parts that lead from the most public part to the most intimate. The ensemble lies between two gardens. One arrives from the southeast, via the exterior room with a tiled floor already mentioned. It is followed by an entry, conceived as a room in which the author can meet with her editors without their penetrating further into the house. The wet and service areas are to the north. The central part of the house is taken up by a large living room with a double orientation, the kitchen straddles that between the service areas and this same living room, a study that opens up to a rear garden, and a "Japanese" room with tatamis, with its own alcove (*tokonoma*) and separated from its veranda (*en*) by sliding paper panels (*shōji*). In the living room, with its papered ceiling, the architect repeats another unusual detail that has no other function than a purely decorative and symbolic one. Despite appearance, it is simply added on to the real structure, which is concealed within the wall. This wood device evokes and copies elements that were found during the Nara period in the temples reserved for women (*amadera* 尼寺). The bedroom, bath, and closets are located at the far end, at the southwest part of the house. An additional wing extends into the garden on the north side, which recalls the traditional *kura*, those outdoor warehouses, with their thick plaster walls which made them more fire-resistant, and where one stored valuables along with unused items depending on the season. In this way, the Yoshiya house affords a Sukiya haven, a veritable *pot-pourri* of stylistic, typological, and constructional references. Yet it is not simply an anecdotal collection of somewhat outdated historicist quotations. In this house, Yoshida sought to affirm a certain Japanese quality, which apparently includes some nostalgia for national traditions, but which primarily calls on artisans from trades that are still alive and well.

The Inomata House (Inomata tei 猪俣邸, fig. b32), built five years later in Tokyo in 1967, is another attempt to renew or even to modernize the Sukiya style by creating spaces inspired by it, but with the help of modern techniques. Yoshida integrated modern heating and air-conditioning

fig b32. Yoshida Isoya, Inomata House, Tokyo, 1967
fig b32-a. exterior view
fig b32-b. interior view

into this house, introducing a previously unheard-of level of comfort in Japanese houses. In a certain way, he sought to get past the dilemma so humorously evoked by the bittersweet author Tanizaki Junichirō, in his descriptions of the difficulties of adapting local dwellings to western modernization thirty years before.[137] But the main point of interest of this work for our arguments lies elsewhere. Yoshida employed metal structural elements at various points, concealed by dropped ceilings, in order to increase the length of uninterrupted spans. In this way, he was able to increase the size of rooms in this luxurious and apparently traditional dwelling, and in so doing, the house raises an important point in relation to wood construction: the concurrence between spans and proportions.

If the grand salon gives the impression of being wood construction, its unusual size for a residential space undermines this illusion, especially in contrast to the attached wing that includes a small salon and other rooms that are actually made of wood. There, the proportions are very different, and their heights and lengths are coordinated by the *kiwari* system. Visitors are struck by the new enlarged dimensions, much as they are in Shinohara's White house (fig. b25) whose famous ceiling serves as much to create an abstract space as to mask the umbrella structure which makes it possible to increase the span. On the other hand, these examples highlight the importance of a system of measurements in conveying the Japanese quality of a space. But there is a certain theoretical weakness in Yoshida, one we have called a *pot-pourri* of relatively subjective references that he blithely lumps together.

Yoshida's contemporary, Murano, calls to us through the variety of his inspirations, that run the gamut between Art Nouveau, Art Deco, the modern, and the traditional according to the programs and periods of his long career. Often thought of (with good reason) as a commercial architect, or more ambiguously as an architect of commercial programs, it is sometimes difficult to distinguish between the real talent he shows in some of his work and a propensity for a certain stylistic eclecticism. Nonetheless, he proclaims his feeling for traditional architecture in most of his residential work and in certain programs such as hotels, tea pavilions, and tea houses. His is essentially a subjective practice, in so many words, in which he feels free to borrow from all cultures, including his own. Indeed, he makes no claim to theorizing his references to the past in Yoshida's overblown manner, but instead plays in his own personal manner at recreating a Japanese architecture. In an interview, he speaks simply of "my Japanese architecture" that he learned from rubbing elbows with artisans in his native region of Kansai.[138] He also quotes Izumioka Sōsuke 泉岡宗助, his mentor as a youth, reading the rules to apply in conceiving a house: "An entry should not be large (…) the exterior (of the house) should appear small and low, the interior large and high (…); the ceiling height should be 7.5 *shaku* (2.25 m), except for the space for preparing meals (…); a square post should be 3 *sun* (9 cm) on a side (…); the posts of the *engawa* should be spaced one *ken* apart (… etc.)." Even though he is an architect, he expresses himself somewhat like an artisan, who refers to his construction recipes without argument, based on the practical and sensible knowledge of his subject, the tradition of construction.

---

[137] See the first pages of Tanizaki Junichirō 谷崎潤一郎, *Inei raisan* 陰翳礼讃, 1933; English edition: *In Praise of Shadows*, translated by Thomas J. Harper and Edward G. Seidensticker (Stony Creek: Leete's Island Books, 1977).

[138] See the interview with Murano Tōgo 村野藤吾 in *Murano Tōgo wafū kenchikushū* 村野藤吾和風建築集 [Collection of *wafū* architecture by Murano Tōgo] (Tokyo: Shinkenchiku-sha, 1978), 103.

fig b33. Murano Tōgo, Kasuien annex, Kyoto, 1959
fig b33-a. exterior view from the garden
fig b33-b. exterior view from the entry

This ease with charming designs, as well his superficial facility for exchanging one set of influences for another, is particular evident in the Japanese-style annex Kasuien 佳水園 that he built in 1959 for the former Miyako Hotel in Kyoto (fig. b33). Hidden behind the large mass of the main part of the building, with its heavily westernized construction, and also designed by Murano, this little annex in the Sukiya style is nestled against the mountain that lies at the edge of Kyoto looking like a surrealist collage. Even if the intent to please the client was a purely commercial one, the intelligence at work in drawing up the annex is undeniable. Keeping within the play of references, its overall plan conforms to the "flying geese formation" inspired by the Katsura Villa (fig. a44). But here the rooms have replaced the *shoin*, and the peripheral galleries (*en*) have been transformed into access corridors. But these changes have more profound consequences. They transform the relation to the exterior, because unlike the *shoin* at Katsura that open on to the gardens through the *en* or *engawa*, here the rooms turn their backs on the garden and face the city. The reference is thus purely a formal one, without retaining any of the original spatial relations. In the center of the courtyard that is hemmed in by the corridors, the architect has placed a gravel garden with a low grassy bulge in the shape of a gourd (*hyōtan* 瓢箪), a good luck motif that he borrowed for the occasion from the Sanbōin 三宝院 temple of the Daigoji 醍醐寺 monastery, located south of Kyoto. While Murano clearly demonstrates his formal facility in the composition of the whole and in the proportions of buildings topped by very shallow sloped roofs—only made possible by the metal details of the framing—the concept relies on a free adaptation of forms from the past, understood only as simple geometrical motifs that the architect has chosen according to his own inspiration.

The career of Taniguchi, the last of the protagonists we will discuss here, touches upon our subject in more ways than one. He was both a faculty member of the Tokyo Institute of Technology as well as a practitioner. Relatively unknown today, he occupies a remote position in relation to the modern movement in Japan, but an important one in the tangle of relations he maintained. He was a classmate of Maekawa Kunio's at the University of Tokyo, a colleague of Horiguchi Sutemi's in an association of adherents to the tea ceremony (*sadō kenkyūkai* 茶道研究会), professor of Shinohara Kazuo with whom he shared the role of outsider, and father of architect Taniguchi Yoshio 谷口吉生 (b. 1937). He was also tied to Itō Chūta, who sent him to Berlin in 1939 to oversee the construction of the new Japanese garden at the Embassy of Japan for him. This also clarifies one of the lessons that informs all the careers of these architects. Whether they turned momentarily to tradition or not, they were all linked to direct knowledge of the West. Taniguchi was no exception to this rule. His educational and industrial buildings that preceded his trip to Berlin were in a pronounced modernist vein, even a rationalist one, that evoked Gropius and the Bauhaus: very strict, white cubic volumes pierced by large glazed planes, strongly emphasized structure, etc. But his exposure in Berlin to the neo-classical architect Karl Friedrich Schinkel (1781–1841), and through him to the beauty of Greek architecture caused him to call the modern architecture of his time into question through two central ideas: the relation of architecture to its milieu (*fūdo* 風土), and the timeless quality of beautiful "form" (*kei* 形). As far as Taniguchi was concerned, Schinkel translated into the present the ideal beauty inherited from the Greeks, and like him, one must remain contemporary while rediscovering the formal principles of one's own culture.

Once the war years were over and he was back in Japan, Taniguchi was able to put his ideas into practice with the 1947 memorial to the writer Shimazaki Tōson 嶋崎東村 (1872–1943) (Tōson kinendō 東村記念堂, fig. b34) in the mountain village of Magome, a stop on the main

fig b34. Taniguchi Yoshirō, Tōson Memorial, Magome, 1947
fig b34-a. entry portico
fig b34-b. memorial gallery
fig b34-c. statue of Tōson

central road, Nakasendō 中山道, which connected the capital Edo to the Kansai across the Japanese alps, in the Gifu region. With the exclusive help of artisans and local residents, who had formed an "Association of the *terroir* and its friends" (Furusato to tomo no kai ふるさと友の会) he created a modest wood structure building on the very same location as the house where Tōson was born, which had been destroyed in a fire. All the materials were locally sourced and the actual foundation stones from the original house were reused in the courtyard that served as a forecourt-garden in front of the building. In addition to the fundamental characteristic of communal work, which gives full meaning to the idea of *milieu*—at once physical, geographical, and social—he employed a traditional architectural vocabulary that he revived. This search for a "form," in other words the archetype that he aspired to, comes to be defined by a long volume with white plastered walls, marked by a rhythm of black posts, and covered in its entirety by a gabled tile roof.

Although the construction is in some ways reminiscent of the elongated buildings of the *narabidō* type from the Heian and Nara periods, the architect composed the organization of the wall in relation to the interior functions of the memorial in an original way (fig. a39). He opted for a *shinkabe* principle, in which the structure of the wall remains exposed, a solution characteristic of the Shoin and Sukiya styles, but which is also closer to the modern rationalist credo of structural truth, and even to the Greek classical canons and tectonics. Yet he also innovated on the theme of the wall as measured out by structure in two ways: for one, he inserted *shōji* of different heights between the posts. This was for both functional and symbolic reasons: the interior is conceived as a long corridor with a statue of the sitting writer at the end, and these sliding panels, when one opens them, give on to a memory garden. The latter affords a view of a simple grey-gravel surface with stones floating on it—the only remaining vestiges of the previous building that burned down. On the other hand, Taniguchi allowed himself to contradict the regularity of the bays by burying the last set of posts behind the plaster so as to extend the apparent length of the white volume. He also arranged another sequence between the memorial and the street. While the building and garden are sited perpendicularly to the street, he placed two parallel screens in a row running along its length. The first of these, which serves to close off the site, is a long wooden palisade painted black, interrupted by a door framed by a monumental portico. Inspired by the earlier control points for travelers taking the Nakasendō road, the door brings the role of the original house to mind. The second screen, placed a few meters back in the plot, is a massive wall finished in white plaster, which creates a chicane and hides the memorial from the street.

While the wooden palisade recalls those of Shintō sanctuaries such as the Ise shrine that reinforce the sacred quality of the place, the wood here is painted black, not left unfinished. This composition is a dramatic and entirely modern abstraction, both in its contrasts between materials and between colors. For a visitor who knows little about architecture, the project simply appears to be an ensemble inspired by tradition that is difficult to pin down by epoch and that evokes a writer from the past in a poetic manner. For the more erudite visitor strolling between the different spaces, it is a work that strikes one by its subtle shifts between a certain primitivism that combines architectural principles derived from historical examples, and a modernism that mythicizes to the place. According to the architect Kuma Kengo, there is "almost nothing" to this project, but according to the historian Fujimori Terunobu,[139] this "almost nothing" makes all the difference and gives the place a timeless quality.

[139] See the interview between the architect and the historian published in Taniguchi Yoshirō 谷口吉郎, "Taniguchi Yoshirō no sekai" 谷口吉郎の世界 [The world of Taniguchi Yoshirō], *Kenchiku bunka* (September 1994): 232–35.

fig b34-d. exterior view of the memorial from the entrance
fig b34-e. exterior view from the garden

CONTEMPORARY SUKIYA ARCHITECTURE: AN EXCEPTION TO THE RULE?   259

fig b34-f. entrance to the memorial

fig b35. Zangetsutei pavilion, Omotesenke house, Kyoto, 1594

Two other projects, one by Taniguchi and the other by Murano, will round out this review of the relation to tradition in which wood plays a central role, even if that role needs to be linked to other actors in this relation. Like Murano, Taniguchi was not content to simply construct buildings out of wood, and there is always in his work a powerful and modular structural expression, beyond functions and dimensions, which unifies his work—a quality absent from the work of the former. They are contemporaries with each other, but do not have any particular relations, even though they have both built several tea pavilions. This type of space, this program one might say, was already described in our first chapter, and constitutes despite its small size, one of the most original archetypes of Japanese spatial culture. Today, it is often fixed in its forms and is an especially instructive example for addressing tradition, its spirit, and its rules; in other words, where is contemporary creative freedom to be located when one is copying existing and ancient prototypes directly?

Here we are particularly interested in different ways of seeing on the part of very dissimilar architects confronting the same case study. One year from each other, in 1969 for Taniguchi and 1970 for Murano, they were each commissioned to design complexes of this type in commercial buildings in the heart of Tokyo, based on a play of explicit references. Both were constrained by pre-existing plans: in Taniguchi's case the ninth floor of a small building with an octagonal plan, located along the edge of the Shinjuku station, and for Murano, the orthogonal structural grid of the rooms at the Imperial Hotel in the Hibiya neighborhood. In both cases, and even though the projects consisted only of interior architecture, the two designers treated the access path, *roji*, as if it were located in a garden. Their compositions included a small pavilion of the *koma* type (between 2 and 4.5 tatamis) for intimate and sober ceremonies, and another more spacious room of the *hiroma* type (more than 4.5 tatamis), that can accommodate ceremonies for larger numbers of guests. For their respective *koma*, Tanaguchi's Kakiden 柿傳 copied the Rokusōan 六窓庵 pavilion, relocated from its original location in the gardens of the Tokyo National Museum (based on the principle of a three-tatami *koma* and a *daime-datami*, fig. a49). Murano's Tōkōan 東光庵 did the same with the Yūin 又隠 pavilion of 4.5 tatamis (fig. a51) from the Urasenke 裏千家 tea school, located in Kyoto and imbued with the spirit of Sen no Rikyū, one of the founders of the tea ceremony and its architecture. As for the *hiroma* of the two authors, they draw on the same reference: the celebrated Zangetsutei 残月亭 of twelve tatamis (fig. b35). That pavilion is one of the principle constructions of the Omotesenke 表千家 school, Urasenke's neighbor, and the other great house devoted to preserving the legacy of Rikyū.[140]

Without going into a lengthy analysis of the original works, all of them going back to the last years of the sixteenth century and the first half of the seventeenth, or to Rikyū, the primary founder of the archetypes, we should still note the similarities and the differences in the approaches of the two designers (fig. b36). We should note that from the outset neither of the two objected to taking part in this exercise, calling for a display of one's knowledge of the model and the mastery of its interpretation. This play between rules to adhere to and creative freedom can seem restrictive at first to a western creator, but it constitutes the very spirit of this manner of creative conception. It is true that the archetype is fixed, but on one hand it is freely chosen, and on the other Taniguchi and Murano assembled *koma* and *hiroma* pavilions they had chosen from different locations and by different authors; they subsequently adapted

---

[140] Horiguchi Sutemi also built his own version of the same Zangetsutei pavilion for the Zangetsu no ma 残月の間 room of the Hasshōkan 八勝館 restaurant, built in a Sukiya style, in Nagoya in 1958. See Itō Teiji, *The Classic Tradition in Japanese Architecture: Modern Versions of the Sukiya Style* (New York-Kyoto, Weatherhill-Tankōsha, 1972), 50–67.

fig b36. variations on the Zangetsutei pavilion
fig b36-a. Taniguchi Yoshirō, Kakiden pavilion, *hiroma*, Tokyo, 1969
fig b36-b. Murano Tōgo, Tōkōan pavilion, Imperial Hotel, Tokyo, 1970

these different archetypes through original combinations in a different context (a hotel or an apartment building instead of a garden); and finally, they redrew the pavilions with slight adaptations to their designs, transforming them in effect, which created a shift between the model and its new form.

The educated user can judge later the prowess at work in this balancing act between respect and adaptation, and it is precisely here that the differences between the two authors come into play. While they brilliantly reinvent the access path (*roji*) within the constrained spaces allocated to them, their approaches to borrowing differ. As he did in his Kasuien hotel annex in Kyoto, Murano plays rather freely in his references. He introduces a lighted ceiling into his version of the Zangetsutei and makes the *jōdan* two-tatami step disappear (space of *jōdan* or *jōdan no ma* type, fig. a47). Not only does he eliminate this platform, but he also replaces the tatamis with planks and completely redraws the elevations of this zone in order to adapt his plan to the adjacent *koma*. Even if the design of the ceiling was elegant, its presence is incongruous in a room meant to maintain some level of obscurity. The elimination of the raised *jōdan* piece and the two-tatami space may not bother today's visitors (primarily foreign tourists staying at this grand hotel) who have come for an introduction to the tea ceremony, and it even allows for an increase in the number of guests, but it makes the room lose its meaning. Taniguchi is more meticulous, working instead as a scholar on behalf of a circle of tea enthusiasts far more enlightened than the visitors to the hotel. He not only keeps this platform, as it initially served as an elevated space for the guest of honor to sit—for Toyotomi Hideyoshi in the original pavilion created by Rikyū for the Jūrakudai palace, since destroyed—in a grand *hiroma* space better suited to receive the nobles of the period in comfort. He went so far as to return to the original version by placing three *shōji* at the end of this same space, while the current Zangetsutei in Kyoto only has two, as a result of an accident and a later repair.

These few examples clarify more precisely the debate in Japan over tradition and this contemporary Sukiya style, whose title often papers over untimely differences in attitude. Murano helps himself with brio to a tradition that he knows in a formal manner, using it as a toolkit of motifs in order to set up scenery. Yoshida has his backward-looking visions of the past, even though he takes advantage of the resources of modern technologies, with a residue of nationalism. Horiguchi and Taniguchi, who have little taste for the two previous examples, advance in their projects and ambiguities what Kenneth Frampton will subsequently formulate as "Critical Regionalism," that attempt to anchor modernity in stories, in places, and in different milieus.

A PARTICULAR STORY

fig c1-a. street view of the EFEO Center in Kyoto, 2014

AN EXAMPLE FROM TODAY

"Sensibility is born from words. One cannot feel something that has no name."[141]

On the twenty-eighth of June 2013, with the summer humidity of Kyoto barely cooled by a light breeze coming off the nearby mountains, some thirty people are gathered under a red-and-white striped tent set up on a small cleared site in the northeast part of the city. They are attending a propitiatory Shintō ceremony (*jichinsai* 地鎮祭), whose intent is to appease the local divinities in view of future construction. At the request of the construction company, two priests from the nearby Yoshida sanctuary, dressed in the bulky clothing (*kariginu* 狩衣) that originated in the Heian period, in cool-colored blue-and-green pastels, proceed with the ceremony. Each in turn—the client, the project manager, and the entrepreneur—lop off the top of a small cone of earth topped with a branch of *sakaki* 榊, using a shovel, a spade, and a hoe. Once the divinities have received their offerings, the priests purify the cardinal points of the plot with sacred saké, salt, and rice—or in this case with confetti to symbolize them. Then each participant lays a branch of *sakaki* on the altar, before sharing a cup of saké. This brief account describes the first steps prior to erecting a building in Japan, be it public or private, that are still followed today, even if the state refrains from invoking any specific liturgy, in order not to favor either Buddhism or Shintō. The construction will be completed by the end of February 2014, in less than eight months… While the two preceding chapters sought to precisely define the essence and originality of wood architecture in Japan, yesterday as well as today, this last chapter addresses the same theme through a specific example: the construction of the École française d'Extrême Orient (EFEO) Center in Kyoto (fig. c1).

The choice of this project was dictated by two considerations. First of all, it was conceived and carried out under the supervision of two of the authors of this work, with the Mikan architectural design office (Mikan-gumi みかんぐみ) giving them special access to the creative sources and the different agents of its construction. But the essential reason for this study was that the building's spatial and structural principles, as well as the choices of materials and assemblies illustrate so many aspects of contemporary Japanese architecture and its dialectical relationship born from the confrontation of local tradition and the modernity imported from the West at the end of the nineteenth century. Beginning at that time, and even more so after overcoming the scarcity of materials tied to the war and the defeat of 1945, most construction abandoned the wooden post and beam principle which had generally been the rule previously, with the notable exception of the single-family home, some religious architecture, and some types of public buildings. The primary cause of this changed situation is to be found in the westernization

---

[141] "La sensibilité naît des mots. On ne saurait sentir ce qui n'a pas de nom," Sekiguchi Ryōko 関口涼子, *Nagori* (Paris: POL, 2018), 21.

fig c1-b. ground breaking ceremony (*jichinsai*)
fig c1-c. the Director of the EFEO, Franciscus Verellen, lopping off the top of the earthen cone with a spade

of Japan, which affected all socio-cultural and economic domains of the country after 1860, starting with the upheaval of the political system. After almost 220 years of authoritarian closure to foreign influence (1639–1854), the new Meiji government from its founding moment in 1868 confirmed the opening of the country that had already begun with the previous Tokugawa shogunate under American military pressure. This new reformist thinking recognized the politico-economic superiority of the West, encouraged the importation of technologies and technicians, teachings and teachers, laws and regulations, and by extension the culture these brought along. During this initial technical (as well as economical) catch-up period, as Basil Chamberlain noted in 1905, the Japanese had doubts as to the validity of their tradition. That professor of Japanese and philology at the Tokyo Imperial University wrote at the time that even if one comes across occasional persons interested in the old traditions, or others that "secretly cherish" the sabers they have inherited from their ancestors, or even those who practice the traditional arts (tea ceremony, *ikebana*, or Nō theater), these traditions are still all being lost. According to him, "educated Japanese are done with their past. They want to be someone or something different from what they have been, and to some extent still remain."[142]

In the realm of architecture, these changes affected views of the historical legacy, both in terms of styles and techniques, and raised questions as to the future Japan to be built. With the new techniques and materials, such as brick, metals, and later, around 1895, concrete—whose use became more widespread starting in the 1920s—new spatial concepts, and new agents overran the field of construction. Even today, many cultural, technological, and regulatory factors from that time continue to shed light on the status of wood construction, with very distinct influences on contemporary Japanese architecture. The EFEO Center in Kyoto was thus conceived as a contemporary example of design thinking expressing a local construction ontology rather than a simple wood building that could have skirted issues of identity. In other words, our example is the result of careful consideration of local conditions of production, all the while avoiding the elusive imagery of "Japan-ness." At the risk of seeming hackneyed, let us call this concept *regionalist*.

---

[142] Basil Hall Chamberlain, *Things Japanese. Being Notes on Various Subjects Connected with Japan. For the Use of Travelers and Others* (London: John Murray, 1905), 2.

fig c2. Kigumi Infinity. Detail of wood assemblage (*kigumi* 木組), Kitagawara Atsushi, Japanese pavilion (Expo Milano, 2015), reconstruction for the "Japan in Architecture" exhibition, Mori Art Museum, 2018

HISTORY AND CULTURE

MASTER TO MASTER: CARPENTERS AND ARCHITECTS

Until the Meiji era (1868–1912), Japan basically only knew wood post and beam construction. The few exceptions that called on other techniques were the imperial tumuli (*kofun*) of antiquity, the fortresses of the medieval period (whose foundations and retaining walls were built of stone), or some buildings built from stacked timbers (such as the storehouse for writings, *kyōzō* 経蔵 of the Tōshōdaiji temple 唐招提寺). These constructions were thus conceived and constructed by carpenters (*daiku* 大工), whose central and unifying role in the development of buildings resembles that of the master masons of medieval Europe. The carpenters were responsible for the general concept and the erection of the structure, but were content to represent any plan as a simple grid with the axes and posts inked onto a plank. This simplified drawing without dimensions (*itazu*), which only shows the abscissas and ordinates, provides a figure of both a structural schema—the grid—and an organizational one—an assemblage of modular rooms (fig. c3-a). Descriptive sketches were also drawn on a plank or borrowed from carpentry manuals (*hinagata-bon*) and were used to resolve the complex assemblies of the roofs (figs. 5, c3-b, c3-c, c3-d). Other tradespeople joining the carpenters literally dressed the construction skeleton. The main artisans were the maker and installer of *tatami* (*tatamiya* 畳屋), the joiner for the sliding panels (*tateguya* 建具屋) of paper (*shōji* and *fusuma*), the cabinetmaker who made the built-in furniture (such as the stepped drawers, the shelving, and storage units), the mason (*sakanya* 左官屋) who set up the cob walls and coated them, and the tile setter (*kawaraya* 瓦屋) who fabricated and installed roof tiles, as well as other craftsmen, who attached cypress weatherboarding or thatch to finish off the roof.

Before the Meiji era, neither the general contractor nor the architect as understood in the West since the Renaissance actually existed, although with the development of the Sukiya-style tea pavilions at the end of the sixteenth century, some of their creators (such as Rikyū, Oribe, or Enshū) gained recognition and claimed the role of form-giver that we have described in the first chapter. At that time, some master carpenters seem to have advanced a claim to the role of artist too.[143] Even so, the sudden appearance (the importation one can say) of this new actor went beyond the simple change of title and had multiple impacts that are still visible today: a relative and long-term lack of interest on the part of most architects in traditional construction (and wood construction by extension), as well as a new separation between the act of designing and drawing on one hand, and that of carrying out and building on the other (acts that had heretofore been shared by the same artisan).

---

[143] Jean-Sébastien Cluzel and Nishida Masatsugu, "*Kenchiku* 建築 l'architecture," in Bonnin, Inaga, and Nishida (eds.), *Vocabulaire de la spatialité japonaise*, op. cit. (2014), 250.

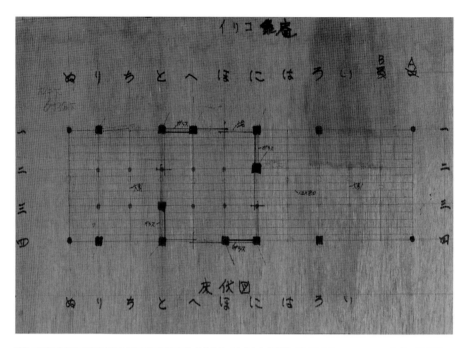

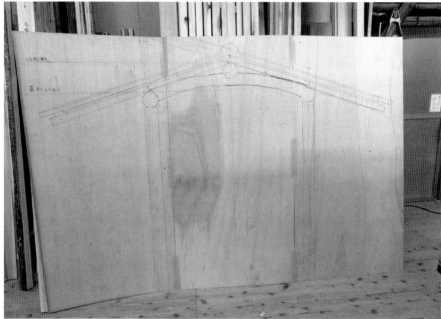

fig c3-a. *itazu*, "drawing on plank"
fig c3-b. descriptive drawing of a portico at full scale. Nakamura Sotoji Workshop, Kyoto, 2014

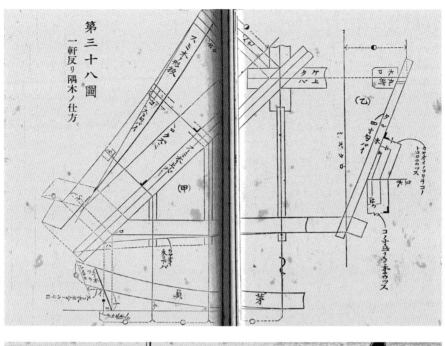

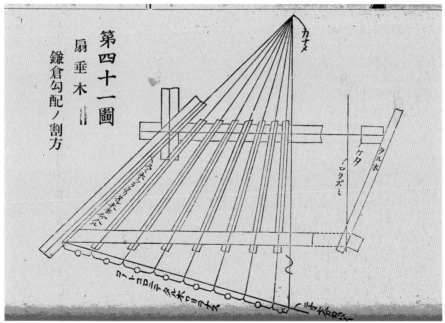

fig c3-c. descriptive drawing of a *sumigi* angle rafter, drawn from a construction manual, Kameyama, 1918
fig c3-d. descriptive drawing of a fanning rafter *ōgitaruki* "in the Zen style of the Kamakura period," Kameyama, 1918

In this new division of competencies, what were the roles of those two key individuals, the architect (*kenchikuka* 建築家) and the carpenter (*daiku*)? The Meiji government was obsessed by the idea of modernizing the country and its image, and it began by emphasizing the Western contribution to many domains, including education. Architects and engineers were thus trained in new university programs rather than in a construction culture based on detailed knowledge of local traditions. The education of the new Japanese elites was conducted by studying Western architecture under foreign masters, the second and most famous of whom was Englishman Josiah Conder, who began his course in 1877 at Tokyo Imperial University. Factories, headquarters for private companies and banks, railroad stations and other large public buildings that were shaping the public face of the country had little in common with the legacy of religious or profane architecture in wood in the minds of the clients or the creators, the architects who first began to practice in the 1880s. For them, the old wooden buildings belonged to an outdated vernacular history, whose possible charms could hardly serve to edify a new country.

Another notable difference was that the separation between architect and carpenter implied a dichotomy between conception and realization. For some time, the survival of technical know-how and the implementation of framing and other construction methods (including knowledge about different species of wood in relation to their required function—structure, partitioning, secondary construction, decoration, built-in furnishings) had rested on the shoulders of framer/carpenters. Moreover, as we have seen in the preceding chapter, one of them, Kiko Kiyoyoshi, began teaching the history and theory of Japanese architecture in 1886 at the very same university, in the absence of architects and historians with the capacity to do so. But more than an exhaustive understanding of the styles, it called for studies of the construction and proportioning systems (*kiwari*) practiced by the carpenters.[144] Aside from wood frame houses—which are predominant much as they are in North America—which they had never ceased drawing up, the renewal of interest on the part of certain architects remains limited or recent and relies on the know-how of construction companies.

The current status of these two avocations of architect and carpenter illustrates the ambiguity of the changes that occurred at the end of the nineteenth century. It is useful to specify more clearly their respective attributes. Since the Edo period, the term *daiku* has included a number of different practices, all specialized in wood construction but different in kind and complexity. Some of the main ones are: the simple carpenter who conceives and builds vernacular buildings (the *wataridaiku* 渡大工, who helped villagers build farms in the countryside), and who might also be itinerant; the *machidaiku* 町大工 or *machibadaiku* 町場大工, who worked on urban buildings, including the city houses; the more skilled *miyadaiku* 宮大工; and the *sukiya daiku* 数寄屋大工. The former specialized in larger buildings, primarily temples and shrines, while the latter concentrated on rich and very refined residences in the Sukiya style.

Despite the fact that the carpenter's scope of work has been reduced since the Second World War with the development of metal and concrete structures (considered more fire resistant by populations traumatized by the bombings of 1945) and enforced by laws that prohibited the use of wood in multiple zones defined by the construction code, the trade has still not disappeared as a result. Today, carpenters are usually employed by general contractors or by builders of private houses. Aside from the construction of smaller buildings, in an unexpected

---

[144] Benoît Jacquet, "Between tradition and modernity. The two sides of Japanese pre-war architecture," in Kohte et al. (eds.), *Encounters and Positions: Architecture in Japan* (Basel: Birkhäuser, 2017), 226–37.

development, they also work on the fabrication of wood formwork for building designs out of concrete that can include complex geometries and still eschew metal formwork. Thus, one can claim (as paradoxical as it might appear), that the achievements in formwork for exposed concrete in the archipelago, which have been such a source of pride, owe much to the carpenters. The architects who work with this material devote much of their talents to the careful layout of the wood panels and the formwork holes. We should also remember that the standard size for wood panels is 182cm by 91cm, which brings us back to the proportional rules of the *kiwari*.

The *miyadaiku* and *sukiya daiku* continue to exist and are highly respected, despite their marginal position in a narrow and very specialized market. The former contribute to the maintenance of a significant religious patrimony as well as the occasional but rare new creation, while the latter maintain the existing residential patrimony and create new houses that are entirely or partly in a style inspired by tradition, either the Shoin or the Sukiya—the very styles that often serve as illustrations in the West of the stereotypical and minimalist Japanese house. In reality, contemporary Japanese regulations have mitigated the dichotomy between concept and construction that was imported and established in the nineteenth century by granting the status of architect to a number of trades. Two types of professional licenses can be obtained (architects of the first or second category), based on practical experience and education, and after passing an examination. The second license in particular gives the bearer (very often a carpenter or builder of private houses) the right to design and build wood constructions less than three stories high, a category which perfectly encompasses residential architecture. So even if the contrary is more rarely the case, the carpenter has become somewhat of an architect.

… 2021, SPACE ODYSSEY

Until the Meiji era, Japanese architecture was characterized by the exclusive perpetuation of the post-and-beam construction system, whose consequences so struck modern architects by its apparent modernity, starting with the German Bruno Taut in the 1930s. Its characteristic features were an open, fluid, and standardized space, and the separation between structure and internal divisions. Although we need to put this interpretation of traditional Japanese space as a precursor to modernity in architecture in proper perspective, we must recognize its influence on many contemporary designers.

Despite differences in function and size, as well as stylistic variations, the construction systems described in the first chapter have always been built with an un-triangulated skeletal structure, in other words, without diagonal bracing in the walls or roof, but consisting only of orthogonal posts and beams. These assemblies are for the most part built from four-sided sections, with the transition from round shafts to squared elements taking place towards the end of the Heian period. These structures supported large and projecting gabled or hipped roofs, whose trusses were constructed without principal rafters or struts and were most often achieved by a series of stacked collar beams. The foundations consisted of posts driven into the soil or rested on stone mountings to prevent their rotting. The floors were raised for the same reason, a principle that is widespread in the humid and tropical southeast of Asia. Walls of cob, either coated or plastered over, were attached to a bamboo trellis core tied together with grasses and freely inserted between posts in both directions, thus stabilizing and bracing the ensemble. The connections between posts and beams consisted of mortise and tenon joints that were often complex, and which contributed to the rigidity of the framing. As bracing by walls occurred only occasionally, non-bearing partitions were inserted between posts—with shutters, swing doors, and (towards the end of the Heian period) sliding doors that were sometimes translucent in the case of white paper *shōji*. Although the structural principles were not the only determining factor, they allowed for "porosity" between adjacent rooms as well as between inside and outside as mediated through the exterior galleries. But technique alone does not suffice in characterizing this traditional wood architecture, for its carpenters had also developed an ensemble of original and consequential references. Previously transmitted orally and through practice, these ancestral techniques were applied through the intermediary of the *kiwari*, a stereotomy of wood whose rules were systematized towards the end of the sixteenth century, as we have seen in chapter one. In other words, it was a system of modular proportions of which the interval between posts (*ken*) was a part, which we will return to.

The passage to a written form of transmission of know-how seems to have first occurred in the fourteenth century through the manuals of carpentry (*hinagata-bon*) which were kept secret and served primarily for the apprenticeship of workmen within a single workshop, like the medieval professional guilds in Europe.[145] Along with direct apprenticeship onsite and paper or wood models, these were the primary vectors of the methods of carpentry (see note 6). The first works in this genre were published, and subsequently disseminated by virtue of the growth of woodcut impressions at the beginning of the Edo period, in the seventeenth century. At that time, the definitive political stabilization of Japan inaugurated a long period of construction, including among other things, the founding of the new capital Edo (the former name of Tokyo), whose population reached one million inhabitants in less than a century.

And yet, like any language, this system (*kiwari*) required an alphabet. What were the units of measure that expressed these principles and their dimensions? At the end of the Asuka period (sixth to eighth centuries) and under the cultural influence of Tang China, Japan imported a particular system of measurement, whose primary units were the *sun* 寸, the *shaku* 尺, the *jō* 丈, and later the *ken* 間. At its origin, a *sun* was approximately the size of a thumb, or approximately 3 centimeters, a *shaku* the width of a hand (the distance between the thumb and the index or major finger) of approximately eighteen centimeters—before it grew to some thirty centimeters, closer in size to a foot or a cubit—and a *jō*, ten *shaku*—in other words close to three meters. As for the *ken*, it was a polyvalent term which originally signified the space between two posts, and eventually supplanted the *jō*, becoming the very measure of the interval that it was meant to define, or ten *shaku* in the Heian period (eighth to twelfth centuries). As was pointed out earlier, in the first chapter of this work, *ken* and *ma* are two readings of the same ideogram 間, which also serves to form the words for space (*kūkan* 空間) and time (*jikan* 時間) For our part, we will use the reading for *ken* that refers concretely to the notion of the interval or spacing between two posts and a unit of measurement at the same time.[146]

By the Kamakura period (twelfth to fourteenth centuries), the *ken* had been reduced to seven and a half *shaku* as a result of rationalization, economies of construction, the increased scarcity of resources in wood, and successive proportional determinations. The *ken* was further reduced to six and a half *shaku* or six *shaku* in some regions during the Edo period (seventeenth to

---

[145] William H. Coaldrake, *The Way of the Carpenter: Tools and Japanese Architecture* (New York-Tokyo: Weatherhill-Heibonsha, 1990), 38–41, 139–40.

[146] Manuel Tardits, "*Sun-shaku-jō-ken* 寸/尺/丈/間 les mesures," in Bonnin et al. (eds.), *Vocabulaire de la spatialité japonaise*, op. cit. (2014), 468–70.

nineteenth centuries). At that point the *shaku* was broken down into ten *sun*, each of them subdivided further into smaller decimal units, the *bu* 分 and the *rin*. These measures were applied to all construction continuously for centuries, despite a certain variability which lasted until the twentieth century, no doubt due to the lack of any central authority capable of imposing a coherent system on all the regions, as well as the resistance of practitioners to share the secrets of their specific workshops. It was only in 1886 that the official conversion to the international metric system permanently set their size: among other things, the *ken* was set at 181.818 cm, or six *shaku* of 30.3 cm (*see* chapter one). But although the metric system became the norm for concrete and steel construction, carpenters nonetheless continued to use traditional notation in wood construction until the 1960s. The true changeover occurred in 1966, when the law insisted that all measurements in *ken* and *shaku* be abandoned, and imposed the metric system on all drawings and contract documents.

These twists and turns would only be of historical interest if they did not implicate an entire system of proportions, which was a particularity of the architecture of wood. *A contrario*, the final and recent abandonment of this system and the translation from one set of units to another entailed a loss of meaning to dimensions, to their relations, and their use. As an initial consequence, architects rounded off their measurements to simpler decimal dimensions on their plans, since they would otherwise be too complicated in the metric system. But this was initially done in the spirit of maintaining *shaku* dimensions, along with their subdivisions. Subsequently, as time and generations passed, they forgot the proportions whose intrinsic features were no longer clear when the measurements were written up in different units. In order to see the fundamentally radical quality of this change and to concretely apprehend these difficulties, one has but to compare the plans for two houses drawn up by Shinohara Kazuo, one of the great masters of residential architecture in the second half of the twentieth century. Among his houses, described in the second chapter, are the "House with an Earthen Floor" (*doma no ie*, figs. b24, c4). Its plans are expressed in *shaku* and *sun*, and these convey simple and clearly repeated dimensions. On the other hand, in the celebrated "House in White" (*shiro no Ie*, figs. b25, c5) the relation to the vernacular habitat (*minka*) is still clearly maintained, but the measurements translated into millimeters seem excessively precise, and their relations are no longer as clear. Shinohara and his carpenters who built this latter house appear to remain aware of the original meaning masked by the notation in millimeters, but for later generations who use only the metric system, the next step was the disappearance of dimensioning linked to the *shaku* (figs. c4, c5).

Today in 2021, interest in this epic story of construction is essentially limited to historians and some artisans involved in construction. Carpenters still use the *shaku* as naturally as the centimeter—their rulers most often include a double graduation—as do those of other masters of traditional arts such as gardens or tea houses, as well as lovers of a patrimony that may also include architects. Contemporary creators are not unaware of these terms or measurements. But they use them in a pragmatic manner to estimate the dimensions of a room or an arrangement of these same rooms like a puzzle, instead of using them as tools for drafting their plans or for deliberate references. For example, it is easier to visualize the size of a parallelepipedic space of ten tatamis or of three *ken* by two than a more or less equivalent space of thirteen square meters (42.6 sf), and even more so if one has most likely lived in this type of space. Beyond this, architects rarely refer explicitly to these spatial systems and their subtleties, and even if the term *tsubo* (3.3 square meters or 10.8 sf, a square with the same area as two tatamis) is still used in real estate and property transactions, this is again for pragmatic reasons.

fig c4. Shinohara Kazuo, House with an Earthen Floor, construction drawings, 1963

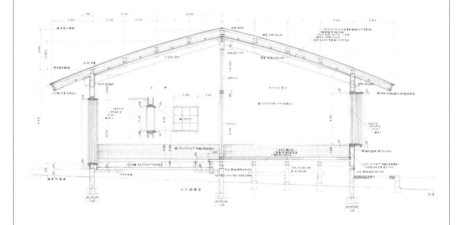

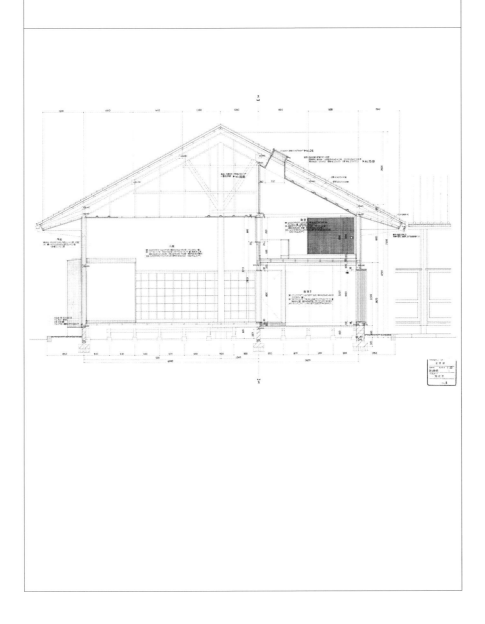

fig c5. Shinohara Kazuo, House in White, construction drawings, 1965

TWO ASSOCIATES: *KEN* AND *JŌ*

A Relative Modularity

Until 1966, architecture in wood—and especially residential architecture—continued to be governed in its measurements and proportions by the relation between stereotomy and the interval between posts, *kiwari* and *ken* (the latter measuring 181.8 cm). The semantic flexibility of this latter term, as the spatial concept of an interval and as its dimensional unit—both bay and span—had in fact facilitated its variation in time and place. In order to better understand the intrinsic qualities of its double meaning, it is useful to compare the *ken* to the bays that provided rhythm to the naves of Western cathedrals. As a standardized bay, the *ken* changed over the course of nine centuries (from the eighth to the seventeenth centuries) from a span of ten *shaku* to six and influenced the size and form of spaces. And yet, like two kingdoms in the same land, two main competing zones persisted over the course of three more centuries, from the seventeenth to the nineteenth. In the first zone, the *ken* was counted out as six and a half *shaku* and called *kyōma* 京間 or *ken/ma* of Kyoto and was developed in that city and region. In the second zone, the *ken* was taken as six *shaku* and called *inaka ma* 伊仲間 or country (*inaka*) *ken/ma* and *Edo ma* after the new capital Edo. The law ended up deciding in favor of the latter in 1886 when it established the correlation with the metric system.

This final geometric uncertainty of a half shaku (approximately 15 cm) between the two zones derived in part from the appearance of another element that has become in the meantime representative of Japanese architecture: the tatami/*jō*. Initially it was a simple mat placed on the plank floors (*itajiki*) of wealthy residences in the Shinden style during the Heian period. The tatami (*jō* 畳), whose size fits a single stretched out human body or two seated individuals, became increasingly thicker and more rigid over time. It ended up replacing wood floor boards altogether by covering whole rooms in aristocratic *shoin* residences starting in the mid-fifteenth century. This newcomer measures approximately 1.82 meters by 91 centimeters, or approximately one *ken* by a half *ken*. Coming after the *ken* that had always defined the size of rooms, the tatamis in turn became essential modular elements governing the size of the rooms whose floors they covered. They inserted themselves between those posts and in turn influenced their spacing. So if the *ken* can be compared to a span, the tatami/*jō* is more like a tile or "brick." All four shared a meaning and constant role, but whose dimensions varied, yet they were dedicated to standards and proportionality.

As we have just indicated, the Edo period was marked by the existence of two principal and competing zones regarding the spacing of posts. The reasons are two-fold: the construction economy and the extent to which the tatami was adopted in dwelling spaces. In other words, a drive for economy conjoined with a competition among different components of spatial structuring (*ken* and *jō*), led to two different forms of resolution to this dilemma which was social, conceptual, and geometric all at once. In Kyoto, with its many aristocratic residences, the tatami—a recent element that functioned as a symbol of prosperity, even of modernity—spread to the bourgeois habitat. It then influenced the size of the *kyōma* (the *ken* of the six and one half *shaku*). In the countryside, on the other hand, a more economical construction based on the smaller grid of six *shaku*, the *inaka ma*, produced smaller rooms, and the spread of the tatami, which remained relatively costly compared to wood plank, proved to be less widespread (figs. c6, c7).

In both of these geographical areas, the carpenter as well as the tatami layer sought to promote a certain standardization[147]. Thus, once the structural skeleton had been set up on a regular grid, along with the roof and wood floor, the tatami installer came to assess the rooms between posts and partitions, without forgetting to verify his measurements by triangulating these same rooms—a step rendered necessary in order to confirm the actual shapes of the rooms, that were not always perfectly orthogonal—before fabricating and laying down his mats, whose dimensional variations he sought to keep to a minimum. While there is a clear consistency to the square rooms, particularly one of the most common—the eight tatamis/jō generic rooms—this will to rationalize did not preclude a multiplication of mat modules, as our illustrations show. Notwithstanding slight geometric inconsistencies, this "unfinished" standardization significantly facilitates the overall spatial comprehension of the rooms and their combinations, despite any differences of a few small *bu* more or less.

The rooms are thus named either according to their number of bays or by the number of tatamis, although the latter calculations are by far simpler and more frequently used. It is much easier to say that a room is eight tatamis in area than to say it is two *ken* by two. The reasons for this are pragmatic: the tatamis provide more useful numbers for the users, and they are simpler to perceive than the structural dimensions. The readings of the latter are often more complicated, because a post does not occur at every *ken* (figs. c6, c7). But the language of the tatami is also a source of confusion, as it generally refers to standard dimensions of 6.3 *shaku* or 5.8 *shaku*, that are the most prevalent in the *kyōma* and *inaka ma* zones respectively. And as is frequently the case, simply speaking of tatami as if they had only one standard size contradicts all the plans.

Intercolumniation and Center-to-center Distance

Another ambiguity results from authors confusing the role of the tatami as well its installation by considering it an element that structures space—a role it does in fact share with the spacing of posts—but also as a possible preliminary step towards construction, a function that it does not serve.[148] There is also talk of two principles for the formation of Japanese spaces of the Shoin and Sukiya styles: the *uchinori* 内法, based on the intercolumniation or space between posts, and the *shinshin* 真々, based on their center-to-center distance (fig. c8). In this schema, the first principle regulated the zone for the large tatamis of the ancient capital Kyoto (*kyōma*) due to the primacy of the tatami over the flooring, and thus a repeated and standardized mat ruled the structural regularity. The prior and intangible dimensions of these "bricks" resulted in forced but slight variations in spans or intercolumniation. According to this *uchinori* principle, the work of the tatami installer using a single module, whose location within the same room can vary according to the season and that is frequently replaced, is facilitated as a result. The carpenter, on the other hand needed to plan for slight variations in the location of posts from the outset, whose small offsets are a function of the number of mats in a room and their arrangement.

---

[147] In addition to tatamis in the *kyōma* and *inaka ma* zones, which were the most widespread, there were other such as the *Edo ma*, the smallest one, in the region of Edo (Tokyo) as well as the *chūkyōma*.

[148] Mizuki Cruz-Saito, Masatsugu Nishida, and Philippe Bonnin, "Le tatami et la spatialité japonaise," in *Ebisu-Études japonaises*, no. 38 (Fall–Winter 2007), 76–8. The article clearly expresses the "to-and-fro" between the parts and the whole, as well as the absence of theoretical thought in the construction methods of the carpenters, but it does not recognize the sequence of tasks. *See also* Jacques Pezeu-Masabuau, "*Shinshin/uchinori* 真々/内法 la mesure entraxe/intérieure," in Bonnin et al. (eds.), *Vocabulaire de la spatialité japonaise*, op.cit. (2014), 438–40, which also tends to confuse the practical application of the two principles.

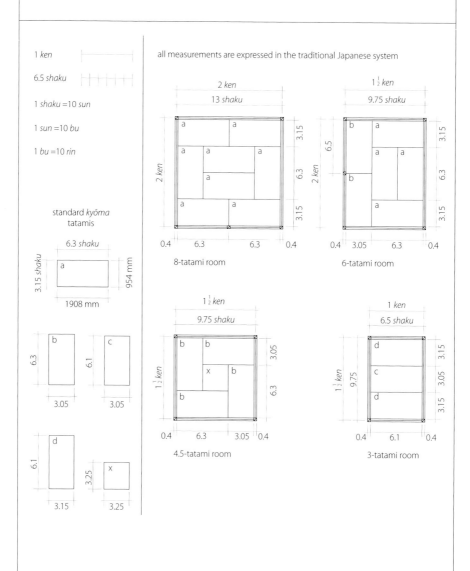

fig c6. *kyōma zone*

size of tatamis and typical rooms

HISTORY AND CULTURE   283

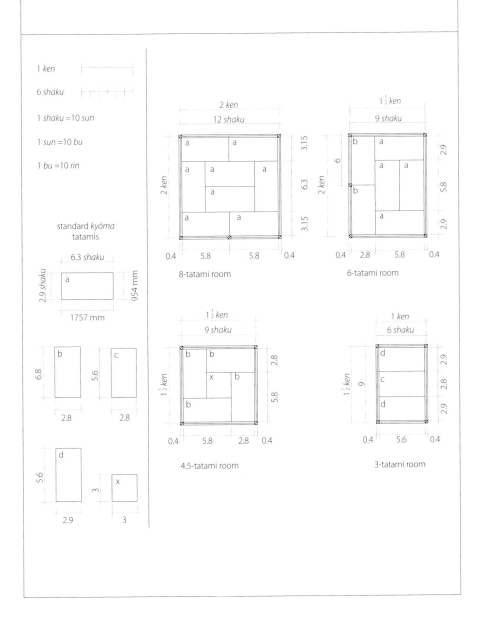

fig c7. *inaka ma* zone

size of tatamis and typical rooms

On the other hand, in the *inaka ma* zone in the countryside, where the tatamis are scarcer, the carpenter's order has the upper hand, with its bays established on a regular grid at the outset and set at the center points of the posts. This is the *shinshin* principle. Here the mats were trimmed ("recut") so as to fit in this rigid structural framework. This rigorous approach to the structural grid consequently facilitates the work of the carpenter.

For practical and socio-historical reasons, let us put in perspective the explanations, often taken up in the West, whose rationality seems to be both theoretical and influenced by ideology. Precise measured plans of buildings almost always reveal small discrepancies in the regularity of rooms and various elements such as structure, tatamis, and sliding panels. These variations have several concrete causes. It has always been and still is unusual for carpenters, despite their skill, to achieve perfection in their grids, and the wood itself can expand or contract. During the course of construction, the measurement of the rooms by the tatami craftsman, a prudent artisan who seeks to bring the mats he will have created in his workshop in keeping with the variations in dimensions, provides the proof. Another reason is that constructions most often consist of a combination of tatami rooms and wood-floored ones. So, with such hybridity, why favor an *uchinori* principle, founded on the tatami module alone? Finally, there is a tendency to think of the Japanese house in generic terms as an autonomous building set in a garden. But in dense urban contexts like Kyoto, buildings for the most part occupy the full width of the plots. Although these are set by property grids, they also affect the modular regularity of the rooms, even if the lateral corridor (*tōri niwa*) of town houses (*machiya*) can absorb some of these irregularities in its width. But at a deeper level, this abusive theorization reflects a modernist vision and analysis of traditional Japanese construction, considered as a precursor to contemporary industrial rationalization, while also confusing architects with carpenters. In terms of the system of production, this explanation misjudges the division of roles on a construction site, the sequence of tasks, and the rationality specific to each agent.

So what is the role of the carpenter, and how does he work? The conceptual work of this master builder is essentially inseparable from the act of construction. His drawings consist of simple structural and organizational schemas (size, position, relations between rooms) in plan form, the *itazu* (fig. c3-a). He does not bother with sections—which is no doubt one of the reasons that Shinohara wrote that the concept of space did not exist in Japanese construction[149]—except for certain details, like the roof awnings. The geometric difficulty of the projecting roof in temples and sanctuaries, consisting of corbelled capitals (*kumimono*) and rafters superimposed on curves, forced the master carpenter (*miyadaiku*) to consult the manuals (*hinagata-bon*) and to make full-scale descriptive construction drawings as well as templates (*tawamijaku* 撓釈) of these parts. Aside from these cases, the carpenter's "plans" sufficed for him to visualize the ensemble out of current construction, to evaluate the number, location, and size of the rooms, to size the different wood structural elements, evaluate the costs, communicate with the other tradespeople, and to consult with and obtain approval from the client. This practice stemmed from his role as designer-builder. It clearly differs from the manner a modern architect proceeds. An architect is a designer first and foremost and seeks a general spatial rationality before handing over the working drawings to contractors, who partly redraw them during construction.

---

[149] Shinohara Kazuo, *Jūtaku kenchiku*, op.cit. (1964), 34 and *Shinohara Kazuo*, op.cit. (1996), 61, translated in fig. b26, chapter 2, supra.

fig c8. two principles

Sequence and actual practice of *shinshin* principle construction

Shinshin (center-to-center) and *uchinori* (intercolumniation) principles

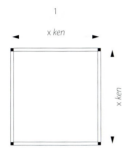

Actions of the carpenter: placing posts on a grid based on multiples of *ken*

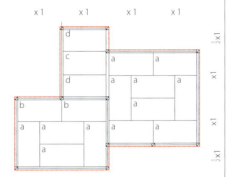

shinshin principle:
the tatamis are inserted into a regular structural grid. Aside from the 8-tatami room, the tatamis vary in size.

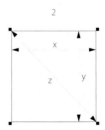

Actions of the tatami installer: measurement of the rooms with triangulation, after the posts are set, in order to verify their precise sizes and to rationalize the fabrication and installation of tatamis (number and dimensions)

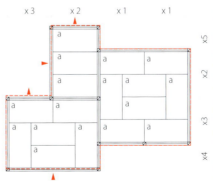

uchinori principle:
the tatamis are fixed in size. In the rooms adjoining the 8 tatamis room, the structural grids are offset.

Although the drive to reduce the variations in tatami size is at work, particularly in the urban zone of Kyoto (*kyōma*), where they became prevalent, the true master builder of construction, the one who manages what one would call today the building fabric and the construction site as a whole, has always been and still remains the carpenter. In the course of construction, the tatami only comes after him, just as the tile layer comes after the mason. The theoretical and rational difference between the two principles, intercolumniation (*uchinori*) or on-center (*shinshin*) has little bearing on the working methods of these two artisans. The tatami installer works on a series of rooms that have already been constructed and verifies their dimensions to locate the usual slight deformations. This meticulous adaptive work does not call into question the general division of the rooms and their surfaces—broken down into numbers of tatamis—whose basic layout has already been agreed on and specified in the carpenter's plans.

On the other hand, obliging the carpenter to account for all the small adjustments inherent in the principle of intercolumniation (*uchinori*) on his plates (*itazu*) would entail additional work, with the potential for error outweighing any real gain in quality. The choice of tatamis is linked more to the goal of reproducing a standard module whose rigor is relative, and whose "faults" are invisible to the untrained eye. It is far from a perfectly modular system in which the rough construction and finish construction would fit together with the precision of architects' drawings and perfect prefabrication. We can leave the use of centerline dimensions (*shinshin*) to the framing carpenter and the intercolumniation (*uchinori*) to the tatami installer and the cabinetmaker who makes the sliding partitions. These two terms serve primarily to qualify two practices, two logics that form an unproblematic sequence over the course of the construction. All of these dimensional vagaries underscore over and over the useful but relative character of standardization—the part left to the artisan as well as the primordial role of the structural system in wood that regulates space.

The dilemma between the tatami and the structure extends beyond the Japanese framework and illustrates one problem that all architects confront. While many of them like to rationalize the structural grids, who does not know the inverse example of architects who despise cutting bricks or cinderblocks—Swede Sigurd Lewerentz or Frenchman Roland Simounet are prime examples—who endow them with a sort of original modular essence to be preserved? What architect has not looked to manage tiled surfaces without cutting into the modular pieces when the partitions had already been located on the plans, or even already built?

Proportionality

In this space conceived through harmonious concurrence, rooms are located and structured by the number of spans—one, one and a half, two, two and a half, and three *ken*—given names, and quantified by their number of tatamis—three, four and a half, six, eight, sometimes ten or twelve *jō*, or even more. Furthermore, the simple spans between posts remain short. The most frequent are one and a half *ken* (2.73 m) and two *ken* (3.64 m). One occasionally comes across three *ken* (5.45 m), as in the reception room *kōnoma* of the Nishi Honganji temple in Kyoto. In this typological register of rooms, it is wood and its system of proportions (*kiwari*) and not the tatami, that sets the dimensional standards that govern the different spatial and constructional elements.

Consider the example of a residence from the Edo period based on a module of 1.82 m (a *ken* of six *shaku*, slightly rounded off) (fig. c9). The square posts are typically four *sun* (12 cm) on a side. The overall height between the two main horizontal structural elements, the eaves purlins (*noki-geta* 軒桁) and the groundsill (*dodai* 土台), is two *ken* (3.64 m). If one then looks at how the heights are composed or broken down amongst themselves, one finds in sequence: a clear height under the lintel of five *shaku* and eight *sun* (1.757 m); a lintel/upper sliding track (*kamoi*)—with notches for the rails of the sliding panels—of one *sun* nine *bu* (5.75 cm), a false lintel/frieze rail (*nageshi*)—a decorative element running around the room, located over the *kamoi* and evoking the structural lintels (*nageshi*) that were to be found in temples—of four *sun* eight *bu* (14.54 cm). The ceiling heights are thus made up on one hand of the sum of the three elements referred to above—six *shaku*, four *sun*, and seven *bu* (1.96 m)—and on the other hand, a fascia (or transom window) of varying height as a function of three *sun* (9 cm) multiplied by the number of tatamis of the room; thus, nine *sun* for a three-tatami room and thirteen *sun*, five *bu* (40.5 cm) for a four-and-a-half-tatami room, etc.

By adding these figures together, one arrives at respective ceiling heights that increase with the surface area of the rooms; seven *shaku*, three *sun* and seven *bu* (2.23 m) for a three-tatami room, seven *shaku*, eight *sun* and two *bu* (2.42 m) for a four-and-a-half-tatami room; eight *shaku*, two *sun* and seven *bu* (2.5 m) for a six-tatami room; eight *shaku*, eight *sun* and seven *bu* (2.68 m) for an eight-tatami room, etc. Similarly, different manuals give the standard dimensions for wooden elements making up the sliding panels such as the sections for the *shōji* frames, the window frames and thresholds, the depth and thickness of the decorative shelving (*tana*), their spacing, etc.[150]

Two final remarks apply to this orderly coordination of dimensions. First of all, there is a mixture of unchanging dimensional values and others that evolve or are proportional. This is a fairly logical economic choice, if one takes into account that the former apply to standardized construction components, while the latter are only concerned with spatial relations, such as those that link the size of rooms with their ceiling height. Furthermore, one understands better why carpenters were content to draw a simple schematic plan on a plank (*itazu*) in order to construct a building.[151] Since the assemblies were regulated by the different sizes of tatamis (*inaka ma* and *kyōma*), there was no need for sections or elevations. In most cases, the master carpenter simply needed to locate the various rooms and their respective sizes on the grid, identify structural points with known spans, and know certain details of the roof projection and joints that were already tried and tested, as described in a manual or by a descriptive drawing (figs. c3-b, c3-c). The other trades came in turn to cover the primary structures or to fit in between the members, with some small adjustments. Thanks to this efficiency in construction and its conceptual simplicity, all creative energies could go into subsequently refining the construction itself, along with the choice of materials. This is not a merely inconsequential story, for it has marked Japanese spatiality over the long term, and still does today, albeit in a more discreet manner.

[150] Heino Engel, *Measure and Construction of the Japanese House* (Tokyo: Tuttle Company Publishing, 1985), 27–33.
[151] Paper or wood models called *okoshiezu* 越し絵図 are other design tools, but they are rarely used. The paper models are built around a plan, with flaps for all the vertical elevations except the ceiling. Thus one can see a plan with its interior elevations lying flat, or the exterior form of a room or series of rooms when they are up. These are primarily used for tea pavilions (*chashitsu*), but their function is less about helping the carpenter in their construction than for making it possible to apprehend the subtle variations in space and the different moldings of the interiors. The wood models, the oldest of which date from the Nara period, are usually at the 1/10 scale. They are remarkably precise and aid the carpenters in understanding the difficulties of construction in larger buildings, particularly pagodas or dungeons.

fig c9. the *kiwari:* a system for setting proportions

variations in the ceiling height as a function of the number of tatamis to the room

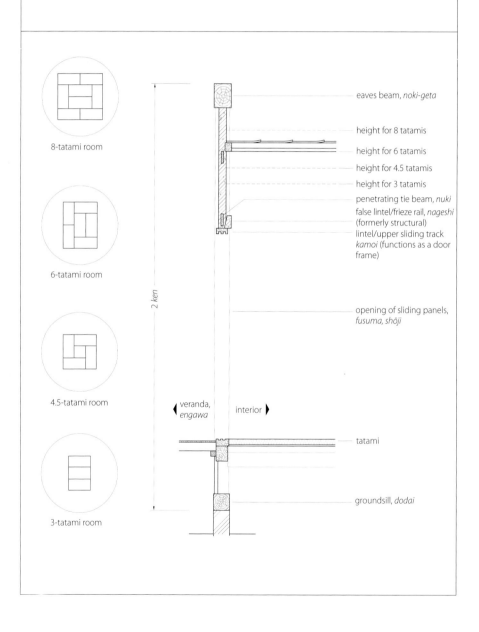

But today, post and beam systems have become one set of options among others, and the international spread of information and techniques has resulted in making the same kinds of assemblies available in Europe, America, and in other Asian countries: triangulated, doubled or sandwiched, with struts, three-dimensional trusses, American balloon framing, prefabricated structural panels with dry construction, etc.

STABILITY

Certain choices linked to the stability and structural rigidity of traditional building can at first sight seem puzzling. In a country with unstable soil conditions, why are foundations so minimal, diagonal structural bracing pretty much absent, and bearing posts so slender in comparison with the heavy beams of framing that does not have a principal rafter?

The Foundations

Archaeological excavations have sometimes revealed the existence of piles in the foundations of buildings from antiquity—several dozens of bases for posts at the Chikamori site in the Shiga prefecture, dating from 2,000 to 2,500 years BC—proof that this method had been known and used since long ago. But most often, however, posts rest on stones whose surface they fit exactly. The advantage of this method is that it avoids the rapid rot of the base of the post. This remains a point of fragility in construction, as is attested by the frequent existence of replacement assemblies for ruined lower parts. And from a more fundamental structural point of view, it is a frequent choice to let a building "float" on the surface of ground that is subject to frequent earthquakes—like one of those great wooden boats that ply the surface of the water without damage—rather than anchoring it more deeply.

The Missing Triangulation

The absence of diagonal bracing in partitions, combined with the limited number of walls, can seem *a priori* to be a structural anomaly in a post and beam system, although even today more stringent building regulations do not specifically require triangulation over other means of bracing. In residential programs, for example, contemporary architects often prefer the use of structural plywood panels in vertical as well as horizontal partitioning. This absence is due to an empirical intent to promote some level of ductility or flexibility capable of absorbing shocks rather than resisting them. It seems difficult to imagine that Japanese carpenters, so expert in geometric construction, could have not been aware of the physical properties of triangles. Nor was the use of struts (*hōzue* 方杖) altogether unusual. But regardless of the function or the epoch, this architecture always relied on orthogonal assemblies, with few exceptions. The distribution of forces in these two directions exclusively prioritized stability over stiffness.

When one examines closely the construction principles of the coated or plastered cob walls of the large religious buildings, the temples and shrines, or the grand homes of the nobility in the Shinden style, one notices a tendency to multiply the encircling elements that tie or strap the construction together: starting from the bottom, one finds the horizontal groundsills (*dodai*) that tie the bottoms of the posts together, continuous structural lintels (*nageshi*) and penetrating tie beams (*nuki*) in the walls, and finally the eaves beams (*keta*) at the beginning of the roof (figs. a33-d, a35, a36, c9). In addition, carpenters favor framing with collar beams (more flexible) over trusses with a principal rafter, even if the former requires larger pieces of wood to permit strong joints between post and beam.

The thin Post

While the posts in certain buildings can appear thin, it is first necessary to distinguish between the function and size of buildings, and whether they are religious or residential in purpose. Starting in the medieval period and the birth of the Shoin style in architecture (towards the fifteenth century), the size of dwellings was significantly reduced, compared to the palaces of antiquity in the Shinden style, whose typologies remained similar to religious buildings. The spans between posts were limited, or even fixed—most often 2.7 m or 3.6 m, in other words one *ken* or one and a half *ken*. The most common post was a 12 cm square section—in other words, four *sun* by four (even if sections of 9 cm or 15 cm—three *sun* by three, and five *sun* by five—are to be found as well). These three types of posts, and especially the first, in combination with modular parts of fixed dimension enabled and were the products of a prefabrication process. The dimensions of the vertical and horizontal bearing elements and their spans, even if they were empirical in origin and codified by aesthetic intention, were considered established and reliable. Modern regulations have not modified these sections (at present 10.5 cm square section or 3 *sun* 5 *rin* also exists).

On some construction sites, especially those whose limited scope do not require building permits or engineers' calculations, the carpenter estimates the weight of the beams as a function of their size and the species of available tree trunks to make sure, for instance, that his posts of 10.5 x 10.5 cm, 12 x 12 cm do not need to reach 15 x 15 cm. Thus the prefabrication linked to modularity provides the key to dimensional choices. In the architecture of large religious buildings, the size requires heavier posts, in which prefabrication and standard dimensions play a lesser role, precisely because these are special buildings. Nonetheless, like Western builders who knew the sizes of vaults and cupolas through experience, even if they sometimes pushed them to their limits (occasionally learning those limits the hard way as in Saint Sophia or the cathedral of Beauvais), the carpenters specialized in this type of construction knew how to dimension longer spans, whose structural principles remained the same.

MATTERS FOR DISCUSSION: WOOD OR WOODS?

We have primarily addressed the structural, dimensional, and modular aspects of wood in relation to construction bays of residential scale, similar in size to the building built to house the EFEO Center, which we shall discuss below. But all of these types of architecture, be they residential or religious, have applied similar principles beyond the styles and periods, as we indicated in the first chapter. Without undertaking an exhaustive exegesis of all the features of the construction culture of wood aside from structure and dimension, we would like to address another remarkable feature: the choice of wood species, the variety and quality of non-structural work and furnishings in particular, where, as Bruno Taut wrote, "This style of work effaces the boundaries between carpenter and joiner."[152] It is still common today for the general

---

[152] Bruno Taut, *Houses and People of Japan* (Tokyo: Sanseidō, 1937), 31.

carpentry contractor to build the furniture, if it does not pose some particular difficulties in fabrication, rather than specifically going to a cabinet or furniture maker. This option is available thanks to the lower cost and the skills of the carpenters.

While construction techniques hardly changed before the twentieth century, the same was not the case for the choice of wood species employed or their application. As in other countries with a rich tradition of wood construction, the term should be used in the plural rather than the singular. It would seem more appropriate to refer to woods rather than wood. This choice, which varies by period, is a function of the construction economy, the species available and their physical properties, their religious and symbolic considerations, not to mention the evolution of technical knowledge and tools.

As the first great capitals were located in the Nara region, carpenters used conifers–"soft" woods with a fine grain and regular fiber like the Japanese cypress (*hinoki*), which grew in the mountainous forests of the south of this region–for the structures. Their tall and thin trunks were well suited for the round posts of the temples, shrines, and monumental palaces of the Heian period (eighth to twelfth centuries). In addition, their great density and mechanical properties allowed them to last until today, if they escaped the vicissitudes of history and its parade of fires. But as early as the eighth century overharvesting obliged carpenters to seek supplies as far as the western part of the island of Honshu, near Yamaguchi, more than seven hundred kilometers away from the main construction zones. Subsequently, between the fourteenth and sixteenth centuries, multiple factors linked to political developments, changes in ceremonies and living issues, the increasing scarcity of resources in wood, and progress in the carpenters' cutting tools resulted in important changes to architecture. The monumental architecture of palaces in the Shinden style built during the Heian period evolved into the Shoin style, more restrained in size. The latter achieved its full flowering in the seventeenth century, before extending to the popular habitat during the Edo period. The ongoing reduction in the size of residential construction of the Shoin and Sukiya styles, the concomitant reduction of the *ken* module which passed from ten to six *shaku* (from 3 m to approximately 1.82 m), and the passage from massive round columns to slimmer, standardized square ones are all symptomatic of this search for economy linked to an aesthetic. Without direct links *stricto sensu* to structure, other arrangements appeared as well, such as the increasing division and partitioning of large rooms, and the replacement of plank floors by tatamis that influenced dimensioning, as we have seen. Spatial elements and furniture by woodworkers proliferated, such as the *shoin*—studies for reading that supplied the name of the new style—as well as shelving and alcoves, *tokonoma*. As described in the first chapter, the advent and formalization of the tea pavilion by Rikyū and his successors also influenced the entire style of Sukiya interiors, by bringing a touch of simplicity and refined rusticity to the Shoin style through the choice and treatment of different woods.

Using available local species and properly matching them is another important component of the construction culture of the archipelago. Around the fifteenth century, the abundance of resinous woods, including red pine (*akamatsu* 赤松), as well as the use of the Japanese zelkova (*keyaki* 槻) occasionally compensated for the exhaustion of the cypresses (*hinoki*) destined for use in structures[153]. The elms are much less consistent and are difficult to harvest, but it became possible to fell them, thanks to the development of new two-person saws that came from China.

---

[153] Coaldrake, *The Way of the Carpenter*, op.cit. (1990), 130–2.

At the end of the nineteenth century with the annexation of Taiwan, it also became possible to use the cypresses of that island, similar in appearance to their Japanese cousins, as ersatz, although their mechanical qualities were not as good, which meant that their sections needed to be heavier. Today, cost and scarcity entail assembling smaller pieces of local cypress and the use of imported exotic woods, either Taiwanese—although these are becoming scarcer in turn—or African woods for the renovation of buildings that are part of the patrimony. In other places, other species: in the countryside, less expensive local species such as chestnut trees (*kuri no ki*), and black pine (*kuromatsu* 黒松) were used in the popular habitat. In the city or in secondary structures, this role often devolved to the Japanese cedar (*sugi*).[154] Contemporary construction relies primarily on imported Douglas fir (*beimatsu*) for the structural parts, and to a lesser extent to Japanese cedar, which was planted in great quantity after the war, as well as the different pines already mentioned for their more figured surfaces and frequent knots.

In looking carefully at the history of these species, the scarcity of local sources occurs repeatedly, to the renewed advantage of faraway or foreign species for economic reasons. This aspect is far from inconsequential, because if the choice of materials qualifies spaces, for the artisans, it is also a source of their claims to qualifications and their knowledge of tradition. Today, a Sukiya carpenter (*sukiya daiku*) will make a display of his craft by showing you that he can still obtain large pieces of Japanese wood of rare quality. Another observation: this culture of wood is homogenous neither in time nor in space. It varies in relation to the type of construction, and today few architects will specify the species to be used for structural purposes, as this role is usually assumed by the construction company, with its network of sources that favor foreign importation.

Finally, let us consider non-structural work in traditional architecture. The variety and refinement of this work is striking, as is the osmosis between the work of the carpenter and that of the woodworker in the frames, the partitioning: including the sliding panels (*shōji* and *fusuma*) and fanlights (*ranma*); the ceilings: coffered, trellised, or latticed; the built-in furniture: primarily shelving, alcoves, and stairs; and the devices for protecting intimacy and controlling light—such as latticed screens. Although all these elements play a part in the standardized spatial arrangements already referred to, the Shoin and Sukiya styles added a layer of complexity to the organization of rooms, as well as a refinement in materials and execution. Beyond an apparent and frequently touted simplicity, it is important to acknowledge a profound mannerism that still affects contemporary architecture. Let us lay out a panorama of the principal operations, keeping solely to wood, that comprise the rich palette of interiors.

— varying the cuts (transverse, rotary, tangential) in order to accentuate or play down the material qualities of the planks (motifs, veining, knots);
— selecting the species, even the individual tree in order to vary the appearance of the planks (flooring, doors, ceilings, etc.) or selecting certain trunks for decorative posts (*toko-bashira* 床柱)—cedar, Kitayama cedar, bamboo, pine, oak, chestnut, camellia, plum tree, cherry, walnut, and more generally all the local or exotic species available;
— expressing the particular mode of fabrication—peeled bark or not, polished finish or deliberately leaving traces of the tools (saw, adze, shears and other planes), covered with molds (*sabi*), simply delimbed, etc.;

---

[154] For a general survey of the different species of wood in Japan, *see* Mechtild Mertz, *Wood and Traditional Woodworking in Japan* (Ōtsu: Kanseisha Press, 2011), and *Japanese Wood and Carpentry: Rustic and Refined* (Ōtsu: Kanseisha Press, 2020).

—choosing the forms, textures, and colors of the posts, twisted trunks or straight, thick or thin, smooth surface, rough or twisted, silky, dark or light, brown, blonde or reddish, etc.; and— matching up the different aspects and materials of the various surfaces and furnishings, without forgetting variations in their patina.

Nonetheless, in Japan as elsewhere, solid wood is tending to disappear in the face of all the new products made from laminated woods—glulam (glue-laminated timber), and more recently CLT (Cross-Laminated Timber)— particle boards, such as MDF (Medium Density Fiberboard) and OSB (Oriented Strand Board)—plywoods, and other laminated boards whose species often come from Southeast Asia, Scandinavia, and North America. The least expensive and most frequently used plywoods are lauan and larch (*karamatsu* 唐松). Limewood (*shina* 科) is in also great demand as it is more even and more delicate in appearance. Other blond woods that are generally available include maple, ash (*tamo*), beech (*buna* 橅), birch (*shirakaba* 白樺), or the hemlock (*tsuga* 栂) native to the central or southern islands of Japan as well as South Korea. Floorboards are most frequently made of light or medium colored species, either laminated or in solid wood form, the most common of which include Japanese oak (*nara* 楢), maple, birch, or cherry (*sakura* 桜 or *kaba-zakura* 蒲桜). Cabinets and frames are often made of cedar (*sugi*) or spruce. If excellence in architectural woodworking remains alive today, it applies to a range of products and species that has been partly transformed.

fig c10. EFEO Center, Kyoto. Exterior entryway

IDENTIFICATION OF A CENTER

WHAT ARE WE MADE OF?

Japan is far from the only country to have wonderful recent achievements in the domain of wood. What interest or originality is there in deciding to build here in this material today? Why call on tradition when information is disseminated on a planetary scale, when structural systems, materials and products are substantially similar in the most industrialized countries? And what tradition are we referring to, given the evolution of styles and layouts according to function, location, and period? The architects who design wood buildings in Japan no longer refer to tradition in an explicit manner. It may be a simple economic, aesthetic, or ecological choice, rather than any historicist view, or even just one choice among many, given the plethora of techniques and references available. The project for the new EFEO research Center in Kyoto is an attempt to answer these questions in a concrete manner within the framework that we have just sketched out. Its conceptual development and construction are clearly a part of a cultural project, for reasons of affinity, economy, and symbolic intent.

PROGRAM

The École française d'Extrême-Orient (EFEO, French School of Asian Studies) was originally founded in Saigon in 1898 and was called the Mission archéologique d'Indochine at the time, before adopting its current name in 1900. Today, it includes eighteen research centers in twelve Asian countries, from India to Japan. It welcomes researchers from fields in the social sciences and humanities. The EFEO Kyoto Center, which is dedicated to the study of ancient and contemporary Japan in particular, opened in 1968 and was first housed in a temple at the Zen monastery of Shōkokuji 相国寺, and relocated to offices near the university of Kyoto some thirty years later[155]. After purchasing a plot in 2010, the EFEO moved in 2014 to its current building. This research center is partnered with numerous Japanese universities. It provides space for colloquia and scholars and houses a library of 20,000 works.

For the construction of this new facility, the program was defined in a first competition and subsequently refined with a second call for applications. It includes a lecture hall, offices for scholars and staff, a space for seminars and colloquia, a terrace for relaxation, and a bicycle parking area. In sum, it is a place for work and exchange between cultures, equipped with an oversized library; an open place, but like any research center, rendered more restricted by the degree of specialization on the part of its users; a place built to enable the study of the material

---

[155] For the history of the EFEO in Japan and the construction of the new Center, *see* the collective work, *Un siècle d'histoire. L'École française d'Extrême-Orient au Japon* (Paris: EFEO, Magellan & Co., 2014), and Benoît Jacquet, "Un nouveau Centre à Kyoto: une chronique du chantier," 21–35.

and cultural patrimony of Japan *in situ*. It is one of those symbols that Kyoto harbors, more than any other city in the archipelago, of a concrete (rather than imaginary) relation to tradition and its most contemporary resurgences.

CONTEXT

While the question of the relation between the architectural object and its environment is not directly related to the subject of wood architecture, it cannot be ignored completely. The idea that there was a greater freedom in construction in Japan than in Europe has been repeatedly raised under the pretext that there is no continuously existing urban context, and that it evolved so quickly as to barely exist, is a simplistic one. Not only is there an important body of laws regulating the relations to the immediate neighborhood and to public space, but if the lifespan of most constructions in Japan is one-half or one-third that of European buildings, the concern for integration into specific sites appears in other forms. The real difference lies elsewhere and stems from a different understanding of public space. In the historical centers of European cities—although much less so in contemporary suburbs—legislators seek to formalize public space by addressing the street and the block. Each building is considered a piece of a figure that is intended to form a harmonious and integrated ensemble. In Japan, public space is historically far less formalized. Zoning is defined in functional terms, and regulations are rarely applied to aesthetics. Most importantly, legislation considers each particular object in relation to its immediate neighbors. The floor area ratios of construction, the height limits, and views all exist in abundance, perhaps in overabundance—to the north, on the street and towards the neighbors—and these then apply to all sides of the building inside the property lines. These rules, in combination with the possibilities for setbacks from the street and for constructing detached buildings, highlight the visual independence of each construction, which leads to visual fragmentation and lack of overall unity. The building for the EFEO Center, for which we managed each of these aspects, illustrates this manner of responding to the physical and regulatory environment.

In July 2010, the EFEO decided to acquire a small plot of 149 square meters (1,600 sf) to the northeast of Kyoto, near the university of Kyoto, as well as near to the Philosopher's Path and the Silver Pavilion, in the Kitashirakawa neighborhood of the Sakyō ward. It is located in a commercial zone (*kinrin shōgyō chiiki* 近隣商業地域), according to the construction code, and as it is less than twenty-five meters from Shirakawa Avenue, the regulations permit the construction of offices around the campus of the university of Kyoto, especially when surrounded by residential zones (*jūkyo senyō chiiki* 住居専用地域). The building's allowable floor area is 357 square meters (3,840 sf), with 119 square meters (1,281 sf) coverage on the ground level—240% and 80% of the plot size respectively—and a maximum height of 10 m. Unlike many commercial zones, building in wood is permitted, but the facade needs to be equipped with a legally approved fire protection outfit that provides 30 minutes of fireproofing. The site is also part of an "aesthetic area" (*bikan chiku* 美観地区), a rare situation outside of Kyoto, that requires adherence to certain formal codes: a palette of natural colors, an inclined roof, the inclusion of planting, and more generally—a rather vague concept—harmony with the immediate context. The building is sited on a narrow and deep plot that adjoins a rear alley and is embedded on three sides: relatively undistinguished small houses on the north and south and the rear elevation of stores on Shirakawa avenue to the east. Rather than taking carefully into account the forms, moldings and trim of the immediately adjacent constructions, that are both disparate and relatively ephemeral, the Center meticulously addresses its own relations— the views, light and ventilation, protection of privacy and expressions of its public character, as well as access—on both sides.

Some simple guiding principles were followed in establishing the relations to the site. The street to the west affords abundant light, but also high heat gain throughout the afternoon. The building had to both take advantage of this exposure and afford protection from it; playing up the public side without exposing the users to the rare but extremely close passerby. On the other hand, the buildings to the east are tall and too overshadowing to allow for proper openings. The houses to the north and south are also close by, although lower and smaller, which made it possible to play with the placement of windows, on the condition of avoiding excessively direct views and taking into account the reciprocal requirements for privacy. On the third floor, it is possible to enjoy views of the horizon and see the sky, over the roofs of the area, as well as to see the ring of mountains that encircle Kyoto in the direction of Arashiyama to the west of the city. Putting the entry and a small parking area for bicycles to the south and setting back the building by one meter created a small distance from the street and a slight gain in light and air. A few openings on the east side take in the breeze from the mountain nearby and cool the inside during the summer (figs. c11, c12).

ORGANIZATION

The vertical organization of the EFEO center as built is didactic. But the rationality of the explanation *post facto* and its division into clearly laid-out chapters is the result of patient efforts of giving form to the project. Its logic is not the result of chance, but only emerged over time, like clouds that progressively expose the high points before finally revealing the coherence of the landscape as a whole. The organization consists of four juxtaposed parts that respond to the program and the context one has just described; each of them has its own function and expression. The ground floor forms the first part, with a hypostyle hall punctuated by exposed structural beams. The central columns are round in section, and their forms, texture, and species were specially chosen to reinforce the public character of this reading room. One flight up, the second part is designed as a series of smaller scale boxes, or protective cases for the scholars' studies. The structure is entirely concealed; the walls and ceilings are lined in soft-toned plywood panels to accentuate an enveloping quality, that suggests both intimacy and comfort. The third part—the top floor with the meeting and conference room, which is freed from the constraints of supporting structure that were required on the lower floors—resembles a long covered and festive hall; long transom windows free the ceiling by separating it from the wall, letting it float like a great protective canopy and affording a view of the roofs of the city and sky; placed above eye level, they do not disturb the concentration of the listeners once they are seated. The last part, established by the vertical circulation, consists of a large built-in piece of furniture that is both stair and bookcase, running up from the entry and landings with their panoramic views. It faces the street and rises up over three floors. It functions as a window display and buffer space for the Center, and as a threshold between the aforementioned spaces and the exterior (figs. c13, c14, c15, c16).

fig c11-a. schematic plan of the city of Kyoto

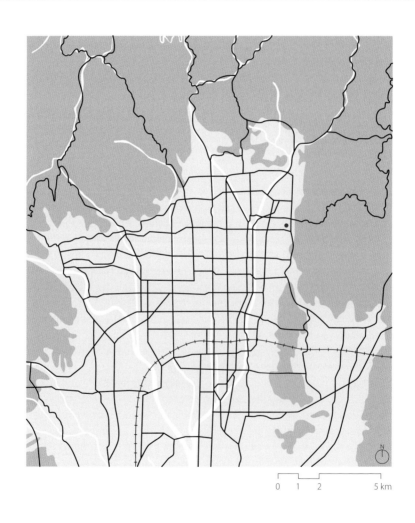

fig c11-b. Kitashirakawa neighborhood

fig c11-c. site plan

fig c12-a. street view of the EFEO Center

fig c12-b. the EFEO Center in its urban context

fig c12-c. site prior to construction

fig c12-d. site built up

fig c13-a. ground floor plan

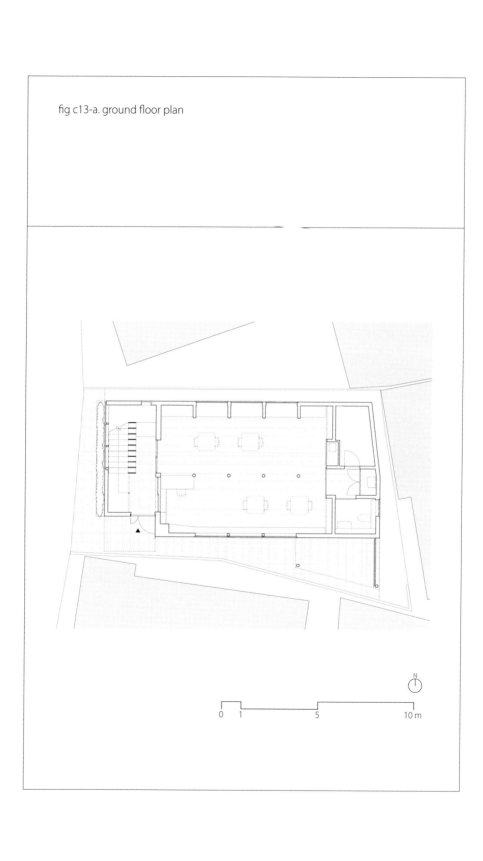

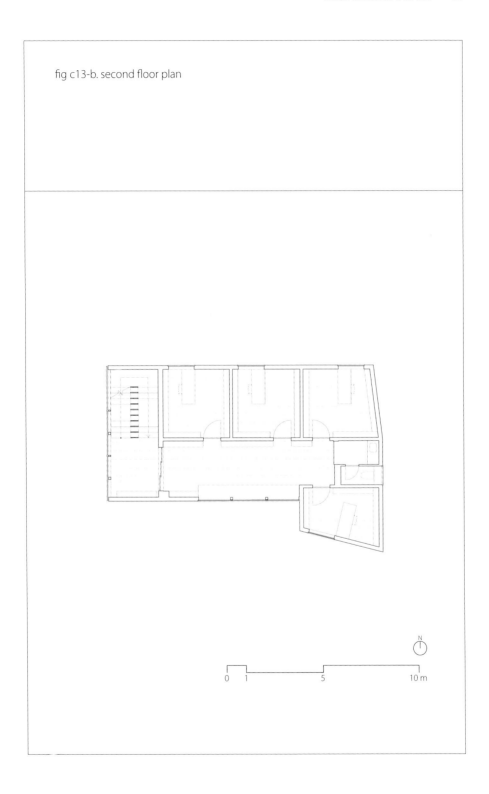

fig c13-b. second floor plan

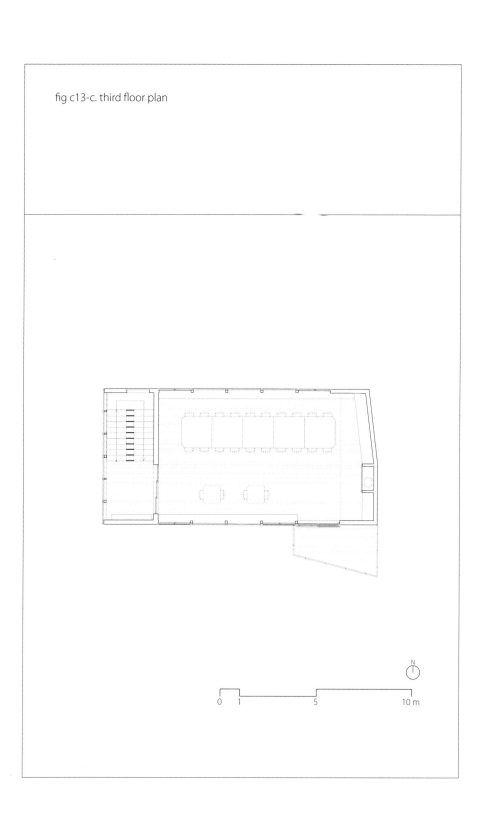

fig c13-c. third floor plan

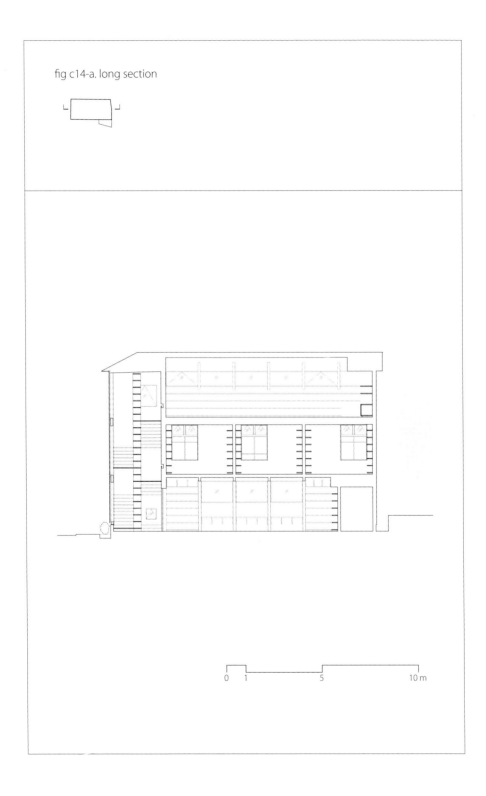

fig c14-a. long section

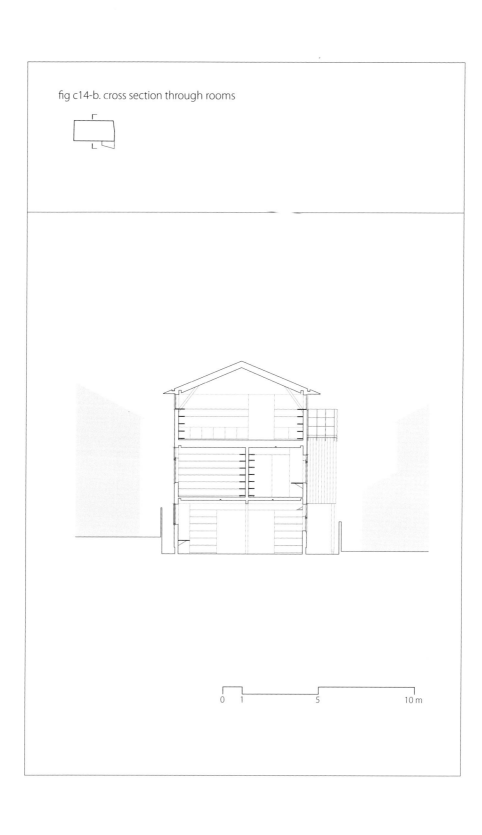
fig c14-b. cross section through rooms

fig c14-c. cross section at stair

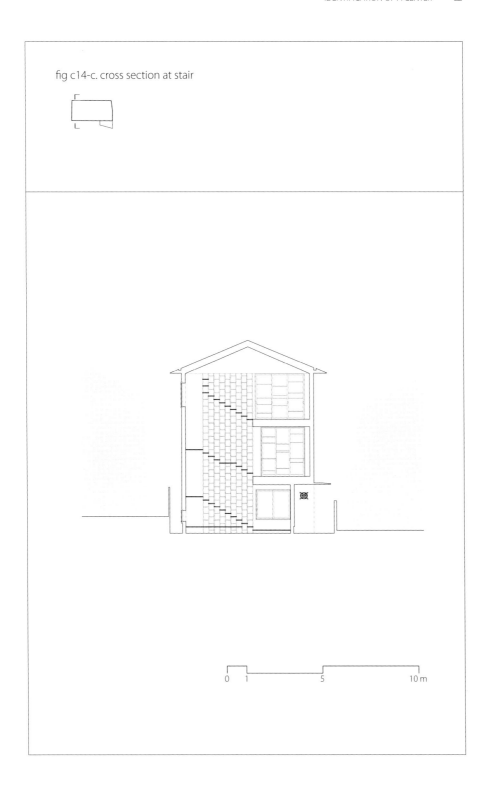

fig c15-a. west elevation at street

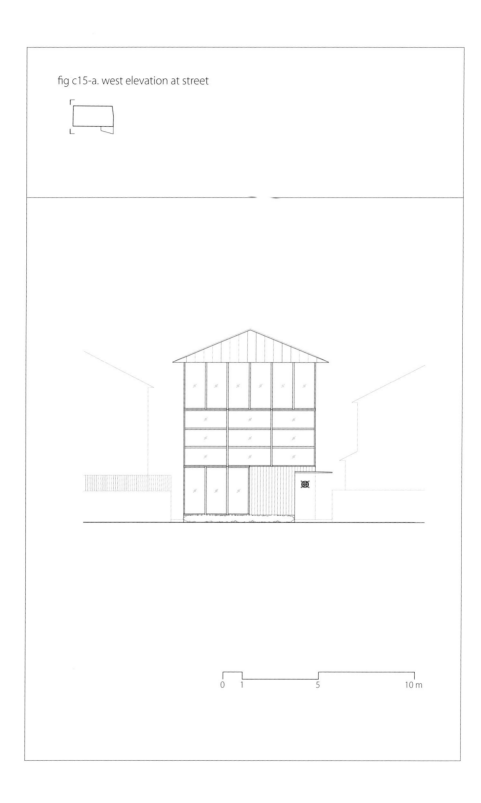

fig c15-b. north elevation

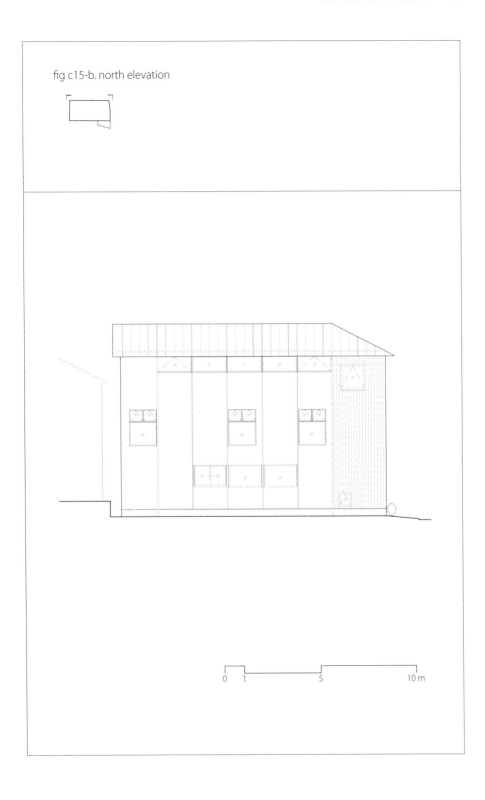

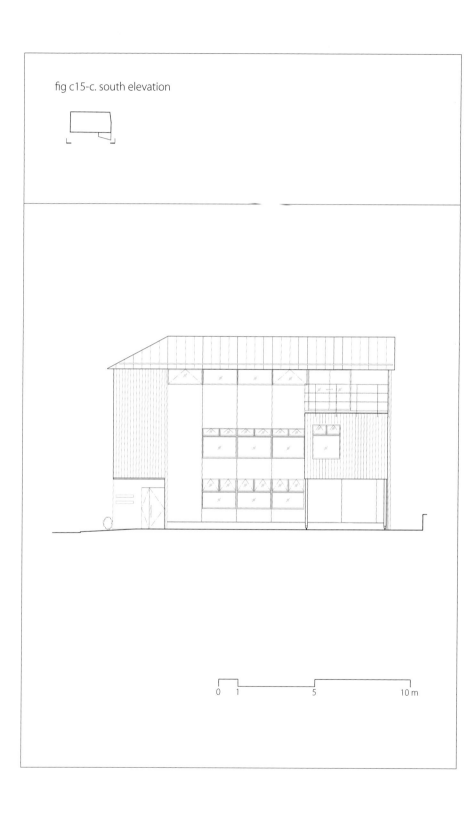

fig c15-c. south elevation

fig c16-a. overall axonometric

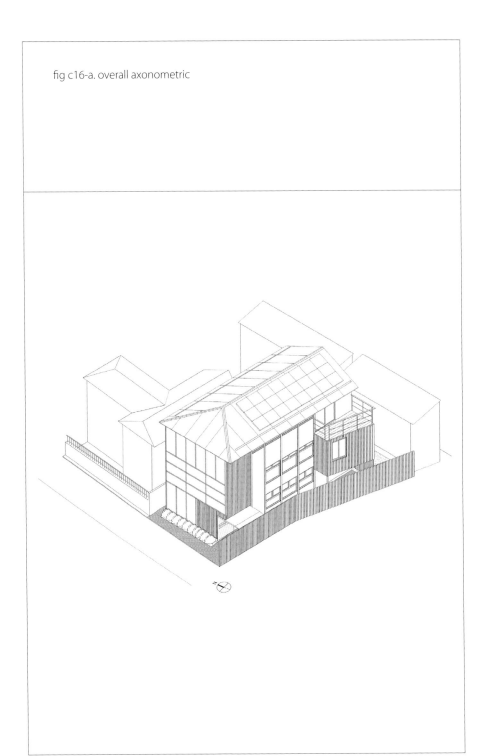

fig c16-b. the two main blocks

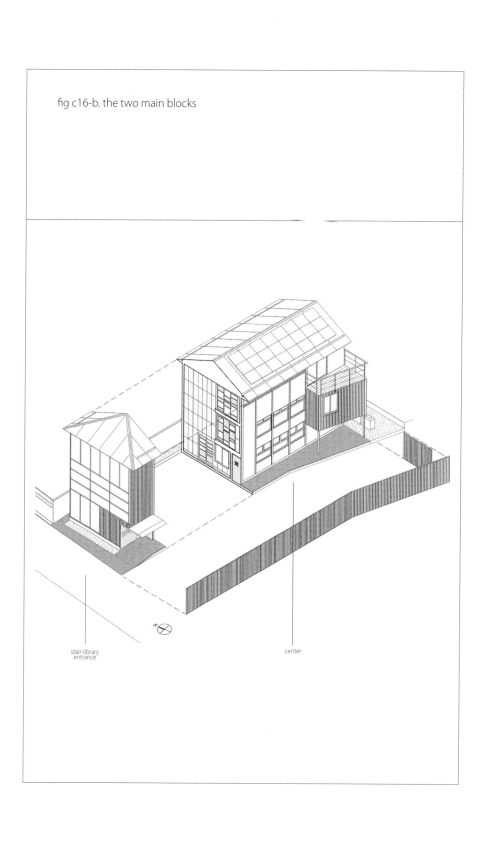

fig c16-c. the four parts

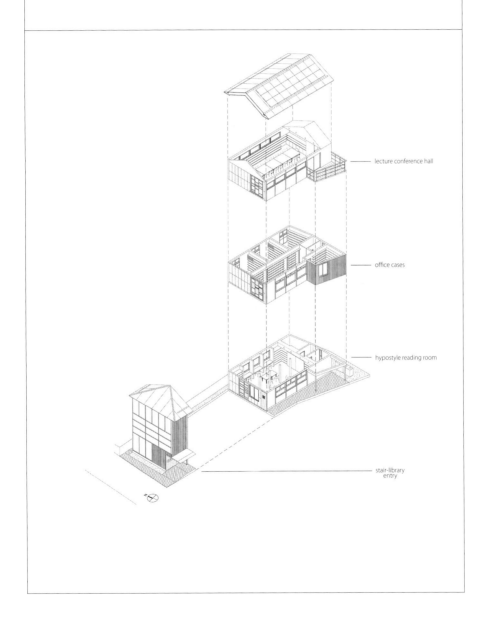

fig c17-a initial structural grid

PRINCIPLES OF AN ONTOLOGY OF CONSTRUCTION

In the first instance, the choice of wood was a matter of construction economy and sustainable development, inherently linked to the expression of a culture and a local tradition: through the project's construction system, dimensioning, choice of materials, and architectural arrangements. Our emphasis on this material is not the expression of an undue attraction to a tradition embodied by Kyoto. It is the result of an analysis of the situation: the program, context, organization, and symbolism. The new EFEO Center was the object of a first competition won by a young Franco-Japanese team, consisting of Shinsaku Munemoto & Associates (SMA, Kyoto) and Olivier Boucheron (Nelobo, Nantes). The team worked on a preliminary draft project before the client (the EFEO) launched consultations with several Japanese architecture firms to restart the plans and complete the project. One of the main selection criteria for this second phase of the architectural project was the ability to reconcile the program and planning of the first version with economic imperatives. The Mikan office found that one of the reasons for the high cost of the initial project came from the choice of the structure. During the first phase of the competition, none of the teams had considered building out of wood. And yet, as was amply confirmed subsequently, a post-and-beam system would make best use of the local resources, both physical and human ones.

GRID AND MODULES

The rather narrow and deep shape of the plot (8 m by a bit over 15 m), and the intention of having a large reading room on the ground floor, near the entry, seemed at first an argument for having a concrete or steel structure that could span the width of the site and provide flexibility for its use. This was the direction chosen by the first team. On the contrary, we counted on the competence of the local carpenters and standardized short-span wood elements. Although traditional dimensions are no longer officially used, having been converted in 1966 to the metric system as previously indicated, they continue to function in a coherent semi-industrialized process, even when the original meanings of these dimensions escape the designers. It was possible to establish repetitive bay sizes in the deep dimension of the plot (ordinate axis), starting with a first span of 2.73 m (one *ken* and a half), followed by six others of 1.82 m (one *ken*), while two spans of 3.64 m (two *ken*) across the site (abscissa axis) allowed the entire plot to be gridded out in a simple and modular manner (fig. c17-a).

These standard dimensions and short spans had the advantage of being moderately priced, and the relative inconvenience of requiring a row of posts down the middle of the reading room on the ground floor. But the disadvantage of this double span is offset by the fact that it has little impact on the functionality of the space, as the reading tables can be laid out without difficulty and with some variations in this simple parallelepiped space. On the second floor, we were able

fig c17-b. deformed and adapted structural grid

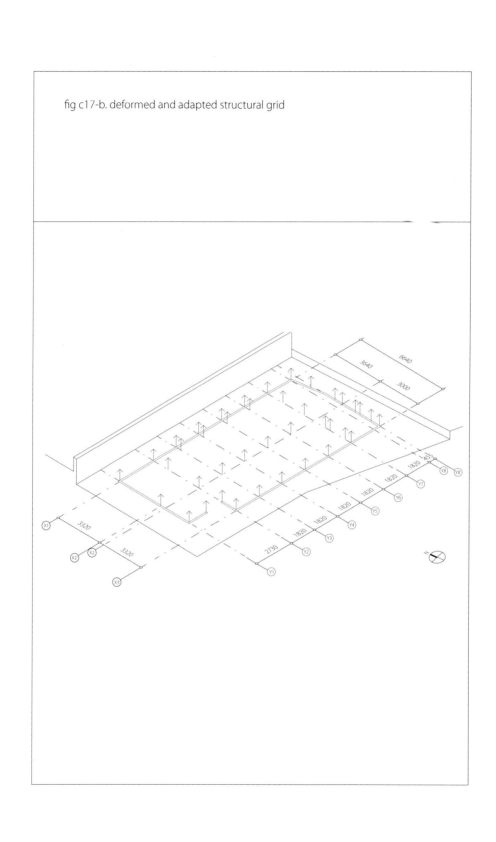

to lay out individual offices for the scholars that take advantage of the regular dimensions of the grid, giving each of them the reasonable dimensions of 3.64 m x 3.64 m (two *ken* by two, or eight tatamis in area), or somewhat greater than 13 square meters (140 sf). As the top floor only supports the roof, simple trusses with struts to brace them and reduce the depth of the beams provide a span of 7.28 m (four *ken*) without intermediate supports and free up the space for a large conference room.

DIMENSIONS, PROPORTIONS, AND EXCEPTIONS

The use of this grid could have been the result of a simple rationality of production, as it is in most wood-structure contractor houses. But like some architects in the West, who look to sublimate the simple economy of cinderblock or brick construction to establish an architectonic order, here the conscious and repeated choice of the *ken*—in the practical sense of a dimensional module and a span—and the *ken*—in the conceptual sense of intercolumniation and thus of spatial scansion—affords expression and proportions that resonate with the construction tradition of post-and-beam structures.

In addition, just as the traditional systems adapted to circumstance—prior to the Meiji period, Japan took free advantage of standards as well as their exceptions—here the modular principle of the *ken* is subject to a deformation in the abscissa axis. In order to satisfy the client's wish to include a bicycle parking area at the south, while maintaining the maximum width of 3.64 m (two *ken*) for the individual offices for scholars on the second floor, the X2-X3' bay was slightly reduced from 3.64 m to 3.32 m. The simultaneous presence of the X2' and X2 grid lines maintains the trace of this contingency: the X2-X3 interval of two *ken* remains unchanged and X2 remains the central column line. But the X1-X2' interval of 3.32 m establishes the new half-width and the median axis of the street facade and ridge line of the roof. The symmetry which has disappeared in plan remains visible from the street thanks to the doubling of the X2 axis (fig. c17-b).

These pragmatic and imperceptible arrangements between regular modules and concrete measures are a measure of play in the relation between principle and contingency, as they were in wood architecture in the past. The architect works with views. The carpenter and cabinetmaker resize and carefully adjust interior dimensions.

ACTORS AND KNOW-HOW

In its cultural acceptation, context can also encourage the choice of wood: for the Mikan architectural office, based in Yokohama, this project was an opportunity to work with trusted professionals in the domain of carpentry-cabinetry, who were referred to us by our local colleagues. The Amuza general contracting company (Amuza kōmuten アムザ工務店) was chosen for those reasons and truly played the role of constructor as well as consultant, with the carpenters maintaining the mission of passing on the tradition of building in wood. A few months before building the EFEO Center, Mikan also had the chance to test young woodworkers from the Geneto company, who were hired as subcontractors to Amuza. They had helped with the assembly of a temporary tea pavilion out of wood panels and framing in the region around Kōbe, on Mount Rokkō, a construction inspired by the famous Joan pavilion of Oda Uraku, described in the first chapter (figs. a53, a54, c18). Represented by Azuma Kōji 東幸史,

Amuza generally kept to, but sometimes amended, the points discussed with the structural engineer, Manda Takashi 萬田隆.

Through the central role they played in the construction process, these practices clearly express the working framework of conception-construction in Japan. First of all, the building tradition relies on the close relationship between the architect and the structural engineer—both of them "modern" professionals—on the one hand, and the carpenter, who maintains a living, practical culture on the other. The project developed around the relations

fig c18. Organ pavilion オルゴル庵, architect: Mikan

between these three main actors, with the agreement of the client, represented in Japan by Benoît Jacquet, in a fragile economic equilibrium that combined the virtues of craftsmanship and those of industrialization, in which standardization lowered the costs, without ruling out exceptions that conveyed an additional architectural spirit. The practical reality of this work is best expressed by what we have called "points of detail" as well as "rooms and materials."

FOUR POINTS OF DETAIL

The main structure, which is left exposed at the ground and the top floors, posed problems for the clarity of architectonic expression. The four main issues were as follows: the design of the framing, the abutments between segments of the posts and beams, and the assemblies of posts and beams with the stair.

Drawing up a Frame

There were several possible solutions to free up the ceiling height of the space on the top floor, which is constrained by the maximum legal height of ten meters to the ridge of the roof these included whether to install collar beams—higher than the eave beams—or struts; the number and orientation of struts per support; the choice of simple beams, double beams, or trellis beams; interrupting the post at the bottom of the glazed bands and replacing it with a series of smaller vertical struts, etc. As the room is not very high and the framing is consequently near eye level—as in an attic with a low ceiling—it was finally decided to let the post continue up to the eave beam located above the row of windows and to add a single strut to the main rafter concealed above the ceiling. Adjoining these roof trusses without collar beams, purlins (with the exception of the eave beam), or rafters, which are rather unusual in Europe, are small beams laid between the main rafters rather than on top of them, which reduces the ultimate thickness of the roof by their own depth. The overhang is supported by console beams, fixed directly to the eave beams, in the absence of rafters. This assembly attempts to balance the expression of support through the posts and struts, and the concept of a large roof with a protective overhang, with a visually continuous band of windows emphasizing its floating quality. Horizontal bracing is achieved by the gables, with the addition of structural plywood panels attached to the main rafters.

Assembling and joining posts and beams

Having chosen short pieces of solid Douglas fir for the beams as well as the posts, it was necessary to manage the many visible ties between segments. A first question arose in the hypostyle hall on the ground floor: should one favor the expression of the posts in the central column line X2 or the beams? In other words, should the beams stop at the posts or interrupt them instead and give the impression of being supported by the posts? The latter option was chosen, in order to emphasize the sense of load and support, which meant that visible abutments would inevitably occur, as the segments of beams did not exceed 3.64 meters (two *ken*). Which axis—abscissa or ordinate—should be highlighted? It was decided to expose the assemblies, with mortise and tenon joints, only in the X2 direction, by far the least noticeable to a person entering in the hall (fig. c-19a).

fig c19-a. assembly and abutment (1)

direction of abutment

fig c19-b. assembly and abutment (2)

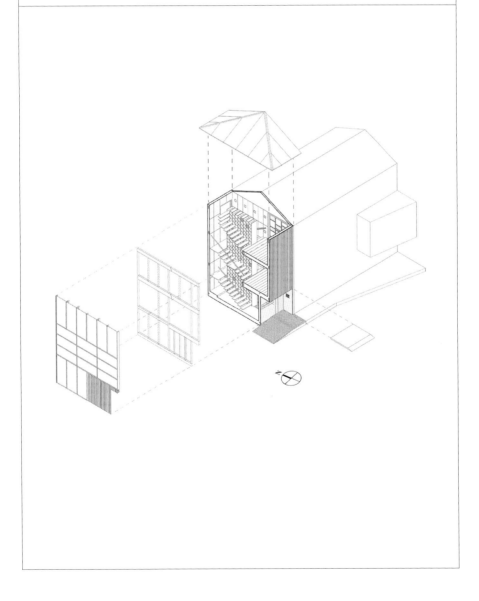

The second problem concerned the expression of structure visible through the glazed facade on the street side. Here, the opposite solution from the inside of the hall was chosen and the posts are given priority over the beams that are interrupted. After consultations with the general contractor's carpenter and the engineer, it turned out to be possible to employ a massive post in a single length of about 5 meters maximum. Although this height was not enough to reach the roof in a single piece, the eye of the passerby is too far, or rather too far below this break for it to be bothersome; so, the post of the X2′ line passes through the beams. They butt against it and the effect is to reinforce the vertical thrust of the facade on the two lower floors (fig. c19-b).

Choosing a Post

The main contribution of the Amuza enterprise, aside from their close attention and quality of execution, relates to two of the high points of the project: the central posts of the hypostyle hall on the ground floor (line X2) and the stair. In their first designs, the Mikan agency had drawn posts that were square in section before turning to round sections, in order to visually reinforce their dominant role in the scansion of the bays of the hall. Azuma Kōji, the director of the construction company suggested that we swap out the Douglas fir, which was intended to be used throughout the structure, for trunks of the famous Kitayama cedar (Kitayama *sugi*) from the mountains north of Kyoto. This choice not only highlighted the particular role of these posts, but it also called on the production of local woods, with their links to the architecture of Sukiya residences from the sixteenth century. We were introduced to a nurseryman from Kitayama (Nakata Osamu 中田治), and much as one might do at the market, we were able to select four trunks with slightly puffy surfaces from his reserve for the four main columns of the room.

Nakata Osamu, the director of the Nakagen 仲源 company that has cultivated cedars for five generations, is the last owner/trader in the village to continue the traditional techniques: the *honjikomi* felling and natural mountain drying (fig. 4). The *honjikomi* takes place in August, on the date of the new moon, during the hottest time in the summer, and when the summer sun's rays at its zenith penetrate the furthest, down to the bottom of the valley. The tree trunks are cut at the base, before being tipped to lay at an angle onto posterns built on the steep slopes. They are then peeled and trimmed by hand, up to about three meters (the length of a standard bole), by local woodsmen who climb up trees. Only the crown of branches at the top is left intact. It extracts as much as 40% of the moisture remaining in the plant's veins during the week that it is left in this state. The trunks are then brought down on sleds or carried on men's backs to the village. There, they are washed by hand with water and sand from the river, generally by the women of the village, in order to maintain their exceptional pallor and a particular luster to the wood. After that, they are left to dry in the warehouse until October. The warehouses are aligned along the river and are equipped with large openings so as to obtain good natural ventilation. They have an ingenious and unusual structure, with planks that get wider on the upper floors. But the carpenters who built them during the 1930s disappeared along with their secrets for fabrication (fig. c20). The natural drying-out process takes about three months, which is relatively little time, but it maintains the structural qualities of the wood, its texture and essential oils, as its moisture content is evacuated vertically, primarily through its fibers (veins). In contrast to this, artificial drying in the factory, which is brutal and accelerated, accomplished while the felled trees are still very humid, has a tendency to make the wood "sweat" and lose more of its natural qualities (fig. c21).

fig c20. warehouses at Nakagawa, Kitayama-chō, Kita-ku, Kyoto, built in 1935

It is often (and wrongly) thought that the occasionally tortured appearance of the famous Kitayama cedars is a result of manipulations of the trunks' surfaces during the drying process. While some of the various types handled by Mr. Nakata have been artificially constrained, most of the variations are normal ones, specific to the species and under the control of the nurseryman. In the Shintō shrine of the village stands the mother tree, a white cedar (*shiro sugi* 白杉) that was recognized as a perfect tree five hundred and fifty years ago. Cuttings were taken from it in order to reproduce the ideal tree. Ever since, new plantings proceed in the same manner, with cuttings selected from the best trees to increase the chances of obtaining a specimen identical to the original. The trees are raised in a nursery at first, for three years, before being replanted in the forest. They start being pruned after six years, and every three years thereafter so that their trunks are not blemished by knots from the branches. The harvest occurs some twenty years later, as a function of the desired thickness (between 15 and 20 cm for a post). Five or six types are available, from the smoothest to the most distressed, including some peeled trunks whose surfaces have been intentionally constricted in order to obtain printed motifs. The most desirable posts, and the most expensive (certain specimens can cost thousands of euros) are those whose fibers are the finest, with the most perfect bole, even if some unusual or curious shape may spark interest in some particular individual (fig. c22).

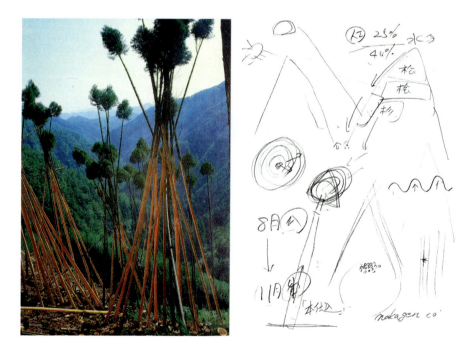

fig c21. sketch by the nurseryman Nakata Osamu of the planting of the mountains north of Kyoto. The foot of the mountain is planted with cedars, then the cypresses and pines

This manner of selection would be unthinkable in the context of industrial production. It is an artisanal manner of working, in which one carefully chooses planks or trunks from specialized tradesmen in order to produce aesthetic effects in tea pavilions or the interiors of Sukiya-style houses—for example for the corner posts (*tokobashira*) of *tokonoma* alcoves—from four centuries ago, that is combined with the most contemporary working methods, of precutting all the structural pieces in the factory. As the thicknesses for the posts of the Center were natural sections, they were slightly augmented from the 15 cm that were structurally necessary to 20 cm, and incised along their full height to create a seasoning check to avoid cracking.

Mounting a staircase

After extensively studying the framing and repeatedly testing the solutions through perspectives and models at different scales: 1/100, 1/50 or 1/30 for overall views, then 1/10 and 1/5 in order to understand the precise dimensions and 1/1 for samples of the beams, planks, and posts in order to experience the different combinations of species of wood, we then turned to various possibilities for the staircase. It had started out only as a functional means of moving from floor to floor and as a buffer space that could control views, intensities of light and temperature, but subsequently the staircase was transformed into a hybrid element of a library and an evocation of stepped furniture from Japanese houses. The deliberate multiplication of landings, aside from facilitating access to the books, also recalls the climbing paths up a mountain, with their aleatory stops or the disjointed stone steps (*tobiishi*) of a garden pathway.

Through mutual encouragement and trust in each other's competence, the two young carpenter/cabinetmakers of the subcontractor Geneto, who had already worked with us on the tea pavilion on Mount Rokko (fig. c18) built a sort of accompanying masterpiece in three weeks: three-centimeter-thick steps of glue-laminated oak extend out from bookcases of the same thickness, like little wings. In spite of the engineer's calculations, the carpenters considered the console by the glazed facade to be too long, so two thin threaded steel rods pick up the loads at the ends of the steps by suspending them. Transcending its basic function, the staircase becomes the symbol of the Center from the outside (fig. c23).

ROOMS AND MATERIALS

The architect Shinohara Kazuo claimed, as we have already said, that traditional Japanese architecture had no concept of space (fig. b26). The argument is not altogether without material basis, as most significant buildings were based on planar compositions of juxtaposed rooms, but this aphorism reduces space to its purely third dimension, so to speak. In this very modern reading, Shinohara appears to accord primacy to spatial experimentation enabled by contemporary techniques and materials and further strengthened by digital tools. And yet, one of the teachings of all this architecture in wood is based on dialogues between structures and cladding (as well as lines and surfaces) that qualify spaces or space just as much. In our building, we played with a restrained palette of woods and tied these choices to the function and meaning of each room. In typological terms, there are four types in the building: the staircase/library (fig. c23), the hypostyle reading room (fig. c24), the office/cases (fig. c25), and the lecture conference hall (fig. c26).

fig c22. various trunks, M. Nakata's warehouse
fig c22-a. fairly smooth trunks of the type chosen by the EFEO   fig c22-b. trunks with irregular surfaces
fig c22-c. trunks with intentionally constricted surfaces   fig c22-d. naturally tortured trunks

The Douglas fir employed for the structure, except for the central posts in the hypostyle hall, has a reddish-brown appearance with a fine grain and few knots. The floors are solid oak planks and glulam for bookcases and the stairs. The slightly darker brown and the solid appearance of the material played a role, but it was the shelving, whose thickness needed to hold up many books without sagging, that dictated the final choice. In all the rooms and especially in the staircase where they extend into the steps, they keep to the relatively thin section of 3 cm of glued laminated (glulam) oak. For the walls and ceilings, with the exception of the top floor and the stairwell, we opted for plywood faced in limewood, a pale but warm wood with a subtle grain. Its tone lightens the rooms and contrasts with the darker lines of the structure and the plank floor surface.

On the other hand, we sought out more expressive materials in three places: the central bay of the hypostyle hall on the ground floor made from Kityama cedar whose Sukiya refinement contrasts with the other exposed structural members; the ceiling of the conference room on the top floor, in Douglas fir planks, reinforces the dynamic character of the room; and finally the choice of OSB boards whose appearance was toned down by sanding, for the walls of the staircase, whose rustic aspect recalls the straw cob of tea pavilions in the Sōan style and highlights the material sobriety of the staircase/furniture. Outside, the cedar siding, installed vertically and varnished dark brown complements the window frames with its coating applied with a trowel rather than being sprayed, giving it a less mechanical appearance.

JOINERIES AND FURNITURE

Four major elements fall into this category: doors, windows, bookcases, and tables. Together, they contribute to the "color" of the spaces. The frames for the sliding doors are cedar. Japanese glass artist Michiyo Durt-Morimoto treated them like stained glass windows and created a contemporary expression which recalls the translucent *shōji* in translucent paper, whose frames were often made of this wood. We should point out that in our "design brief," we requested that the artist eschew colored glass and seek to give "color" through texture instead. The choice of various artisanal glasses that we approved in her workshop cast transparent and opalescent tones and their compositions were an ideal response to this idea of freely reworking tradition—as represented by paper *shōji*—and in counterpoint to the "high tech" glass (see below) used on the west facade, as well as the idea of defining the different spaces by their respective materials. Here the patterns of the wooden rail and the dark tones of the frames and moldings emphasize the presence of the openings cut into the partitions, clad in light and calm limewood. The window frames of Canadian spruce play the same role for the windows cut into the walls.

The bookshelves, tabletops, and countertops are glue-laminated oak, with a constant thickness of 3 cm. Nonetheless, the tabletops are beveled in order to make them appear lighter, and the desktops in the individual offices were factory-cut from the solid wood to create a small ridge separating the researcher and a possible interlocutor. The legs of the tables in the reading and conference rooms were made out of limewood plywood to give them a precious touch and to minimize the dimensions that would have been difficult to obtain with solid wood at a reasonable cost (fig. c27).

fig c23-a. staircase: the volume

fig c23-b. staircase: the stair-library insert

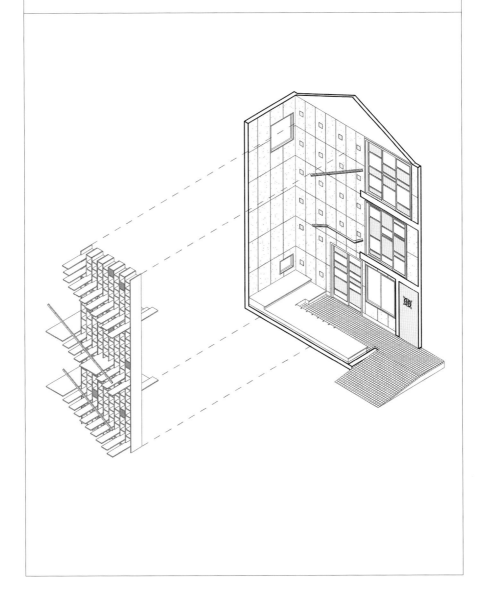

fig c23-c. staircase: the occupied volume

fig c23-d. exterior at entry

fig c23-e. interior at entry

fig c23-f. bottom of stair

fig c23-g. staircase, 2nd floor landing
fig c23-h. staircase, reference elements

PRINCIPLES OF AN ONTOLOGY OF CONSTRUCTION 339

fig c23-i. staircase: reference elements

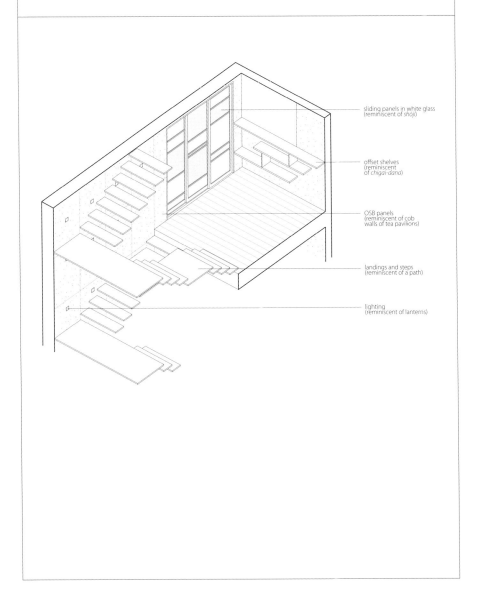

fig c23-j. staircase, reference elements

fig c24-a. hypostyle reading room

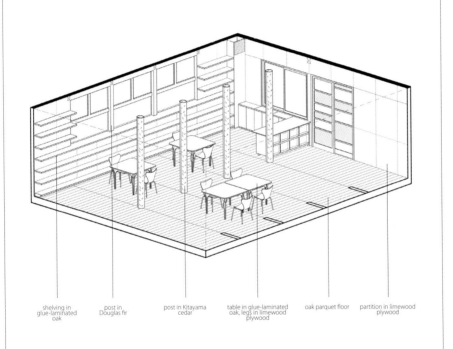

shelving in glue-laminated oak | post in Douglas fir | post in Kitayama cedar | table in glue-laminated oak, legs in limewood plywood | oak parquet floor | partition in limewood plywood

fig c24-b. hypostyle reading room
fig c25-a. office/cases

PRINCIPLES OF AN ONTOLOGY OF CONSTRUCTION   343

fig c25-b. office/cases

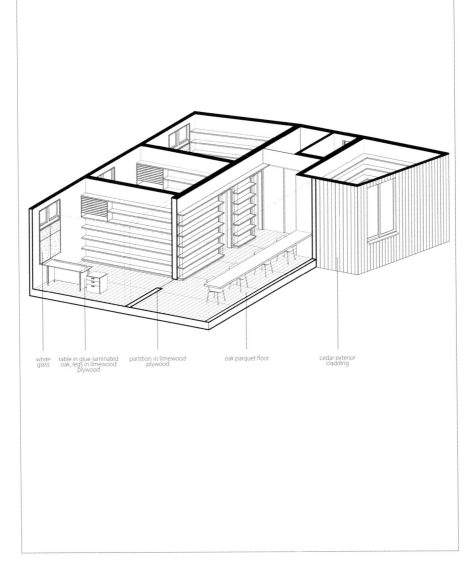

white glass | table in glue-laminated oak, legs in limewood plywood | partition in limewood plywood | oak parquet floor | cedar exterior cladding

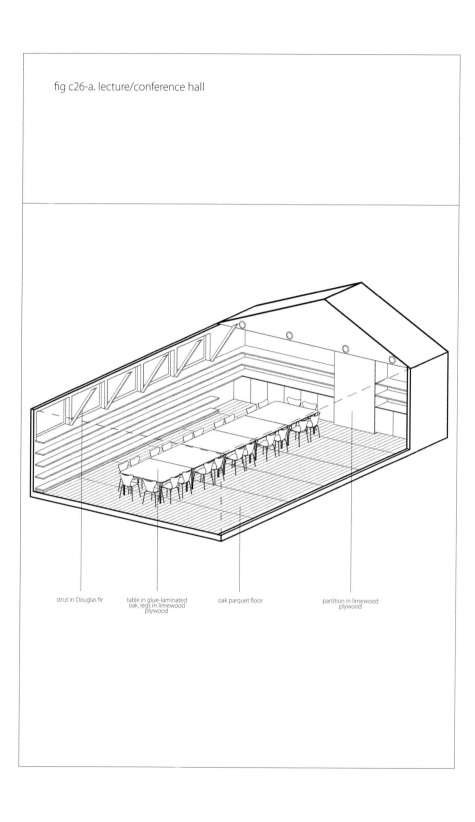

fig c26-a. lecture/conference hall

fig c26-b. lecture/conference hall

SPACE AND PASSIVE SYSTEMS

The choice of wood for the structures, cladding, and furniture was not the only one to be made with economy in mind. A number of other elements, not directly related to this material, also contribute to the general concept of an ecology of the whole that favors passive systems: the earth tube (geothermal ventilation), solid walls on three sides (north, east, and south), projecting canopies on the south, based on calculations for the latitude of Kyoto, low-emissivity glass (low-E), natural ventilation by convection at the buffer space and staircase at the west, and solar protection on that side, for the first time in Asia, by a facade in SAGE electrochromic glass, developed by Saint-Gobain whose variable tint is controlled by sensors and managed by computer (fig. c28).

fig c27-a. leg at reading room table, ground floor
fig c27-b. scholar's desk, 2nd floor

fig c27-c. conference room table, 3rd floor
fig c28-a. buffer space, darkened day mode

fig c28-b. sustainable development, general principles

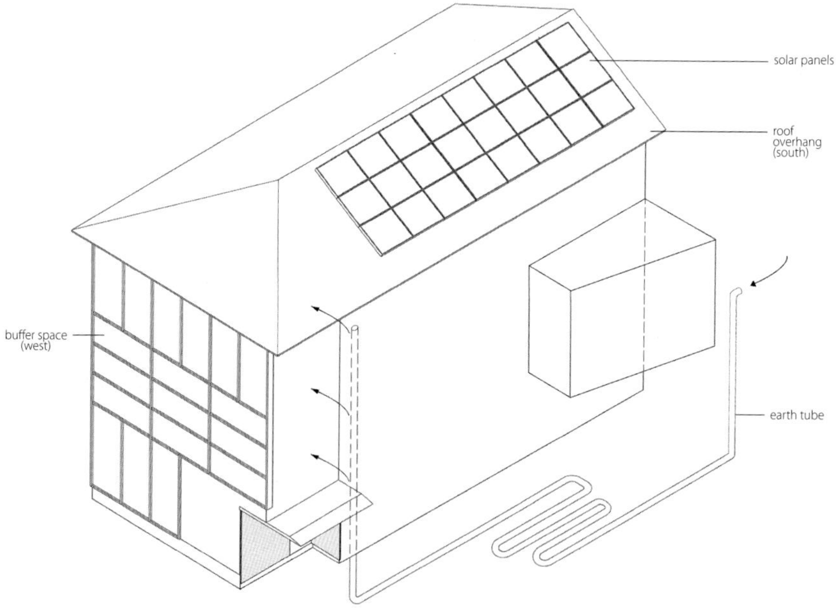

solar panels

roof
overhang
(south)

buffer space
(west)

earth tube

fig c28-c. west facade by night

fig c28-d. treatment of south light

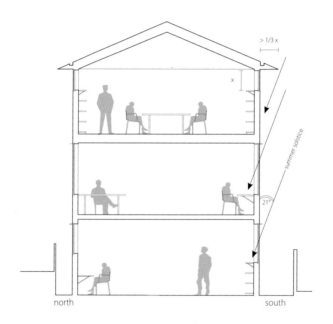

fig c28-e. treatment of west light

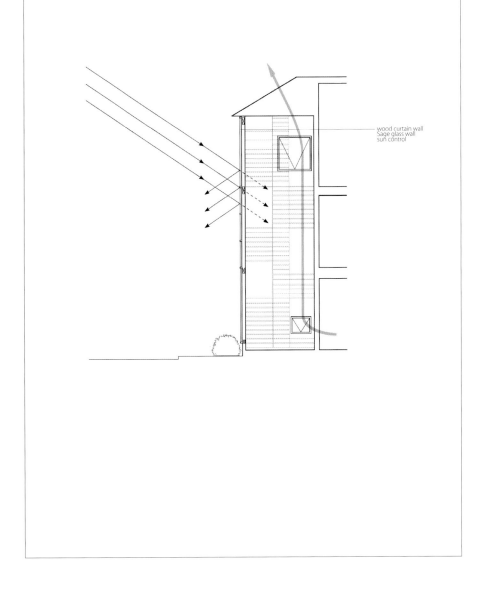

fig c28-f. west facade transparent mode

fig c28-g. west facade darkened mode

fig c28-h. sliding panels in blown glass, closed position

fig c28-i. sliding panels in blown glass, open position

fig c29. structure: foundations

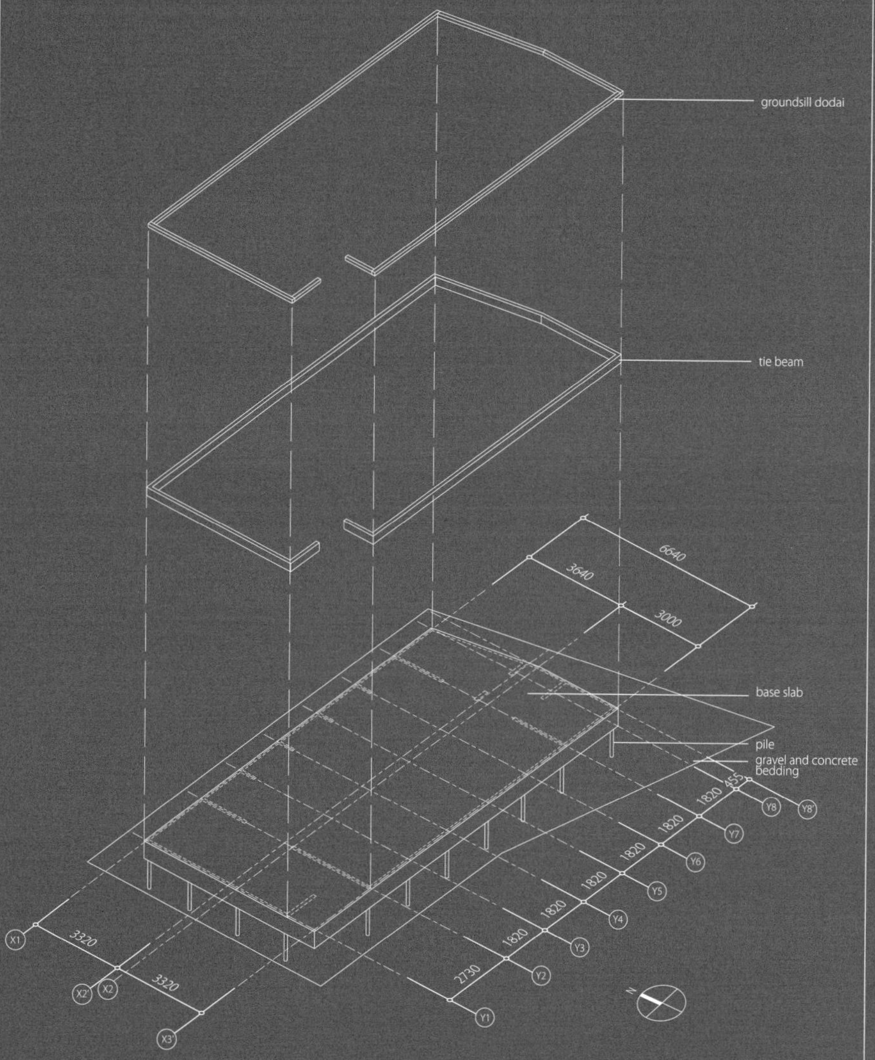

groundsill dodai

tie beam

6640

3640

3000

base slab

pile

gravel and concrete
bedding

Y8' Y8"

1820 655

1820

1820 Y7

1820 Y6

1820 Y5

1820 Y4

1820 Y3

1820 Y2

2730 Y1

X1 3220

X2' X2 3220

X3

PAST-PRESENT

OVER THE COURSE OF CONSTRUCTION

On September nineteenth and twentieth 2013, approximately three months after the initiating ceremony of *jichinsai*, another event was held to celebrate the completion of the carpentry of the shell, the *jōtōshiki* 上棟式. The assembly and installation of the wood structure (*tatekata* 建方) onsite was in fact extremely rapid: it was erected over the course of two days and completed by securing the ridge beam (*muneageshiki* 棟上式 or *jōtōshiki*). As all the wood pieces: posts, beams, joists, purlins, rafters, etc. had been precut and numbered in the factory, the work of the carpenters during those days, aside from assembly and installation, consisted of making adjustments onsite to any imperfect joints or profiles of specific pieces, using saws and wood shears. For example, the posts of Kitayama cedar, which had come directly from the nursery without further milling, needed preparation of their ends. We should note in passing that the wonderful work on mortise and tenon joints remains the prerogative of carpenters, and that they prepare them in the pre-cutting phase in the mill, or sometimes onsite with hand tools. We will return to the issue of joints in the afterword.

The architect is primarily concerned with verifying with the engineer the appearance of the pins and metal connecting pieces that are required by contemporary regulations, and seeks to minimize their visual presence. Once the roof has been set, the finish work begins, which takes much more time: the waterproofing of the building, which consists of closing up the walls, belongs in a certain way to the finish work, that extended here until the end of February 2014, a period of close to five months. In conclusion, it is clear that the layout of the structure and its installation required industrial techniques and sequences, while the meticulous corrections and the second phase of work was more artisanal. And while the gods may have been helpful to the different trades for launching and mastering the construction process, they were absent, or perhaps simply ineffable, from the glass raised to celebrate the final delivery (figs. c29, c30, c31, c32).

YOUNG AND OLD COUPLES

The use of a post and beam structural skeleton turned out to be economical, respectful of a sense of space that was both contemporary and traditional, and so in that sense, timeless. Over the course of the process, it resulted in an aesthetic logic bringing together the competences of the different actors. The final result is not so much due to a historicist or Japanese-inspired intent, but rather an embodiment of a concrete ecological vision—an ontological one we might say— to make the best use of local resources. And these are part of a living and dialectical tradition: the metric system and the modules in *ken*; standard and exception; structure and cladding; richness

fig c30. structure: connections

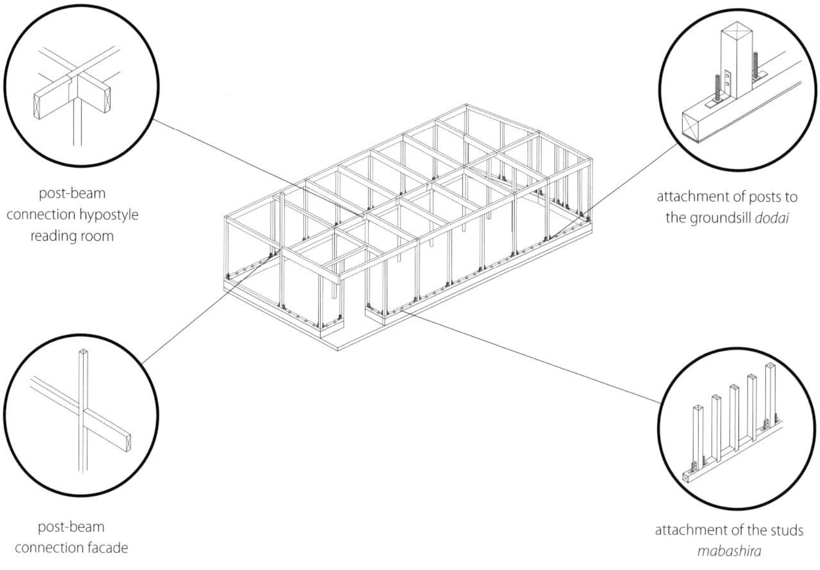

post-beam
connection hypostyle
reading room

attachment of posts to
the groundsill *dodai*

post-beam
connection facade

attachment of the studs
mabashira

of textures and materials, simplicity of implementation; free and coordinated use of local and imported material (old or new); and reliance on contemporary techniques for shaping wood as well as the excellence of craftmanship. These are a few of the concrete lessons of wood architecture in Japan today.

fig c31. construction site
fig c31-a. precut structure waiting to be installed
fig c31-c. preparation of the ends of the Kitayama cedar posts

fig c31-b. installation of the groundsill *dodai*

fig c31-d. mortise and tenon joint between beams
fig c31-e. installation of a beam

fig c31-f. main skeleton at the time of the *jōtōshiki*
fig c31-g. secondary structure

fig c32-a. structure: main skeleton ground floor

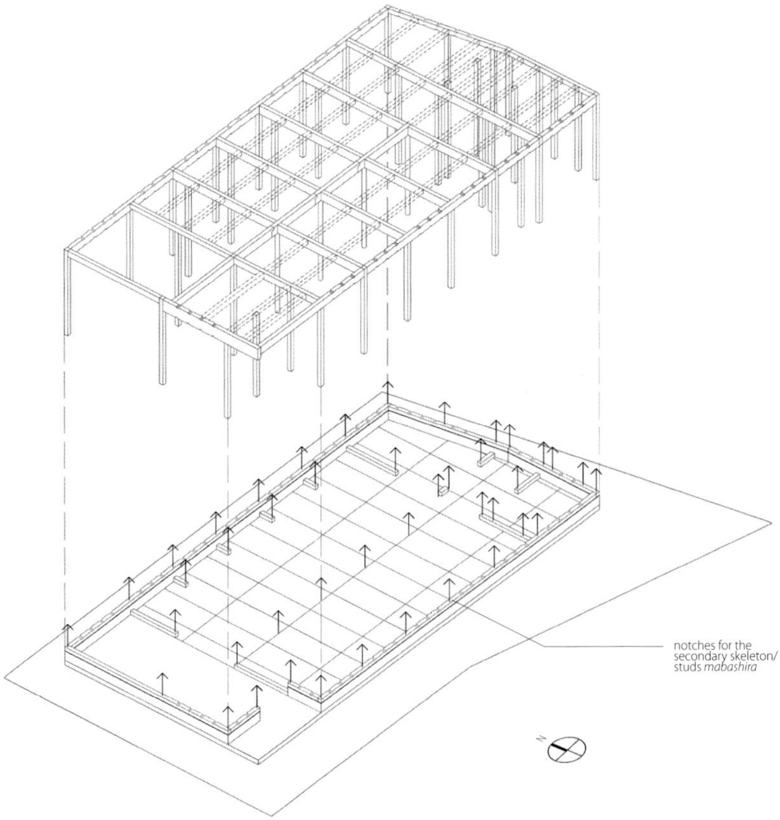

notches for the
secondary skeleton/
studs *mabashira*

fig c32-b. structure: main skeleton 2nd floor

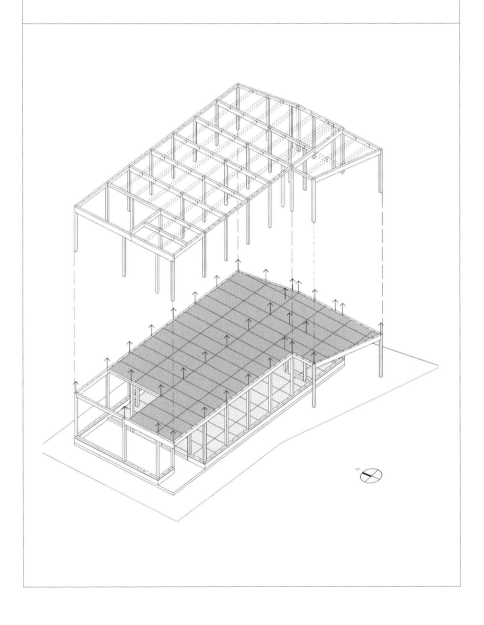

fig c32-c. structure: main skeleton 3rd floor and roof

fig c32-d. structure: main skeleton building

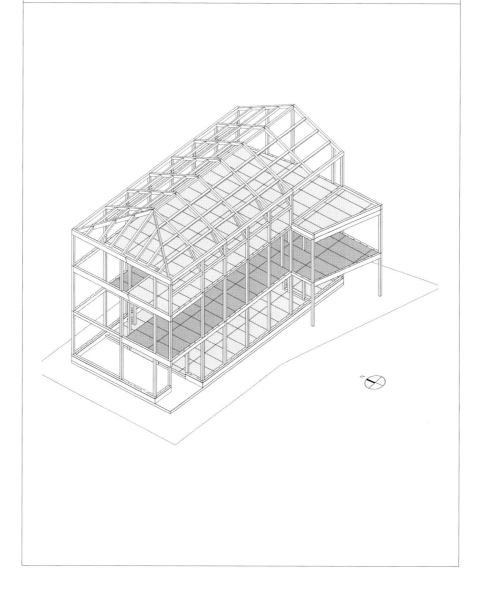

fig c32-e. structure: north-south section

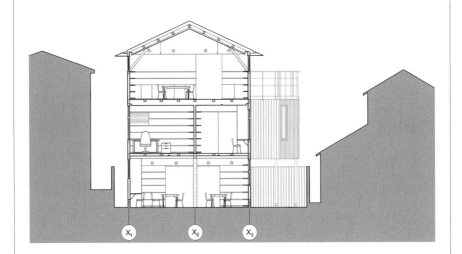

fig c32-f. structure: detailed section

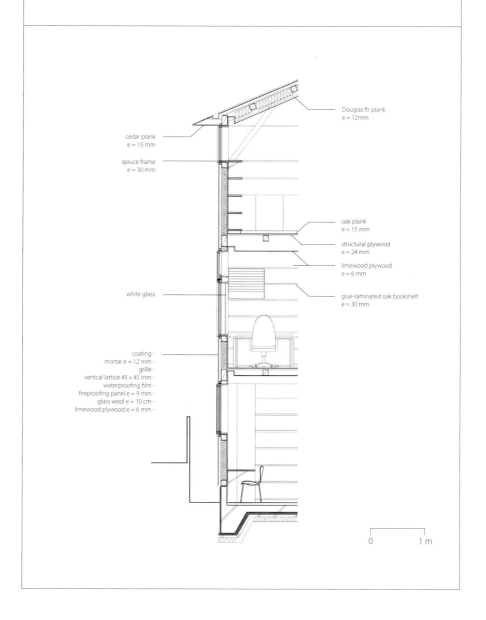

fig d1. cedars spared by the tsunami of 2011, to serve for the construction of Asahi children's playgrounds by Tezuka Architects, Minamisanriku

POSTSCRIPT: TRADITION, WHO ARE YOU?

As every culture is alive, and every tradition and view of it is alive as well; any concrete definition requires a precise analysis of the terms that characterize it. In the present volume, we have thus considered the actors, their training, the physical and legal frameworks of their work, structural and construction systems, typologies and their evolution, as well as the available array of materials and their implementation. While attempting to describe the history of wood construction in Japan from its beginnings, we have also sketched out a history of Japanese spatiality, or perhaps of spatialities.

What is the status of wood construction today? The situation is ambiguous and full of contrasts. Local historians of architecture have long since rehabilitated their own culture, and the patrimony is well maintained and present in physical and mental landscapes, although the very sense of what constitutes tradition is always being reformulated. Nonetheless, the teaching of architecture, if it does not prize Western architecture unduly—to the extent to which it did at its beginnings barely a century ago—generally refers the study of traditional constructions to the disciplines of historians and engineers. One can see a certain lack of culture, even if it is offset by the wealth and variety of very precise architectural details and examples of construction to consult. No doubt, we should think of these as contemporary versions of the manuals of carpentry (*hinagata-bon*) and thereby one of the many offshoots of tradition. These publications are not limited to the use of wood exclusively, and they address all types of construction. One might also see in them a rather Japanese determination, for practical purposes, to classify, or even compile past knowledge of a subject amalgamated with modern Western influences, as exemplified in Ernst Neufert's dictionary.[156] While the craft of master carpenter has lost some of the preeminence that it held until the Meiji era, its know-how has been conserved, and many architects make good use of it while still taking advantage of contemporary technical possibilities.

Timber structures have generally been avoided in large buildings since the Second World War, after the traumas of experiencing entire cities being reduced to ash by bombing. But interior work, cabinetry and houses, has never ceased turning to this material for historical reasons of economy and quality. In addition to the masters of the postwar period: Horiguchi, Raymond, Yoshimura, Murano, Taniguchi, Maekawa, Tange, Yoshida, Shinohara, who were mentioned or described in the second chapter—as well as others we did not name—we have witnessed a new renewal of interest in wood architecture over the past twenty years or so. This tendency is due at least in part to a new planetary ecological awareness, as well as to the influence of media, and to a recognition of the richness of its history. Nonetheless, as an indication of the difficulties raised here by wood, the architect Ban Shigeru (born in 1957) did not hesitate to castigate

---

[156] Ernst Neufert, *Bauenentwurfslehre* (Berlin: Ullstein Verlag, 1936); English edition: *Architects' Data*, Fifth edition (Hoboken: Wiley-Blackwell, 2019).

the lack of innovation in this type of construction, frustrated as he was by local regulations.[157] Although there are recent examples of multi-storied buildings in Europe or North America with wood structures, thanks to construction systems of CLT panels, these are often hidden or require significant increase of their thickness to conform to fire codes. As floors are often covered by soundproofing in order to avoid possible complaints from future users, wood is part of the economy of building, but it often receives scant visual attention.

In looking closely at construction and spatial arrangements, we see signs of a certain resilience there. The traditional units of measurement, and consequently the systems of proportions that were subject to them, have not been officially in use since 1966. While they still survive among carpenters specialized in restoration—the *miyadaiku* and *sukiya daiku*—for the clear purpose of consistent preservation of the patrimony of cultural buildings and houses in the Shoin and Sukiya styles, the same often holds true of simple local carpenters (*daiku*) as well. The old measurements in *ken* and *shaku* still play a role in residential construction, most of which are constructed with wood structures, in which modules of 91 cm and their multiples remain in common use. Even though it is a matter of industrial production, and more concerned with standardization than with tradition, the latter extends its influence in the proportions of rooms and spaces. Rooms often continue to be accounted for in *ken* and *jō* (tatami), units that make it possible to apprehend spatial dimensions concretely and directly.

On the other hand, this relation no longer holds true for larger buildings, even if tradition permeates contemporary practices in the most unexpected ways—for example through the recrudescence of certain practices, in a manner both ironic and tenacious but not deliberate. The drawings of the SANAA architecture office, in their schematic simplicity, remind us of carpenters' construction drawings on boards (*itazu*). In our day, tools like these are still in use on small construction sites, such as the board established *a posteriori* by a carpenter for his own understanding, based on our architectural plans for a pavilion, despite their being dimensioned in millimeters in the contract working drawings (fig. c3-a).

Another resurgence occurs in the very contemporary and famous "Silver Hut" house, designed in 1984 by Itō Toyō and built entirely out of glass and metal, in which the architect used spans of 3.64 m, in other words two *ken*, for his structural grid. Materials and their implementation also demonstrate certain lasting qualities. New products employed by designers today do not prevent them from maintaining traditional features. Contemporary plywood panels, that replace the solid wood planks of the past at a lower cost, come in panels 1.82 m by 91 cm, in other words one *ken* by one half *ken*, or one tatami/*jō*! The architecture of Andō Tadao, constructed almost completely from exposed concrete, is imprinted by its plywood formwork. The concrete is a perfect illustration of the quality (and recurring dimensions) of the local plywood panels, their fine joinery, and their formwork holes, as well as their underlying relation to tradition.

In the end, the study of wood construction deals only indirectly with the issue of Japanness—an over-used and often poorly defined term—in architecture.[158] Let us not forget that the master builders for almost two thousand years of the monuments we admire were not architects, but artisan carpenters (*daiku*). Some of them, especially those who worked on the construction

---

[157] Shigeru Ban 坂茂, "Wood Architecture in the Expanded Field," *The Japan Architect*, no. 89 (2013), 32.

[158] The architect Isozaki Arata employs the term *nihonteki na mono* 日本的なもの, translated as Japan-ness into English. See Isozaki Arata, *Kenchiku ni okeru "nihonteki na mono"* 建築における「日本的なもの」 (Tokyo: Shinchōsha, 2003); English edition: *Japan-ness in Architecture*, translated by Sabu Kohso, edited by David B. Stewart, foreword by Toshiko Mori (Cambridge: The MIT Press, 2006).

of significant cultural buildings and impressive residences in the Sukiya style (the *miyadaiku* and *sukiyadaiku*), seem to have had a high regard for their work and their attribution, although they did little to theorize their practice aside from the construction manuals that appeared in the sixteenth century (*hinagata-bon*). The tea and garden masters[159] were somewhat more prolix, and in their own way, they came closer to the theoreticians of the Renaissance in Europe. Paintings and some literary masterpieces written between the twelfth and fourteenth centuries also give us some idea of the creators or the spirits of those who lived in these places, such as the poet Kamo no Chōmei[160] or the monks already cited, Saigyō and Urabe.

The establishment of historical and stylistic perspectives and the work of theorization are in reality relatively recent developments. They are the achievements of numerous historians and architects from the end of the nineteenth and the twentieth centuries, that were referred to in the first and second chapters. There are thus two different ways of looking at the works and texts of Itō Chūta, in his research into the origins of Japanese architecture; Horiguchi Sutemi, in his studies of tea pavilions; or Shinohara Kazuo, in his analysis of the popular habitat (*minka*). These can be seen on the one hand, as a determination to know and understand the traditions transmitted by wood construction, in order to be inspired by them; and on the other hand, as an attempt to respond to the temptation of the West seen through a Japanese vision of reality—in other words, as an attempt to propose a Japanese definition of spatiality and of this new and initially foreign discipline of architecture.

This determination is particularly striking with Shinohara and his contemporary Isozaki Arata, and the metaphysical sense that the latter accords to the concept of *ma* 間 for a Western audience—a French one to begin with, rather than a local one.[161] Although he himself has constructed few projects out of wood (could this be an underlying reason for his bias?), his definition of *Japan-ness* is based on a semantic analysis of this term. Influenced by the philosophical debates of 1960–1970, Isozaki focuses *a posteriori* on the reading of *ma* as the spacing or interval between things, over the reading of the same Japanese character 間 as *ken* which is more closely linked to construction. The association between the ideograms such as space (*kūkan* 空間) as emptiness or spacing, and time (*jikan* 時間) as time or interval, demonstrate for him that a notion of space-time is a characteristic feature of Japanese architecture. This reading of *ma* and its combinations is certainly important, but Isozaki constructs an amalgam that detracts from a demonstration that is in reality rather aphoristic and anachronistic: he tends to confuse architects with carpenters, when for the latter, concept and construction were intimately bound together. Despite the multiplication of meanings of this ideogram, it seems more reasonable to think that the builders of the past undoubtedly had a more pragmatic and concrete vision of the term. The *ken/ma*, in its double acceptation as span and bay, or room and surface unit was an instrument for the planning, standardization, control, and ultimately the actualization of construction, linked to the *kiwari*, the general system of establishing proportions in construction. One of the great original features of wood construction in Japan is the fact that this concept is simultaneously a part of practical construction and a spatio-structural system.

---

[159] Tachibana no Toshitsuna 橘俊綱, *Sakuteiki* 作庭記 (*Records of Garden Making*, eleventh century). English edition: *Sakuteiki: Visions of the Japanese Garden*, translated by Jiro Takei and Marc. P. Keane (North Clarendon: Tuttle, 2008).

[160] Kamo no Chōmei, *Hōjōki, The Ten Foot Square Hut*, op. cit. (1999).

[161] Isozaki Arata, "Ma: Espace-Temps du Japon," exhibition at the Festival d'automne, Paris, Musée des Arts Décoratifs, 1978; and "MA, Space/Time in Japan," New York, Cooper-Hewitt Museum, 1979. See also Michael Lucken, "Les limites du *ma*" in *Nouvelle revue d'esthétique*, vol 1., no. 13 (2014): 45–67.

To conclude our study, let us finally address the current situation. Aside from reservations regarding legislation, as articulated by Ban Shigeru, and problems in the supply chain of wood that we have already mentioned, what about this return of interest in wood that we have been talking about? Japanese architects of today have little interest in the conceptual play we have been invoking. While they may be aware of it, they borrow ideas freely from multiple sources. Their work does not necessarily refer to a local architectural tradition. In fact, just the opposite is sometimes the case—a strong urge to avoid commonplaces and to affirm a contemporary creative freedom. And yet the recent work of Japanese architects often touches upon one or more aspects of wood construction that have been invoked in this book. These include:

— exposed and modular structure;
— dimensions and proportions of construction systems;
— establishing relations between rooms with each other or with the exterior, and their spatial fluidity;
— the influence of certain historical styles: the mannerism of the Sukiya, the dryer rigor of the Shoin style, or the rusticity of the Sōan tea pavilions;
— the work on materials and elements of joinery; and
— the selection of species of wood.

Sometimes this relation to tradition remains quite literal, as we have pointed out in the case the Sukiya style, which still thrives in the residential sector and in *ryokan* guest houses. But in these latter buildings, either in their construction as a whole or only in their interior design, carpenter/cabinetmakers (*sukiya daiku*) often replace architects. Without any claims to being comprehensive, we have selected an assortment of works from the last two decades that are both significant and symptomatic. While these examples are meant to illustrate the whole range of fluctuating relations to tradition that we sought to invoke, they nonetheless illustrate relations between programs and places in a deeper manner, without being excessively didactic.

The sizes of the structural members, posts and beams, especially when they consist of solid wood, and the various plywood panels, structural or not, that clad the walls and ceilings, adhere to the dimensions we have repeatedly described. Very large modules of 3.6 m (two *ken*) are at work in the Bunraku theater of the town of Seiwa, as proposed in 1992 by Ishii Kazuhiro 石井和紘 (1944–2015). Conversely, an orthogonal assembly of small pieces of cypress was employed to achieve spans of 7.2 m (four *ken*) in the archery halls and the boxing rooms of Kōgakuin university in Tokyo, in 2013, designed by FT architects (Fukushima Kazuya 福島加津也, and Tominaga Yōko 富永洋子), with evident and explicitly acknowledged references to the superposed collar beam roof structures of temples (figs. d2, d3, d4). But in one of their earlier buildings, offices for a specialized fabricator of glue-laminates in Nagoya, the catenary curves of the roof, held up by cables running through an assembly of imported Douglas fir pieces, explicitly demonstrate the know-how of a contemporary enterprise (fig. d5). This serves as a reminder that the same architects often express themselves in different registers, in response to the particular context for each project. Similarly, the Asahi kindergarten by Tezuka Architects (Tezuka Takaharu 手塚貴晴 and Tezuka Yui 手塚由比), even if it consists of large geometric spaces without posts and covered by superposed beams of solid wood or glulam, is entirely based on modules of 1.8 m, 3.6 m, or 7.2 m (fig. d6). Although the spans and the stacked roofs are untraditional, the underlying modules and the detailing of the beams, on the other hand, create an image that interferes with this impression.

In his project for a kindergarten near Chiba, Yoshimura Yasutaka 吉村靖孝 relied exclusively on plywood panels made with *lauan*—a species from Southeast Asia, which is one of the least expensive materials available in Japan for wood partitions, along with American larch. While economic constraints were the primary consideration, subtle references are still apparent: the emphasis on the modules with the studs left exposed, a fluid space regulated by an exclusively orthogonal geometry, and a membrane enclosure that evokes a Japanese lantern, as the architect almost reluctantly tells it—as if he was embarrassed by this almost involuntary reference and a reading that seemed to him to be pushed too far (fig. d7). But one could just as easily read this exterior membrane as the cladding of a contemporary service building. The curious wood beams placed on top of the interior room volumes, which function as horizontal bracing, bring to mind a surrealist collage, far removed from any reference to the past.

Several projects deliberately incorporate local cedar and cypress at the behest of the architects and clients, both for symbolic and economic reasons to support the wood industry. The elements are either in solid wood or in glulam when the spans increase. *Local* is too vague a term. It would be better to say *regional*: Akita cedar for the three-dimensional members for the Odate dome (Itō Toyō), located in the same prefecture; cedar from the coasts affected by the Tsunami of 2011 for the structures in the playground for Asahi kindergarten in Minamisanriku (fig. d6), one of the ports destroyed in the catastrophe; or cedars from the center of the island of Kyūshū for the Bunraku theater constructed for the small rural community of Seiwa, close to Kumamoto (fig. d2).

Sometimes, on the other hand, the finish work calls on species from the region. In botanist Makino Tomitarō's 牧野富太郎 Museum of Plants and People, located in Kōchi, Naitō Hiroshi 内藤廣 used cedar panels for the ceilings and cypress for the terraces, all from the Kōchi region, on the south of Shikoku island (fig. d10). While the expressivity of hybrid structures combining wood and steel has little to do with "Japan-ness," and Naitō rejects any stylistic or vernacular reference in favor of the idea of an archetype of "protoform," the fact remains that his ethnographic Sea-Folk Museum in Toba south of Nagoya evokes the nearby houses of fishermen (fig. d9). In part, this is a choice linked to the local ecology. Near the Makino museum is the columbarium of the Chikurinji temple 竹林寺 by Horibe Yasushi 堀部安嗣, whose sober appearance is similar to the Shoin style and showcases the simplicity of its hipped roofs and the exposed structural relationships of posts and beams (fig. d11). As in most of the houses of Horibe that emphasize the use of wood, the finish work is inserted or placed on top of structures where the choice of species and bay sizes recalls older examples.

At the intersection of these different paths, the built work of the architectural historian Fujimori Terunobu conveys a more celebratory vision, full of cultivated verve, which applies a critique of contemporary architecture and a cultured dilettantism to a personal rereading/reconstruction of the past. His variations on tea pavilions are formally fairly successful, and they recall in a very free manner some of the architects of the new Sukiya style of the preceding period. One of his first projects, the Too-High tea pavilion (Takasugian 高過庵) perched in a tree clearly demonstrated his love for the past that was both iconoclastic and reverential (fig. d12). A number of his buildings appear outrageous on closer examination, but in the end, they often turn out to be simply a local and belated version of the "decorated sheds" of postmodern architect Robert Venturi, when one understands that the wall that appear to be wattle and daub actually consists of metallic structures covered with plasterboard panels and finished off with an earthy brown coating, and that the trees only seem to be alive. While he may appear to be less "inventive" than Fujimori and is visually closer to traditional architecture's structural truthfulness, through his experiments with materials—in this case wood and metal—the architect Suzuki Ryōji 鈴木了二 proposes nothing less than an exquisite rereading of the past in the new pavilions he added to the Konpira sanctuary 金刀比羅宮 near Takamatsu in Shikoku island's northern part (fig. d13).

With the proliferation of material, technical procedures, and the ever-faster circulation of information, it makes little sense to ferret out some Japanese spirit in each and every new project that calls on wood. This is the case of the small Sun-Pu protestant church in Shizuoka designed by Nishizawa Taira 西沢大良, whose geometry is stripped down to a very simple box, clad in vertical planks of rough-cut red cedar left unvarnished on the exterior, and horizontal pine strips on the inside. The panels are joined together near the floor, and are spaced increasingly far apart going up the wall. Further up the wall, they function as louvers to break up the sunlight, creating a transcendental composition with the light from above. Ten years later, the untreated exterior has weathered to a uniform grey, unlike the interior, which retains its original blonde tone. While the play of material and light establishes a direct connection to the spiritual aspects of a religious building of foreign origin, one might still find a trace of the Sukiya spirit in its rustic and rather precious qualities, although Nishizawa has not advanced the claim (fig. d14).

On the other hand, at the risk of overplaying their hand, some architects knowingly stress a Japanese aesthetic that borrows from various registers in which wood plays a decorative, demonstrative, or structural role. After a series of projects that reflected a particular concern with joints—Cidori at the Salone del Mobile in Milan, the research center of the GC Prostho museum at Kasugai, the Starbucks café in Fukuoka—developed with the engineer Satō Jun 佐藤淳, Kuma Kengo proposed a series of trellises formed from small lengths of cypress to partially support and cover over the SunnyHills Japan store in Tokyo (fig. d15). Although the proliferation of layers visually overwhelms the structural aspect and gives a shapeless appearance to this "object," that has resulted in criticism for the excessive and decorative use of wood, one cannot help but admire the delicate work of connection between the sections, which establishes a successful link between contemporary engineering and traditional carpentry/cabinetry. The great difficulty that this jewel-like work entails resides in the joints. In fact, this particular type, in which the different parts lay in the same plane is called the "hell joint" (*jigokukumi* 地獄組), and is a perfect illustration of an understanding between the engineer, the architect, and the carpenters on site. This interest in the expressive possibilities of joints is promising in itself, but it also demonstrates that architects and engineers can be part of a field of excellence belonging to the carpenters. The book on the joints of Seike Kiyoshi, a modernist architect who happens to have been Shinohara's former professor, reminds us that architects can be interested in these procedures, which are not normally their prerogatives. Two main reasons can explain this situation. The first is a lack of knowledge about traditional architecture in wood. The second is the fact that in this particular case, the joint is a structural one—as in wood architecture everything is made out of joints in a certain way—and is concealed or barely visible and can be left to the care of the person building it, in other words the carpenter. These details were born from the need to manage the prolongation of beams (abutment joint *tsugite* 継手) (fig. a62-k), the meeting of two angled beams, between beams and posts (angle joint *shiguchi* 仕口), or between several joists that join together to form the angles of canopies (figs. a62-i, a62-l). They generally disappear within the intersection itself, or above false ceilings that conceal the framing. But this was not the case during the Heian period, where the latter often remained visible, or even in the vernacular habitat (*minka*), until recently.

According to Seike, this joining technique, which was particularly developed in Japan, was linked to the increased scarcity of wood in the medieval period. The butt joints (*tsugite*) thus compensated for the difficulty of finding trees with thick enough trunks.[162] Returning to the present, the paradox of the projects mentioned above lies precisely in this new determination, and a rather Sukiya style mannerism, to display the virtuosity of certain joints (Kuma Kengo) or of complex assemblies of joists (Ishii Kazuhiro, FT architects).

We will complete the loop with a contemporary project by a master builder (*tōryō*) specialized in the construction of temples (*miyadaiku*). We should not forget to note that aside from the scope and quality of the project, it was also the fruit of a contemporary collaboration between a well-regarded carpenter, Nishioka Tsunekazu 西岡常一 (1908–1995), and one of the principal historians of Japanese architecture, Ōta Hirotarō, the editor of the modern version of the *Shōmei*, the construction manual (*hinagata-bon*) referred to early in this book. While the *miyadaiku* are primarily called upon to maintain the patrimony, as we have noted, they are sometimes commissioned for a new creation. Nishioka, who was in charge of the restoration of the Hōryūji monastery, started reconstructing the Yakushiji monastery 薬師寺 (seventh and eighth centuries)[163] in the 1970s as well. Only its east pagoda was original. His careful study made it possible to undertake new constructions in the same Wayō style: the new central gate (*chūmon*), the cloister, the west pagoda, the main pavilion (*kondō*), and the study pavilion (*kōdō*).

This reconstruction was completed in 2003, while the construction of another completely new ensemble, the Sanzōin temple 三蔵院 behind the complex, was built during the 1980s. It was dedicated to the memory of the Chinese monk Genzō Sanzō 玄奘三蔵 (Xuanzang in Chinese), the founder of the Hossō school of Buddhism, whose principal monastery had been the Yakushiji. It consists of a cloister, an octagonal pavilion (*genjodō* 玄奘), and a picture hall (*e-den* 絵殿), built at the back of the main complex (fig. d16). But unlike a reconstruction, this is a new project entirely, as it did not exist previously. Ōta and Nishioka decided to draw on a different register. Instead of scrupulously copying some existing ancient pagoda, they were inspired—still in the Wayō style, but more freely this time around—by medieval buildings of the Kamakura period, when the Chinese influence was less evident. One cannot help but draw a parallel to the manner in which some modern architects, including Murano, Yoshida, Horiguchi, or even Taniguchi, to name a few, engaged in a clever game of references to tea pavilions. But the choice here is significant, for even when looking to the past, the choice is for what is most Japanese and least Chinese. Another illuminating point: the interior architecture of the refectory (*jikidō* 食堂), which was completed in 2017, was designed by the architect Itō Toyō, a contemporary designer if there ever was one. Once again, one is forced to recognize the permeability of styles and practices.

All of these works provide evidence as to the variety of the local scene and the multiplicity of relations to a tradition that is multiple in itself. Even if the proliferation of cross-laminated timber (CLT) panels in Japan as well as elsewhere, might seem to be a cause for alarm—for it seems to globalize certain practices and forms of expression—nonetheless, the originality of these different approaches should ultimately prevail, and without expressive one-upmanship, convey a specificity and sensibility particular to Japan. The double parenthesis of carpenter and architect characterizes the best in wood construction in Japan, and its Japan-ness remains doubtlessly one of its best guarantees.

---

[162] Seike Kiyoshi, *Nihon no kigumi* 日本の木組 (Kyoto: Tankōsha, 1979). English edition: *The Art of Joinery* (New York-Kyoto: Weatherhill-Tankōsha, 1977), 20.

[163] Azby Brown, *The Genius of Japanese Carpentry: Secrets of an Ancient Craft*, revised edition (Tokyo: Tuttle, 2013), 28–35.

fig d2. Ishii Kazuhiro, Seiwa Bunraku Theater, Kumamoto prefecture, 1992
fig d2-a. exterior view

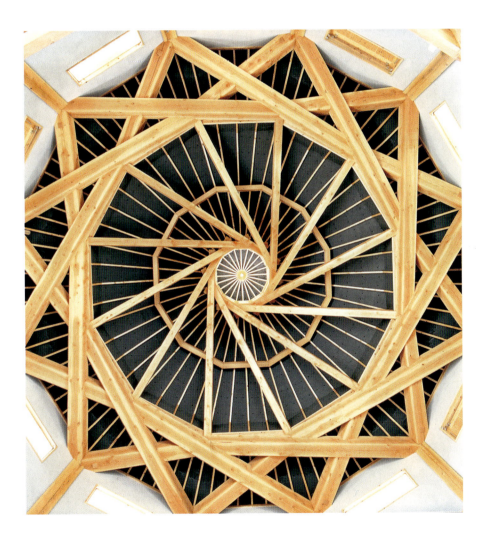

fig d2-b. interior view

fig d2-c. interior view

fig d3. FT Architects, Timber structure II (boxing hall), Kōgakuin University, Tokyo, 2013
fig d3-a. exterior view
fig d3-b. interior view

fig d4. FT Architects, Timber structure I (archery hall), Kōgakuin University, Tokyo, 2013, interior view

POSTSCRIPT: TRADITION, WHO ARE YOU? 381

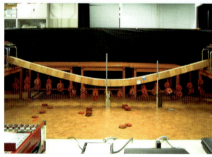 

fig d5. FT Architects, c-Office, Nagoya 2004
fig d5-a. exterior view
fig d5-b. structural principal: catenary and post-tensioning   fig d5-c. construction process

POSTSCRIPT: TRADITION, WHO ARE YOU? 383

fig d5-d. interior view
fig d5-e. construction process   fig d5-f. construction process

fig d6. Tezuka Takaharu and Yui, Asahi 1 and 2 kindergarten, Minamisanriku, 2012-2017
fig d6-a. overall view
fig d6-b. street facade

fig d6-c. exterior view
fig d6-d. interior view of a classroom

fig d7. Yoshimura Yasutaka, Fukumasu base and kindergarten, Chiba, 2016
fig d7-a. exterior view
fig d7-b. interior view

fig d7-c. interior view

fig d8. Itō Toyō, dome, Odate, 1997
fig d8-a. exterior view
fig d8-b. interior view

fig d9. Naitō Hiroshi, Sea-Folk Museum, Toba, 1992
fig d9-a. exterior view
fig d9-b. interior view

fig d10. Naitō Hiroshi, Makino Museum of Plants and People, Kōchi, 1999
fig d10-a. view of interior courtyard
fig d10-b. view of a gallery

fig d10-c. view of a gallery
fig d10-d. interior view

fig d11. Horibe Yasushi, columbarium of the Chikurin-ji monastery, Kōchi, 2013
fig d11-a. exterior view
fig d11-b. view of entry

fig d11-c. interior view with basin

fig d12. Fujimori Terunobu, Takasugian, Suwa, Nagano prefecture, 2004

fig d13. Suzuki Ryōji, Konpira sanctuary, Kagawa prefecture, 2004
fig d13-a. exterior view of entry pavilion
fig d13-b. detail of awning and *kumimono* capital
fig d13-c. detail of awning and *kokera-buki* cedar bark shingle roofing

fig d14. Nishizawa Taira, Sun-Pu church, Shizuoka, 2008
fig d14-a. exterior view

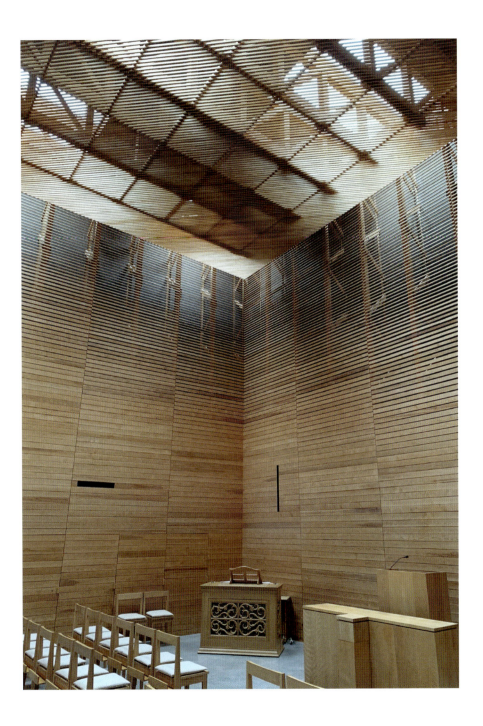

fig d14-b. interior view

fig d15. Kuma Kengo, SunnyHills Minamiaoyama store, Tokyo, 2013
fig d15-a. exterior view   fig d15-b. facade detail
fig d15-c. interior view

fig d15-d. exterior view

fig d16. Reconstruction of the Yakushiji monastery, Nara, 1970–2017
fig d16-a. west pagoda

fig d16-b. *kondō*
fig d16-c. *genjōdō* and *e-den*

JAPANESE TERMS

A

akari shōji 明障子: sliding panel with translucent paper and a wood frame that appeared in Shoin-style construction. Called *shōji* by extension today. See *fusuma, shōji*.

amadera 尼寺: temple reserved for women during the Nara period in the eighth century.

amado 雨戸: sliding wood shutter that is stored in *tobukuro* 戸袋, caissons, attached to the exterior of walls.

amidadō 阿弥陀堂: pavilion in Buddhist temples devoted to the worship of the Amida Buddha.

aita アイタ: clear distance between capitals.

B

beimatsu 米松: literally, American pine; Douglas fir or Oregon pine.

betsugū 別宮: main auxiliary shrine of a Shintō sanctuary. See *massha, seiden, sessha*.

bu 分: a traditional unit of measurement. One hundred *bu* make one *shaku*. See *jō, ken, shaku, sun, rin*.

butsuden 仏殿: pavilion in Buddhist monasteries presided over by a statue of a seated Buddha.

byōbu 屏風: folding screen.

C

cha-date tatami 茶立畳: generic term for the tatami mat on which the tea master officiates in a tea pavilion See *daime-datami, tatami*.

chanoyu 茶の湯: tea ceremony. See *chayoriai*.

chashitsu 茶室: recent term (from the Meiji era) to name the tea pavilion or the room, *shitsu*, where the tea ceremony, *cha*, takes place. Earlier terms: *kakoi, kozashiki, chazashiki, sukiya* room.

chawan 茶碗: tea bowl.

chayoriai 茶寄合: festive gatherings for the first tea ceremonies. The *yoriai* appeared towards the end of the twelfth century, during the Kamakura period. See *chanoyu*.

chazashiki 茶座敷: large formal room, *zashiki*, for the tea ceremony.

chidorihafu 千鳥破風: a "seated dog" or dormer bargeboard which resembles the cut gable of *irimoya*-type roofs. See *hafu, karahafu, noki karahafu*.

chigai-dana 違棚: asymmetric shelving, *tana*, characteristic of the Shoin style. See *haizen-dana, tana, to-dana*.

chinjusha 鎮守社: Shintō shrines, *sha*, that appeared in Buddhist monasteries in the eighth century. These buildings illustrate the syncretism of the two main religions. See *jingū-ji*.

chō 町: an ancient measurement unit, of agrarian origin (equivalent in size to a rice paddy), that became a measure of a street or urban block in the Heian period. A *chō* is 360 *shaku* (60 *ken*), or 109.09 meters long.

chūmon 中門: a porch or main entry gate to different buildings. See *mon*.

chūmonrō 中門廊: a passageway connecting the various pavilions in a Shinden palace.

chūmon-zukuri 中門造: a type of framing characterized by its *chūmon*-type roof. See *honmune-zukuri, kabuto-zukuri*.

D

daibutsuyō 大仏様: literally, Great Buddha style. The name given to Buddhist temples that appeared at the time of the reconstruction of the Tōdaiji temple in Nara, in the twelfth century, during the Heian period. Also known as *tenjikuyō*. See *tenjikuyō, setchūyō, wayō, zenshūyō*.

daime-datami 台目畳, 大目畳: *cha-date tatami*, or the tatami mat on which the tea master officiates in tea pavilions, whose length has been reduced by about a third. Sen no Rikyū was the first to propose this new type of tatami in order to reduce the size of the room. See *cha-date tatami, tatami*.

daikoku-bashira 大黒柱: in popular dwellings, *minka*, a central post that is both symbolic and structural. Literally, the post, *hashira*, of the great blackness (*Daikoku*), the god who ensures the prosperity of the household. Originally the post referred by homonymy to the *daigoku-bashira* 大極柱, the central post of ceremonial imperial buildings. See *hashira*.

daiku 大工: a generic term for capenters, who were the principal managers and builders of all wood architecture in Japan until the Meiji era. The term includes several categories of craftsmen of varying competence, according to the type of construction: ordinary dwellings or not, rural or urban, as well as religious. They still exist today, most often as part of construction companies. See *machibadaiku, machidaiku, miyadaiku, sukiya daiku, tōryō, wataridaiku*.

daitō 大塔: literally, the great tower; pagoda in the Shingon Buddhist school. See *tō, tahōtō*.

denya 殿屋: palace.

dō 堂: Buddhist pavilion.

do-bisashi 土庇: canopy, *hisashi*, which covers over the exterior room with a beaten earth floor, *doma*, in front of a tea pavilion, and by extension, that space. See *doma, hisashi*.

dodai 土台: groundsill in wood which makes the structural connection between the grade/tie beam (previously flat stones placed under each post) in concrete foundations and the wood posts.

doma 土間: a space or room, *ma*, with a (beaten) earthen floor, *do*.

E

edoma 江戸間: name given to the *ken/ma* interval between posts in the Edo region, the new shôgun's capital at the beginning of the period by the same name. Its most standard length was six *shaku*, during the Muromachi period (fourteenth to sixteenth centuries). See *ma, inaka ma, kyōma*.

en 縁: space linking inside and outside, a perimeter gallery/veranda, with plank flooring, usually three *shaku* (approx. 90 cm) wide. It also serves as a corridor leading to rooms one next to each other, generally separated by sliding *shōji* panels. See *engawa, nureen, ochien, hiroen*.

engawa 縁側: a more recent term (from the Edo period) with the same meaning as *en*. See *en*.

F

fūdo 風土: literally, wind and earth. The environment as human context or milieu.

fukihanachi 吹き放ち: hypostyle hall free of partitions in residences from the Nara period of the eighth century.

fushi 節: wood knot.

fusuma 襖: previously called *fusuma shōji*, these opaque sliding panels between rooms appeared in the fourteenth century, during the Muromachi period, in Shoin-style buildings.

G

gankō haichi 雁行配置: plan layout in the form of "flying geese formation," or in a staircase pattern.

garan 伽藍: Buddhist monastery.

gedannoma 下段の間: low, *gedan*, room or salon. See *jōdanoma*.

gekan 下間: low, *ge*, reception chamber, *kan*, for receiving familiar guests in the abbot's residence, *hōjō*, in Zen Buddhism. Along with the *jōkan* and *shichū*, it is one of three chambers in *enfilade*, dedicated to receptions and rituals. It is located on the garden side of residences, facing south. See *jōkan, shichū*.

geya 下屋: low perimeter roof in the popular habitat, *minka*, which recalls the low exterior gallery *hisashi* in Shinden palaces. See *jōya*.

gohai, **kōhai** 向拝: low exterior space under a canopy, in front of shrines and temples.

gojūnotō 五重塔: five-story pagoda. See *tō*.

gōsei-bari 合成梁: composite beam.

H

hafu 破風: cut gable end of *irimoya*-type roofs. See *chidorihafu, karahafu, noki karahafu*.

haizen-dana 配膳棚: cupboard. See *chigai-dana, tana, to-dana*.

hanare 離れ: annex. Smaller house detached from the main "mother" house (*moya* 母屋).

hanegi 桔木: console beam which allows canopies to extend far past the roof, and that reinforce the rafters.

hanikamu kōzō ハニカム構造: bee hive structure (contemporary period).

hari 梁: beam. See *kōryōhari*.

hashira 柱: post. See *daikoku-bashira, hashiratate, hashirawari, hottate-bashira, ma-bashira, maru-bashira, munamochi-bashira, naka-bashira, shin-bashira, sō-bashira, toko-bashira*.

hashiratate 柱立て: erection of posts. In other words, the symbolic and physical beginning of the construction of a wood-structure building. See *hashira*.

hashirawari 柱割: construction principle for dividing up rooms by modular grids of posts, based on spans in *ken*. As opposed to the *tatamiwari*, or division of rooms by tatamis, which appeared in the sixteenth century. See *hashira, shinshin, tatamiwari, uchinori*.

hafu 破風: cut gable in *irimoya*-type roofs. See *chidorihafu, noki karahafu*.

haiden 拝殿: oratory in a Shintō shrine. See *heiden, honden, seiden, shōden*.

heichishiki jūkyo 平地式住居: presumably the first type of habitat *jūkyo*, on level ground, *heichishiki*. Although the partly buried buildings, *tateana jūkyo*, or the buildings with raised floors, *takayuka jūkyo*, are considered the two primary habitats of prehistoric times in Japan, it is likely that this type existed as well. See *takayuka jūkyo, tateana jūkyo*.

heiden 幣殿: pavilion for receiving offerings in a Shintō sanctuary. See *haiden, honden, seiden, shōden*.

hijiki 肘木: corbel. Initially making up the *kumimono*, corbelled capitals. See *kumimono, sashihijiki*.

hinagata-bon 雛形本: carpentry manual whose earliest examples seem to date from the fourteenth century. They were used to transmit secret knowledge within a workshop, but starting in the seventeenth century, during the Edo period, they began to be published more freely. One of the best-known examples is the *Shōmei*, published in 1608.

hinoki 檜: Japanese cypress.

hiwada-buki 檜皮葺: cypress bark shingle roofing. See *kaya-buki yane, kokera-buki yane*.

hiratenjō 平天井: flat, *hiratai*, ceiling, *tenjō*. See *kakekomitenjō, tenjō*.

hiroen 広縁: literally, a wide, *hiroi*, veranda, *en*. See *engawa, nureen, ochien*.

hiroma 広間: literally, great reception room, as opposed to the smaller, *koma*, reception rooms in Shoin-style buildings. These rooms are often *kokonoma*: rooms that are nine *ma* or eighteen tatamis. See *ōhiroma, kokonoma, koma, zashiki*.

hisashi 庇: canopy, and by extension a gallery/space under the canopy in Shinden-style architecture. One can compare this semantic affinity with the French *pilotis*, which designates both the post and the space that is structured by these same posts. See *do-bisashi, ichimen hisashi, mago-bisashi, nimen hisashi, sanmen hisashi*.

hōjō 方丈: abbot's residence in Zen monasteries. The symbolic origin of the term comes from a square room (*hō*, or side of a square) one *jō* on a side (ten-foot-square), approximately three meters by three meters, 29.5 sf, that recalls the mythical shelter of the Indian Buddhist hermit Vimalakīrti, a contemporary of the Buddha. See *tachū hōjō, jōma*.

hokkedō 法華堂: Buddhist oratory. In our text we mention the oratory of the Enryakuji monastery. See *Enryakuji, jōgyōdō*.

honden 本殿: main building (holiest of holy) of Shintō shrines. Over time the term has come to replace the older terms of *seiden, shōden*.

hondō 本堂: main building (holiest of holy) of Buddhist temples. See *kondō, seidō, shōdō*.

honmune-zukuri 本棟造: Framing characterized by the style of its roof, of the *honmune* type. See *chūmon-zukuri, kabutozukuri*.

honjikomi 本仕込み: felling, stripping, and drying of Kitayama cedars (Kitayama sugi) in the forest, at the beginning of August, as practiced in the village of Nakagawa, Kitayama-chō in Kyoto. This traditional technique has been practiced for about four hundred years and enables the wood to have a better "finish" (*honjikomi*), with a natural polish and brilliance.

hosodono 細殿: literally, a long and narrow building.

hottate-bashira 掘立柱: a structural post, originally driven into the ground. This primitive method was not particularly long-lasting and was replaced by posts set on flat stones functioning as footings.

hōzue 方杖: strut

I

ichinoma 一の間: first, *ichi*, room, *ma*. Another name for the *jōkan* hall in the tripartite spatial arrangement of ceremonial chambers in Shoin-style edifices. The most honored guests were received in these rooms. See *jōkan, gekan, shichū*, and *ninoma, sannoma, jōdannoma*.

ima 居: literally, room for living. A type of living room.

Inaka ma 田舎間: the name given to the *ken/ma* interval between posts in the provinces or countryside, *inaka*, as opposed to *kyōma*. Smaller than its Kyoto homologue, its standard size was most frequently six *shaku*, during the Muromachi period (fourteenth to sixteenth centuries). See *ma, edoma, kyōma*.

isshi 一枝: distance between parallel rafters.

irimoya, irimoya-zukuri 入母屋, 入母屋造: hipped gable roof type. See *kirizuma, moya, yosemune*.

itajiki 板敷き: plank floor.

itazu 板図: thin wood board that a carpenter uses to represent the schematic plan of the building he is working on. Only the numbered centerlines (abscissa and ordinates) and the points indicating the locations of posts are represented. Traditionally, this was the only document, except for purely descriptive full-scale drawings and framing details, that carpenters relied on in their work.

izumidono 泉殿: the spring pavilion in Shinden-style residences. See *tainoya, tsuridono*.

J

jichinsai 地鎮祭: Shintō propitiatory ceremony which precedes the construction of a building.

jigokukumi 地獄組: joints between wood profiles in the same plane. They are very difficult to make and are known as Hell, *jigoku*, joints. See *kigumi, shiguchi, tsugite*.

jikidō 食堂: refectory pavilion in monasteries.

jingūji 神宮寺: Buddhist temple, *ji*, built inside a Shintō shrine, *jingū*, in the eighth century. These edifices illustrate the syncretism of the two major religions. See *chinjusha and shinbutsu konkō*.

jinja 神社: Shintō shrine.

jō 丈: an ancient unit of length, measuring ten *shaku*, or approximately three meters during the Muromachi period (fourteenth to sixteenth centuries). Over time, it was abandoned for the *ken*. See *ken* and *shaku*.

jō 畳: another reading of "tatami," when it is used for counting. For example, a three, *san, tatami* room or a *sanjō* room. See *tatami*.

jōdannoma 上段の間: a rostrum or elevated section, *jōdan*, in the *ichinoma* reception room, where the highest-ranked guest is seated in Shoin-style edifices. See *ichinoma*.

jōgyōdō 常行堂: Buddhist oratory. In our text we refer to the one in the Enryakuji monastery. See *Enryakuji, hokkedō*.

jōkan 上間: tall, *jō*, hall, *kan*, for receptions that serves to seat the most distinguished guests, in the abbot's residence, *hōjō*, for Zen Buddhism. Along with the *jōkan* and *shichū*, it is one of three chambers in *enfilade* which are dedicated to receptions and rituals and are located across from the south garden in these residences. See *gekan, shichū*, and *ichinoma, ninoma, sannoma, jōdannoma*.

jōma 丈間: a room, *ma*, measuring one *jō* on a side. The name is given to a small reception room, *kozashiki*, that appeared in the fourteenth century, during the Muromachi period, which measured one and a half *ken* on a side, or approximately three meters at the time, whence the appellation of *jōma*. See *hōjō, ma*.

jōtōshiki 上棟式: see *muneageshiki*.

jōya 上屋: tall central roof in the popular habitat, *minka*, which recall the *moya* of Shinden palaces. See *geya*.

juraku tsuchi 聚楽土: covering of cob walls. See Sukiya style and *tsuchi kabe*.

jūtakuron 住宅論: essay or theory of dwelling (contemporary period).

K

kabe 壁: wall. See *sodekabe, sujikai kabe, tsuchi kabe*.

kabuto-zukuri 兜造: type of framing characterized by the style of its roof, the *kabuto* type. See *chūmon-zukuri, honmune-zukuri*.

kaishō 会所: festive meeting room in residences of the nobility and clergy, that appeared in the twelfth century, during the Kamakura period. By extension, the term applies to pavilions that contain those halls where the *tsukeshoin* and other spatial arrangements characteristic of the Shoin style later appear.

kakejiku 掛軸: hanging scroll, most often in the *tokonoma*.

kakekomitenjō 駆込天井: high sloped ceiling in a tea pavilion. The oblique plan is in reality the underside of the roof, whereas the other ceilings are false dropped ceilings. See *tenjō*.

kake-zukuri 懸造: a style of religious buildings that appeared in the eighth century, at the beginning of the Heian epoch, supported on pilotis, seemingly fastened, *kakeru*, to rocky cliffs in remote areas. They harbored syncretic cults linked to the mountain.

kakoi 囲い: originally a temporary space, defined by a screen on a veranda, *en*, for practicing the tea ceremony. By extension, the term has come to refer to the room used for the tea ceremony, also called the *chazashiki*. See *chazashiki, chashitsu kozashiki, zashiki*.

kaku 閣: belvedere.

kamachi 框: piece of solid hardwood, which serves as a nosing to a step: usually a thick piece, sometimes as thick as the step itself, used where there are differences in height between floors of different rooms.

kami 神: Shintō divinity.

JAPANESE TERMS

kanejaku 矩尺・曲尺 or **sashigane** 差金: metal set square, graduated in *sun* and *shaku* on one side, and in millimeters on the other one—used by carpenters.

kanbatsuzai 間伐材: pruned wood.

kanjōdō 灌頂堂: prayer pavilion of the Shingon school of Buddhism. See *mandaradō*.

karahafu 破風: See *noki karahafu*.

karamatsu 唐松: larch. Widely used in plywood panels (contemporary period). See *lauan, shina*.

karamono 唐物: precious objects, often imported from China or Korea, *kara*, that were displayed in the interiors on different kinds of shelves, *tana*.

kata 形: form, archetype.

katanagare yane 片流れ屋根: single-slope roof.

katō-guchi 花頭口: rounded opening in the partition, *sodekabe*, that separates the tea master from his guests in a tea pavilion.

katōmado 花頭窓: a rounded window that can be found, among other places, in tea pavilions. See *mado*.

katte-guchi 勝手口: service entry from the preparation area, *mizuya*, used by the tea master to enter the pavilion.

kaya-buki yane 茅葺屋根: thatched roof, *yane*. See *hiwada-buki, kokera-buki yane*.

kayoi-guchi 通口: passage door.

kawaraya 瓦屋: tile, *kawara*, roofer. Fabricates and installs roof tiles.

ken 間: along with *jō, shaku, sun, bu*, and *rin, ken* constitutes the main measure of length, imported from China in the sixth century, at the beginning of the Asuka period, at the time of the arrival of Buddhism from the continent. The system was thus used for the construction of new religious buildings before becoming an integral part of all Japanese wood architecture. The *ken* represented the interval between two posts, the intercolumniation. It was both a unit of measurement and an interval, and carried the double meaning of span and bay. The sino-Japanese character 間 is a compound of two basic ideograms: a sun 日 seen between the two posts of a gate 門. In 1886, during the Meiji period, its conversion into the international system set it, once and for all, at 1.81818 meters, or six *shaku. Ken* is along with *ma* the primary reading of the character 間. See *ma* and *jō, shaku, sun, bu*, and *rin*.

kenchiku 建築: a term created during the Meiji period, at the end of the nineteenth century, to translate the word architecture into Japanese.

kenchikuka 建築家: architect.

kenmen kihō 間面記法: a method that served to describe buildings—primarily residences and temples—during the Nara and Heian periods (eighth to twelfth centuries) as a function of the numbers of bays, *ken*, and of the galleries on the facade, *men*. Also called *kenmen hō*.

keta 桁: cross bar/purlin. See *moya, noki-geta*.

ki 木: wood. Can also be read as *moku*. See *mokuzō*.

kichō 几帳: silk curtains that provide separation in Shinden-style residences.

kigumi 木組: joint (generic term). See *jigokukumi, shiguchi, tsugite*.

kireisabi 奇麗さび: this term which literally signifies beautiful *sabi*, (refined simplicity), refers to the aesthetic developed by Kobori Enshū in his tea pavilions. As opposed to the sober and rustic style of Sen no Rikyū, known as *wabisabi*, Enshū sought a certain ornamental richness that more closely conformed to the tastes of the elites. See *wabisabi*.

kirizuma, kirizuma-zukuri 切妻, 切妻造: gable roof. See *irimoya, yosemune*.

kiwari 木割: a system of stereotomy of wood and proportional relations between the different constructive and spatial elements of wood buildings. The dimensions of constituent parts (posts, beams, etc.) and the relations of their height, length, and width are managed in a modular and proportional manner. Yet this system, which has been in effect since the sixth century and the Asuka period, varied in its proportions as well as the basic modular elements. In the Asuka and Heian periods, the spacing between posts played this role, but beginning in the twelfth century in the Kamakura period, carpenters took the distances beween two rafters, *isshi*, more into account.

kōdō 講堂: study pavilion for monks in Buddhist monasteries.

kokera-buki yane 柿葺屋根: roof, *yane*, of wood shingles (often *sawara* cypress or *hinoki*). See *hiwada-buki, kayabuki yane*.

kokonoma 九間: large reception room nine *ma* in size. See *hiroma, koma*.

kokumin jūtaku 国民住宅: national housing (contemporary period).

koma 小間: small room as apposed to the *hiroma* in Shoin-style architecture. See *hiroma, kokonoma*.

kondō 金堂: literally, treasure pavilion; main religious pavilion of Buddhist temples. Also called *hondō* or *shōdō*.

kōryōhari 虹梁: collar beam. See *hari, koya-bari*.

kōshi 格子: wood lattice. See *shitomido*.

koshikake 腰掛: sofa.

koya-bari 小屋梁: primary beams of the roof (tiebeam). See *hari*, *kōryōhari*.

kozashiki 小座敷: little *zashiki*. See *kakoi*, *zashiki*.

kumimono 組物: capital with a corbel consisting of several pieces of wood, supports, *masu*, and corbels, *hijiki*. These capitals can support long roof canopies. See *hijiki*, *masu* and *sashihijiki*.

kusunoki 楠: camphorwood.

kura 倉: warehouse, attic.

kuri 庫裏: pavilion housing the kitchens in temples.

kurinoki 栗の木: chestnut tree.

kuroshoin 黒書院: black *shoin* or black study, so-called as it is often decorated with China ink paintings. Along with the *shiroshoin*, it is one of the most intimate complex of reception rooms, *hiroma*, in Shoin-style residences. See *hiroma*, *shoin*, *shiroshoin*.

kusarinoma 鎖の間: In Shoin- and Sukiya-style edifices, an intermediate room, both in style and function, between the small *koma* rooms, where the tea ceremony takes place, and the large, formal *hiroma* rooms. At the beginning of the Edo period, in the seventeenth century, tea masters like Furuta Oribe and Kobori Enshū created new spatial arrangements using these rooms so as to vary the ways of organizing the tea ceremony.

kyakuden 客殿: a reception hall that appeared during the medieval period.

kyōma 京間: a name given to the *ken/ma* interval between posts, in Kyoto, as opposed to the *inaka ma*. It was longer than the latter, with a typical standard length of six and one half *shaku*, during the Muromachi period (fourteenth to sixteenth centuries). See *ma*, *edoma*, *inaka ma*.

kyōzō 経蔵: reserved for writing.

L

lauan ラワン: wood imported from Southeast Asia. Frequently used in the fabrication of plywood panels (contemporary period). See larch, *shina*.

M

ma 間: like the *ken*, the sino-Japanese character 間 is a compound of two basic ideograms: the sunlight 日 seen between the two posts of a gate 門; *ma* represents an interval between two posts—their intercolumniation. It constitutes a spatial unit linked to the tatami, simultaneously in the sense of length (of one tatami) and of area (the square area of two tatami mats). But in the spatial domain that concerns us, it also refers to a space or room, whence this plethora of semantic associations like *kokonoma* (a nine-*ma* room), *ichinoma* (the primary room), *hitoma* (a room one *ma* squared) or *kusarinoma* (the *kusari* room). See *ken*; *edo ma*, *inaka ma*, *kyōma*; *hiroma*, *jōma*, *kokonoma*, *koma*; *ichinoma*, *jōdannoma*, *ninoma*, *sannoma*; *hitoma*, *futama*, *mima*, *muma*; *kusarinoma*, *tokonoma*, *tsuginoma*.

ma-bashira 間柱: stud. See *hashira*.

machibadaiku 町場大工: another name for the *machidaiku*. See *daiku* and *machidaiku*.

machiya 町屋: urban residence. See *minka*.

machidaiku 町大工: carpenter specialized in the construction of urban residences, *machiya*. See *daiku*.

mado 窓: window. See *katōmado*, *shitajimado*.

mago-bisashi 孫庇: canopy and supplementary gallery added to the exterior of a gallery, *hisashi*. See *hisashi*.

mandaradō 曼荼羅堂: prayer pavilion in which mandalas were displayed in the Shingon school of Buddhism. See *kanjōdō*.

maru-bashira 丸柱: round post, common during the Heian period (eighth to twelfth centuries) in Shinden-style edifices. This type was replaced by square posts in later periods. They are still to be found in certain pieces of Sukiya influence when Kitayama cedars is used. *Kitayama sugi*. Also called *maruta-bashira* 丸太柱.

massha 末社: low auxiliary structure in a Shintō shrine. See *betsugū* and *sessha*.

masu 斗: supporting element in the composite capitals of canopies. See *kumimono*.

matsu 松: pine.

michō 御帳: a sort of temporary podium on tatamis, surrounded and protected by curtains, for the most honored guest to sit, in Shinden-style residences.

minka 民家: popular habitat. See *machiya*, *nōka*.

miyadaiku 宮大工: carpenter specialized in the construction of religious buildings, especially temples, *miya*. Along with the *sukiya daiku*, they are considered to be the best craftsmen in their profession. See *daiku*.

mizuya 水屋: literally, the room, *ya*, for water, *mizu*; space for preparing the tea, adjacent to the main room in the tea pavilion.

mokuzai 木材: wood, *moku*, taken in its material sense, *zairyō*. See *ki*.

mokuzō 木造: construction system with wood structure. Wood construction or wood architecture are thus called *mokuzō kenchiku*. See *ki*, *mokuzai*.

mon 門: Entrance gate or portico for different edifices.

moya 母屋: literally, the mother frame, or the central room located under this frame, free of posts, and generally two *ken* deep. It is surrounded by exterior galleries/verandas, *hisashi*, in Shinden-style edifices. Although it is archaic, it already highlights the breakdown of barriers between rooms, and the role of transitional spaces, *hisashi*, between inside and outside, that establish certain recurring features of wood architecture in Japan. The term *moya* is also used to name the purlins of the roof. See *hisashi*.

muna-gi 棟木: ridge beam of a roof; *mune*, ridge, and *ki*, wood. See *keta*.

munamochi-bashira 棟持柱: post supporting the ridge capping or the ridge beam in Shintō shrines.

muneageshiki 棟上式: ceremonial laying of the ridge beam, which concludes the *tatekata* phase in the early part of construction. Also called *jōtōshiki*. See *tatekata*.

mukuri 起り: convex form characteristic of Sōan tea pavilion roofs.

N

narabikuradō 並倉堂: complex of pavilions/storehouses, *kuradō*, aligned, *narabi*, inside temples. Heian period (eighth to twelfth centuries). See *narabidō*.

nagare-zukuri 流造: type of gable roof, with two planes, *kirizuma*, one of which is very elongated at the entry side. See *kirizuma*, *irimoya*, *yosemune*.

nageshi 長押: lintel beam which forms a sort of structural chainage line in the walls, located over the opening parts of edifices from the Heian period, (eighth to twelfth centuries). The term is still used even when it is merely decorative, as in Shoin-style residences.

naka-bashira 中柱: literally, the center post. In reality it is a decorative post that terminates the *sodekabe* in the tea pavilion. See *hashira*, *sodekabe*.

nakanoma 中の間: span between the posts of the central bay in religious buildings.

nando 納戸: storeroom.

nara ナラ or **naranoki** 楢の木: oak or Japanese oak.

narabidō 並堂: complex of pavilions, *dō*, aligned, *narabi*, in temples of the Heian period (eighth to twelfth centuries). See *narabikuradō*.

nijiri-guchi 躙口: lowered or crouching entry to a tea pavilion for guests. An arrangement attributed to Sen no Rikyū.

ninaidō にない堂: corridors that link the oratories in Tendai Buddhism.

ninoma 二の間: second *ni*, room, *ma*. Another name for the *gekan* chambers in the tripartite spatial arrangement of the ceremonial parts of edifices in the Shoin style. The guests received in these rooms were less distinguished than those received in the *ichonoma* (first) chamber. See *jōkan*, *gekan*, *shichū*; *ichinoma*, *jōdannoma*, *sannoma*.

nōka 農家: rural habitat, farm. See *minka*.

noki 軒: canopy or edge of the roof.

noki-geta 軒桁: eave beam or purlin, *keta*, at the leading edge of the roof or canopy. See *keta*.

noki karahafu 軒唐破風: a type of curved canopy of Chinese inspiration (*kara*). See *chidorihafu*, *hafu karahafu*.

nokisaki 軒先: edge of a canopy. See *noki*.

nuki 貫: penetrating tie beam that crosses through the posts.

nureen 濡れ縁: open air extension to the *en* space/veranda. See *en*.

O

ōgitaruki 仰垂木: fanning rafters often used in Zen Buddhist edifices. See *taruki*.

ōhiroma 大広間: literally, great *hiroma* and by extension the pavilion that accomodates this room. See *hiroma*.

ōkabe 大壁: this term is formed from two characters ō–for grand, or rather thick in this case—and *kabe*, wall. It is used as a name for constructing a cob wall whose exterior layer (plaster of planks) covers over the main wood structure. See its opposite, *shinkabe*.

oki-datami 置畳: a tatami mat placed over the plank floor of buildings of the Heian period.

okoshiezu 越し絵図: a paper model consisting of a plan with all the facades around it folded down, with the exception of the ceiling. Mainly used for tea pavilion.

oshiita 押板: a long tablet, narrow and thick, which is at the origin of the *tokonoma*. Often laid out in an L-shape during the Muromachi period (fourteenth to sixteenth centuries).

ochien 落縁: low exterior veranda. See *en*.

R

raiden 礼殿: oratory in the syncretic complexes of the *shinbutsu konkō* during the Muromachi period (fourteenth to sixteenth centuries). Compound term composed from *raidō* (Buddhism) and *haiden* (Shintō). See *haiden* and *raidō*.

raidō 礼堂: oratory placed in front of the *shōdō* in Buddhist temples. See *shōdō*.

ranma 欄間: transom located above *fusuma* and *shōji* sliding panels.

reibyō 霊廟: mausoleum built in the Muromachi and the early Edo periods (seventeenth century) according to the syncretic doctrine of the *shinbutsu konkō*. The most famous of them is the Tōshōgū in Nikkō.

rin 厘: traditional unit of measurement. One thousand *rin* make up one *shaku*. See *shaku*.

rōdai 露台: uncovered terrace in front of a building.

rōka 廊下: corridor. See *en*.

roji 露地: path leading to a tea pavilion.

S

sakanya 左官屋: craftsman who puts up cob walls and applies coatings to them.

sangakujiin 山岳寺院: mountain temple.

sannoma 三の間: third, *san*, room, *ma*. Another name for the *gekan* rooms in the tripartite spatial arrangement of ceremonial rooms in Shoin-style edifices. The status of the guests received in these rooms was lower than those received in the *ichinoma* (first) rooms. See *jōkan, gekan, shichū; ichinoma, jōdannoma, ninoma*.

sashihijiki 挿肘木: corbel with strut. See *hijiki, kumimono*.

saiden 祭殿: place of worship in prehistoric times.

setchūyō 折衷様: name given to the late composite style of Buddhist temples that appeared in the Kamakura period (twelfth to fourteenth centuries). See *daibutsuyō, wayō, zenshūyō*.

sekisō gōhan 積層合板: plywood (contemporary period).

seiden 正殿: literally, a building in which public life takes place. Also called *shōden*. The main building of Shintō shrines, it is part of a complex that includes the oratory, *haiden*, a pavilion for offerings, *heiden*, and annexes: *bessha, massha* and *sessha*. See *haiden, heiden, honden, shōden*.

seikatsu kūkan 生活空間: space required for daily life.

sessha 摂社: auxiliary building in a Shintō shrines. See *bessha* and *massha*.

shakkei 借景: a spatial arrangement used in gardens called "borrowed landscape." It consists of managing the distant view—for example a mountain—and using it as a visual background, while masking an unwanted view in the middle ground. This technique, which appeared during medieval times, makes it possible to link inside and outside, to increase the apparent size of the garden, and sometimes to select and establish a relationship with some important element in the surrounding landscape.

sha 社: Shintō shrine.

shaku 尺: a traditional unit of measurement imported from China by way of Korea towards the end of the Asuka period (sixth to eighth centuries), that was originally close to a span (the distance between the thumb and index or middle finger), or approximately 18 cm. Its size subsequently increased to be close to a cubit. The *ken* played an important dimensional and conceptual role, which made it possible to manage the size and relation between pieces, while the *shaku* was the primary unit of measure used by builders on site. In 1886, during the Meiji period, it was converted into the international system and its value set as 30.3030 centimeters. Its decimal subdivisions are the *sun*, the *bu* and the *rin*. See *bu, jō, ken, rin, sun*.

shichū 室中: central reception room in the abbot's residence, *hōjō*, in Zen Buddhism. See *gekan, jōkan*.

shiguchi 仕口: angle joint. See *jigokukumi, kigumi, tsugite*.

shikinen sengū 式年遷宮: periodic rite of reconstruction of Shintō shrines, like Ise, that is linked to the transfer of the divinity. This rite goes back to the year 690 and takes place almost every twenty years.

shikkui 漆喰: whitewash. The lime coating applied to cob walls, *tsuchi kabe*.

shina シナ or ***shinanoki*** 科の木: linden or Japanese linden tree (*tilia japonica*). Frequently used as limewood plywood panels (contemporary period). See *larch, lauan*.

shin-bashira 心柱: central post whose function is more symbolic than structural. It establishes an axis, *shin*, for the display of relics of the Buddha in the pagodas. See *hashira*.

shinbutsu konkō 神仏混淆: a syncretic doctrine that appeared during the Muromachi period (fourteenth to sixteenth centuries) and the beginning of the Edo (seventeenth century), that mixes elements borrowed from Shingon Buddhism and Shintō. See *reibyō*.

shinden*, *shinden-zukuri 寝殿, 寝殿造: a term used to designate a type of edifice, a method of construction, and an architectural style. The Shinden style was characteristic of noble residences of Chinese inspiration during the Heian period. The *shinden* designates the main body of these palaces. Oriented to the south and facing a courtyard/garden, it consists of a central room, *moya*, without fixed partitions, and surrounded by peripheral galleries, *hisashi*, whose bearing structure consists of posts round in section, *maru-bashira*. It is connected by corridors to annexed pavilions, *tainoya*, arranged symmetrically. The entire palace complex is also called *shinden* by extension, but no original examples survive, as they were replaced by Shoin-style residences in the medieval period.

shingyōsō 真行草: this term is formed from three characters that describe the three principal styles of classical sino-japanese calligraphy: *shin* for the formal and angular type, *gyō* for the semi-cursive, and *sō* for the cursive, fluid, and free one. During the Muromachi period (fourteenth to sixteenth centuries), these terms characterized three types of rooms by analogy: *shin* for large, extremely formal reception rooms, *hiroma*; *gyō*, for intermediary rooms; and *sō*, for the uncluttered and rustic rooms of the tea pavilion, *koma*.

shinkabe 真壁: this term is formed from two characters: *shin*, axis, and *kabe*, wall. It refers to the most common method of construction for cob walls that are inserted between wood posts that remain exposed as a result, along with the rest of the main structure. For the opposite, see *ōkabe*.

shinshin 真々: this term is the name of the working method of the carpenters who were until the end of the nineteenth century (Meiji era) the only master builders of wood architecture in Japan. *Shin* signifies an axial line, and thus *shinshin* signifies the center interval (*ken*) between posts. In other words, the carpenters proceeded by setting up a spatial, organization, and structural grid of posts based on multiples of the center-to-center distance. See *uchinori*.

shinwayō 新和様: literally, the new *wayō* style. Name given to the style of Buddhist temples that combined *wayō* and *daibutsuyō* influences during the Kamakura period (twelfth to fourteenth centuries) See *wayō*.

shinzashiki 真座敷: literally, *zashiki* (formal hall) in *shin* style, according to the principles of *shingyōsō*. See *shingyōsō* and *zashiki*.

shiroshoin 白書院: white *shoin* or white study. Along with the *kuroshoin*, it makes up one of the complexes of reception rooms, *hiroma*, the most intimate ones in Shoin-style edifices. See *hiroma, shoin, kuroshoin*.

shitajimado 下地窓: a window, *mado*, which leaves exposed the bamboo lattice that makes up the internal structure, *shitaji*, of cob walls, *tsuchi kabe*, in tea pavilions, *chashitsu*. See *mado*.

shitaji 下地: internal structure (studs, etc.) of walls (with wood or metal structures).

shitomido 蔀戸: wooden shutter suspended between posts in *Shinden*-style residences.

shitsurai 室礼: seasonal arrangements and decoration of residential interiors in the Shinden style.

shōbanseki 相伴席: Initially a room or space a single tatami in size that served to slightly enlarge the small tea pavilion as Sen no Rikyū had conceived it. Subtly separated from the main space, it served to hold a greater number of guests, possibly of a lower rank.

shōden 昇殿: main building of Shintō shrines, also called *seiden*. See *honden* and *seiden*.

shōdō 正堂: another name for the *kondō*, or *hondō* in Buddhist temples.

shoin, shoin-zukuri 書院, 書院造: designates a room, a type of edifice, a method of construction, and an architectural style. The Shoin style that developed in the Muromachi period (fourteenth century) characterized the residences of the nobility and supplanted the previous Shinden style. The *moya-hisashi* pair was gradually replaced by a series of asymmetrical pavilions in which the main rooms, recently covered in tatamis, were separated by sliding partitions with thinner square-shaped posts. The term *shoin* designated at the time a *tsukeshoin*, an alcove for reading and writing that included a tablet, and a *shōji* (for natural illumination) before extending to the room or study which contained it, and finally to pavilions for the nobility built in this style. See *kuroshoin, shiroshoin*.

shōji 障子: a name which originally applied to all types of partitioning. Today, the term only applies to wood-framed sliding panels with translucent paper, as opposed to the opaque *fusuma*. See *akari shōji, fusuma, wakishōji, yarido*.

shuden 主殿: a type of medieval aristocratic residence, an intermediary between the Shinden and Shoin styles. No building of this type survives today.

shūseizai 集成材: glue-laminated or cross-laminated (contemporary period).

sōan 草庵: rustic style of tea pavilions known through the *wabisabi* precepts of Sen no Rikyū, *Sōanfu* or *Sōan* type. See *wabisabi*.

sō-bashira 総柱: ancient construction type in which the entire structural grid is filled in, as opposed to buildings that omit some posts. For example, the *shinden*, in which the central *moya* omits some posts, is not an example of the *sō-bashira* type. See *hashira*.

sodekabe 袖壁: wall, *kabe*, or non-structural partition that partly conceals the *cha-date tatami* occupied by the tea master during the ceremony. It originally separated the room in which the ceremony is held from the adjacent *tsuginoma*, the space used for the preparation. It was subsequently integrated into the main room by Sen no Rikyū.

sori 反り: convex curvature of roofs in keeping with the archetypes of Buddhist temples imported from China during the Asuka period (sixth to eighth centuries).

sōzashiki 草座敷: literally, a *zashiki* (salon) in the *sō* style, according *shingyōsō* principles. In fact, a small room, *koma*, which serves as an informal living room. See *shingyōsō* and *zashiki*.

sudare 簾: a sort of suspended shade made from slats of bamboo, reed, or other modest materials. It allows air to pass but blocks the view.

sugi 杉: Japanese cedar, cryptomeria.

sukiya, **sukiya-zukuri** 数寄, 数寄屋造: designates an architectural style from the Azuchi-Momoyama period, during the late sixteenth century, with tea pavilions also known as *sukiya* rooms. The new style featured the refinement of these new rooms that influenced the entire aesthetic of aristocratic residences.

sukiya daiku 数寄屋大工: carpenter specialized in the construction of rich and highly refined residences in the Sukiya style, the archetypes of which appeared with the first tea pavilions at the end of the sixteenth century. Along with the *miyadaiku*, the *sukiya daiku* is considered the best craftsman in his profession. See *daiku*, *miyadaiku*.

sujikai kabe 筋交い壁: from *sujikai*, bracing. In the Joan tea pavilion designed by Oda Uraku, the angled wall, *kabe*, that evokes bracing even though it is non-structural.

sumigi 角木: angled corner rafter at a canopy.

sun 寸: a traditional unit of measurement. Ten *sun* equal one *shaku*. See *jō, ken, shaku, bu, rin*.

sunoko 簀の子: wood strip flooring for terraces.

sunpō 寸法: dimensions, values (usually in *sun* and *shaku*, or millimeters) for a construction drawing.

T

tachū hōjō 塔頭方丈: complex from the Kamakura period (twelfth to fourteenth centuries) consisting of several edifices for the tombs *tachū* of the Zen abbots which also served as their residences, *hōjō*. See *hōjō*.

tahōtō 多宝塔: pagoda with multiple roofs in the Shingon Buiddhist school (a circular tower placed on a square base) and the Tendai school (tower with square plan placed on a homothetic base). This edifice is an element of monastic complexes, *garan*. The word *tō*, tower, is derived from the term *sotōba*, which is itself a phonetic transcription of the Sanscrit *stupa*, the sepulcher in which relics of the Buddha were first conserved. See *tō, daitō, shin-bashira*.

taimenjo 対面所: reception and audience room in residences in the Shoin style.

tainoya 対屋: annex pavilon in palaces of the Shinden style. The pavilions were named according to their placement in the cardinal directions: the east pavilion, *higashinoya* 東の屋, the west, *nishinoya* 西の屋, and the north, *kitanoya* 北の屋; or according to their location and function, such as the fishing pavilion, *tsuridono*, and the spring pavillon, *izumidono*. See *shinden*.

tana 棚: generic term to refer to shelving. Originally, the shelving units were used to display the bowls, teas, as well as other objects and utensils in the gathering rooms, *kaisho*, during the Muromachi period (fourteenth to sixteenth centuries) See *chigai-dana, haizen-dana, to-dana*.

takayuka jūkyo 高床住居: type of archaic habitat, *jūkyo*, with a raised wooden floor, *takayuka*. See *heichishiki jūkyo* and *tateana jūkyo*.

taruki 垂木: common rafter. See *ōgitaruki*.

tatami, **jō** 畳: initially a simple rush mat, *igusa*, similar in size to a man lying down. (approximately one meter eighty by ninety centimeters) The tatami gradually became thicker and more rigid to become a floor tile approximately five centimeters thick made of compressed rice straw—often replaced today by a polyurethane foam mat. The long side is usually reinforced by a band of fabric. Beginning in the Muromachi period (fourteenth to sixteenth centuries), the tatami was used as a modular element to cover the floors of rooms in residences of the nobility. This use subsequently extended to most construction, with the mat playing a spatial and dialectical role in relation to the grid of posts. Although its dimensions were standardized, its size could very according to its location in rooms, as well as in different regions and periods. See the three main types of intercolumniation called *edoma, inaka ma* and *kyōma*. The tatami is less used in the contemporary habitat today, and it is only used in so-called Japanese rooms, *washitsu*. See *cha-date tatami, daime-datami, jō, oki-datami* and *tatamiwari*.

tatamiwari 畳割: a principle of dividing up space by tatamis and their modules that appeared during the Muromachi period (fourteenth to sixteenth centuries) with the creation of small *jōma* or *koma* rooms, based on tatami modules and no longer on structural bays. This principle also serves to organize and measure spaces. See *tatami* and *hashirawari*.

tatamiya 畳屋: a craftsman who fabricates and lays tatamis.

tateana jūkyo 縦穴住居: an archaic type half-buried, *tateana*, habitat, *jūkyo*, from the Jōmon period. See *heichishiki jūkyo* and *takayuka jūkyo*.

JAPANESE TERMS

tateguya 建具屋: a craftsman and woodworker who fabricates and installs doors and sliding partitions (*tategu*).

tatekata 建方: the set-up and assembly of the prefabricated skeleton of a wood structure at the beginning of construction.

tawami-jaku 撓尺: a long curved wooden jig or template that makes it possible to adjust the height of the rafters and make them rise up to meet the corners of the roof, so as to make curved canopies.

tenjikuyō 天竺様: literally, the Indian style. A name previously applied to the *daibutsuyō* style. See *daibutsuyō*.

tenjō 天井: a generic term for the ceiling of a room. From a strictly construction point of vew, these are for the most part false, or dropped ceilings. See *hiratenjō, kakekomitenjō, tokotenjō*.

tera 寺: Buddhist temple.

tō 塔: pagoda (or tower). See *daitō, gojūnotō, tahōtō*.

tobiishi 飛石: garden pathways in Japanese gardens, consisting of disjointed stone steps, *ishi*, (literally, jumping, *tobi*).

to-dana 戸棚: shelving unit with doors. See *chigai-dana, haizen-dana, tana*.

toko-bashira 床柱: decorative post marking the angle of the *tokonoma* alcove in Shoin-style architecture. See *hashira*.

tokonoma 床の間: an alcove, often raised up a step, for the display of different ornaments in buildings in the Shoin and Sukiya styles and in tea pavilions (*chashitsu*).

tokotenjō 床天井: ceiling, *tenjō*, of the *tokonoma*.

torii 鳥居: gateway that leads to a Shintō shrine.

tōriniwa 通庭: an interior lateral corridor, perpendicular to the street, often in beaten earth, which developed in city residences, *machiya*, built on narrow and deep lots.

tōryō 棟梁: the master carpenter. See *daiku*.

tsubo 坪: a unit of surface area equivalent to one *ma* squared, or two tatamis, equivalent to 3.3 square meters (35.5 sf).

tsubo niwa 坪庭: literally, a garden, *niwa*, of one *tsubo* (or two tatamis) in area, or 3.3 square meters (35.5 sf). In other words, a small interior garden in town houses, *machiya*.

tsuchi kabe 土壁: cob wall. See *kabe*.

tsuginoma 次の間: a room adjoining the area in which the master officiates in a tea pavilion. Along with the *mizuya* room, it is often the place where tea is prepared prior to the master's presentation to the guests.

tsugite 継手: butt joint. See *jigokukumi, kigumi*.

tsukeshoin 付書院: a study (of Chinese origin) for the learned that forms a kind of projecting alcove with a tablet. This frequently used manner of juxtaposing a projecting space into the exterior corridor, *en*, or into a next room of lesser importance, makes it possible to retain the formal regularity of the main space covered in tatamis. This space, often simply called *shoin*, provides the name for the pavilions that contain it as well as the eponymous style. This aesthetic first appeared during the medieval period and gradually replaced the Shinden style in residences of the nobility and became widespread in the seventeenth century. See *shoin*.

tsukue 机: desk.

tsuridono 鶴殿: the fishing pavilion in Shinden-style residences. See *izumidono, tainoya*.

U

uchinori 内法: this term refers to a principle of conceiving and comprehending buildings based on the distance between posts, or intercolumniation, as defined by the size of tatamis that can be inserted between them. It was the intent of completely covering multiple rooms with these thick and standardized mats at the end of the sixteenth century that led to the organization of plans into modular compositions based on this principle. This term is complementary—and not opposed—to *shinshin*, the principle of on-center dimensions, which refers more specifically to the work of the carpenter and is more prevalent during construction. See *shinshin*.

uraku mado 有楽窓: literally, a window, *mado*, à la Uraku. A type of window in tea pavilions attributed to Oda Uraku. The window consists of a lattice of bamboo behind a sliding panel in translucent paper.

W

wabicha 侘茶: tea, *cha*, in the *wabi* style. In other words, the tea, and by extension the tea ceremony, as it was practiced in the tea pavilions of the *wabisabi* style.

wabisabi 侘び寂び: a composite term based on the words *wabi*, uncluttered, and *sabi*, patina. A rustic and austere style, embodying an ideal of simplicity in the tea pavilions attributed to Sen no Rikyū, or following his aesthetic in small rooms, *koma*. These rooms thus contrasted with the luxury of the main reception rooms, *hiroma*, of aristocratic residences in the Shoin style. See *kireisabi, wabicha*.

wakishōji 脇障子: sculpted wood panels that terminate the exterior galleries of shrines and of *shoin*, starting in the Muromachi period (fourteenth to sixteenth centuries). See *shōji*.

wataridaiku 渡大工: itinerant, *watari*, carpenter, who helped construct farmhouses in the countryside. See *daiku*.

wayō 和洋: literally, Japanese style. The name given to the first Buddhist temples that appeared in the sixth century, during the Asuka period. See *daibutsuyō, setchūyō, shinwayō, zenshūyō*.

Y

yarido 遣戸: temporary sliding partition, as opposed to *shōji*, in Shinden-style residences. See *shōji*.

yōkan 洋館: literally, Occidental building or construction built in an European style from the Meiji era.

yosemune, **yosemune-zukur**i 寄棟, 寄棟造: hipped roof. See *kirizuma, irimoya*.

Z

zashiki 座敷: Originally a grand reception room with a floor covered in tatamis, in the *shoin*. Since the seventeenth century and the Edo period, this room spread to all types of habitat and constitutes a salon for reception, in which one finds the *tokonoma* and the various shelving units that appeared with the Shoin style. See *chazashiki, kozashiki, hiroma*.

zenshūyō 禅宗様: literally, the style of the Zen schools. The name given to the style of Zen Buddhist temples that appeared in the thirteenth century, during the Kamakura period. See *daibutsuyō, setchūyō, wayō*.

INDEX OF PROPER NAMES

A

Aikawa Haruki 相川春喜 (1909–1953): Japanese historian. 194

Andō Tadao 安藤忠雄 (born 1941): Japanese architect. 9, 21, 370

Ashikaga Yoshimitsu 足利義満 (1358–1408): political leader during the Muromachi period, third Ashikaga shōgun. 109

Ashikaga Yoshinori 足利義教 (1394–1441): political leader during the Muromachi period, sixth Ashikaga shōgun. Son of Yoshimitsu. 60

Ashikaga Yoshimasa 足利義政 (1435–1490): political leader during the Muromachi period, eighth Ashikaga shōgun. 115, 120

B

Ban Shigeru 坂茂 (born 1957): Japanese architect. 369, 372

C

Chamberlain Basil Hall (1850–1935): British Japanologist. 269

Chōgen 重源 (1121–1206): Buddhist monk, responsible for the reconstruction of Tōdaiji. 29, 33, 38

Conder Josiah (1852–1920): British architect, considered to be the first professor of architecture at the Imperial University of Tokyo. 173, 274

D

Dōgen Kigen (Zenji) 道元希玄 (禅師) (1200–1253): Buddhist monk, founded the Sōtō school (Sōtōshu 曹洞宗) of Zen Buddhism. 195

F

Frampton Kenneth (born 1930): British historian of architecture. 263

Fróis Luis (1532–1597): Portuguese Jesuit and historian. 117

Fujii Kōji 藤井厚二 (1888–1938): Japanese architect. 179, 180

Fujimori Terunobu 藤森照信 (born 1946): architectural historian and Japanese architect. 21, 169, 171, 179, 181, 193, 257, 373, 374, 394

Fujiwara no Michinaga 藤原道長 (966–1028): political leader during the Heian period. 99, 100

Fujiwara no Toyonari 藤原豊成 (704–765): political leader during the Nara period. 150

Fukushima Kazuya 福島加津也 (born 1968): Japanese architect. 372

Furuta Oribe 古田織部 (1544–1615): tea master, disciple of Sen no Rikyū. 67, 125, 128, 135

Futagawa Yukio 二川幸夫 (1932–2013): Japanese photographer. 222

G

Genshin 源信 (942–1017): Buddhist monk, author of Ōjōyōshū 往生要集, The Essentials of Rebirth in the Pure Land. 100

Go Shirakawa (tennō) 道元希玄 (禅師) (1127–1192): emperor. 100

Gropius Walter (1883–1969): German-born American architect. 203, 204, 255

H

Heinouchi Masanobu 平内政信 (1583–1645): master carpenter, author of the Shōmei 匠明 treatise on carpentry (1608). 19, 84

Hirayama Chūji 平山忠治 (born 1909): Japanese photographer. 218

Horibe Yasushi 堀部安嗣 (born 1967): Japanese architect. 373, 392

Horiguchi Sutemi 堀口捨己 (1895–1984): Japanese architect and historian. 22, 64, 67, 113, 124, 176, 177, 179, 181, 187, 247-249, 255, 261, 263, 369, 371, 375

Hosokawa Sansai 細川三斎 (1564–1646): tea master, disciple of Sen no Rikyū. 124

I

Inoue Mitsuo 井上充夫 (1918–2002): historian of Japanese architecture. 64, 231

Inoue Shōichi 井上章一 (born 1955): historian of Japanese architecture. 204

Ishii Kazuhiro 石井和紘 (1944–2015): Japanese architect. 372, 375, 376

Ishimoto Yasuhiro 石元泰博 (1921–2012): Japanese-American photographer. 202-206, 231

Isozaki Arata 磯崎新 (born 1931): Japanese architect. 21, 248, 370, 371

Itō Chūta 伊東忠太 (1867–1954): Japanese architectural historian and architect. 10, 11, 168, 172, 173, 177, 255, 371

Itō Toyō 伊東豊雄 (born 1941): Japanese architect. 9, 370, 373, 375, 388

Itō Yōtarō 伊藤要太郎 (1922–2004): Japanese architectural historian and architect. 19, 84

K

Kamo no Chōmei 鴨長明 (1155–1216): poet, author of the Hōjōki 方丈記 (*The Ten Foot Square Hut*). 22, 371

Katagiri Sekishū 片桐石州 (1605–1673): tea master of the fourth Tokugawa shōgun. 141

Kawazoe Noboru 川添登 (1926–2015): Japanese architectural historian and critic. 30, 204

Kishida Hideto 岸田日出刀 (1899–1966): Japanese architectural historian and architect. 177, 187, 203, 205, 247

Kiko Kiyoyoshi 木子清敬 (1845–1907): master carpenter *miyadaiku* and architect. 172, 173, 274

Kjaerholm Poul (1929–1980): Danish furniture designer. 233

Kobori Enshū 小堀遠州 (1579–1647): tea master, disciple of Furuta Oribe. 67, 125, 128, 134-139, 141, 231, 274

Kūkai 空海 (774–835): founded Shingon 真言 school of Buddhism (of the true word or *mantra*). 96, 98, 99

Kuma Kengo 隈研吾 (born 1954): Japanese architect. 9, 257, 374, 375, 398

L

Lévi-Strauss Claude (1908–2009): French anthropologist. 30

Lewerentz Sigurd (1885–1975): Swedish architect. 286

M

Mackintosh Charles Rennie (1868–1928): Scottish architect. 179

Maekawa Kunio 前川国男 (1905–1986): Japanese architect. 22, 23, 193-198, 200, 201, 203, 205, 210, 218, 243, 247, 249, 255, 369

Makino Tomitarō 牧野富太郎 (1862–1957): Japanese botanist. 373

Matsukuma Hiroshi 松隈洋 (born 1957): historian of Japanese architecture. 193-195

Motono Seigo 本野精吾 (1882–1944): Japanese architect. 187

Murano Tōgo 村野藤吾 (1891–1984): Japanese architect. 22, 248, 249, 253-263, 369, 375

Murata Jukō 村田珠光 (1423–1502): tea master, Sen no Rikyū's predecessor. 67, 109, 117

N

Nakamura Masao 中村昌生 (born 1927): Japanese architectural historian and architect. 67, 124

Nakamura Sotoji 中村外二 (1906–1997): Sukiya master carpenter. 18, 248, 272

Naitō Hiroshi 内藤廣 (born 1950): Japanese architect. 373, 389, 390

Niijima Jō 新島襄 (1843–1890): known as Joseph Hardy Neeshima, founder of Dōshisha university. 169, 171

Niemeyer Oscar (1907–2012): Brazilian architect. 25

Nishioka Tsunekazu 西岡常一 (1908–1995): *miyadaiku* master carpenter. 375

Nishizawa Ryūe 西沢立衛 (born 1966): Japanese architect. 215

Nishizawa Taira 西沢大良 (born 1964): Japanese architect. 374, 396

O

Oda Nobunaga 織田信長 (1534–1582): political and military leader. 125

Oda Uraku 織田有楽 (1548–1622): tea master. Contemporary of Sen no Rikyū, younger brother of Oda Nobunaga. 67, 125-128, 135, 136, 151, 321

Ono Kaoru 小野薫 (1903–1957): Japanese structural engineer. 195, 198

Ōtsuji Kiyoji 大辻清司 (1923–2001): Japanese photographer. 222

Ōta Hirotarō 太田博太郎 (1912–2007): Japanese architectural historian and architect. 19, 33, 81, 84, 99, 107, 143, 375

R

Raymond Antonin (1888–1976): or Antonín Reimann, Czech-American architect. 22, 186-194, 205, 245, 247, 248, 369

S

Sakakura Junzō 坂倉準三 (1901–1969): Japanese architect. 23

Sakamoto Hanjirō 坂本繁二郎 (1882–1969): Japanese painter. 144

Sakatoku Kinnosuke 酒徳金之助 (1896–1946): Japanese carpenter. 181

Saichō 最澄 (767–822): Buddhist monk. Founder of the Tendai Buddhist school 天台 (of the Celestial Terrace). 99

Saigyō Hōshi 西行法師 (1118–1190): Buddhist monk from the end of the Heian period. 29, 30, 371

Sasaki Dōyo 佐々木道誉 (1296–1373): feudal lord (*daimyō*) at the beginning of the Muromachi period. 109

Satō Jun 佐藤淳 (born 1972): Japanese structural engineer. 374

Seike Kiyoshi 清家清 (1918–2005): Japanese architect. 219, 374, 375

Sejima Kazuyo 妹島和世 (born 1956): Japanese architect. 9, 215

Sekiguchi Ryōko 関口涼子 (born 1970): translator and Japanese poetess. 267

Sen no Rikyū 千利休 (1522–1591): tea master, creator of the Sōan style and *wabisabi* aesthetic. 67, 116, 117, 119, 120, 124-126, 135, 137, 139, 141, 151, 179, 261, 263, 271, 291

Schinkel Karl Friedrich (1781–1841): German architect. 255

Shimazaki Tōson 嶋崎東村 (1872–1943): Japanese writer. 255

Shinoda Tōkō 篠田桃紅 (1913–2021): Japanese artist and calligrapher. 212, 213

Shinohara Kazuo 篠原一男 (1925–2006): Japanese architect. 22, 214-216, 218-220, 222-224, 228, 230-233, 235-238, 241, 243, 245, 247, 249, 253, 255, 277-279, 284, 329, 369, 371, 374

Simounet Roland (1927–1996): French architect. 286

Suzuki Ryōji 鈴木了二 (born 1944): Japanese architect. 374, 395

T

Tachibana no Toshitsuna 橘俊綱 (1028–1094): presumed author of the *Sakuteiki* 作庭記 (*Records of Garden Making*). 371

Taira no Kiyomori 平清盛 (1118–1181): military leader at the end of the Heian period. 100

Taira no Shigemori 平重盛 (1138–1179): military leader at the end of the Heian period, son of Taira no Kiyomori. 103

Takeda Goichi 武田五一 (1872–1938): Japanese architect. 179

Takenaka kōmuten 竹中工務店: construction company. 179, 249

Takeno Jōō 武野紹鴎 (1502–1555): tea master, teacher of Sen no Rikyū. 67, 119-120, 139

Tanabe Hajime 田辺元 (1885–1962): Japanese philosopher. 194

Tange Kenzō 丹下健三 (1913–2005): Japanese architect. 22, 23, 25, 203-205, 207-213, 215, 218, 222, 243, 247, 249, 369

Tanikawa Shuntarō 谷川俊太郎 (born 1931): Japanese poet. 236-238

Taniguchi Yoshirō 谷口吉郎 (1904–1979): Japanese architect. 22, 248, 249, 255-257, 261-263, 369, 375

Taniguchi Yoshio 谷口吉生 (born 1938): Japanese architect, son of Taniguchi Yoshirō. 255

Tanizaki Junichirō 谷崎潤一郎 (1886–1965): Japanese writer, author of *In'ei raisan* 陰翳礼讃 (*In Praise of Shadows*). 253

Taut Bruno (1880–1938): German architect. 177, 203, 247, 275, 290

Tezuka Takaharu 手塚貴晴 (born 1964): Japanese architect, associate of Tezuka Yui. 368, 372, 384

Tezuka Yui 手塚由比 (born 1969): Japanese architect, associate of Tezuka Takaharu. 368, 372

Tokugawa Ieyasu 徳川家康 (1543–1616): political and military leader, first. 76

Tokugawa shōgun. 63, 113, 125

Tokugawa Hidetada 徳川秀忠 (1579–1632): political and military leader, second Tokugawa shōgun. 83, 125, 269

Tominaga Yōko 富永洋子 (born 1967): Japanese architect. 372

Toyotomi Hideyoshi 豊臣秀吉 (1537–1598): political and military leader. 63, 76, 124, 125, 263

Tsukamoto Yoshiharu 塚本由晴 (born 1965): Japanese architect. 215

V

Vimalakīrti (in Japanese Yuima Koji 維摩居士): Buddhist hermit. Contemporary of the Shakyamuni Buddha, who is said to have lived in a square hut, the mythical archetype of the *hōjō* space. 115, 116

W

Watanabe Yoshio 渡辺義雄 (1907–2000): Japanese photographer. 204, 231

Wright Frank Lloyd (1867–1959): American architect. 179, 187, 191

Y

Yamanoue Sōji 山上宗二 (1544–1590): tea master, disciple of Sen no Rikyū. 67, 116, 117, 119, 139

Yoshida (Urabe) Kenkō 吉田兼好 (*ca.* 1283–*ca.* 1352): monk, author of the *Tsurezuregusa* 徒然草, *Essays in Idleness*. 31, 85, 371

Yoshida Isoya 吉田五十八 (1894–1974): Japanese architect. 22, 23, 25, 246, 248-253, 263, 369, 375

Yoshimura Junzō 吉村順三 (1908–1997): Japanese architect. 18, 193, 242, 243, 245, 248, 369

Yoshimura Yasutaka 吉村靖孝 (born 1972): Japanese architect. 373, 386

PLACE NAMES

A

Asuka-dera 飛鳥寺: Shingon Buddhist monastery, Asuka, Nara prefecture. Another name for Hōkōji. 33

B

Byōdō-in 平等院: ancient palace in the Shinden style; Buddhist temple, Uji, Kyoto prefecture. Its most celebrated building is the "Phoenix Hall," Hōōdō 鳳凰堂, mythological bird (*fenghuang, hōō* 鳳凰 in Japanese). 54

C

Chikurinji 竹林寺: Shingon Buddhist monastery, Mont Kôdai, Kôchi. 373

D

Daibutsuden 大仏殿: pavilion of the Great Buddha. Name given to the treasure pavilion (*kondō*) of the Tōdaiji monastery, Nara. 38

Daigoji 醍醐寺: principal monastery of Shingon Buddhism, Kyoto. 89, 255

Daitokuji 大徳寺: principal monastery of Rinzai Zen Buddhism, Kyoto. 18, 134, 135, 139, 141, 231

Danjō garan 壇上伽藍: Shingon Buddhist monastery (*garan*) of Mount Kōya, Wakayama prefecture. 96

Denpōdō 伝法堂: study pavilion (*kōdō*) of the Hōryuji monastery, Ikaruga, Nara prefecture. 49, 149, 150

Dōjinsai 同仁斎: study cabinet (*shoin*) in the Tōgudō pavilion of the Jishōji temple, Kyoto. 116, 120

E

Enan 燕庵: tea pavilion built by Furuta Oribe for the Yabunouchi house 藪内家, Kyoto. 125, 128, 151

Enjōji 円成寺: Shingon Buddhist monastery, Nara. 95

Enryakuji 延暦寺: principal monastery of Tendai Buddhism, Mount Hiei, Kyoto. 100, 101

F

Fushimi bugyō yashiki 伏見奉行屋敷: lost governor's residence (*bugyō*), Kyoto.

Fushimi Inari taisha 伏見稲荷大社: Shintō shrine, Kyoto. 50

G

Gepparō 月波楼: tea pavilion, Katsura Villa, Kyoto. 151

Ginkakuji 銀閣寺: "Silver Pavilion," Higashiyama Jishōji Rinzai Zen Buddhist monastery, Kyoto. Another name for the Jishōji temple. 115, 147, 150, 243

Gokokuji 護国寺: Shingon Buddhist monastery, Tokyo. 64

Gosho or **Kyōto Gosho** 京都御所: imperial palace of Kyoto. 53, 56, 58, 94, 99, 164, 169

H

Hase-dera 長谷寺: Shingon Buddhist monastery, Shinri, Nara prefecture. 156, 157

Hassōseki 八窓席: tea pavilion in the Konchiin temple of the Nanzenji monastery, Kyoto. 128, 135, 136

Heian jingū 平安神宮: modern Shintō shrine of the Meiji period, Kyoto. 172,173

Heiankyō 平安京: imperial capital of the Heian period, Kyoto today. 33

Heijō 平城 or **Heijōkyū** 平城宮: imperial palace of Heijōkyō, the imperial capital during the Nara period. 150

Heijōkyō 平城京: imperial capital of the Nara period. 150

Heisenji 平泉寺: Tendai Buddhist monastery, the Heisenji hakusan jinja 平泉寺白山神社 shrine today. Katsuyama, Fukui prefecture. 103

Higashi sanjō dono 東三条殿: lost Shinden-style residence of the Heian period. 59, 60, 99

Hiunkaku 飛雲閣: pavilion in the Nishi Honganji monastery, Kyoto. 51, 151, 156

Hōkōji 法興寺: see Asuka-dera. 33

Hōryūji 法隆寺: Shōtoku Buddhist monastery, Ikaruga, Nara prefecture. 10, 19, 32, 33, 49, 81,95, 97, 149, 150, 173, 174, 175, 375

PLACE NAMES

I

Ikkyūji 一休寺: alternative name for the Shūonan pavilion 酬恩庵, Rinzai Zen Buddhist temple of the Daitokuji monastery, Kyōtanabe, Kyoto prefecture. 105

Ise jingū 伊勢神宮: great Shintō shrine, Ise, Mie prefecture. 30

Ishiyama-dera 石山寺: Shingon Buddhist monastery of Tōji, Ōtsu, Shiga prefecture. 156, 157

Itsukushima jinja 厳島神社: Shintō shrine, Itsukushima, Hiroshima prefecture. 47

Iwashimizu Hachiman 石清水八幡宮: Shintō shrine, Yawata, Kyoto prefecture. 134,135

Izumo taisha 出雲大社: great Shintō shrine, Izumo, Shimane prefecture. 43–45

J

Jikōin 慈光院: Rinzai Zen Buddhist temple of the Daitokuji Monastery, Yamatokōriyama, Nara prefecture. 139–141

Jingoji 神護寺: Shingon Buddhist monastery of Kōyasan, Mount Takao, Kyoto. 98, 99

Jishōji 慈照寺: see Ginkakuji. 115, 120, 150

Jōruriji 浄瑠璃寺: Shingon-risshū Buddhist monastery, Kizugawa, Kyoto prefecture. 100

Joan 如庵: tea pavilion built by Oda Uraku in the Kenninji monastery (1618), located today in the Urakuen park 有楽苑, Inuyama, Aichi prefecture. 121, 125, 126, 128, 151, 321

Jūrakudai 聚楽第: palace initially built in 1586, on the site of the former imperial palace in Kyoto, for Toyotomi Hideyoshi. 66, 125, 263

K

Kamo jinja 賀茂神社: Shintō shrine, Kyoto. 29, 43

Kanshinji 観心寺: Shingon Buddhist monastery, Kawachinagano, Osaka prefecture. 42, 47, 51, 89, 98, 146

Kanshinin 観智院: Shoin-type pavilion in the Tōji monastery, Kyoto. 64, 94

Kakehashi izumi tei 掛橋和泉邸: Kakehashi izumi house, Yuzuhara, Kōchi prefecture. 73

Kanunken 閑雲軒: tea pavilion in the Iwashimizu Hachiman sanctuary, Yawata, Kyoto prefecture. 134, 135

Karakasatei 傘亭: tea pavilion in the Kōdaiji monastery, Kyoto. 219

Kasuga taisha 春日大社: Shintō shrine, Nara. 29, 43, 97, 143

Katsura, Katsura rikyū 桂離宮: Katsura Imperial Villa, princely palace. Katsura, Kyoto. 63, 67, 68, 85, 106, 107, 130, 133, 151, 162, 177, 202-205, 210, 222, 230, 247, 255

Kazuragawa Myōōin 葛川明王院: Tendai Buddhist monastery, Ōtsu, Shiga prefecture. 88

Keihoku 京北: mountainous plateau, Kyoto. 12, 14

Kenninji 建仁寺: principal monastery of Rinzai Zen Buddhism, Kyoto. 125

Kikugetsutei 掬月亭: Kikugetsu residence, Ritsurin garden, Takamatsu, Kagawa prefecture. 94

Kinkakuji 金閣寺: "Golden Pavilion," Rinzai Zen Buddhist monastery, Kyoto. Alternative name for the Rokuonji. 142, 150, 152, 243

Kitano Tenmangū 北野天満宮: Shintō shrine, Kyoto.

Kiyomizu-dera 清水寺: Hossō Buddhist monastery, Kyoto. 77, 156, 158

Kōdaiji 高台寺: Rinzai Zen Buddhist monastery, Kyoto. 219

Kohōan 孤篷庵: tea pavilion built by Kobori Enshū in the Daitokuji monastery, Kyoto. 139, 141, 231

Koke-dera 苔寺: "Moss Temple," Kyoto. Another name for Saihōji. 150

Konchiin 金地院: temple in the Nanzenji monastery, Kyoto. 128, 135

Kōnoma 鴻の間: meeting room in the Nishi Honganji monastery, Kyoto. 232, 286

Konpira (Kotohiragū) 金刀比羅宮: Shintō shrine, Mount Kotohira, Kagawa prefecture. 374, 395

Kōrakuen 後楽園: one of the three most famous gardens (sanmeien 三名園) in Japan, Okayama. 151, 155

Kōya or **Kōyasan** 高野山: center of Shingon Buddhism, mountain of the Wakayama prefecture. 96, 99

Kōzanji 功山寺: Sōtō Zen Buddhist monastery, Shimonoseki, Yamaguchi prefecture. 38, 146

Kunōzan Tōshōgū 久能山東照宮: Shintō shrine, Shizuoka. 51

Kusakabe tei 日下部邸: Kusakabe house, Takayama, Gifu prefecture. 89

M

Manshuin 曼殊院: Tendai Buddhist monastery, Kyoto. 146

Meimeian 明々庵: tea pavilion, Matsue, Shimane prefecture. 119

Mikami jinja 御上神社: Shintō shrine, Yasu, Shiga prefecture. 47

Mittan 密庵: tea pavilion of the Ryōkōin temple in the Daitokuji monastery, Kyoto. 134, 135

Murōji 室生寺: principal monastery of Shingon Buddhism, Uda, Nara prefecture. 39, 40

Myōkian 妙喜庵: Rinzai Zen Buddhist monastery, Yamazaki, Kyoto prefecture. Temple where the Taian tea pavilion is located. See Taian. 119, 120

N

Nageiredō 投入堂: another name for the Okuin-zaōdō 奥院蔵王堂, pavilion in the Sanbutsuji monastery, Misasa, Tottori prefecture. See Sanbutsuji. 160, 161

Nandaimon 南大門: Great Southern Gate. Name given to the southern entry of the Tōdaiji monastery, Nara. 36–38, 86

Nanzenji 南禅寺: principal monastery of Rinzai Zen Buddhism, Kyoto. 128, 135

Nijōjo 二条城: shōgun's castle of Nijō, Kyoto. 62, 64–66

Ninomaru kyakuden 二の丸客殿: suite of pavilions and reception spaces (*kyakuden*) built in the Ninomaru palace of Nijō castle, Kyoto. 62, 64

Nishi Honganji 西本願寺: Jōdoshinshū Buddhist monastery, Kyoto. 51, 66, 151, 156, 232, 286

O

Omotesenke 表千家: one of the two tea schools, along with Urasenke, founded by descendants of Sen no Rikyū, Kyoto. 260, 261

Onjōji 園城寺: Tendai Buddhist monastery; also called Miidera 三井寺, Ōtsu, Kyoto prefecture. See Kōjōin. 66, 151

R

Rengeōin 蓮華王院: Tendai Buddhist monastery, Kyoto. Another name for Sanjūsangendō. 100

Rokuonji 鹿苑寺: See Kinkakuji. 150

Rokusōan 六窓庵: tea pavilion relocated to the Tokyo National Museum. 261

Ruriden 瑠璃殿: lost pavilion constructed in the Saihōji, Kyoto. 150

Ryōginan 龍吟庵: pavilion in the Tōfukuji monastery, Kyoto. 61, 64, 93, 94, 105

Ryōkōin 龍光院: temple in the Daitokuji monastery, Kyoto. 135

Ryūten 流店: pavilion in the Kōrakuen garden, Okayama. 151, 155

S

Saihōji 西芳寺: See Koke-dera. 150

Sakamoto Hanjirō tei 坂本繁二郎邸: Sakamoto Hanjirō house, Kurobe, Fukuoka prefecture. 144

Samita Takarazuka kofun 佐味田宝塚古墳: megalithic graves (*kofun*) and archaeological site, Kawai, Nara prefecture. 150

Sanbōin 三宝院: Daigoji monastery temple, Kyoto. 255

Sanbutsuji 三仏寺: Tendai Buddhist monastery, Misasa, Tottori prefecture. See Nageiredō. 160, 161

Sanjūsangendō 三十三間堂: see Rengeōin. 100, 102

Sanzōin 三蔵院: temple of the Yakushiji monastery, Nara. 375

Seikōken 清香軒: pavilion in the Seisonkaku villa, Kanazawa, Ishikawa prefecture. 151, 154

Seiryōden 清涼殿: "pavilion of purity and freshness," residence of the emperor, imperial palace (Gosho) of Kyoto. 56, 58, 94

Seisonkaku 成巽閣: "villa" in the Kenrokuen garden, Kanazawa, Ishikawa prefecture. 151, 154

Shinnyodō 真如堂 or **Shinshōgokuraku-ji** 真正極楽寺: Tendai Buddhist Monastery, Kyoto. 8

Shishinden 紫宸殿: "Polar star pavilion," hall for state ceremonies, imperial palace (Gosho) of Kyoto. 53, 56, 99

Shōdenin 正伝院: pavilion in the Kenninji monastery, Kyoto. 125

Shōiken 笑意軒: tea pavilion at the Katsura Villa, Kyoto. 133, 151

Shōkintei 松琴亭: tea pavilion at the Katsura Villa, Kyoto. 130, 151, 162

Shōkokuji 相国寺: principal monastery of Rinzai Zen Buddhism, Kyoto. 295

Shōsōin 正倉院: treasure house of the Tōdaiji monastery, Nara. 29, 205

Shūonan 酬恩庵: pavilion, another name for the Ikkyūji temple, Kyōtanabe, Kyoto. 105

Shunsōro 春草盧: tea pavilion constructed by Oda Uraku, Sankeien park, Yokohama. 132, 136

Sumiyoshi jinja 住吉神社: Shintō shrine, Shimonoseki, Yamaguchi prefecture. 97

Sumiyoshi taisha 住吉大社: great Shintō shrine, Osaka. 29, 43

T

Taian 待庵: tea pavilion attributed to Sen no Rikyū in the Myōkian temple, Yamazaki, Kyoto prefecture. See Myōkian. 119-121, 124-126, 179

Tenryūji 天龍寺: principal monastery of Rinzai Zen Buddhism, Kyoto. 110, 114

Tōdaiji 東大寺: principal monastery of Kegon Buddhism, Nara. 29, 33, 36, 42, 81, 83, 86, 87, 143, 146, 173

Tōfukuji 東福寺: principal monastery of Rinzai Zen Buddhism, Kyoto. 61, 64, 93, 94, 105, 107, 146

Tōgudō 東求堂: pavilion in the Jishōji (Silver Pavilion), Kyoto. See Ginkakuji. 115, 116, 120

Tōin or **Tōin teien** 東院庭園: garden of the Heijōkyō Imperial Palace, Nara. 150

Tōji 東寺: principal monastery of Shingon Buddhism, Kyoto. 64, 88, 94

Toro or **Toro iseki** 登呂遺跡: archeological site where first century *tateana* and *takayuka* type buildings have been discovered, Shizuoka.

Tōshōdaiji 唐招提寺: principal monastery of Ritsu Buddhism, Nara. 49, 50, 271

Tōshōgū 東照宮: Shintō shrine, Nikkō, Ibaraki prefecture. 51, 76, 77, 173

Toyokuni jinja or **Hōkoku jinja** 豊国神社: Shintō shrine, Kyoto. 76

U

Urakuen 有楽苑: garden, Inuyama, Aichi prefecture. See Joan. 125

Urasenke 裏千家: one of the two tea schools, along with Omotesenke, founded by par descendants of Sen no Rikyū, Kyoto. 120, 261

Usa jingū 宇佐神宮: Shintō shrine, Usa, Oita prefecture. 97

Y

Yakushiji 薬師寺: principal monastery of Hossō Buddhism, Nara. 81, 148, 375, 400

Yoshijima tei 吉島邸: Yoshijima house, Takayama, Gifu prefecture. 113

Yoshino Mikumi jinja 吉野水分神社: Shintō shrine, Yoshino, Nara prefecture. 51

Yūin 又隠: tea pavilion of 4.5 tatamis (*koma* type) in the Urasenke house, Kyoto. 120, 261

Z

Zangetsutei 残月亭: tea pavilion of 12 tatamis (*hiroma* type) in the Omotesenke house, Kyoto. 260–263

Zuiganji 瑞巌寺: Rinzai Zen Buddhist monastery, Matsushima, Miyagi prefecture. 104, 105

BIBLIOGRAPHY

Aikawa Haruki
1940   *Gendai gijutsuron* 現代技術論 (A theory on contemporary techniques). Tokyo: Mikasa shobō.

Aikawa Hiroshi
2003   *Hikaku kenchikuron: Rikyū to Aruberuti no sakui* 比較建築論:利休とアルベルティの作意 (A comparative architectural study: the conceptions of Rikyū and Alberti). Tokyo: Chūōkōron bijutsu shuppan.

Aoki Jun, Gotō Osamu, Tanaka Sadahiko, Nishi Kazuo, Nishizawa Taira, eds.
2005   *Nihon no kenchiku kūkan* 日本建築空間 (The architectural space of Japan). *Shinkenchiku*, special edition (November 2005).

Ban Shigeru
2013   "Wood Architecture in the Expanded Field." *The Japan Architect*, no. 89 (June).

Berque, Augustin, ed.
1987   *La qualité de la ville: urbanité française, urbanité nippone*. Tokyo: Maison franco-japonaise.
1994   *La maîtrise de la ville: urbanité française, urbanité nippone*. Paris: EHESS.

Bonnin, Philippe, Nishida Masatsugu, Inaga Shigemi, eds.
2014   *Vocabulaire de la spatialité japonaise*. Paris: CNRS Editions.

Brown, Azby
1989   *The Genius of Japanese Carpentry: Secrets of an Ancient Craft. Revised edition.* Tokyo: Tuttle, 2013.

Chamberlain, Basil Hall
1905   *Things Japanese. Being Notes on Various Subjects Connected with Japan. For the Use of Travelers and Others.* London: John Murray.

Cluzel, Jean-Sébastien, ed.
2014   *Hokusaï le vieux fou d'architecture*. Paris: Bibliothèque nationale de France and éditions du Seuil.

Cluzel, Jean-Sébastien, Nishida Masatsugu, eds.
2015   *Le sanctuaire d'Ise. Récit de la 62ᵉ reconstruction*. Brussels: Mardaga.

Coaldrake, William H.
1990   *The Way of the Carpenter: Tools and Japanese Architecture*. New York-Tokyo: Weatherhill-Heibonsha.
1996   *Architecture and Authority in Japan*. London: Routledge.

Collectif, EFEO, ed.
2014   *Un siècle d'histoire. L'École française d'Extrême-Orient au Japon*. Paris: EFEO, Magellan & Co.

Compagnon, Antoine
1994   *The 5 Paradoxes of Modernity*. Translated by Franklin Philip. New York: Columbia University Press.

Cruz-Saito, Mizuki, Masatsugu Nishida, Philippe Bonnin
2007   "Le tatami et la spatialité japonaise." *Ebisu*, no. 38: 55–82.

Detienne, Marcel, ed.
1994   *Transcrire les mythologies*. Paris: Albin Michel.

Dōgen, Hashida Kunihiko (trans.)
1939–1950   *Shōbōgenzō shakui* 正法眼藏釋意 (Translation and interpretation of the *Shōbōgenzō*), 4 volumes. Tokyo: Sankibō busshorin.

Engel, Heino
1985   *Measure and Construction of the Japanese House*. Tokyo: Tuttle Company Publishing

Faure, Bernard, D. Max Moerman, Gaynor Sekimori, eds.
2009   *Shugendō. The History and Culture of a Japanese Religion. Cahiers d'Extrême-Asie*, no. 18.

Fiévé, Nicolas
1996   *L'architecture et la ville du Japon ancien. Espace architectural de la ville de Kyôto et des résidences shôgunales aux 14ᵉ et 15ᵉ siècles*. Paris: Maisonneuve & Larose.

Fiévé, Nicolas, ed.
2008   *Atlas historique de Kyôto. Analyse spatiale des systèmes de mémoire d'une ville, de son architecture et de ses paysages urbains*. Paris: Centre du Patrimoine Mondial, Editions de l'UNESCO – Editions de l'Amateur.

Fiévé, Nicolas and Benoît Jacquet, eds.
2013   *Vers une modernité architecturale et paysagère. Modèles et savoirs partagés entre le Japon et le monde occidental.* Paris: Collège de France.

Fiévé, Nicolas, Yola Gloaguen and Benoît Jacquet, eds.
2020   *Mutations paysagères de l'espace habité au Japon, de la maison au territoire.* Paris: Collège de France.

Fróis, Luís
1998   *Européens et Japonais. Traité sur les contradictions et différences de mœurs, écrit par le R.P. Luís Fróis au Japon, l'an 1585.* Paris: Chandeigne.
2014   *The First European Description of Japan, 1585: A Critical English-Language Edition of Striking Contrasts in the Customs of Europe and Japan by Luis Frois, S.J.* Edited by Daniel T. Reff, Richard K. Danford, Robin D. Gill. Japan Anthology Workshop Series. New York: Routledge.

Fujii Keisuke
1998   *Mikkyō kenchiku kūkanron* 密教建築空間論 (A spatial analysis of the architecture of Esoteric Buddhism). Tokyo: Chūōkōron bijutsu shuppan.

Fujii Kōji
1932   *Zoku: Chōchikukyo zuanshū* 続・聴竹居図案集 (Catalogue of plans of Chōchikukyo. Annex). Kyoto: Tanaka Heiando.

Fujimori Terunobu
1993   *Nihon no kindai kenchiku* 日本の近代建築 (The modern architecture of Japan), 2 volumes. Tokyo: Iwanami shoten.

Fujimori Terunobu, Shimomura Junichi
2002   *Fujimori Terunobu no gen, gendai jūtaku no saiken* 藤森照信の原・現代住宅再見 (Fujimori Terunobu's re-reading of the origins of contemporary housing). Tokyo: TOTO shuppan.

Fujimori Terunobu, Andō Tadao, Isozaki Arata, eds.
2007   *The Contemporary Tea House: Japan's top Architects Redefine a Tradition.* Tokyo: Kōdansha International.

Fujimori Terunobu, Mitsumasa Fujitsuka
2017   *Japan's Wooden Heritage: A Journey through a Thousand Years of Architecture.* Tokyo: Japan Library: Japan Publishing Industry Foundation for Culture.

Fukuyama Toshio
1984   *Fukuyama Toshio chosakushū 4. Jinja kenchiku no kenkyū* 福山敏男著作集4. 神社建築の研究 (Collected works of Fukuyama Toshio, volume 4. Studies on the architecture of sanctuaries). Tokyo: Chūōkōron bijutsu shuppan.

Futagawa Yukio
1962   *Nihon no minka* 日本の民家 (Japanese popular houses). Tokyo: Bijutsu shuppan-sha.
2012   *Nihon no minka 1955 nen* 日本の民家一九五五年 *Minka 1955 Japanese Traditional Houses.* Tokyo: ADA Edita Tōkyō.

Gloaguen, Yola
2016   *Les villas réalisées par Antonin Arthaud dans le Japon des années 1920-1930. Une synthèse entre modernisme occidental et habitat vernaculaire japonais*, PhD dissertation, EPHE, January 13.

Hayashiya Tatsusaburō, Nakamura Masao, and al.
1974   *Japanese Arts and the Tea Ceremony.* New York-Tokyo: Weatherhill-Heibonsha.

Helfrich, Kurt and William Whitaker, eds.
2007   *Crafting a Modern World: The Architecture and Design of Antonin and Noémi Raymond.* New York: Princeton Architectural Press.

Hirai Kiyoshi
1965   *Shiro to shoin* 城と書院 (Castles and *shoin*). Tokyo: Heibonsha.
1973   *Feudal Architecture of Japan.* New York-Tokyo: Weatherhill-Heibonsha.
1986   *Nihon jūtaku no rekishi* 日本住宅の歴史 (History of the habitat in Japan). Tokyo: NHK shuppan.

Horiguchi Sutemi
1924   *Gendai Oranda kenchiku* 現代オランダ建築 (Contemporary Dutch architecture). Tokyo: Iwanami shoten.
1927   *Shiensō zushū* 紫烟荘図集 (Catalogue of the plans of Shiensō). Tokyo, Kōyōsha.
1978   *Shoin-zukuri to sukiya-zukuri no kenkyū* 書院造と数寄屋造の研究 (Studies on the Shoin and Sukiya styles). In *Horiguchi Sutemi hakase chosakushū* 堀口捨己博士著作集 (Collected works of professor Horiguchi Sutemi). Tokyo: Kajima shuppankai.
1987   *Rikyū no chashitsu* 利休の茶室 (The tea pavilions of Rikyū). In *Horiguchi Sutemi hakase chosakushū* (Collected works of professor Horiguchi Sutemi). Tokyo: Kajima shuppankai.

Inagaki Eizō

2008 *Jinja kenchikushi kenkyū* 神社建築史研究 (Historical studies on the architecture of sanctuaries). In *Inagaki Eizō chosakushū* 稲垣榮三著作集 (Works of Inagaki Eizō), vol. 2. Tokyo: Chūōkōron bijutsu shuppan.

Inoue Mitsuo

1969 *Nihon kenchiku no kūkan* 日本建築の空間. Tokyo: Kajima shuppankai.

1985 *Space in Japanese Architecture*. Translated by Hiroshi Watanabe. New York: Weatherhill.

Inoue Shōichi

1995 *Senjika Nihon no kenchikuka: āto, kitchu, japanesuku* 戦時下日本の建築家：アート、キッチュ、ジャパネスク (Japanese architects during the war: art, kitsch, Japanesque). Tokyo: Asahi shinbunsha, Asahi sensho, no. 530 [Seidosha, 1987].

Isozaki Arata

2003 *Kenchiku ni okeru "nihonteki na mono"* 建築における「日本的なもの」. Tokyo: Shinchōsha.

2006 *Japan-ness in Architecture*. Translated by Sabu Kohso, edited by David B. Stewart. Cambridge: The MIT Press.

Itō Chūta

1893 "Hōryūji kenchikuron" 法隆寺建築論 (A study of the architecture of Hōryūji). *Kenchiku zasshi* 建築雑誌, vol. 7, no. 83 (November): 317–50.

Itō Nobuo

1977 *Bunkazai kōza. Nihon no kenchiku 1. Kodai* 文化財講座：日本の建築1古代 (Lectures on cultural property, Japanese architecture, vol. 1, Antiquity). Tokyo: Daiichi hōki.

1977 *Bunkazai kōza. Nihon no kenchiku 3. Chūsei* 文化財講座：日本の建築3中世 (Lectures on cultural property, Japanese architecture, vol. 3, The Middle Ages). Tokyo: Daiichi hōki.

Itō Teiji

1969 *The Elegant Japanese House: Traditional Sukiya Architecture*. New York-Kyoto: Weatherhill-Tankōsha.

1972 *The Classic Tradition in Japanese Architecture: Modern Versions of the Sukiya Style*. New York-Kyoto: Weatherhill-Tankōsha.

1973 *Kura: Design and Tradition of the Japanese Storehouse*. Tokyo: Kōdansha International.

1977 "The Development of the Shoin-Style Architecture." In Hall & Toyoda (eds.), *Japan in the Muromachi Age*. Berkeley: University of California Press.

Jacquet, Benoît

2010 "*À la croisée des chemins: l'ambivalence des discours sur les villas impériales de Kyōto*." In Dejanirah Couto and François Lachaud, eds., *Empires éloignés. L'Europe et le Japon (XVIᵉ-XIXᵉ siècles)*. Paris: EFEO, 255–77

2011 "Dans les secrets du pavillon de thé, d'hier et d'aujourd'hui." *Sigila*, no. 28 (November 2011): 91–104.

2013 "La villa Katsura et ses jardins: l'invention d'une modernité japonaise dans les années 1930." In Fiévé & Jacquet, eds., *Vers une modernité architecturale et paysagère. Modèles et savoirs partagés entre le Japon et le monde occidental*. Paris: Collège de France, 99–139.

2015 "Itō Chūta et son étude architecturale du Hōryūji: comment et pourquoi intégrer l'architecture japonaise dans une histoire mondiale." *Ebisu*, no. 52: 89–115.

2017 "*Between tradition and modernity. The two sides of Japanese pre-war architecture*." In Kohte and al. eds. *Encounters and Positions: Architecture in Japan*. Basel: Birkhäuser, 226–37

Jacquet, Benoît, Philippe Bonnin and Nishida Masatsugu, eds.

2014 *Dispositifs et notions de la spatialité japonaise*. Lausanne: EPFL Press.

Kamo no Chōmei

1989 *Hōjōki* 方丈記. Edited by Ichiko Teiji 市古貞次. Tokyo: Iwanami shoten.

1999 *Hōjōki: The Ten Foot Square Hut*. Translated by A.L. Sadler. North Clarendon: Tuttle.

2007 *An Account of a Ten-Foot-Square Hut*. Translated by Anthony H. Chambers. In *Traditional Japanese Literature: An Anthology*, edited by Haruo Shirane. New York: Columbia University Press.

2020 *Hōjōki: A Hermit's Hut as Metaphor*. Translated and annotated by Matthew Stavros. Kyoto: Vicus Lusurum.

Kawabata Yasunari

1962 *Koto* 古都. Tokyo: Shinchōsha.

2006 *The Old Capital*. Translated by J. Martin Holman. Berkeley: Counterpoint Press, reprint edition.

Kawakami Mitsugu

1967 *Nihon chūsei jūtaku no kenkyū* 日本中世住宅の研究 (Studies of residences in medieval Japan). Tokyo: Kokusui shobō. 2002 Reprint edition. Tokyo: Chūōkōron bijutsu shuppan.

Kawamoto Shigeo

2012　*Shinden-zukuri no kūkan to gishiki* 寝殿造の空間と儀式 (Space and ceremony in the *Shinden*). Tokyo: Chūōkōron bijutsu shuppan.

Kawazoe Noboru

2010　*Ki to mizu no kenchiku. Ise jingū* 木と水の建築・伊勢神宮 (The architecture of wood and water: Ise Jingū). Tokyo: Chikuma shobō.

Kishida Hideto

1927　*Ottō Wagunā: kenchikuka toshite no shōgai oyobi shisō* オットー・ワグナー：建築家としての生涯と思想 (Otto Wagner: The life and thought of an architect). Tokyo: Iwanami shoten.

Kohte, Susanne, Adam Hubertus, Daniel Hubert, eds.

2017　*Encounters and Positions: Architecture in Japan*. Basel: Birkhäuser.

Koizumi Kazuko

1979　*Kagu to shitsunai ishō no bunkashi* 家具と室内意匠の文化史 (A cultural history of furniture and interior design). Tokyo: Hōsei daigaku shuppansha.

Kōjiro Yūichirō

1986　*Nihon kenchiku no kūkan. Nihon no bijutsu 9 No. 244* 日本建築の空間・日本の美術 9 No. 244 (Space in Japanese architecture. Art in Japan, vol. 9, no. 244). Tokyo: Shibundō.

1989　*Ma: Nihon kenchiku no ishō* 間(ま):日本建築の意匠 (*Ma*, the conception of Japanese architecture). Tokyo: Kajima shuppankai.

Kuwata Chikatada

1977　*Sadō koten zenshū dai 6 kan* 茶道古典全集第6巻 (The Classics of the tea ceremony. Complete works, volume 6). Revised and annotated edition. Kyoto: Tankōsha.

Kuwata Chikatada, Kumakura Isao

1977　"Nanpō roku seiritsu to sono haikei" 南方録成立とその背景 (The Nanpō roku: its genesis and context). *Chanoyu* no. 11.

Kyoto kyōiku inkai (Educational committee of Kyoto)

1965　*Kokuhō jishōji Tōgudō shūri kōji hōkokusho* 国宝慈照寺東求堂修理工事報告書 (Report on the repair work of the Tōgudō national treasure in the Jishōji temple).

Le Corbusier and Pierre Jeanneret

1964　*Œuvre complète de 1929-1934*, ed. Willy Boesiger. Zurich: Les Éditions d'Architecture [Artemis, 1935].

Lévi-Strauss, Claude

2013　*The Other Face of the Moon*. Translated by Jane Marie Todd. Cambridge: Harvard University Press.

Lucken, Michael

2014　"Les limites du *ma*." *Nouvelle revue d'esthétique*, vol 1., no. 13: 45–67.

Maekawa Kunio, Sakakura Junzō, Tange Kenzō, Yoshida Isoya

1953　"Kokusaisei, fūdosei, kokuminsei. Gendai kenchiku no zōkei o megutte"(Internationalism, mediance, nationality. Around the formation of contemporary architecture). *Kokusai kenchiku* (March): 2–15.

Maruyama Shigeru

2001　*Jinja kenchikushi ron: Kodai ōken to saishi* 神社建築史論:古代王権と祭祀 (History of sanctuary architecture: Imperial authority and the rituals of antiquity). Tokyo: Chūōkōron bijutsu shuppan.

Masaki Akira

2012　*Kūkai to mikkyō bijutsu* 空海と密教美術 (Kūkai and the art of Esoteric Buddhism). Tokyo: Kadokawa gakugei shuppan.

Matsukuma Akira

2015　*Chōchikukyo. Fujii Kōji no mokuzō modanizumu kenchiku* 聴竹居:藤井厚二んの木造モダニズム建築 (Chōchikukyo: the modernist wood architecture of Fujii Kōji). Tokyo: Heibonsha.

Matsukuma Hiroshi and al., ed.

2006　*Kenchikuka Maekawa Kunio no shigoto* 建築家前川國男の仕事—*The Work of Kunio Maekawa: A Pioneer of Japanese Modern Architecture*. Tokyo: Bijutsu shuppan dezain sentā.

Matsuyama Ginshoan (ed.) and Kumakura Isao (revised)

1974　*Chatō koten sōsho 1* 茶湯古典叢書1 (Classics of the tea ceremony, vol. 1). Kyoto: Shibunkaku shuppan.

Matsuzaki Teruaki

1989　"Kake-zukuri to iu meishō ni tsuite" 懸造と言う名称について (On the the appellation *kake-zukuri*). In *Nihon kenchiku gakkai ronbun hōkokushū* 日本建築学会論文報告集 [Annual symposium of the Architecture Institute of Japan].

1991　"Kodai chūsei no kakezukuri" 古代中世の懸造 (The *Kake-zukuri* in ancient and medieval times). In *Nihon kenchiku gakkai ronbun hōkokushū*, 日本建築学会論文報告集 [Annual symposium of the Architecture Institute of Japan].

2020 *Yama ni tatsu kami to hotoke* 山に立つ神と仏 (The constructions in the mountains for Shinto gods and Buddha). Tokyo: Kōdansha sensho Métier

Mertz, Mechtild
2011 *Wood and Traditional Woodworking in Japan*. Ōtsu: Kanseisha Press.
2020 *Japanese Wood and Carpentry: Rustic and Refined*. Ōtsu: Kanseisha Press.

Mitsui Wataru
2001 *Kinsei jisha keidai to sono kenchiku* 近世寺社境内とその建築 (Temples and shrines of the modern period and their architecture). Tokyo: Chūōkōron bijutsu shuppan.

Miyamoto Nagajirō
1996 *Nihon genshi kodai no jūkyo kenchiku* 日本原始古代の 住居建築 (Primitive residential architecture in Japan). Tokyo: Chūōkōron bijutsu shuppan.
2007 *Shutsudo kenchiku buzai ga hodoku kodai kenchiku* 出土建築部材が解く古代建築 (Architecture revealed through archaeological discoveries). *Nihon no bijutsu* 日本の美術 490 (Japanese art, vol. 490). Tokyo: Shibundō.

Mori Art Museum, Tsuchiya Takahide and al., eds.
2018 *Kenchiku no Nihonten: sono idenshi no katarasu mono* 建築の日本展：その遺伝子のもたらすもの – *Japan in Architecture : Genealogies of Its Transformation*. Roppongi Hills and Mori Art Museum 15th Anniversary Exhibition. Tokyo: Echelle-1.

Murano Tōgo
1978 *Tōgo wafū kenchikushū* 村野藤吾和風建築集 (Collection of *wafū* architecture by Murano Tōgo). Tokyo: Shinkenchiku-sha.

Murano Tōgo kenkyukai, ed.
2009 *Murano Tōgo kenchiku annai* 村野藤吾建築集案内 (Guide of the architecture of Murano Tōgo). Tokyo: Murano Tōgo kenkyūkai and TOTO Shuppan.

Nakagawa Takeshi
2002 *Nihon no ie: kūkan, kioku, kotoba* 日本の家：空間・記憶・言葉. Tokyo: TOTO Shuppan.
2005 *The Japanese House: In Space, Memory and Language*. Tokyo: I-House Press.

Nakahara Yasuo
1967 *Kenchiku mokkōzō kōsaku zushū* 建築木構造工作集図 (Compilation of technical drawings of wooden structure of architecture). Tokyo: Rikōgakusha.

Nakahara Yasuo, Satō Hideo
1995 *The Complete Japanese Joinery,* transl. Koichi Paul Nii. Vancouver: Hartley & Marks.

Nakamura Masao
1971 *Chashitsu kenkyū* 茶室研究 (Studies on the tea pavilion). Tokyo: Bokusui shoten.

Nakamura Masao, ed.
1989 *Sukiya koten shūsei* 数奇屋古典集成 (Collection of Sukiya classics), vol. 2. Tokyo: Shōgakkan.

Naitō Akira, Nishikawa Takeshi
1977 *Katsura: A Princely Retreat*. Tokyo: Kōdansha.

Nara bunkazai kenkyūjo, Nara National Research Institute for Cultural Properties, ed.
2003 *Heijōkyō hakkutsu chōsa hōkokusho 15: Heijōkyō Sakyō sanjō-nibō teien* 平城京発掘調査報告書15 平城京左京三条二房宮跡庭園 (Report on the archaelogical excavations of the Heijōkyō, no. 15. Garden of the remains of the Heijōkyō Sakyō sanjō-nibō Palace). Nara: Nara bunkazai kenkyūjo.

Neightbour Parent, Mary
1983 *Roof in Japanese Buddhist Architecture*. Tokyo: Kajima.

Neufert, Ernst
1936 *Bauenentwurfslehre*. Berlin: Ullstein Verlag.
2019 *Architects' Data*, Fifth edition. Hoboken: Wiley-Blackwell.

Ōta Hirotarō
1957 *Chūsei no kenchiku* 中世の建築 (Architecture of the Middle Ages), vol. 2.Tokyo: Shōkokusha.
1983 *Nihon kenchiku no tokushitsu* 日本建築の特質 (The characteristics of Japanese architecture). In *Nihon kenchikushi ronshū* 日本建築史論集 (Collected studies on the history of Japanese architecture). Tokyo: Iwanami shoten.
1984 *Nihon jūtakushi no kenkyū* 日本住宅史の研究 (Study on the history of the habitat in Japan). In *Nihon kenchikushi ronshū* (Collected studies on the history of Japanese architecture), vol. 2. Tokyo: Iwanami shoten.
1986 *Shaji kenchiku no kenkyū* 社寺建築の研究 (A study of the architecture of shrines and temples). In *Nihon kenchikushi ronshū* (Collected studies on the history of Japanese architecture), vol. 3. Tokyo: Iwanami shoten.

Ōta Hirotarō, ed.
1971 *Shōmei* (1608). Annotated and translated into modern Japanese by Itō Yōtarō. Tokyo: Kajima shuppankai, 2 volumes.

Ōta Hirotarō (ed.), Nishi Kazuo
1990 *Zukai kokenchiku nyūmon. Nihon kenchiku wa dō tsukurarete iru ka* 図解古建築入門：日本建築はどう造られているか (Illustrated introduction to ancient architecture. How are Japanese buildings constructed?). Tokyo: Shōkokusha.

Ōta Seiroku
1987 *Shinden-zukuri no kenkyū* 寝殿造の研究 (Study of the Shinden style). Tokyo: Yoshikawa kōbunkan.

Pezeu-Masabuau, Jacques
1966 *La maison japonaise et la neige. Études géographiques sur l'habitation du Hokuriku (Côte occidentale du Japon central)*. Bulletin de la Maison franco-japonaise, New Series, vol. 8, no. 1. Paris: PUF.
1981 *La maison japonaise*. Paris: POF.

Plutschow, Herbert
2003 *Rediscovering Rikyu and the Beginnings of the Japanese Tea Ceremony*. Folkestone: Global Oriental.

Raymond, Antonin
1938 *Architectural Details*. Tokyo: Kokusai kenchiku kyōkai.

Reynolds, Jonathan
2001 *Maekawa Kunio and the Emergence of Japanese Modernist Architecture*. Berkeley: University of California Press.

Saigyō
1991 *Sankashū* 山家集. English edition: *Poems of a Mountain Home*. Translated by Burton Watson. New York: Columbia University Press.

Saitō Hidetoshi
1990 *Katsura rikyū* 桂離宮 (The Katsura villa). Tokyo: Shōgakkan.

Sasaki Hiroshi
2000 *Kyoshō e no shōkei: Ru korubyuje ni miserareta Nihon no kenchikukatachi* 巨匠への憧憬：ル・コルビュジエに魅せられた日本の建築家たち (Drawn to the master: The Japanese architects fascinated by Le Corbusier). Tokyo: Sagami shobō.

Satō Shigeru, Takamizawa Kunio, Itō Hirohisa, Ōtsuki Toshio, Mano Yōsuke
1998 *Dōjunkai no apātomento to sono jidai* 同潤会のアパートメントとその時代 (The Dōjunkai apartments and their times). Tokyo: Kajima shuppankai.

Seike Kiyoshi
1977 *The Art of Joinery*. New York-Kyoto: Weatherhill-Tankōsha.
1979 *Nihon no kigumi* 日本の木組 (The joinery in Japan). Kyoto: Tankōsha.

Sekiguchi Ryōko
2018 *Nagori*. Paris: POL.

Sekiguchi Kinya
2011 *Chūsei zenshūyō kenchiku no kenkyū* 中世禅宗様建築の研究 (Studies in medieval Zen architecture). In *Sekiguchi Kinya chosakushū* 関口欣也著作集 (Works of Sekiguchi Kinya), vol. 1. Tokyo: Chūōkōron bijutsu shuppan.
2016 *Gozan to zenin* 五山と禅院 (The Five Mountains and the Zen monasteries). In *Sekiguchi Kinya chosakushū* (Works of Sekiguchi Kinya), vol. 3. Tokyo: Chūōkōron bijutsu shuppan.

Shimizu, Christine
1998 "Origins of the Tea Pavilion." In *Acta Universitatis Ouluensis, Humaniora*, special issue: "Japani: Culturi, Nainen, Murros": 25–38.

Shimizu Hiroshi
1992 *Heian jidai bukkyō kenchikushi no kenkyū. Jōdokyō kenchiku o chūshin ni* 平安時代仏教建築史の研究浄土教建築を中心に (Historical studies on Buddhist architecture during the Heian period. The architecture of Pure Land Buddhism). Tokyo: Chūōkōron bijutsu shuppan.

Shinohara Kazuo
1957–1964 *Nihon kenchiku no hōhō* 日本建築の方法 (The Methodology of Japanese Architecture). *Nihon kenchiku gakkai ronbun hōkokushū* 日本建築学会論文報告集 *Transactions of the Architectural Institute of Japan*.
1962 "Jūtaku wa geijutsu de aru" 住宅葉芸術である (The house is an art). *Shinkenchiku* (May): 77–8.
1962 "Karakasa no ie" から傘の家 (The umbrella house). *Shinkenchiku* (October): 149–51.
1964 *Jūtaku kenchiku* 住宅建築 (*Residential architecture*). Tokyo: Kinokuniya shinsho.
1964 "The Japanese Conception of Space." *The Japan Architect* (June): 57

1971 *Shinohara Kazuo 16 no jūtaku to kenchikuron* 篠原一男16の住宅と建築論 *(16 houses and architectural reflections by Shinohara Kazuo)*. Tokyo: Bijutsu shuppansha.

1975 "Ragyō no kūkan o ōdan suru toki" 裸形の空間を横断するとき *(When we traverse a naked space)*. *Shinkenchiku* (April): 34.

1976 "When Naked Space is Traversed." *The Japan Architect* (February): 64–9.

1996 *Shinohara Kazuo*. Tokyo, TOTO shuppan.

Souyri, Pierre-François

2010 *Nouvelle histoire du Japon*. Paris: Perrin.

Stewart, David

1987 *The Making of a Modern Architecture: 1868 to the Present*. Tokyo, New York: Kōdansha International.

Tachibana no Toshitsuna

2018 *Sakuteiki: Visions of the Japanese Garden*. Translated by Jiro Takei and Marc. P. Keane. North Clarendon: Tuttle.

Takenaka daiku dōgukan, Takenaka Carpentry Tools Museum

2012 *Sukiya daiku: bi o sōzō suru takumi* 数奇屋大工：美を創造する匠 – *Sukiya Carpenter: The Creator of Beauty*. Kobe: Takenaka Carpentry Tools Museum.

2014 *Jōsetsuten zuroku* 常設展図録 (Catalogue of the permanent exhibition). Kobe: Takenaka Carpentry Tools Museum.

Takenaka kōmuten, Takenaka daiku dōgukan, Shinkenchiku-sha, eds

2019 *The Thinking Hand: Takenaka Corporation and Takenaka Carpentry Tools Museum*. A+U no. 581 (February).

Tanabe Hajime

1937 *Tetsugaku to kagaku to no aida* 哲学と科学との間 (Between philosophy and science). Tokyo: Iwanami shoten.

Tange Kenzō, Walter Gropius, Ishimoto Yasuhiro

1960 *Katsura: Tradition and Creation in Japanese Architecture*. New Haven: Yale University Press.

Tange Kenzō, Kawazoe Noboru, Watanabe Yoshio

1962 *Ise: Nihon kenchiku no genkei* 伊勢：日本建築の原形 (Tokyo: Asahi Shinbun, 1962); English translation: *Ise: Prototype of Japanese Architecture* (Cambridge: MIT Press, 1965).

Tange Kenzō, Fujimori Terunobu

2002 *Tange Kenzō*. Tokyo: TOTO shuppan.

Taniguchi Yoshirō

1994 "Taniguchi Yoshirō no sekai" 谷口吉郎の世界 (The world of Taniguchi Yoshirō). *Kenchiku bunka* (September): 232–5.

Tanizaki Junichirō

1933 *Inei raisan* 陰翳礼讃. *Keizai ōrai* 経済往来 (December–January 1934).

1977 *In Praise of Shadows*. Translated by Thomas J. Harper and Edward G. Seidensticker. Stony Creek: Leete's Island Books.

Taut, Bruno

1937 *Houses and People of Japan*. Tokyo: Sanseidō.

Urabe Kenkō

1998 *Tsurezuregusa* 徒然草. *Essays in Idleness*. Translated by Donald Keene. New York: Columbia University Press, paperback edition.

Varley, H. Paul, Kumakura Isao (eds.)

1995 *Tea in Japan: Essays on the History of Chanoyu*. Honolulu: University of Hawaii Press.

Vendredi-Auzanneau, Christine

2012 *Antonin Raymond: un architecte occidental au Japon*. Paris: Picard.

Wasokamori Tarō

1972 *Shugendōshi kenkyū* 修験道史研究 (Historical studies on the *shugendō*). *Tōyō bunko* 東洋文庫, no. 211. Tokyo: Heibonsha.

Yamato Satoshi

2000 *Shiro to goten* (Castles and palaces). Tokyo: Shibundō.

ILLUSTRATIONS

FOREWORD: HISTORY, STORIES

fig 1. View of the Shinnyodō monastery 真如堂, from the Yoshida hill, Kyoto © Andrea Flores Urushima

fig 2. Landscape of the Keihoku 京北 plateau, northwest of Kyoto, 2016 © François Azambourg

fig 3. Precut and numbered pieces (floor by floor), delivered to the construction site of the EFEO Center in Kyoto, 2014 © Benoît Jacquet

fig 4. At the start of the traditional felling (*honjikomi* 本仕込み) of the Kitayama cedars (Kitayama *sugi*), a woodcutter cuts the tree at its base, while another pulls it in order to make it tip onto the postern where it can dry. Kyoto, August 2016 © François Azambourg

fig 5. Stripping the bark off a Kitayama *sugi*, Kyoto © François Azambourg

fig 6. Example of measurements and proportions for the construction of a Shintō sanctuary (*jinja*). Plate from the carpentry treatise *Shōmei* 匠明 (1608), republished in 1971 in the *Shōmei gokankō* 匠明五巻考 [An analysis of the five rolls of the *Shōmei*], plate 3 © Itō Yōtarō

fig 7. A combination of contemporary and traditional materials, techniques, and tools on the construction site of the EFEO Center in Kyoto, 2014 © Benoît Jacquet

— A STORY OF PRINCIPLES

fig a1. Ise shrine, Ise © John Barr

fig a2. Wayō-style temple, Hōryūji monastery, Nara prefecture

fig a2-a. *kondō* © John Barr

fig a2-b. from left to right, *kondō* and *gojūnotō* © John Barr

fig a3. Daibutsuyō-style temple, Tōdaiji monastery

fig a3-a. capitals and penetrating tie beams, Nandaimon gate © John Barr

fig a3-b. *kondō*, Nara © John Barr

fig a-3c. Nandaimon gate © John Barr

fig a4. Zen-style temple

fig a4-a. Kōzanji monastery, *butsuden*, Yamaguchi prefecture © Teruaki Matsuzaki

fig a4-b. Murōji monastery, *hondō*, Nara prefecture © Manuel Tardits

fig a4-c. Murōji monastery, *hondō,* Nara prefecture © Manuel Tardits

fig a5. Setchūyo-style temple, Kanshinji monastery, *kondō*, Osaka prefecture © Teruaki Matsuzaki

fig a6. central room (Asuka/Nara period)

fig a7. Izumo taisha sanctuary, Shimane prefecture

fig a7-a. *honden* © John Barr

fig a7-b. *honden* and *sessha* © John Barr

fig a8. central room (Heian period)

fig a9. canopies in front of the *moya*

fig a9-a *nagare-zukuri* style, with *gohai* space, Mikami jinja sanctuary, *sessha*, Shiga prefecture © Teruaki Matsuzaki

fig a9-b. Kasuga style with *gohai* space, Kanshinji monastery, Kariteimotendō, Osaka prefecture © Teruaki Matsuzaki

fig a10. Itsukushima jinja Sanctuary, Hiroshima prefecture © Teruaki Matsuzaki

fig a11. roof construction principles

fig a12. roof types

fig a12-a *kirizuma* roof type, Hōryūji monastery, *denpōdō*, Nara © Teruaki Matsuzaki

fig a12-b. *irimoya* roof type, Tōshōdaiji monastery, *kōdō*, Nara © Teruaki Matsuzaki

fig a12-c. *yosemune* roof type, Tōshōdaiji monastery, *kondō*, Nara © Teruaki Matsuzaki

fig a12-d. *kirizuma* roof type, *nagare-zukuri* style, Fushimi Inari taisha sanctuary, *honden*, Kyoto © Teruaki Matsuzaki

fig a13. architectural details

fig a13-a. "seated dog" *chidorihafu*, Yoshino Mikumi jinja sanctuary, *honden*, Nara prefecture © Teruaki Matsuzaki

fig a13-b. curved canopy (*noki karahafu*), Hiunkaku pavilion, Nishi Honganji monastery, Kyoto © Nicolas Fiévé

fig a13-c. *wakishōji* screen, Kunōzan Tōshōgu sanctuary, Tochigi prefecture © Teruaki Matsuzaki

fig a13-d. *wakishōji* screen, Kanshinji monastery, Kariteimotendō, Osaka prefecture © Teruaki Matsuzaki

fig a-14. residential architecture

fig a15. Shinden-style palace

fig a15-a. Gosho imperial palace, Shishinden, Kyoto © Teruaki Matsuzaki

fig a15-b. Byōdō-in temple, "Phoenix Hall," Kyoto prefecture © John Barr

fig a15-c. Gosho imperial palace, Shishinden, *irimoya-zukuri* roof type, Kyoto © John Barr

fig a15-d. Gosho imperial palace, Seiryōden, Kyoto © Teruaki Matsuzaki

fig a15-e. framing and spatial structure

fig a-16. Shinden palace, interior view

fig a-16-a. Gosho imperial palace, Seiryōden, view from the *moya*, Kyoto © Yuichirō Kōjiro

fig a-16-b. *shinden* of the Higashi sanjō dono residence. Example of typical layout (*shitsurai*) according to the roll of illustrations of the "ruijū zatuyōshū sashizukan" 巻類聚雑要指沙巻 © Archives of the National Museum of Japanese History (Kokuritsu rekishi minzoku hakubutsukan 国立歴史民俗博物館)

fig a17. aristocratic residential architecture: evolutionary principles (1)

fig a18. aristocratic residential architecture: evolutionary principles (2)

fig a19. Shoin architectural details

fig a19-a. from left to right: *kuroshoin* and *ōhiroma* pavilions, Nijō Castle, Ninomaru, *kyakuden*, Kyoto © John Barr

fig a19-b. from left to right: the new palace, the music room, the main Shoin and the old Shoin, Katsura Villa, Kyoto © John Barr

fig a19-c. Tōfukuji monastery, Ryōginan, Kyoto © Manuel Tardits

fig a19-d. *tokonoma* alcove with a flower vase and a *kakejiku* hanging roll and *tsukeshoin* study cabinet, Tōji monastery, Kanshinin, Kyoto © Manuel Tardits

fig a19-e. *jōdannoma* high room in the *ōhiroma* pavilion, Nijō castle, Ninomaru kyakuden, Kyoto © Teruaki Matsuzaki

fig a19-f. *chigai-dana* shelving, Gokokuji monastery, *gekkōden*, Tokyo © Teruaki Matsuzaki

fig a20. aristocratic residential architecture: evolutionary principles (3)

fig a21. archetypes and variations of upper-class residences.

fig a22. Katsura Villa (exterior view), Kyoto © John Barr

fig a23. *tateana* construction type (on the right) © Teruaki Matsuzaki

fig a24. *takayuka* construction type © Teruaki Matsuzaki

fig a25. residential architecture

fig a26. *nōka* farm (Kakehashi house, Kōchi prefecture)

fig a26-a. exterior view © Manuel Tardits

fig a26-b. *doma* room © Manuel Tardits

fig a26-c. living room (*ima*) © Manuel Tardits

fig a26-d. salon (*zashiki*) © Manuel Tardits

fig a26-e. roof detail. In rural architecture, the purlins and rafters are often bound together, without joints. © Manuel Tardits

fig a27-a. urban house, *machiya*, Murata house, Kyoto, early twentieth century

fig a27-b. urban house, *machiya*, Gion neighborhood, Kyoto © Teruaki Matsuzaki

fig a28. construction of the *kake-zukuri* type, Kiyomizu-dera monastery, Kyoto © John Barr

fig a29. mausoleum of the Shintō sanctuary of Tōshōgū, *haiden*, Nikkō, Tochigi prefecture © Nicolas Fiévé

fig a30. surface area units

fig a31. *moya* archetype

fig a32. principal layouts of central room/galleries (*kenmen kihō* method)

fig a33. architectural details

fig a33-a. fanning rafters (*ōgitaruki*) Tōdaiji monastery, Nandaimon, Nara © John Barr

fig a33-b. rafter (*taruki*), Tōdaiji monastery, *daibutsuden*, Nara © John Barr

fig a33-c. console beam (*hanegi*) Kazuragawa monastery, *gomadō*, Shiga prefecture © Teruaki Matsuzaki

fig a33-d. lintel (*nageshi*) Tōji monastery, *gojūnotō*, Kyoto © Manuel Tardits

fig a33-e. capital (*kumimono*) Daigoji monastery, *kondō*, Kyoto © Teruaki Matsuzaki

fig a33-f. penetrating tie beam (*nuki*), Kanshinji monastery, *kondō*, Osaka prefecture © Teruaki Matsuzaki

fig a33-g. collar beam frame, Kusabe house, Takayama, Gifu prefecture © Manuel Tardits

fig a34. structural principles in the Heian period: roof truss and foundations

fig a35. capitals, *kumimono*. Principles (1)

fig a36. capitals, *kumimono*. Principles (2)

fig a37. structural principles in the Momoyama period: sections through a *tachu hōjō*

fig a38. architectural details

fig a38-a. from left to right: central room (*moya*); canopy (*hisashi*); veranda or large terrace (*hiroen*); low terrace (*ochien*), Gosho imperial palace, Seiryōden, Kyoto © Teruaki Matsuzaki

fig a38-b. Tōfukuji monastery, Ryōginan, Kyoto © Teruaki Matsuzaki

fig a38-c. Tōji monastery, Kanshinin, Kyoto © Manuel Tardits

fig a38-d. Kikugetsutei residence, Takamatsu, Kagawa prefecture © Manuel Tardits

fig a39. methods of enlargement

fig a39-a. pavilion with multiple wings, Enjōji temple, Kasuga and Hakusan sanctuaries, Nara © Teruaki Matsuzaki

fig a39-b. aligned pavilions *narabidō*, Hōryūji monastery, *jikidō* and *hosodono*, Nara prefecture © Teruaki Matsuzaki

fig a40. attempts to establish symmetry in Shingon Buddhism

fig a40-a. the only pagoda built out of two originally proposed by Kūkai: Konpon *daitō* of the Danjō garan monastery, Kōya, Wakayama prefecture © Manuel Tardits

fig a40-b. two *mandalas* symmetrically arranged in the main room, Kanshinji monastery, *kondō*, Osaka prefecture © Bunkazai

fig a41. attempts to establish symmetry in Tendai Buddhism

fig a41-a. exterior view © Benoît Jacquet

fig a41-b. hokkedō and jōgyōdō oratories, Enryakuji monastery, plan, Kyoto © Yuichirō Kōjiro

fig a42. Sanjūsangendō temple, Kyoto

fig a42-a. exterior view © Teruaki Matsuzaki

fig a42-b. plan

fig a43. Zuiganji monastery, Matsushima, Miyagi prefecture

fig a44. aristocratic residential architecture: evolutionary principles (4)

fig a45. *hiroma* and *koma*

fig a46. *hiroma* room in the *shoin*, Tenryūji monastery, Kyoto © Manuel Tardits

fig a47. *shoin*: reception room

fig a48. architectural details

fig a48-a. translucent paper sliding panel (*shōji*) and blind (*sudare*), Yoshijima house, Takayama, Gifu prefecture © Manuel Tardits

fig a48-b. hanging shutter (*shitomido*) and lattice (*kōshi*), Tenryūji monastery, Kyoto © Manuel Tardits

fig a48-c. sliding exterior shutter (*amado*), Rinshukaku villa, Sankeien park, Yokohama © Manuel Tardits

fig a49. Sōan tea pavilion: principles

fig a50. tea pavilion, Sōan style, Meimeian, Matsue, Shimane prefecture © Teruaki Matsuzaki

fig a51. tea pavilion (1)

fig a52. Taian pavilion, Kyoto prefecture

fig a52-a. exterior view (reconstruction for the "Japan in Archi-tecture" exhibition, Mori Art Museum, 2018) © Manuel Tardits

fig a52-b. interior view © Shōgakukan (2002 ed.)

fig a53. Joan pavilion, Aichi prefecture

fig a53-a. exterior view © Teruaki Matsuzaki

fig a53-b. interior view showing the angled *sujikai kabe* wall with the *tokonoma* alcove © Fujitsuka Mitsumasa

fig a53-c. interior view from entry, with the *sodekabe* partition terminated by a *naka-bashira* ornamental post and "*Uraku*" windows © Fujitsuka Mitsumasa

fig a53-d. "*Uraku*" windows © Fujitsuka Mitsumasa

fig a54. tea pavilion (2)

fig a55. architectural details

fig a55-a. full-sized model of a tea pavilion. Detail of internal structure of the walls before being covered in cob, Takenaka Carpentry Tools Museum (*Takenaka daiku dōgukan*), Kobe © Manuel Tardits

fig a55-b. squatting entry (*nijiri-guchi*), Shōkintei pavilion, Katsura Villa, Kyoto © John Barr

fig a55-c. *tokonoma* alcove with its *toko-bashira* angle post, Shunsōro pavilion, Sankeien park, Yokohama © Teruaki Matsuzaki

fig a55-d. ornamental post *naka-bashira* in front of a *daime-datami* and the *sodekabe* partition, Shunsōro pavilion, Sankeien park, Yokohama © Teruaki Matsuzaki

fig a55-e. *shitaji mado* window, Takenaka Carpentry Tools Museum (*Takenaka daiku dōgukan*), Kobe © Manuel Tardits

fig a55-f. earthen floor entry space (*do-bisashi*), Shōiken pavilion, Katsura Villa, Kyoto © John Barr

fig a-56. the tea pavilion (3)

fig a-57. example of the multiplication of windows leading to Oribe and the *kireisabi* of Enshū. Oda Uraku, Shunsōro pavilion, Sankeien park, Yokohama © Teruaki Matsuzaki

fig a-58. *kusarinoma* space

fig a-58-a. example of a *kusarinoma* room in plan

fig a-58-b. example of *kireisabi*. Kobori Enshū, reconstruction of Kobori Enshū's residence in Fushimi. Fuji no kuni cha no miyako Museum, Shizuoka, *kusarinoma* © Fuji no kuni cha no miyako bijutsukan

fig a-58-c. example of *kireisabi*. Kobori Enshū © Fuji no kuni cha no miyako bijutsukan

fig a-59. Jikōin temple, Nara prefecture

fig a-59-a. view of the garden from the *shoin* © Manuel Tardits

fig a-59-b. view of the *shoin* from the garden © Manuel Tardits

fig a-59-c. *hiroma* room with a *tokonoma* alcove, a *tsuke shoin* alcove on the right, and the entry of a tea pavilion from the *engawa* veranda © Manuel Tardits

fig a-59-d. *shakkei* principle © Manuel Tardits

fig a60. Kohōan pavilion, Daitokuji monastery, Kyoto © Teruaki Matsuzaki

fig a61. jetty, Golden Pavilion (Kinkakuji), Kyoto © John Barr

fig a62. architectural details

fig a62-a. convex roof (*mukuri*), Sakamoto Hanjirō house, Fukuoka prefecture © John Barr

fig a62-b. extremity of the canopy (*nokisaki*), Kōzanji monastery, Yamaguchi prefecture © Teruaki Matsuzaki

fig a62-c. concave roof (*sori*), Tōdaiji monastery, *hokkedō*, Nara © Teruaki Matsuzaki

fig a62-d. convex roof (*mukuri*), Manshuin monastery, great *shoin*, Kyoto © Benoît Jacquet

fig a62-e. gable (*hafu*), Kanshinji monastery, *kondō*, Osaka prefecture © Teruaki Matsuzaki

fig a62-f. *katōmado* window, Tōfukuji monastery, *zendō*, Kyoto © Benoît Jacquet

fig a62-g. wood shingle roofing (*kokera-buki*), Silver Pavilion (Ginkakuji), Kyoto © Teruaki Matsuzaki

fig a62-h. template (*tawamijaku*), Silver Pavilion, Nara © Azby Brown

fig a62-i. three-dimensional assembly of beams with the angle rafter (*sumigi*), Yakushiji monastery, Nara © Azby Brown

fig a62-j. assembly of a roof canopy with the angle rafter (*sumigi*), Takenaka Carpentry Tools Museum, Kobe © Manuel Tardits

fig a62-k. (*tsugite* type) joint between two collar beams © Manuel Tardits

fig a62-l. assembly at top of angle capital (*kumimono*), Yakushiji monastery, Nara © Azby Brown

fig a63. study pavilion, Hōryūji monastery, *denpōdō*, Nara prefecture

fig a63-a. elevation, initial and current state

fig a63-b. exterior view © Teruaki Matsuzaki

fig a64. overall view, Golden Pavilion (Kinkakuji), Kyoto © Nicolas Fiévé

fig a65. Seikōken tea pavilion, Seisonkaku villa, Kanazawa

fig a65-a. plan

fig a65-b. exterior view © Seisonkaku Foundation (kōeki zaidan hōjin Seisonkaku)

fig a66. Ryūten pavilion, Kōrakuen garden, Okayama

fig a66-a. view from the interior © Nicolas Fiévé

fig a66-b. view from the exterior © Nicolas Fiévé

fig a67. Hiunkaku pavilion, Nishi Honganji monastery, Kyoto © Nicolas Fiévé

fig a68. Ishiyama-dera monastery, Shiga prefecture © Teruaki Matsuzaki

fig a69. Hase-dera monastery, Nara prefecture © Teruaki Matsuzaki

fig a70. Kiyomizu-dera monastery, Kyoto © John Barr

fig a71. Nageiredō pavilion, Sanbutsuji monastery, Tottori prefecture © Teruaki Matsuzaki

fig a72. Shōkintei tea pavilion, Katsura Villa, Kyoto © John Barr

fig a73. proportion system, Gosho imperial palace, Kyoto © John Barr

fig a74. plank barrier and cypress (*hinoki*) post, Ise shrine © John Barr

二 A MODERN STORY

fig b1. Honganji dentōin honkan 本願寺伝道院本館 building (formerly Shinshū shinto seimei hoken 真宗信徒生命保険 "Life insurance for adherents of the Shinshū Buddhist school"), built by Itō Chūta, Kyoto, 1912 © Benoît Jacquet

fig b2. Christian Orthodox church of Kyoto (Kyōto Harisutosu seikyōkai 京都ハリストス正教会), built by Matsumuro Shigemitsu 松室重光, Kyoto, 1903 © Benoît Jacquet

fig b3. Former Niijima house, Teramachi street, east of the Imperial Palace, Kyoto, 1870 © Benoît Jacquet

fig b4. Example of a *machiya* facade, Kyoto. Hata House (Hatake 秦家), Aburanokōji street, Bukkōji, Kyoto, 1869. Registered as a tangible cultural property of the City of Kyoto (Kyōto-shi tōroku yūkei bunkazai 京都市登録有形文化財) © Benoît Jacquet

fig b5. Kiko Kiyoyoshi and Itō Chūta, Heian Shrine, Kyoto (Okazaki), 1895 © Benoît Jacquet

fig b6. Buddhist monastery of Hōryūji, Ikaruga, Nara prefecture, seventh century

fig b7. Horiguchi Sutemi, Shiensō Clubhouse, Saitama, 1926

fig b7-a. Horiguchi Sutemi, Shiensō Clubhouse, Saitama, 1926

fig b7-b. exterior view (1926) © Archives of Architecture Horiguchi Sutemi Meiji University

fig b7-c. exterior view (1926) © Archives of Architecture Horiguchi Sutemi Meiji University

fig b8. Fujii Kōji, Chōchikukyo House, Kyoto, 1928

fig b8-a. Fujii Kōji, Chōchikukyo House, Kyoto, 1928

fig b8-b. exterior view © Furukawa Taizō; Takenaka kōmuten

fig b8-c. living room, dining room, and tatami room © Furukawa Taizō; Takenaka kōmuten

fig b8-d. dining room © Furukawa Taizō; Takenaka kōmuten

fig b8-e. annex, *tsuginoma* room 次の間, cabinet (*haizen-dana* 配膳棚), passage (*kayoi-guchi* 通口), author's print; Fujii (1932), plate 18 © Fujii Kōji Archives, Department of Architecture, Kyoto University

fig b8-f. annex, low room (*gedannoma* 下段の間) or salon; storage shelving with door (*to-dana* 戸棚); desk (*tsukue* 机), sofa (*koshikake* 腰掛), author's print; Fujii (1932), plate 13 © Fujii Kōji Archives, Department of Architecture, Kyoto University

fig b9. Antonin Raymond, Karuizawa Summer House, Karuizawa, 1933

fig b9-a. Antonin Raymond, Karuizawa Summer House, Karuizawa, 1933

fig b9-b. interior view of the living room © The Architectural Archives, University of Pennsylvania

fig b9-c. exterior view © The Architectural Archives, University of Pennsylvania

fig b10. Antonin Raymond, Adachi House, Karuizawa, 1966

fig b10-a. interior view of living room © Yola Gloaguen

fig b10-b. interior view of living room and dining room © Yola Gloaguen

fig b11. Construction details for traditional roof types, Antonin Raymond, *Architectural Details*, 1938 © The Architectural Archives, University of Pennsylvania

fig b12. Maekawa Kunio, Kasama House, Tokyo, 1938 © Yoshimi Chiaki

fig b13. Maekawa Kunio, Maekawa House, Tokyo, 1942

fig b13-a. Maekawa Kunio, Maekawa House, Tokyo, 1942

fig b13-b. reconstruction of the Maekawa House in the garden of the Edo-Tokyo buildings (Edo Tōkyō tatemonoen), exterior view © Jérémie Souteyrat

fig b13-c. interior view © Jérémie Souteyrat

fig b14. PREMOS (Maekawa, Ono, Sanin) prefabricated housing, 1946–1951

fig b14-a. plan © Archives of Kunio Maekawa; Archives of Architecture, National Museum of Modern and Contemporary Art (Kokuritsu kingendai kenchiku shiryōkan 国立近現代建築資料館)

fig b14-b. sections and elevations © Archives of Kunio Maekawa; Archives of Architecture, National Museum of Modern and Contemporary Art

(Kokuritsu kingendai kenchiku shiryōkan 国立近現代建築資料館)

fig b14-c. details © Archives of Kunio Maekawa; Archives of Architecture, National Museum of Modern and Contemporary Art (Kokuritsu kingendai kenchiku shiryōkan 国立近現代建築資料館)

fig b14-d. exterior view under construction © Archives of Kunio Maekawa; Archives of Architecture, National Museum of Modern and Contemporary Art (Kokuritsu kingendai kenchiku shiryōkan 国立近現代建築資料館)

fig b15. Maekawa Kunio, Kinokuniya bookstore, Tokyo, 1947

fig b15-a. front elevation © Maekawa Kunio kenchiku sekkei jimusho 前川國男建築設計事務所

fig b15-b. perspective © Maekawa Kunio kenchiku sekkei jimusho 前川國男建築設計事務所

fig b16. photograph of the Katsura Villa by Ishimoto Yasuhiro in 1953 © Ishimoto Yasuhiro; Ishimoto Yasuhiro photographic fund, The Museum of Art Kochi (Kōchi kenritsu bijutsukan 高知県立美術館)

fig b17. photograph of the Hiroshima Peace Memorial, by Ishimoto Yasuhiro (circa 1953) © Ishimoto Yasuhiro; Ishimoto Yasuhiro photographic fund, The Museum of Art Kochi (Kōchi kenritsu bijutsukan 高知県立美術館)

fig b18. Tange Kenzō, Hiroshima Peace Memorial, 1949–1955

fig b18-a. site plan © Tange Associates

fig b18-b. model showing the state of the project during the competition phase,1949 © Tange Associates; Sera Shigeru 瀬良茂

fig b19-a. Tange Kenzō, Tange house, Tokyo, 1953

fig b19-b. main facade with artificial mound © Uchida Michiko

fig b19-c. main facade © Uchida Michiko

fig b19-d. a heightened focus on Japanese wood in a 1/3 scale model built out of cedar by a carpenter specialized in the construction of temples (*miyadaiku*); reconstruction for the "Japan in Architecture" exhibition, Mori Museum, 2018 © Uchida Michiko

fig b20-a. The Tange family with painting on the *fusuma* by Shinoda Tōkō in the *tokonoma* of the main room © Uchida Michiko

fig b20-b. reception room (ST-LR on the plan) © Uchida Michiko

fig b21. Frontal view of the post, the door, and the wall. Shinohara Kazuo, House in White, Tokyo, 1966 © Ueda Hiroshi

fig b22. Shinohara Kazuo, Kugayama House, Tokyo, 1954

fig b22-a. Shinohara Kazuo, Kugayama House, Tokyo, 1954

fig b22-b. main facade © Hirayama Chūji

fig b22-c. interior view © Hirayama Chūji

fig b23. Shinohara Kazuo, Umbrella House, Tokyo, 1961

fig b23-a. Shinohara Kazuo, Umbrella House, Tokyo, 1961

fig b23-b. interior view © Murai Osamu, rights reserved

fig b24. Shinohara Kazuo, House with an Earthen Floor, Kita-Saku, 1963

fig b24-a. Shinohara Kazuo, House with an Earthen Floor, Kita-Saku, 1963

fig b24-b. interior view © Ōtsuji Kiyoji

fig b24-c. exterior view © Ōtsuji Kiyoji

fig b25. Shinohara Kazuo, House in White, Tokyo, 1966

fig b25-a. Shinohara Kazuo, House in White, Tokyo, 1966

fig b25-b. exterior view © Shōkokusha Photographers

fig b25-c. interior view © Ueda Hiroshi

fig b26. "In Japan, there was no space" and "The *minka* is a mushroom," in Shinohara (1996), 61–2

fig b27. Living room (*hiroma*) of the House in White © Murai Osamu, rights reserved

fig b28. Shinohara Kazuo, House for Mister Tanikawa (Tanikawa san no jūtaku), Naganohara, 1974

fig b28-a. interior view © Manuel Tardits

fig b28-b. Shinohara Kazuo, House for Mister Tanikawa, Naganohara, 1974

fig b28-c. exterior view © Taku Sakaushi

fig b28-d. exterior view of gable © Enric Massip-Bosch

fig b28-e. interior view © Taku Sakaushi

fig b29. Yoshimura Junzō, villa at Karuizawa, Karuizawa, 1962

fig b29-a. Yoshimura Junzō, villa at Karuizawa, Karuizawa, 1962

fig b29-b. exterior view © Manuel Tardits

fig b29-c. interior view © Hashimoto Hisamichi

fig b30. Yoshida Isoya, villa Inomata, Tokyo, 1967 Entry door to the *roji* 露地 pathway that leads to the tea pavilion © Manuel Tardits

fig b31. Yoshida Isoya, Yoshiya House, Kamakura, 1962

fig b31-a. Yoshida Isoya, Yoshiya House, Kamakura, 1962

fig b31-b. exterior view © Manuel Tardits

fig b31-c. interior view © Manuel Tardits

fig b32. Yoshida Isoya, Inomata House, Tokyo, 1967

fig b32-a. exterior view © Manuel Tardits

fig b32-b. interior view © Manuel Tardits

fig b33. Murano Tōgo, Kasuien annex, Kyoto, 1959

fig b33-a. exterior view from the garden © John Barr

fig b33-b. exterior view from the entry © John Barr

fig b34. Taniguchi Yoshirō, Tōson Memorial, Magome, 1947

fig b34-a. entry portico © Manuel Tardits

fig b34-b. memorial gallery © Manuel Tardits

fig b34-c. statue of Tōson © Manuel Tardits

fig b34-d. exterior view of the memorial from the entrance © Manuel Tardits

fig b34-e. exterior view from the garden © Manuel Tardits

fig b34-f. entrance to the memorial © Manuel Tardits

fig b35. Zangetsutei pavilion, Omotesenke house, Kyoto, 1594 © Fushinan Omotesenke

fig b36. variations on the Zangetsutei pavilion

fig b36-a. Taniguchi Yoshirō, Kakiden pavilion, *hiroma*, Tokyo, 1969 © Teruaki Matsuzaki

fig b36-b. Murano Tōgo, Tōkōan pavilion, Imperial Hotel, Tokyo, 1970 © Teruaki Matsuzaki

三 A PARTICULAR STORY

fig c1-a. street view of the EFEO Center in Kyoto, 2014 © Jérémie Souteyrat

fig c1-b. ground breaking ceremony (*jichinsai*).

fig c1-c. the director of the EFEO, Franciscus Verellen, lopping off the top of the earthen cone with a spade © Andrea Flores Urushima

fig c2. Kigumi Infinity. Detail of wood assemblage (*kigumi* 木組), Kitagawara Atsushi, Japanese pavilion (Expo Milano, 2015), reconstruction for the "Japan in Architecture" exhibition, Mori Art Museum, 2018

fig c3-a. *itazu*, "drawing on plank" © Manuel Tardits

fig c3-b. descriptive drawing of a portico at full scale. Nakamura Sotoji Workshop, Kyoto, 2014 © Manuel Tardits

fig c3-c. descriptive drawing of a *sumigi* angle rafter, drawn from a construction manual, Kameyama, 1918

fig c3-d. descriptive drawing of a fanning rafter *ōgitaruki* "in the Zen style of the Kamakura period," Kameyama, 1918

fig c4. Shinohara Kazuo, House with an Earthen Floor, construction drawings, 1963

fig c5. Shinohara Kazuo, House in White, construction drawings, 1965

fig c6. *kyōma* zone

fig c7. *inaka ma* zone

fig c8. two principles

fig c9. the *kiwari:* a system for setting proportions

fig c10. EFEO Center, Kyoto. Exterior entryway © Jérémie Souteyrat

fig c11-a. schematic plan of the city of Kyoto

fig c11-b. Kitashirakawa neighborhood

fig c11-c. site plan

fig c12-a. street view of the EFEO Center © Jérémie Souteyrat

fig c12-b. the EFEO Center in its urban context © Jérémie Souteyrat

fig c12-c. site prior to construction

fig c12-d. site built up

fig c13-a. ground floor plan

fig c13-b. second floor plan

fig c13-c. third floor plan

fig c14-a. long section

fig c14-b. cross section through rooms

fig c14-c. cross section at stair

fig c15-a. west elevation at street

fig c15-b. north elevation

fig c15-c. south elevation

fig c16-a. overall axonometric

fig c16-b. the two main blocks

fig c16-c. the four parts

fig c17-a initial structural grid

fig c17-b. deformed and adapted structural grid

fig c18. Organ pavilion オルゴル庵, architect: Mikan © Manuel Tardits

fig c19-a. assembly and abutment (1)

fig c19-b. assembly and abutment (2)

fig c20. warehouses at Nakagawa, Kitayama-chō, Kita-ku, Kyoto, built in 1935 © Manuel Tardits

fig c21. sketch by the nurseryman Nakata Osamu of the planting of the mountains north of Kyoto. The foot of the mountain is planted with cedars, then the cypresses and pines © Benoît Jacquet

fig c22. various trunks, M. Nakata's warehouse

fig c22-a. fairly smooth trunks of the type chosen by the EFEO © Manuel Tardits

fig c22-b. trunks with irregular surfaces © Manuel Tardits

fig c22-c. trunks with intentionally constricted surfaces © Manuel Tardits

fig c22-d. naturally tortured trunks © Manuel Tardits

fig c23-a. staircase: the volume

fig c23-b. staircase: the stair-library insert

fig c23-c. staircase: the occupied volume

fig c23-d. exterior at entry © Jérémie Souteyrat

fig c23-e. interior at entry © Jérémie Souteyrat

fig c23-f. bottom of stair © Jérémie Souteyrat

fig c23-g. staircase, 2nd floor landing © Jérémie Souteyrat

fig c23-h. staircase, reference elements © Jérémie Souteyrat

fig c23-i. staircase: reference elements

fig c23-j. staircase, reference elements © Jérémie Souteyrat

fig c24, c25, c26. rooms

fig c24-a. hypostyle reading room

fig c24-b. hypostyle reading room © Jérémie Souteyrat

fig c25-a. office/cases © Jérémie Souteyrat

fig c25-b. office/cases

fig c26-a. lecture/conference hall

fig c26-b. lecture/conference hall © Jérémie Souteyrat

fig c27. furnitures

fig c27-a. leg at reading room table, ground floor © Manuel Tardits

fig c27-b. scholar's desk, 2nd floor © Jérémie Souteyrat

fig c27-c. conference room table, 3rd floor © Jérémie Souteyrat

fig c28. sustainable development

fig c28-a. buffer space, darkened day mode © Jérémie Souteyrat

fig c28-b. sustainable development, general principles

fig c28-c. west facade by night © Jérémie Souteyrat

fig c28-d. treatment of south light

fig c28-e. treatment of west light

fig c28-f. west facade transparent mode © Jérémie Souteyrat

fig c28-g. west facade darkened mode © Jérémie Souteyrat

fig c28-h. sliding panels in blown glass, closed position © Jérémie Souteyrat

fig c28-i. sliding panels in blown glass, open position © Jérémie Souteyrat

fig c29. structure: foundations

fig c30. structure: connections

fig c31. construction site

fig c31-a. precut structure waiting to be installed © Benoît Jacquet

fig c31-b. installation of the groundsill *dodai* © Benoît Jacquet

fig c31-c. preparation of the ends of the Kitayama cedar posts © Benoît Jacquet

fig c31-d. mortise and tenon joint between beams © Benoît Jacquet

fig c31-e. installation of a beam © Benoît Jacquet

fig c31-f. main skeleton at the time of the *jōtōshiki* © Benoît Jacquet

fig c31-g. secondary structure © Benoît Jacquet

fig c32. structure

fig c32-a. structure: main skeleton ground floor

fig c32-b. structure: main skeleton 2nd floor

fig c32-c. structure: main skeleton 3rd floor and roof

fig c32-d. structure: main skeleton building

fig c32-e. structure: north-south section

fig c32-f. structure: detailed section

POSTSCRIPT: TRADITION WHO ARE YOU?

fig d1. cedars spared by the tsunami of 2011, to serve for the construction of Asahi children's playgrounds by Tezuka Architects, Minamisanriku © Tezuka architects

fig d2. Ishii Kazuhiro, Seiwa Bunraku Theater, Kumamoto prefecture, 1992

fig d2-a. exterior view © Kumamoto Art Polis

fig d2-b. interior view © Sōichi Ishimaru

fig d2-c. interior view © Sōichi Ishimaru

fig d3. FT Architects, Timber structure II (boxing hall), Kōgakuin University, Tokyo, 2013

fig d3-a. exterior view © Shigeo Ogawa

fig d3-b. interior view © Shigeo Ogawa

fig d4. FT Architects, Timber structure I (archery hall), Kōgakuin University, Tokyo, 2013, interior view © Shigeo Ogawa

fig d5. FT Architects, c-Office, Nagoya 2004

fig d5-a. exterior view © Hiroyasu Sakaguchi

fig d5-b. structural principal: catenary and post-tensioning © Nihon University

fig d5-c. construction process © Hiroyasu Sakaguchi

fig d5-d. interior view © Hiroyasu Sakaguchi

fig d5-e. construction process © Hiroyasu Sakaguchi

fig d5-f. construction process © Hiroyasu Sakaguchi

fig d6. Tezuka Takaharu and Yui, Asahi 1 and 2 kindergarten, Minamisanriku, 2012-2017

fig d6-a. overall view © Katsuhisa Kida/FOTOTECA

fig d6-b. street facade © Katsuhisa Kida/FOTOTECA

fig d6-c. exterior view © Katsuhisa Kida/FOTOTECA

fig d6-d. interior view of a classroom © Katsuhisa Kida/FOTOTECA

fig d7. Yoshimura Yasutaka, Fukumasu base and kindergarten, Chiba, 2016

fig d7-a. exterior view © Yoshimura Yasutaka

fig d7-b. interior view © Yoshimura Yasutaka

fig d7-c. interior view © Yoshimura Yasutaka

fig d8. Itō Toyō, dome, Odate, 1997

fig d8-a. exterior view © Kamijo Yoshie

fig d8-b. interior view © Kamijo Yoshie

fig d9. Naitō Hiroshi, Sea-Folk Museum, Toba, 1992

fig d9-a. exterior view © Miao Si

fig d9-b. interior view © Miao Si

fig d10. Naitō Hiroshi, Makino Museum of Plants and People, Kōchi, 1999

fig d10-a. view of interior courtyard © Miao Si

fig d10-b. view of a gallery © Miao Si

fig d10-c. view of a gallery © Miao Si

fig d10-d. interior view © Miao Si

fig d11. Horibe Yasushi, columbarium of the Chikurin-ji monastery, Kōchi, 2013

fig d11-a. exterior view © Manuel Tardits

fig d11-b. view of entry © Miao Si

fig d11-c. interior view with basin © Miao Si

fig d12. Fujimori Terunobu, Takasugian, Suwa, Nagano prefecture, 2004

fig d13. Suzuki Ryōji, Konpira sanctuary, Kagawa prefecture, 2004

fig d13-a. exterior view of entry pavilion © Manuel Tardits

fig d13-b. detail of awning and *kumimono* capital © Manuel Tardits

fig d13-c. detail of awning and *kokera-buki* cedar bark shingle roofing © Manuel Tardits

fig d14. Nishizawa Taira, Sun-Pu church, Shizuoka, 2008

fig d14-a. exterior view © Satoru Yamashiro

fig d14-b. interior view © Satoru Yamashiro

fig d15. Kuma Kengo, SunnyHills Minamiaoyama store, Tokyo, 2013

fig d15-a. exterior view © Manuel Tardits

fig d15-b. facade detail © Manuel Tardits

fig d15-c. interior view © Manuel Tardits

fig d15-d. exterior view © Manuel Tardits

fig d16. Reconstruction of the Yakushiji monastery, Nara, 1970–2017

fig d16-a. west pagoda © Azby Brown

fig d16-b. *kondō* © Azby Brown

fig d16-c. *genjōdō* and *e-den* © Azby Brown

CHRONOLOGY

Prehistory: fifteenth century BCE to third century CE

Jōmon period 縄文 (fifteenth century BCE to third century BCE)
Yayoi period 弥生 (third century BCE to third century CE)

Antiquity: third century to 1185

Kofun period 古墳 (third century to seventh century)
Asuka period 飛鳥 (592–710)
Nara period 奈良 (710–794)
Heian period 平安 (794–1185)

Middle Ages: 1185–1573

Kamakura period 鎌倉 (1185–1333)
Kenmu Restoration 建武 (1333–1336)
Muromachi period 室町 (1336–1573)

Modern period: 1573–1868

Azuchi-Momoyama period 安土桃山 (1573–1603)
Edo period 江戸 (1603–1868)

Contemporary period: 1868 to present

Meiji era 明治 (1868–1912)
Taishō era 大正 (1912–1926)
Shōwa era 昭和 (1926–1989)
Heisei era 平成 (1989–2019)
Reiwa era 令和 (2019 to present)

ACKNOWLEDGEMENTS

This book project was born at the beginning of spring 2014, during a shared meal at the restaurant (*ryōtei*) Wakuden, which is located in a house renovated in 1952 by the famous carpenter (*sukiya daiku*) Nakamura Sotoji. Ever since that long and slow moment enjoyed in such a timeless place, located on the Nene Pathway (Nene no michi) leading to the Kōdaiji monastery, the idea of collaborating to write a book, to describe the evolution of wood construction from antiquity up to the current day, has developed and has been nourished by numerous encounters and collaborations with many people. This book would not have been the same without:

– the photographs of François Azambourg, John Barr, Azby Brown, Nicolas Fiévé, Andrea Flores Urushima, Fujii Kōji, Yola Gloaguen, Hashimoto Hisamichi, Hirayama Chūji, Horiguchi Sutemi, Ishimaru Sōichi, Ishimoto Yasuhiro, Kamijo Yoshie, Kida Katsuhisa, Enric Massip-Bosch, Miao Si, Murai Osamu, Ogawa Shigeo, Ōtsuji Hiroshi, Sakaushi Taku, Sera Shigeru, Jérémie Souteyrat, Sakaguchi Hiroyasu, Uchida Michiko, Ueda Hiroshi, Yamashiro Satoru, Yoshimi Chiaki, Yoshimura Yasutaka, and Kōjiro Yuichirō;
– the illustrations, which have benefited from the help of Egawa Tōru (Atelier Maekawa Kunio), Fukushima Kazuya, Hirose Kazumi, Itō Yōtarō Kimura Giichi, Matsukuma Akira (Takenaka kōmuten; Chōchikukyo Fondation), Matsukuma Hiroshi, Shinozaki Taijin, Sogabe Masashi, Suzuki Akira, Taji Takahiro, Tezuka Takaharu and Tezuka Yui, Tominaga Yōko, and Uchida Michiko, the architectural archives of Horiguchi Sutemi at Meiji University, the archives of the Graduate School of Architecture of Kyoto University, the Architectural Archives of University of Pennsylvania School of Design, Maekawa Kunio Archives at the National Archives of Modern Architecture, Agency of Cultural Affairs, the Ishimoto Yasuhiro Collection at the Museum of Art in Kōchi, and at the Canadian Center for Architecture in Montréal, the Association for the preservation of architectural techniques classified as Cultural property (Bunkazai kenzōbutsu hozon gijutsu kyōkai), of Kumamoto Art Polis, of the Fuji no kuni chanomiyako Museum, of the publisher Shōgakukan, of Shōkokusha Photographers, and of Tange Associates;
– the drawings of Caroline Claudé, Jonathan Decaillon, Arthur Deplanck, Manon Dol, Amandine Fitte-Duval, Zoé Gervais, Cécile Gottardi, Lucas Grisoni, Kido Kōta, Pauline Le Basse, Fabien Mauduit, Inès Saïdi, and Sacha Wiedmaier;
– the translations of Christian Hubert, Matthew Stavros, and Jean-Noël Lecomte, the advice and proofreading of Jean-Louis Cohen, Nicolas Fiévé and Francine Joris; and
– the JSPS Kakenhi Grant Number JP18K18477, JP18H00629.

Finally, this book would never have existed without the support of Olivier Babel (the first person to have asked us for a study on wood construction in Japan), of Lucas Giossi (presently at the head of the EPFL Press), of Luca Ortelli (director of their Architecture collection), of Sylvain Colette and Christophe Borlat (who ensured its successful implementation), and of the attentive work of our book designer, architect Véronique Hours.

We sincerely acknowledge all the persons mentioned here, as well as all those we met, read, or watched during these past years, and also the representatives of the institutions who generously accorded funding for the publication of this book.

Benoît JACQUET, MATSUZAKI Teruaki, Manuel TARDITS